CW00549936

Nazi Germany

Nazi Germany

Society, Culture, and Politics

Pamela E. Swett and
S. Jonathan Wiesen

BLOOMSBURY ACADEMIC
LONDON • NEW YORK • OXFORD • NEW DELHI • SYDNEY

BLOOMSBURY ACADEMIC
Bloomsbury Publishing Plc
50 Bedford Square, London, WC1B 3DP, UK
1385 Broadway, New York, NY 10018, USA
29 Earlsfort Terrace, Dublin 2, Ireland

BLOOMSBURY, BLOOMSBURY ACADEMIC and the Diana logo are
trademarks of Bloomsbury Publishing Plc

First published in Great Britain 2024

A catalogue record for this book is available from the British Library.

A catalog record for this book is available from the Library of Congress.

ISBN: HB: 978-1-3501-1262-9
          PB: 978-1-3501-1261-2
          ePDF: 978-1-3501-1263-6
          eBook: 978-1-3501-1264-3

Typeset by Integra Software Services Pvt. Ltd.
Printed and bound in Great Britain

To find out more about our authors and books visit www.bloomsbury.com
and sign up for our newsletters.

For our teachers:
Volker Berghahn, Jane Caplan, Gerald Feldman,
and Margaret Lavinia Anderson

CONTENTS

PLATES

FIGURES

ACKNOWLEDGMENTS

From the start of this project, we have benefited from the assistance, support, and helpful criticism of many people. Our colleagues at the German Historical Institute in Washington, DC, Insa Kummer, Kelly McCullough, and Gabe Moss, permitted us to use the maps they produced for the GHI's terrific online resource German History in Documents and Images. The United States Holocaust Memorial Museum also provided access to several of the images in their collection gratis, and Professor Bernd Sösemann at the Free University of Berlin was kind enough to allow the inclusion of two reworked tables from his masterful collection on Nazi propaganda. Keren Li generously lent us his time and expertise in the preparation of the tables for publication, and Christine Brocks produced the excellent index. Our editor at Bloomsbury, Rhodri Mogford, has been with the project from the beginning, and we want to thank him for his support, patience, and responsiveness to all our questions along the way.

We are also grateful to our friends in the field who offered to read one, two, or many chapters before publication. They saved us from more than one error and helped to make the arguments and presentation clearer and more compelling. Thanks go to Frank Biess, Moritz Föllmer, Neil Gregor, Benjamin Hett, Eric Kurlander, Mark Roseman, Nathan Stolzfus, Julia Torrie, and Jonathan Zatlin. We also benefited from the efforts of the anonymous peer reviewers of the proposal and full manuscript. Our graduate students, Ryan Heyden (McMaster) and John Stephen Hutchinson (University of Alabama at Birmingham), did much of the heavy lifting on the images and helped us identify some of the key sources that found their ways into the text. And we can never thank enough our spouses, Matt Leighninger and Natasha Zaretsky, for everything they do, including their assistance with this project. Finally, we are grateful (and relieved) that our friendship has survived co-authorship.

ABBREVIATIONS AND GERMAN TERMS

Anschluss	Adjoining of Austria to Germany
BDM	League of German Girls
Center	Catholic Center Party
DAF	German Labor Front
DAP	German Workers' Party
DNVP	German Nationalist People's Party
DVP	German People's Party
Einsatzgruppen	Mobile killing units
Führer	Leader
Führerprinzip	Leader principle
Gauleiter	Nazi Party regional leader
Gestapo	Secret State Police
Gleichschaltung	"Synchronization"
HJ	Hitler Youth
IOC	International Olympic Committee
Judenrein	"Jew-free"
KdF	Strength through Joy
Kindertransport	Children's transport
KL	Concentration camp
KLV	Children's Relocation to the Countryside
KPD	Communist Party of Germany
Kripo	Criminal Police
Lebensraum	Living space
Leistungsgemeinschaft	Performance community

MSPD	Majority Social Democratic Party of Germany
Napola	National Political Institutes of Education
NSBO	National Socialist Factory Cell Organization
NSDAP	National Socialist German Workers' Party (Nazi Party)
NSFO	National Socialist Leadership Officers
NS-Lehrerbund	National Socialist Teachers' League
NSV	National Socialist People's Welfare
Orpo	Order Police
RAD	Reich Labor Service
RAF	Royal Air Force of the United Kingdom
Reichskonkordat	Treaty negotiated between Nazi Germany and the Vatican, 1933
RKK	Reich Chamber of Culture
RMVP	Reich Ministry for People's Enlightenment and Propaganda
RSHA	Reich Security Main Office
RV	Reich Representation of German Jews
SA	Stormtroopers
SD	Security Service
SOPADE	SPD in exile
SPD	Social Democratic Party of Germany
SS	Security Echelon
T4	Code name for the Nazi forced "euthanasia" program
USPD	Independent Social Democratic Party of Germany
VE	People's Radio
Volksgemeinschaft	National community
Volksgenosse	National comrade
Waffen SS	Armed SS

Introduction

Eighty years after the collapse of National Socialist Germany, interest in this subject remains strong. School classes, television shows, movies, novels, and video games offer depictions of the Nazis, the people who fought against them, and those who suffered under their brutal control. Most people in the UK and the United States can say something about Hitler, the Gestapo, the Holocaust, and the Second World War. Public attention to this period is welcome, but it has also resulted in widespread confusion about what National Socialism stood for and what specific policies it enacted. If you were to ask a person on the street what they know about Nazism, they might tell you that Adolf Hitler seized the government in a military coup, established a reactionary regime based on the occult, brainwashed the German population over twelve years, and planned the extermination of European Jews from the start of his regime. None of this would be correct. This textbook seeks to challenge such myths that surround the period in German history, sometimes known as the "Third Reich."[1] It offers students a multidimensional picture of the Nazi dictatorship, which used repression to maintain power, but which also tried to create a society where those people it deemed acceptable could prosper and enjoy themselves. This was a regime that relied on experimentation and a combination of forward-thinking and reactionary policies. In the aim of building a biologically pure "national community," it invited some people to enjoy a resurgent post-Depression Germany, but it also violently expelled other people and sought to build a territorial empire through war.

In order to reveal these dynamics, the book relies on three approaches. First, it balances social and cultural history with the political and military history of the regime. By doing so, it encourages readers not just to explore how the Nazis thrust the world into a global war, but also to unravel the complexities of Germans' daily lives before, during, and immediately after the Second World War. It looks at soldiers, policymakers, perpetrators, victims, and bystanders, and those who defied easy categorization. Second, it highlights the voices of these people, as heard in their speeches, diaries, letters, and memoirs. What did people think and say about National Socialism at the time? How might their views reflect a multifaceted understanding of Nazism? Third, this book places National Socialism in a wider European and global context. In recent years, historians have shown convincingly that Nazi Germany was less isolated than people often remember today. By this we mean that Nazism had its supporters abroad before 1939, that the regime relied on non-Germans throughout the occupied territories to build and maintain its empire, and that Nazi ideologues integrated aspects of racial and social thinking from other countries, including the United States and the UK, into their own worldview and policies. While this textbook draws attention to this international engagement with the Nazi regime and some parallels to other countries, it also notes the unique horror of Nazi Germany, a sophisticated police state that was responsible for millions of dead over its twelve years and for a legacy that continues to affect international relations and fuel online hatred.

The narrative in this book reflects a specific scholarly debate about the Nazi period. It concerns, roughly, the balance between "coercion" and "consent" in the Third Reich. Until relatively recently, scholars of National Socialism emphasized the oppressive nature of the regime, which filled concentration camps and prisons with political opponents and with racial, religious, and sexual minorities. But many Germans also remembered the Nazi years fondly, as a time of economic recovery and personal gratification. What was the balance between the coercive nature of the regime and the fact that, in historian Peter Fritzsche's words, Germans had the freedom to make "deliberate, self-conscious, and knowledgeable political choices" and thus actively embrace the Nazi regime?[2] We hope readers of this book will find the material with which to reflect on this question. A related point is that in Nazi Germany and in occupied Europe people did not uniformly support or reject all aspects of National Socialism. Love of country, belief in Hitler, racist ideals, and concern for loved ones on the battlefield could rise and fall at different points, and a range of emotions and attitudes shaped the population's—and each individual's—attitudes toward Nazism. People could look on with horror at the persecution of "internal enemies" but celebrate the "rebirth" of the German nation under Hitler. A teenager with Jewish ancestry could not only suffer under the regime's antisemitic acts but also envy the sense of belonging members of the Hitler Youth enjoyed. People could both fear the regime and enjoy lives that demanded a certain social and political conformity. In short, this was a dynamic society based on exclusionary and inclusionary practices, and most Germans were touched by both.

Ultimately, by exploring Nazi society, politics, and ideology in depth, students will be prompted to consider key questions: How did German democracy give way to a brutal dictatorship so quickly? What was daily life like for "average" Germans and for those labeled as biological and political outsiders? What did the world think of Hitler and the Nazi regime? Why did the Nazi dictatorship embark on a genocidal war that led to the deaths of tens of millions of Europeans and to the demise of a political order that had become exceedingly popular by 1939? Why did Germans support Hitler for so long, even when they were losing the Second World War? Whatever answers readers come to, we hope they will consider the challenges faced by other people around their age who lived during this earlier period. At the height of the Second World War, some students at the University of Munich faced up to the reality of what National Socialism had wrought. "Isn't it true," they wrote in a leaflet, "that every honest German is ashamed of his government these days? … Who among us can imagine the degree of shame that will come upon us and upon our children when the veils fall from our faces and the awful crimes that infinitely exceed any human measure are exposed to the light of the day?"[3]

Notes

1   This is a term that Nazis used to portray their regime as a successor state to the "first" Reich (or empire), the Holy Roman Empire (800–1806), and the "second one," the German Empire (1871–1918). The term has entered scholarly and everyday usage, but readers should be aware that its origins are with right-wing nationalists.

2   Peter Fritzsche, *Life and Death in the Third Reich* (Cambridge, MA: Belknap Press, 2008), 18.

3   White Rose, Pamphlet #1 (June 1942), https://whiteroseinternational.com/leaflet-1/

Additional Reading

Baranowski, Shelley, Armin Nolzen, and Claus-Christian W. Szejnmann, eds. *Companion to Nazi Germany*. Hoboken, NJ: John Wiley & Sons Ltd., 2018.

Childers, Thomas. *The Third Reich: A History of Nazi Germany*. New York: Simon & Schuster, 2017.

Eley, Geoff. *Nazism as Fascism: Violence, Ideology, and the Ground of Consent in Germany, 1933–1945*. London: Routledge, 2013.

Evans, Richard J. *The Coming of the Third Reich*. New York: Penguin Books, 2003.

Evans, Richard J. *The Third Reich in Power*. New York: Penguin Books, 2005.

Evans, Richard J. *The Third Reich at War*. New York: Penguin Books, 2008.

Gregor, Neil. *How to Read Hitler*. London: Granata Books, 2005.

Kershaw, Ian. *Hitler: Hubris, 1889–1936*. Volume 1. New York: W.W. Norton, 1998.

Kershaw, Ian. *Hitler: Nemesis, 1936–1945*. Volume 2. New York: W.W. Norton, 2000.

Peukert, Detlev. *Inside Nazi Germany: Conformity, Opposition, and Racism in Everyday Life*. Translated by Richard Deveson. New Haven: Yale University Press, 1987.

Rabinbach, Anson, and Sander L. Gilman, eds. *The Third Reich Sourcebook.* Berkeley: University of California Press, 2013.

Stackelberg, Roderick, and Sally A. Winkle, eds. *The Nazi Germany Sourcebook.* London: Routledge, 2002.

Ulrich, Volker. *Hitler: Ascent, 1889–1939*. Volume 1. Translated by Jefferson Chase. New York: Vintage Books, 2017.

Ulrich, Volker. *Hitler: Downfall, 1939–1945*. Volume 2. Translated by Jefferson Chase. New York: Alfred A. Knopf, 2020.

1

The German Reich, Weimar, and the Birth of National Socialism

Selecting a starting point for this story about Germany's National Socialist era is not easy. One could begin with the naming of Hitler as chancellor at the end of January 1933 or with the founding of his political party in 1920. We could go further back to the intellectual origins of right-wing nationalism and early eugenics in the nineteenth century, or even farther to the long violent history of antisemitism in Europe. All these options offer fruitful avenues for exploration, though here we have chosen a slightly different path, which allows us to integrate these themes. Historical change is always contingent on many factors—both long-term developments and immediate actions. In this chapter, the goal is to look at what sort of society and state Germany had become by the early twentieth century and how subsequent events aided (and also undermined) the establishment and growth of the early Nazi movement.

Our story begins in Germany around 1900. At the dawn of the new century, Germany was evolving rapidly owing to the power of industrialization and urbanization, though traditional norms around class, gender, and religion retained considerable strength. The first section of the chapter focuses on the push and pull between the forces of change and the status quo that accompanied economic modernization at the turn of the century. It also explores the status of Germany's minorities, particularly its Jewish community. Nineteenth-century-style antisemitic political parties were on the decline in a liberalizing Germany, but pseudo-scientific racial theories were lending new legitimacy to this form of prejudice.

The second section turns to Germany's defeat in the First World War and its legacy in the 1920s. We discuss demobilization, the revolutionary years of 1918 and 1919, the Treaty of Versailles, and the crises that led to hyperinflation and parliamentary instability as examples of the intense upheaval of the early 1920s. The Weimar Republic that emerged from this turmoil mid-decade embodied both the humiliation and revanchist attitudes that accompanied defeat in 1918–19, and an optimism that stability and national prosperity could finally be achieved. The final section of this chapter looks at the founding of the National Socialist German Workers' Party (NSDAP, or Nazi Party). We provide some biographical material on Hitler, but our focus is on the context and content of the party's early belief system and early activism. The NSDAP remained a fringe party for the better part of the decade with little name recognition beyond Bavaria, and few observers believed it would ever become much more.

Germany around 1900

By the start of the new century, Germany had left behind the authoritarianism of the Iron Chancellor, Otto von Bismarck, who had succeeded in forging a unified state by 1871 but after locking horns with the new Kaiser, Wilhelm II, had left office in 1890. The forty-one-year-old Kaiser Wilhelm II was a forceful but pompous ruler. Guided by his aristocratic inner circle, he overpowered the chancellors who followed Bismarck. However, the Hohenzollern monarch was no absolute ruler; Wilhelm II was at the helm of a system of monarchical constitutionalism. The crown controlled the army and foreign policy and safeguarded law and order at home. Importantly, the chancellor answered directly to the Kaiser, rather than to the parliament, known as the Reichstag. While this structure weakened the Reichstag's power, the parliament did determine taxes, and the Kaiser could not govern without it. In short, all major expenditures, including those for the military, needed parliamentary approval. The Reichstag was elected by universal manhood suffrage, which bolstered political engagement throughout the country. By the 1890s, the Social Democratic Party (SPD) had become Germany's most popular party. In the 1903 election, the SPD received nearly one of every three votes cast. At the time, the SPD was the most important Marxist party in Europe and the largest party to advocate for female suffrage.

For decades, historians argued that the formal limits on the Reichstag's power meant that Germany remained illiberal and anti-democratic and that this "backwardness" paved the way for Nazism. But scholars have since provided convincing evidence that by the start of the twentieth century, Germany's political culture was increasingly democratic; men across class and regional divides felt engaged in the political process, either through the franchise or through their ability to voice their political opinions in the public realm. The possibility that an unhappy monarch might simply outlaw political parties or repeal universal manhood suffrage was no longer likely. And the outlook for further democratization looked bright. After almost two decades of drafting and lively public debate, a new unified Civil Code went into effect in 1900, regulating family law, property, and commerce, though German feminists remained dissatisfied with the ways the Civil Code upheld gender inequality. Innovations like the introduction of voting booths and ballot envelopes made elections freer and fairer.

Germans were also active in civic life beyond party structures. Membership in social clubs, patriotic societies, charities, and other types of civic associations was extremely popular and did much to shape daily life and German culture more broadly. As one resident of the capital recalled: "Berliners went to their factories or business in the morning, worked hard during the day, but used their evening hours to enjoy the pleasant things in life. Quite apart from going to the theaters and concerts, I could tell Berliners were also interested in associational life."[1] By the start of the new century, orderly governance at all levels—from local municipalities to the regional states (*Länder*) to the national level—also meant that Germany was among the most literate and highly educated countries in the world. German primary and secondary schools were models for educators everywhere, and the country's universities attracted students from abroad. African American scholar and activist W. E. B. Du Bois sought an education there as a haven from racism in his home country. Jews and non-Jews from Russia like poet Boris Pasternak did the same. German scientists won more Nobel prizes in the first twenty years of the twentieth century than most major countries combined.

The stability described above and investments in social and cultural institutions were made possible by an expanding economy. While there were periods of downturn, one of which met the threshold of a depression, the overall trend was positive in the decades between 1871 and 1914 in terms of agricultural output—for Germany's agricultural sector remained strong and growing—and in terms of its industrial might. By 1893 the last major downturn was in the past, and two decades of unprecedented economic growth began. By 1913 the ever-increasing agricultural labor force had reached 10.7 million workers, and the country's grain was still sought in foreign markets, despite increased international competition. Simultaneously, more Germans than ever earned their wages in industry. The number of workers employed in mining, metal production, textiles and clothing, chemical manufacturing, and construction all skyrocketed in the decades before the First World War.

Germany experienced a large increase in its population in this era. The first census of the new German empire was taken in 1872, and the count registered just over 40 million. In 1900, the total had risen to 56 million, and on the eve of the First World War there were 67 million Germans. The country had become a popular destination for immigrants, attracted by economic opportunity, political stability, and a culture of tolerance. While only 200,000 foreigners were living within Germany's borders in 1871, by 1910 the country had become far more cosmopolitan, with 1.3 million newcomers living on German territory. Not everyone, however, believed their best opportunities remained in Germany. About 3 million individuals left the country in these decades, choosing to build their lives instead in North and South America, Australia, and elsewhere.

One conclusion to draw from this data is that it reflects a dynamic population—a lot of new faces and much change. But if only a small percentage was born outside of German territory, what else explains the rapid population growth? Life expectancy was up and mortality rates down. In the 1870s men and women lived on average only thirty-seven years. By 1905 this average had risen to about forty-six years. While mortality rates were decreasing, birth rates were rising. Importantly, however, population growth was distributed very unevenly. In 1871 about 31 percent of all Germans lived in the wide-open spaces to the east. In the decades that followed, though the overall population continued to climb, the percentage of Germans living in the rural east was falling. The cities, chiefly Berlin and those in the west around the Rhine River and adjacent Ruhr valley, became the sites of massive population growth, meaning that Germany's urbanization accompanied this demographic boom.

The rapid and uncontrolled expansion of the cities produced a debate about urbanism. There is no ignoring the fact that Germany's cities were unprepared for this intense growth. Basic infrastructure was lacking. Schools, hospitals, electricity, sewage, transportation, clean water sources, and housing were often unavailable to large numbers of people. Squalor had always existed in the countryside, but now it was more concentrated— and more visible to privileged urbanites and government leaders. Wealthy conservatives critiqued the cities as dens of sin, anonymous wastelands which undermined the values of rural life. One conservative theologian lamented "the sacrifice of human beings with immortal souls, living limbs of the social body, who are degraded into means for the satisfaction of self-centered lust."[2] Baked into their criticism of urban life was a romanticization of rural life as peaceful, moral, and healthy. But new arrivals had not experienced the countryside that way—most left because of crippling poverty and insecurity.

Bourgeois reformers also criticized the industrial cities. They defended urban centers as cultural and economic beacons, but they pointed to what they saw as a dark side of unfettered growth, including crime and homelessness. Another key target for criticism of urban life was socialism. With increasingly large numbers of industrial workers crammed together in substandard housing conditions, many middle- and upper-class Germans feared that a socialist revolution was inevitable without proactive measures. Many social democratic workers hoped they were right. One Chemnitz factory worker wrote in 1890 about the "coldness, the estrangement and mistrust" he felt toward the "distinguished classes," who didn't need to work but instead spent their days "eating, drinking, traveling, reading, looking at beautiful things and places." He perceived an "insurmountable chasm" that had opened between the classes. A friend summarized his own feelings as "objective hate."[3]

During this period of industrialization and urbanization, Germany was attracting immigrants looking for opportunity in the newly unified Reich.

There was also internal migration westward to the steel factories and coal mines of the Ruhr valley. A large portion of those arriving in and around Essen and Dortmund were ethnically Polish peasants from Silesia, Poznan, and West and East Prussia. Most of the young men who ventured to the Ruhr were desperate for work and unfamiliar with trade unions. Resentment toward the new arrivals was fueled by their willingness to take lower wages and cross picket lines. Their Catholicism, language, and other cultural differences also made them targets of "Germanization" measures in the 1870s, such as legislation that prohibited all languages except German from being used in classrooms.

Germany's Jewish Minority

Germany's Jewish community also experienced great change. The legal emancipation of Jews in Germany took place three times. In the first two cases, during the Napoleonic era and then during the revolutionary fervor of 1848, the civil rights they gained were later retracted. The process began again in the 1860s, when various German kingdoms and independent states passed legislation ensuring Jews' rights. These rights were eventually enshrined in the constitution of the united German Reich in 1871. That year, there were 512,000 Jews in the Reich, which amounted to about 1 percent of the population. By 1910 that number had risen to 615,000, including about 79,000 Jews who had moved to Germany largely from eastern Europe to take advantage of the freedoms upheld by the new German constitution. However, as a percentage of the total population, the Jewish community fell below 1 percent by 1913, in part because Jewish couples married later and opted for smaller families than their non-Jewish counterparts. Although the number of German Jews remained very small, hovering around 1 percent of the population into the 1930s, one needs to understand their place in German society, because they will figure so centrally in the Nazi worldview.

Assimilation was possible for Jews in Germany. In the last years before the First World War, 13 percent of Jewish women took Christian husbands, and 22 percent of Jewish men chose Christian wives. In some cities, intermarriage was far more common. In Hamburg, for example, over 70 percent of Jews were marrying Christians. Intermarriage can be seen as an attempt to flee persecution, but scholars who have studied German Jews in this period draw a different conclusion. In many cities and towns Jews and gentiles lived side by side and did not shy away from interaction or even from falling in love. The fact that conversion to Christianity remained rare is seen as further proof that most Jews did not feel the need to escape their religious identities.

In the centuries before industrialization and urbanization, Jews in central Europe mostly made their living as traders or moneylenders. In the German-speaking lands, few could speak the dominant language, and they were forced to settle in overcrowded ghettos in Frankfurt, Trier, Mannheim, and other towns. Reflecting on the conditions of Frankfurt's Jewish quarters, Goethe wrote that "the closeness, the dirt, the crowd, the sound of the disagreeable language, all this made the most unpleasant impression."[4] Jews were limited in their choice of occupation because before emancipation they could not own land and they were not allowed into craftsmen guilds. Without access to these most common occupations, Jews were forced into less well-respected careers in trade and moneylending. Many worked as cattle traders, as dealers in grain and hops, or as traveling salesmen who brought household goods to rural peasants. The wife of a Jewish moneylender in the eighteenth century described her husband's life as follows: "He was a money changer. Every money changer rushes around all day for his living, and towards evening, at the time of afternoon prayer goes home and thence to synagogue. Each one belongs to a chevra [group to study rabbinic texts] and, with other members, studies, and after studying returns home."[5]

After unification in 1871, ghetto walls started coming down, and Jews could purchase property for the first time. Civil rights created opportunities. Traveling salesmen could become shop owners, and traders could become wholesalers. The number of Jews in Berlin tripled by 1910 to around 90,000. The Jewish community grew even faster in other cities. Many Jews continued to work in trade and commerce where they had strong reputations for their experience and business contacts. Now settled in densely populated areas with the freedom to expand their businesses, some Jews became prosperous retailers. The Jewish families of Tietz, Israel, and Wertheim, for example, became pioneers in the establishment of Germany's first department stores. Some who had gained experience in moneylending could now establish banking institutions. As a group, Jewish Germans achieved a high rate of social mobility. Through the period before 1914 most Jewish families were middle class, but Jews did account for 20 percent of Germany's richest families.

Like non-Jewish Germans who became prosperous during this period of economic growth, successful German Jews amassed the savings necessary to send their children to university. Education had always been central to Jewish tradition, and it was prized in Germany as essential to *Bildung*—a combination of formal education and cultural sophistication. Therefore, it is not surprising that German Jews prioritized education for their sons and later their daughters. By 1900 about 10 percent of all German university students were Jews, even though the number of Jews in the population continued to hover around 1 percent. The eldest sons took over the family shop or manufacturing firm, while younger sons went into the professions. By 1907, 14.7 percent of Germany's attorneys were Jews, and in Berlin almost half of the attorneys were Jewish. Medicine, journalism, and higher education were also popular career choices among Germany's middle-class Jews.

Although Jews in Germany and elsewhere in central Europe entered universities and the professions at rates higher than their small numbers would predict, antisemitism had not disappeared, and Jews struggled to attain the highest positions in their fields. Attorneys were plentiful in private practice, but few were appointed to the bench. Jewish academics were numerous, but only 2 percent of full professors were Jewish, and some disciplines had no Jewish chair holders before 1918. Two other high-status sectors in which Jews faced discrimination were the civil service and the armed forces. Talented and educated Jews were welcomed into public and military service, but they were consistently overlooked for promotions. At the outbreak of war in 1914, there were no Jewish officers in the Prussian army. One Jewish Berliner, Artur Brandt, chose to transfer out of his guard regiment during the war in order to become an officer, after a friendly captain told him it would never be possible in his unit.[6] Despite such prejudice, German Jews supported the nation's call to arms in 1914 with the same level of patriotism as others. A different Jewish volunteer for the war effort explained at the outset of hostilities: "Love for the Jewish people does not conflict with love for the German Fatherland."[7] Indeed, some Jewish servicemen saw the war as a welcome opportunity to demonstrate their love of country and to disprove antisemitic charges that Jews were unpatriotic. One Jewish officer wrote of this "double duty" when he explained, "I am putting my fate in God's hands ... I am not afraid, and our people are burning to receive their baptism of fire. As a Jewish officer I have a double responsibility to prove myself courageous and diligent."[8] Despite their commitment, charges that Jews were shirking their duty were rife. In 1916, the army conducted a "Jewish census" meant to illustrate that Jews avoided frontline combat. While the report was never published because the charges could not be substantiated, an antisemitic pamphlet making the same claims circulated widely. By the end of the conflict, about 100,000 Jewish men had served in the Imperial forces, roughly 12,000 of them perished.

Well-integrated, urban, middle-class and upper-class Jews played a critical role in shaping Germany's development in the nineteenth and early twentieth centuries. We can easily find the names of prominent German Jewish scholars, artists, politicians, and business leaders in these decades. However, we should not forget that there were also poor Jews, who like other impoverished Germans remained on the fringes of society. Many of them were recent arrivals from the Russian Empire, having fled widespread antisemitic violence in 1881 and 1905. In 1880 there were only about 20,000 non-German Jews in the Empire. By 1910 the number had quadrupled to 79,000. Estimates for 1914 show the number at 90,000. Among this cohort were Jews who dressed differently, spoke Yiddish, and chose not to assimilate. Some lived in rural communities while others lived in inexpensive dwellings in the old city quarters. These were some of Germany's most visible immigrants, and many of Germany's assimilated Jews themselves looked down upon the "*Ostjuden*" (Jews from the east) because of their poverty and cultural and linguistic differences. They feared that the presence of pauperized Jews would provoke an antisemitic backlash against all.

Hatred of Jews was a cornerstone of National Socialism and the motivation for the Holocaust during the Second World War. Antisemitism, however, is a complicated set of beliefs, which predates National Socialism. The particular ways that National Socialists gave life to antisemitic ideology after 1933 through law, policy, and cultural manifestations will be the focus of later chapters, but because Nazi antisemitism was the by-product of several older existing strains of antisemitism, some background is warranted. These can be characterized as religious, socio-cultural, and economic forms of antisemitism.

The oldest form of hatred toward Jews was religious in nature. At the start of the twentieth century it remained popular among religious members of the peasantry and some members of the German lower middle classes and the clergy. For these people, the Biblical notion that Jews murdered Jesus Christ continued to be a powerful stigma that led to persecution, as it had for centuries especially when unexplained crises hit rural villages— deaths of children, poor harvests, epidemics. The synagogue in Neustettin was burned to the ground in 1881, and ritual murder accusations and trials took place near Danzig, in Breslau, and Xanten in the 1880s and 1890s. Violent communal attacks against Jewish neighbors in the German empire and elsewhere in Europe continued in the early twentieth century. Nazis would later traffic in these prejudicial tropes.

Social and cultural antisemitism was more common among elites. Aristocrats and other wealthy Germans still considered Jews (even elite ones) as inferior. Such antisemites were happy to do business with Jews or go to a Jewish doctor, but they would not invite Jews to dinner. To them, Jewish Germans remained outsiders, regardless of their legal status as equals or their personal achievements. As the Jewish industrialist and later Foreign Minister during the Weimar Republic, Walther Rathenau, put it in 1911: "The Jew carries a social blemish [Makel]. In the associations and social circles of the better Christian middle classes, he will not be accepted."[9] A third form of antisemitism that was increasing particularly in towns and cities around the turn of the century was economic in nature. Rapid industrialization meant that some small shopkeepers and craftsmen struggled to maintain their livelihoods and status in their communities when larger firms, chain stores, and industrial manufacturing arrived. For those who saw their businesses drying up in the face of new competition, Jewish businessmen were a convenient scapegoat. Prosperous Jews became symbols of industrial capitalism and exploitation, even though only a small portion of Germany's wealthy business leaders were Jews. Wilhelm Marr, who coined the term "antisemitism" in the 1870s, declared in his oft-reprinted pamphlet, "The Victory of Judaism over Germandom" that the country's Jews held a "controlling position in commerce," along with the press, the theater, and increasingly in politics. At times the lines between these various forms of hatred blurred with antisemites believing all or a combination of these falsehoods. Taken together, Marr concluded that Germans suffered under "alien domination."[10]

Contributing to this dangerous mixture, a new racist-biological variant of antisemitism also came on the scene in the last decades of the nineteenth century. It divided the world into superior and inferior races and used pseudo-scientific language to lend legitimacy to this hierarchy. Jews were easily targeted because they were viewed as a "race without a nation," which lived off the resources of other nations. In this era of rapid change, some Germans were susceptible to the lie that Jews were not only an inferior race but also a dangerous one. Their mere presence as lesser organisms among the superior German race, it was falsely argued, weakened Germany's racial health. There was also a political dimension to this claim. Antisemites believed that Jews conspired to weaken the German race in order to bring it under their control. Jewish bankers and industrialists were key to this plan, helping to achieve domination by enslaving their workers and ruining small businesses. Intermarriage and assimilation were attacked as strategies to disguise Jews' conspiratorial intentions to "dilute" the German gene pool. After the First World War, the Nazis co-opted this idea that Jews were a parasitic race that fed off German society to the point of ruin. And as we will see, they also made use of religious, economic, and social-cultural stereotypes in their attacks on Jewish Germans.

The National Socialists were not the first antisemitic political party in Germany. There were a number of anti-Jewish parties that formed after unification. One of these was Adolf Stoecker's Christian Social Party formed in 1878. Stoecker was the court chaplain to Wilhelm I and a charismatic speaker whose mix of Protestantism and social reform gained adherents among the lower middle classes during the economic downturn of the 1880s. Stoecker and his supporters found a scapegoat for their hardships in "Jewish capitalism." The firebrand also labeled socialism as Jewish, by portraying the Jewish-born Karl Marx and other Jewish social reformers and leftists as having brought a dangerous, foreign ideology to Germany. Seeing capitalism and socialism as a two-pronged Jewish conspiracy remained common in antisemitic circles well into the twentieth century. Stoecker's party and lesser-known right-wing groups lost their popular support during the economic upswing after 1893. Thereafter, antisemitic political parties like Stoecker's remained on the fringes, but the so-called "Jewish Question" remained a strongly contested political issue and cultural touchstone. Heinrich von Treitschke, Germany's most prominent historian of the age, railed against Jews in his uncritical hyper-nationalist history of the nation in 1879. As an esteemed historian and Reichstag member, Treitschke lent an air of legitimacy to prejudicial writings about Jews well into the twentieth century, and the Nazis used the historian's hateful words in their own propaganda: *Die Juden sind unser Unglück* ("The Jews are our misfortune"). Despite such antisemitism, by 1900 the German Jewish community had reason to be optimistic: "We are doing well here," wrote one Jewish memoirist: "We are Germans."[11]

What did German Jews think the future held for them? When the empire was founded, most thought of themselves as simply a religious minority— as Germans of Jewish faith. Over time, under the pressure of antisemitism and the racist-biological language of the day, Jews in Germany began to see their religion as just one aspect of their Jewish identity. They considered their history and cultural identity, combined with their religious faith, to be an ethnic category. This process was sped up by the fact that the vast majority of German Jews were very secular. Still, they experienced prejudice. One young Jewish lawyer, Arthur Ruppin, recalled his experiences working for nine months in the town of Klötze between Hanover and Berlin in 1902. At first his district court colleagues were warm, inviting him out to drinks and meals. But when he reported his religion as Jewish in his personnel file, the atmosphere changed dramatically, and he was treated with "icy civility." Over time, however, "the ice melted" and once again he was included in community activities.[12] Many like Ruppin began to believe their Jewishness and Germanness contributed to a unique but stable identity, like Asian American, Italian Canadian, or Black British today. In contrast to this majority view, there was also a minority of Jews who believed they would never be fully accepted in Germany. These men and women were the first Zionists—those who believed that the founding of a Jewish state was necessary for freedom. Theodor Herzl, who penned the most important treatise on the subject, *Der Judenstaat* (The Jewish State) in 1896, campaigned for this position throughout Europe. Most Jewish Germans, however, looked forward to a future, which they thought was in their grasp, when there would no longer be a "Jewish Question."

Defeat, Revolution, and the Early Republic

The First World War was the twentieth century's first "total war." Between 1914 and 1918 it was not only the German Imperial army and navy that together with their Austrian allies squared off against the Entente Powers of Britain, France, Russia, and their allies. Across the European continent, civilians felt the effects of war like no other conflict before. The boundary between the battlefront and the homefront grew thin as governments mobilized all national resources, including human power, in factories and on farms. How did Germans respond to the outbreak of war? While many greeted the hostilities with enthusiasm, others, particularly socialist workers and farmers, were less keen to see their nation becoming embroiled in conflict. Overall, in 1914 Germans did rally around the common cause, and the country's leaders touted the strength of the *Burgfrieden*, or "peace of the fortress," in which the social classes seemingly set aside their hostilities and supported the war effort together (Figure 1.1). The Nazis would later cite this moment of unity as a goal they strove to recreate in the Third Reich.

Germany's plan for victory—a modified version of the pre-existing Schlieffen Plan—entailed overcoming the country's disadvantageous location, sandwiched as Germany was between France and Russia. A quick victory over France would allow the Kaiser's army to concentrate its forces in the east and defeat the far larger, if less materially sophisticated, Russian army. This plan, however, faltered on day 1, when Belgian resistance slowed the German advance westward, and by autumn it had completely unraveled. The Germans were unable to overcome the French and British at the First Battle of the Marne in 1914, and soon a war of attrition unfolded along a front that ran for roughly 450 miles from Belgium to the Swiss border, on which 8 million men fought (and died). The gruesome conditions at the front left soldiers desperate and terrified. As one young German soldier wrote in spring 1915:

> On every Easter from now on, the pitiful image of my regiment called for inspection will swim before my eyes. Nine out of every ten who had gone out to battle lay strewn across the killing field, as the insatiable Earth drank their blood. And we—the survivors? Dead tired, no clothes, only mud—and blood-spattered rags [standing at attention] on the square.

FIGURE 1.1 *Departure from Berlin of the first German regiments, 1914 (Bundesarchiv, Bild 183-B0527-0001-726).*

Unable to summon a clear thought, each wanting only to find a small place to sleep—sleep to forget the horror of the last days, happy for the god of dreams to carry him home to mother—until the reality of waking comes back to him again.[13]

Despite their greater success on Russian territory, Germany could not avoid the two front land war. At sea the British retained their naval superiority throughout the conflict, choking Germany's trade routes, and pushing the country to resume unrestricted submarine warfare in early 1917. This led to American forces pouring into Europe to aid the Entente. Time and resources were not on the side of the German military. The German government tried to address this dire situation by enlisting civilians in its total war. The so-called Hindenburg Program of 1916 (named after Field Marshal and Chief of the German General Staff Paul von Hindenburg) had the goal of doubling war materiel production. And the Auxiliary Labor Law called all men from ages seventeen to sixty into war-related industries and limited their ability to change jobs. Now called to sacrifice, workers were wooed with new rights. For the first time, the Kaiser's government agreed to work with the SPD and trade unions to achieve production goals.

In the end, the *Burgfrieden* never came to be. Despite concessions to workers, class divisions remained. Most middle-class women stayed out of the factories, though some young single middle-class females did volunteer as nurses, while working-class women shouldered a heavy burden in the factories and at home. Civil servants and other white-collar workers saw their incomes lose ground in the face of rising costs, while workers in war-related industries saw their wages go up. Thanks to the British blockade, Germans experienced severe food shortages in 1917. Crop failures and the lack of imported goods affected the population unevenly. Wealthy Germans could buy or barter on the black market, while the poor went hungry. As a result, support for the war, which had been widespread in the first two years, began to weaken in 1917. The most significant political consequence of the deepening disillusionment was the split in the SPD in April of that year. The more radical wing, known thereafter as the Independent Social Democratic Party (USPD), left behind what became the Majority Social Democrats (MSPD), by declaring their unwillingness to continue support for the government's military campaign.

The desire to bring about an end to the conflict resulted in mass strikes and protests at home, and desertion and feigned illness on the battlefield. In July, the Reichstag passed a resolution in favor of ending the war by a roughly 2 to 1 margin. Only the Conservatives and National Liberals voted against it. Germany was not the only nation facing political turmoil in 1917. Russia underwent a revolution in February and again in October. The second led to the creation of a Bolshevik government that lived up to its promises of pulling Russia out of the war. The Treaty of Brest Litovsk, which Germany imposed on revolutionary Russia in exchange for peace in early 1918, obliged Russia to give up large swaths of territory in exchange for peace with Germany. The end of the conflict in the east created a false sense of optimism among the German High Command. They concentrated their forces in the west and began what they hoped would be a final offensive in March that had to be called off in July (see Plate 1). In the weeks that followed the Allied powers made quick gains. Assuming a negotiated peace was not far away, the High Command returned powers to a new parliamentary government led by the reform-minded Prinz Max von Baden on October 3, 1918.

The carnage, however, was not over. In late October the High Seas Fleet stationed in the North Sea at Wilhelmshaven was ordered out to battle. There was little to gain militarily; it would instead be a glorious display of naval might and self-sabotage that would deny the victor powers the joy of scuttling the ships after victory. About 1,000 German sailors, however, saw this suicide mission for what it was and refused to comply. When they were arrested, other sailors began defying their military orders, and a revolutionary spirit spread from the northern naval cities of Wilhelmshaven and Kiel through the countryside, with soldiers and workers joining the fray. By November 9 the movement had reached Berlin, and the Kaiser was forced to abdicate. Oskar Münsterberg, a businessman and art historian in Berlin, recounted the day in his diary. As he walked to work, he picked up the morning paper, which declared the Kaiser was still on the throne. Münsterberg worried further delay would mean civil war. By midday a second edition had arrived with the news of abdication. "Everyone exhaled with relief. Finally!" But what would come next was still unclear. In the afternoon Münsterberg described crowds of people gathered throughout the governmental quarter and rumors of shots fired. He later reported dramatically, "soldiers and civilians with and without weapons were like bees filling the inside and hanging on the outside of cars and cheering 'Long live the republic.' Now I understood that in Berlin the socialist republic had been declared."[14] Max von Baden happily stepped aside, as Social Democrat Friedrich Ebert was named head of a provisional government called the Council of the People's Deputies, composed of three MSPD and three USPD representatives.

With the army leadership sidelined, Ebert's government negotiated an armistice that took effect on November 11, 1918. This development allowed Hindenburg and others to claim that the military had been "stabbed in the back" by a civilian government, which they asserted was composed of disloyal Jews and socialists who prematurely surrendered while German boys were still fighting. Signed seven months later, on June 28, 1919, the Versailles Treaty that emerged from peace negotiations in Paris stipulated that a defeated Germany turn over 14 percent of its territory and pay substantial reparations. The treaty also contained the infamous Article 231, which blamed the war solely on Germany. These humiliating terms provided further fodder for the right to label the civilian leadership traitors (Figure 1.2). In the 1920s and all through Hitler's rule, civilians' and their parliamentary leaders' alleged betrayal of German troops served as ammunition for the radical right in its plans to revoke the Treaty of Versailles, dismantle the Weimar Republic, and later to defend dictatorship and military aggression. During the Second World War, Nazi propagandists employed the myth of the "stab in the back" and the humiliating surrender of 1918 to shame Germans into supporting the Nazi war machine.

Domestically, Ebert and his colleagues were keen to shore up the SPD-led provisional government. Not only did they worry about those on the right who met the news of the Kaiser's abdication with shock and anger, but they competed politically with parties to their left. When the SPD had split into the MSPD and the USPD, a more radical splinter group, known as the Spartacist movement, had struck out on its own. Led by Rosa Luxemburg and Karl Liebknecht, the Spartacists hoped to organize the workers' and soldiers' councils, which seized control of several towns and cities across the country in the wake of the first mutinies in Wilhelmshaven and Kiel, into a socialist state based on the new Soviet model. To counter this threat, Ebert and his deputy Philipp Scheidemann quickly moved to establish a constituent assembly to formalize the new German republic. Elections to the body were held on January 19, 1919, and women aged twenty and above were given the right to participate for the first time in a national contest (Figure 1.3). Henning Wenzel remembered protectively accompanying his sister as she went door to door encouraging women to vote and explaining that their choice was theirs alone: "If the man of the house votes Scheidemann, you can

FIGURE 1.2 *Mass protest against the Treaty of Versailles in front of the Reichstag, Berlin, May 15, 1919 (Public domain, via Wikimedia Commons).*

still vote for a different party."[15] Thirty-seven elected female representatives sat in the town of Weimar the following spring as members of the assembly tasked with forging a new national constitution.

It was not a foregone conclusion that this first postwar election would be peaceful or that Ebert's SPD would remain in control. Through December and particularly in the first half of January, the Spartacists (after January 1 known as the German Communist Party (KPD)) had engaged the council movement to lead mass strikes and protests, particularly in Berlin. General Wilhelm Groener, who had replaced Erich Ludendorff, as second in command, offered Ebert military assistance to quell the revolutionary actions. Ebert accepted. Both regular troops and demobilized soldiers organized into paramilitary Free Corps squadrons responded with violence. Most infamously, Luxemburg and Liebknecht were abducted and brutally murdered days before the National Assembly elections. Violence continued sporadically throughout the spring of 1919 until the last Soviet-style republic, based in Munich, fell in early May.

The recourse to state-sanctioned violence that ended the revolution had lasting repercussions. First, it deepened animosities within the left among the SPD, USPD, and KPD. While fundamental ideological differences made

FIGURE 1.3 *Election of delegates to the National Assembly that drafted the Weimar Constitution, January 19, 1919. The election marked the first time women were able to stand as candidates and vote in a national election. Armed soldiers were enlisted to keep the peace (United States Holocaust Memorial Museum, courtesy of Dottie Bennett).*

cooperation difficult under the best of circumstances, the assassination of the far left's leaders permanently damaged the relationship between the SPD and KPD. Second, accepting the aid of the military and right-wing Free corps in the early days of the Republic hampered the new government's ability to introduce democratic reforms to the military and judiciary. As a result, throughout the Weimar years anti-republican Germans continued to hold key positions of authority. At the local level, many of those who would join the ranks of the new NSDAP had either participated in this right-wing crackdown on the political left in 1919 and 1920 or sympathized with it.

Ebert and his allies struck a second compromise that supported the status quo when they backed an agreement between the representative of the trade unions, Carl Legien, and the representative of employers, Hugo Stinnes, on November 15, 1918, just four days after the armistice was signed. The Stinnes-Legien agreement was considered a substantial SPD victory. The unions won important concessions from the employers: recognition of union authority to represent workers; acceptance of the long sought eight-hour workday; the creation of factory committees to discuss workplace conditions; and the establishment of a central body to facilitate the return of demobilized soldiers and negotiate wages. In return—and this point divided the SPD from its critics further to the left—the employers also got what they most desired. The new Republic would enshrine the right to private property. There would be no nationalization of industry as in the Soviet Union, and capitalism remained intact.

The Weimar Constitution, which was written and ratified quickly on August 11, 1919, has been heralded for its progressive elements. It explicitly confirmed the individual rights of men *and* women, and granted women the vote. It outlawed noble privilege. The federal structure remained, but the chancellor answered to the democratically elected parliament, as he had since October 1918. The parliament used proportional representation to fill its ranks. While the rationale for this electoral system was to make sure all voices were heard, proportional representation meant that even the smallest political party was guaranteed at least one seat, based on the proportion of the popular vote it had secured. Building and maintaining governing coalitions became a perennial struggle. An elected president had the power to appoint or dismiss chancellors and could rule by decree in times of emergency, if one minister co-signed. The monarchy and all its trappings were gone for good.

For those on the far left in Germany's Communist Party the results of the revolutionary unrest that toppled the Kaiser were a disappointment and a betrayal by the leaders of Social Democracy. The KPD remained an enemy of the Republic until its demise at the hands of the Nazis in early 1933. Despite its marginalized status as a party of the unemployed, particularly during the Depression years from 1929 to 1933, many Germans feared a renewal of KPD-led violence, and they turned a blind eye to growing radicalism on the right. The Free Corps troops that quashed the Spartacist revolt were in turn emboldened by this "victory" and were convinced that the Republic too must be toppled. From its beginning the moderate Weimar Republic had enemies on both sides.

Those demobilized troops who joined the Free Corps found supporters among civilians who shared their antisemitic, anti-republican, anti-socialist, anti-Versailles political views. With the Spartacist threat eliminated and the republican constitution in place, now-President Ebert sought to dismantle the Free Corps in March 1920. On learning of this plan Reichswehr General Walther von Lüttwitz, who commanded several of the Free Corps units, gathered enough troops to occupy the capital on March 13 and claim the right-wing former parliamentarian Wolfgang Kapp and First World War hero and General Erich Ludendorff, as the nation's new leaders. The elected government fled Berlin after the defense minister acknowledged that he could not be sure the military would defend the Republic against the rogue general Lüttwitz. Several high-ranking Reichswehr officers had refused to give orders for their men to shoot former or current soldiers now serving in the ranks of the putschists.

After escaping arrest in Berlin, members of the government called upon the population to engage in a general strike; this was seconded by the central trade unions and the three main workers' parties (SPD, USPD, and even the KPD). As many as 12 million Germans across the country, save for Bavaria, refused to work. The country ground to a standstill, and within two days, Kapp, who had taken the mantle of chancellor, was forced to negotiate. The legacy of the Kapp Putsch and its undoing by popular protest is mixed. On the one hand, it remains a testament to the democratic spirit that had taken hold among many Germans by 1920. They wished to have their opinions heard and for the democratic process to be respected. The Republic did have its supporters, and they were willing to act to save it. On the other hand, the leaders of the putsch and the soldiers and police who supported them were amnestied. Indeed, following the putsch, Ebert's government sent some units to the industrial Ruhr valley to break up striking workers, who had issued their own demands in light of the successful general strike. The soldiers and paramilitaries attacked with ferocity, and a segment of Germany's working class was gravely disappointed by the SPD-sanctioned violence, further deepening divisions within the political left.

Some of the political aims of the putschists were realized. Alongside amnesties for their supporters, the government also agreed to move up to June 6 the date of the first Reichstag election, which the right saw as a referendum on the terms of the Versailles Treaty. The Social Democrats lost their majority, and the parties on both ends of the spectrum, the KPD and the German Nationalists (DNVP), increased their support markedly. The military, despite showing a remarkable lack of loyalty to the new democratic system, was never purged of disloyal officers. The Free Corps were eventually disbanded, but many members remained politically active, joining the numerous small right-wing political parties sprouting up around the country. Some continued their violent tactics. In the summer of 1921 right-wing activists assassinated the Republic's former finance minister and signatory of the Versailles Treaty Matthias Erzberger. The following year, they murdered the country's foreign minister, Jewish industrialist Walther Rathenau, and attempted to kill Social Democratic member of parliament Philipp Scheidemann. For the next ten years, the parties that fully supported the Republic never held a majority of seats in parliament. And every governing coalition included at least one party that was at best indifferent and at worst hostile to the Republic.

The Arrival of National Socialism

Amid the turmoil of the surrender and demobilization, a locksmith from the Bavarian city of Munich named Anton Drexler founded the German Workers' Party (DAP) in 1919. Adolf Hitler was living in Munich at the time. Born in Braunau, Austria, in 1889, he had moved from Linz to Vienna as a young man in the hopes of enrolling in the capital's Academy of Fine Arts. He failed the entrance exam and spent the following years at loose ends, burdened by disappointment and without direction. In 1913 he fled to Munich to escape the Austro-Hungarian military draft. He was eventually arrested and returned to Austria. It was in multi-ethnic Vienna that Hitler later claimed to have begun formulating his hatred for Jews, socialism, and liberalism. He blamed the weaknesses of the Austro-Hungarian Empire on its diversity and its Catholicism. He believed that uniting ethnic Germans in the region was the only path to national greatness. By the time the Great War broke out in July 1914, Hitler was back in Germany. The conflict was a tremendous opportunity for the directionless Hitler, who quickly enlisted in the Bavarian army and served as a dispatch runner in the List regiment. This assignment was not without risk. He was wounded once in 1916 and temporarily blinded by a mustard gas attack in 1918. He spent time in hospital after both incidents and was commended for his service with the Iron Cross, First and Second Class.

Without other prospects at war's end, the thirty-year-old Hitler stayed connected to the military as a political liaison. His task was to keep tabs on the flourishing right-wing networks that were sprouting up in and around the Bavarian capital. It was this job that took him to his first German Workers' Party meeting, where he met Drexler and was enthralled by the ideas he encountered. What he heard was not particularly original at the time, but it was enough to inspire him to quit his job and devote himself full time to the small organization, which updated its name to the National Socialist German Workers' Party (NSDAP) in February 1920 in order to broaden its political base, especially among workers. His later friend and supporter, the German American Ernst Hanfstaengel, remembered meeting Hitler for the first time ahead of an early party rally. "In his heavy boots, dark suit and leather waistcoat, semi stiff white collar and odd little mustache, he really did not look very impressive—like a waiter in a railway station restaurant." But once Hitler spoke, Hanfstaengel was captivated. "That night I could not sleep for a long time. My mind still raced with the impressions of the evening."[16] Hitler quickly became one of the party's most prized speakers, and on July 29, 1921, he was elected party chairman.

Members of the DAP, like others on the far right, aimed to rebuild pride in the German nation. They were eager to blame others for Germany's humiliation, and they accused the Jewish minority at home—rather contradictorily—of being both capitalist war profiteers and socialist strikers and revolutionaries. Jews, they claimed, were also behind the finance capitalism and liberal political orders of the victor nations of France, Britain, and the United States—states seen as Germany's oppressors after the signing of the Versailles Treaty. Drexler, Hitler, and others connected the dots for those willing to listen: Jews had never been loyal to Germany and had stabbed Germany in the back in 1918 in concert with their co-religionists abroad who built and profited from the Allies' war machine. In other words, for those around Hitler what amounted to a global Jewish conspiracy had led to Allied victory and the shameful Weimar Republic, which had empowered Germany's enemies at home to enshrine into law the country's international enslavement.

Most right-wing Germans shared these beliefs, but the NSDAP packaged this worldview into a clear framework for its supporters. The party's program, presented in Munich on February 24, 1920, emphasized three key themes among its twenty-five points. They were racial antisemitism, a hyper-nationalism that called for a uniting of all ethnic Germans in Europe into a "Greater Germany," and anti-capitalism, which demanded both an attack on real and perceived Jewish economic interests. With its new name, the NSDAP hoped to provide a new political home for conservative nationalists, whose parties had let Germany down. The mainstream parties on the right, the Nazis argued, lacked the courage to stand up to their enemies or mobilize the masses. In addition, unlike most radical nationalist groups, the Nazis also made appeals to industrial workers by arguing that only the NSDAP would take on big business and the Jewish interests that allegedly controlled it, while also promising social welfare measures.

This combination of hyper-nationalism, antisemitism, and social reform piqued public curiosity. In the early 1920s the NSDAP did not have a national reputation, but it was gaining a regional one in Bavaria. Hitler's personal photographer and friend, Heinrich Hoffmann, joined the party in April 1920, believing that "its program seemed to offer the only possible solution to the chaotic problems with which my country was overwhelmed."[17] An early membership list from 1920 shows that the party had succeeded in drawing adherents from all employment categories and classes: from workers and soldiers to office clerks and low-level civil servants to doctors and other professionals. We can take a step back for a moment to view the broader context in which these rabble-rousing politicians were making a name for themselves. In 1922 and 1923 the new Republic was very unstable, and some historians have even argued that the conditions were riper for collapse at that time than a decade later, when the Republic was in fact replaced by dictatorship. Following Foreign Minister Walther Rathenau's assassination in June 1922, the government sought to rein in radical, anti-republican paramilitary forces. In the months that followed, the NSDAP was banned in almost every German state, including Prussia (where Berlin was located), though not in Bavaria, where the NSDAP was headquartered.

The ban prompted a backlash from the far right, leading to the first discussions of a possible Nazi-led coup. This radicalism was exacerbated by a growing economic crisis. The Rathenau assassination had shocked the markets, and soon thereafter the French invaded the Ruhr to collect coal and steel that Germany owed to them according to the terms of the Versailles Treaty. The government encouraged civil disobedience among the Ruhr's miners and steelworkers and printed money to pay wages and fuel the economy during the shutdown. A period of hyperinflation was quickly underway (Figure 1.4). The currency was soon rendered worthless, which struck members of the middle classes and those on fixed incomes, like pensioners, most severely. For the middle classes, individual and family savings were to a great extent what differentiated them from workers. That a family had disposable income that could be saved for a child's education or old-age security, or spent on leisure pursuits or in emergencies, was a hallmark of a middle-class lifestyle. Seeing those savings rendered worthless by the collapsing currency further undermined middle-class support for the Republic. It was in this chaotic atmosphere, with the middle classes also worried about KPD gains in the states of Thuringia and Saxony, that Hitler began to conspire with officers in the Bavarian military to overthrow the Republic and install himself as the head of a new nationalist dictatorship, with General Erich Ludendorff leading the army. In October of 1922 Benito Mussolini had successfully seized power in Italy with similar populist rhetoric and a "March on Rome." His success emboldened the Nazi insurgents to seize the moment in Munich and march to Berlin in a similar fashion. In front of a rowdy beer hall crowd, the Nazis detained conservative and anti-republican Bavarian Governor Gustav Kahr and tried to convince him to enable safe passage of the plotters and their troops through Munich, as well as to join the march to Berlin, which would supposedly pick up more and more anti-government putschist along the way.

In a moment of duress, Kahr agreed, only to renege on his promise after exiting the beer hall. The next day on November 9, 1923, Erich Ludendorff and Ernst Röhm, both of whom were party members and army officers, remained committed to the plan, but without Kahr's blessing Hitler could not count on the police and Bavarian military to allow the coup to proceed. There was some local military support around Röhm, but higher-ranking

FIGURE 1.4 *Bank official counts stacks of Reichsmark notes in Berlin during the hyperinflation of 1923 (Library of Congress, Prints & Photographs Division, Bain News Service, publisher, Public domain, via Wikimedia Commons).*

military officers largely kept their distance. Hitler mustered about 2,000 supporters who took to the streets that day, but the police closed in. Several men on both sides were shot and others injured, and the leaders of the putsch, including Ludendorff and an injured Hitler, were arrested. In the short term, what became known as the Beer Hall Putsch was an embarrassing failure for Hitler. But it launched him and his party into the national spotlight.

The German press closely followed Hitler's and his co-conspirators' arrests and subsequent trial. Through regular multiple-page spreads dedicated to court testimony, Germans around the country became familiar with the ambitious and charismatic Hitler. The leaders of the young Nazi movement also learned a valuable lesson from the debacle: the military and governmental elites who had promised to support the putsch failed to follow through. Kahr and others had taken the stand against Hitler to offer evidence for the prosecution. In return, Hitler and his circle vowed not to rely next time on conservative insiders. They could not be trusted to risk their own positions of power for change. In his hours-long defense statement Hitler leaned into his role in the failed putsch, admitting his guilt but explaining it away as the action of a patriotic citizen. He hinted at the quality of the mass movement that he now sought. With supreme confidence Hitler declared the following:

For, gentlemen, it is not you who pronounce judgment upon us, it is the external Court of History which will make its pronouncement upon the charge that it brought against us. The verdict that you will pass I know. But that court will not ask of us, "Did you commit high treason or did you not? That court will just judge us ... as Germans who wanted the best for their people and their fatherland, who wished to fight and to die. You may pronounce us guilty a thousand times, but the Goddess who presides over the Eternal Court of History will with a smile tear in pieces the charge of the Public Prosecutor and the verdict of this court. For she acquits us.[18]

Right-leaning judges acquitted Ludendorff, and Hitler was given the minimum sentence of five years, though he was released on probation after less than one year. The trial coverage had captured the attention of a young writer, Joseph Goebbels, who referenced the proceedings in his diary on March 13, 1924. He wrote excitedly that he "was absorbed by [the news of] Hitler and the Nazi movement and will probably be so for a long time."[19] Ultimately, the publicity around the Beer Hall Putsch and the trial that followed allowed Hitler to gain a national following. His new admirers did not have long to wait for his release and the relaunch of a movement that had already gained roughly 55,000 members and many more fans in just three years.

Notes

1   Quoted in *Jewish Daily Life in Germany, 1618–1945*, Marion Kaplan, ed. (Oxford: Oxford University Press, 2005), 176.

2   Andrew Lees, *Cities, Sin, and Social Reform in Imperial Germany* (Ann Arbor: University of Michigan Press, 2002), 79.

3   Jens Flemming, Klaus Saul, and Peter-Christian Witt, eds., *Quellen zur Alltagsgeschichte der Deutschen, 1871–1914* (Darmstadt: Wissenschaftliche Buchgesellschaft, 1997), 118–19.

4   Quoted in Robert Liberles, "On the Threshold of Modernity" in *Jewish Daily Life*, Kaplan ed., 9.

5   Ibid., 19.

6   Artur Brandt, interview with Südwest Rundfunk, November 4, 1979, Jungfer Archiv. Many thanks to Dr. Benjamin Hett for providing this source.

7   Quoted in Tim Grady, *The German-Jewish Soldiers of the First World War* (Liverpool: University of Liverpool Press, 2011), 28.

8   Letter by Poldi to his father in Eugen Tannenbaum, ed., *The Great War Letters of German and Austrian Jews* (New York: Dannan Books, 2018), 7.

9   Flemming, *Quellen zur Alltagsgeschichte des Deutschen*, 84–5.

10 Wilhelm Marr, "The Victory of Judaism over Germandom" (1879), *GHDI— Document* (ghi-dc.org).

11 Kaplan, ed., *Jewish Daily Life in Germany*, 181.

12 Flemming, *Quellen zur Alltagsgeschichte des Deutschen*, 85–8.

13 "Erlebnis eines Frontsoldaten. Niedergeschrieben in einem Poesiealbum einer Lazarettkrankenschwester aus Berlin," Easter 1915, *Lebendiges Museum Online* and *Deutsches Historisches Museum*, www.dhm.de/lemo/zeitzeugen/ frontsoldat-osterschlacht-1915.html

14 Aufzeichnung aus dem Tagebuch des Unternehmers und Kunsthistorikers Oskar Münsterberg, https://www.dhm.de/lemo/zeitzeugen/oskar-muensterberg-novemberrevolution-1918.html

15 Henning Wenzel on the revolution and election of 1918/19, https://www.dhm. de/lemo/zeitzeugen/henning-wenzel-revolution-und-wahl-191819.html

16 Ernst Hanfstaengl, *Hitler: The Missing Years* (New York: Arcade, 1994), 33–7.

17 Heinrich Hoffmann, *Hitler Was My Friend: The Memoirs of Hitler's Photographer* (Barnsley: Pen and Sword, 2012), 41.

18 Adolf Hitler, court testimony, February 26, 1934, in *Nazism, 1919–1945*, Vol. I, Jeremy Noakes, and Graham Pridham, eds. (Exeter: Exeter University Press, 1994), 35.

19 Elke Fröhlich, ed., *Die Tagebücher von Joseph Goebbels, Aufzeichnungen, 1923–1941*, Vol. I, Band I (Munich: Saur, 2004), excerpt from March 13, 1924, 107.

Additional Reading

Berghahn, Volker. *Imperial Germany, 1871–1918: Economy, Society, Culture, and Politics*. New York and Oxford: Berghahn Books, 1994.

Bessel, Richard. *Germany after the First World War*. Oxford: Oxford University Press, 1993.

Blackbourn, David, and Geoff Eley. *The Peculiarities of German History: Bourgeois Society and Politics in Nineteenth-Century Germany*. Oxford: Oxford University Press, 1984.

Boak, Helen. *Women in the Weimar Republic*. Manchester: Manchester University Press, 2013.

Chickering, Roger. *Imperial Germany and the Great War, 1914–1918*. Third Edition. Cambridge: Cambridge University Press, 2014.

Eley, Geoff. *Reshaping the German Right: Radical Nationalism and Political Change after Bismarck*. Revised Edition. Ann Arbor, MI: University of Michigan Press, 1991.

Frevert, Ute. *A Nation in Barracks: Conscription, Military Service, and Civil Society in Modern Germany*. Translated by Andrew Boreham and Daniel Brückenhaus. Oxford: Berg, 2004.

Fritzsche, Peter. *Reading Berlin 1900*. Cambridge, MA: Harvard University Press, 1996.

Peukert, Detlev. *The Weimar Republic. The Crisis of Classical Modernity*. Translated by Richard Deveson. New York: Hill and Wang, 1993.

Weitz, Eric. *Weimar Germany: Promise and Tragedy*. Princeton and Oxford: Princeton University Press, 2007.

2

The National Socialist
Rise to Power

The Weimar Republic survived the chaos and violence of 1923. For the moment, economic turmoil and Nazi putschism belonged to the past, and a new optimism took hold, allowing the country to rebuild its image abroad and engage in social and cultural experimentation. But this stability was only relative compared to the crises that had just passed and that would soon come. Even while it lasted, the optimism and cultural flourishing of the mid-Weimar period masked underlying economic weaknesses and fundamental disagreements about the direction of the nation. The Nazi Party took advantage of these weaknesses.

The first part of the chapter explores the cultural and social backdrop to the Nazis' rise. It then turns to the growth of the NSDAP. After Hitler's release from Landsberg prison, the Nazis continued to hold nothing but disdain for the Republic, but they too benefited from the energy and openness to change that characterized the period. As we will see, like other Weimar innovators, National Socialists aimed to create a new world. They hoped to forge a "Greater Germany" rooted in racism and a will to violence. The chapter's final section brings together the themes of Weimar experimentation and the Nazis' political rise during the Great Depression. Buoyed by mass support and weakened opponents, by the early 1930s the Nazi Party and its leaders were better prepared than a decade earlier to take advantage of the political opportunities that emerged.

Stability Comes to Germany's First Republic

Some historians have argued that the First World War did not really end until after the Ruhr Crisis of 1923. The French occupation and German passive resistance were direct outcomes of the animosity and mistrust that had fueled the war and the peace process. In the fall of 1923, a new government led by Gustav Stresemann admitted the failure of the German position on debt repayment, and the international Reparations Commission drafted a new payment schedule, supported by the extension of credit from US financiers. What came to be known as the 1924 Dawes Plan also enabled Germany to reform its currency, thus ending the hyperinflation. The days of burning bundles of worthless banknotes to heat apartments were over. But suspicions of German intentions lingered. France charged that Germany had still not fulfilled the disarmament conditions of Versailles, but Britain and the United States encouraged the French to accept Stresemann's invitation to negotiate a Franco-German security agreement in 1925. In October the two sides met at Locarno, Switzerland, where Germany, France, and Belgium agreed not to use force to challenge the existing borders between the countries. The Locarno Pact also paved the way for Germany to join the League of Nations in 1926, officially ending eight years of international isolation.

Those who supported the center-right Stresemann viewed these developments as an indication that the Republic had a real chance at survival. Germany now had a voice within the international community through its seat at the League of Nations and a powerful supporter in the United States (itself not a League member). But the Republic's enemies did not see the situation as positively. National Socialists and others on the far right despised the League, which they viewed as a tool wielded by the victors of the Great War to limit Germany's sovereignty. Locarno, too, in their minds did little more than reconfirm the realities of the *Versailles Diktat*, a treaty they promised to tear up.

Republicans' optimism with respect to foreign affairs was mirrored in the domestic situation. In 1924 relative calm replaced the disorder of the prior six years. Within the political realm, however, lasting parliamentary coalitions remained a challenge. There were five governments between 1924 and 1929, admittedly a far better record than the ten cabinets in the Republic's first three years. And while a revolving leadership slowed parliamentary debate and decision-making, the legislation passed in Weimar's middle years enabled the realization of many principles enshrined in the constitution of 1919. For example, that document affirmed the duties of the state to ensure that the sexes were treated equally, that mothers and war widows were protected, and that young people—supported by their families and the state—could grow into healthy and productive citizens.

Key paragraphs also demonstrated the constitution's commitments to economic reform. To the disappointment of the communists, the constitution protected the right to private property. But it made the state responsible for regulating capitalism by expanding labor laws and enabling co-determination between employers and trade unions. The constitution committed the state to protecting society's most vulnerable "against the economic consequences of old age, infirmity and the vicissitudes of life" by maintaining and extending existing social insurance programs: "Every German shall be given the opportunity to earn his living through productive work. If no suitable opportunity for work can be found, the means necessary for his livelihood will be provided."[1]

Legislative efforts to sustain Germans in times of need took several years to bear fruit, but by 1927 a complex welfare system was in place, especially with the passage of the Unemployment Insurance Law. Employers, employees, and the state contributed directly to a national fund that would support those without jobs. The amount and length of support varied according to one's previous employment. Once these generally meager benefits were exhausted, the unemployed could turn to local emergency relief funds. Separate programs for those most disadvantaged by the recent war—disabled veterans, war widows, and orphans—remained in place. The importance of the Weimar welfare system cannot be overestimated. On the one hand, it exemplified the Social Democratic principles on which the Republic had been founded. Historically, poor relief was based on charitable principles that judged the moral deservedness of those who sought support. Now the state protected citizens regardless of character. On the other hand, the financial system on which this social welfare relied was precarious. The global economic crisis and depression of the early 1930s made the new welfare benefits impossible to sustain. It could not live up to its promise of protecting all citizens from despair, and, as we will see, it left the Republic fundamentally vulnerable to those parties that sought its demise.

The Weimar Republic's stable middle years are remembered today more for their cultural and social achievements than the legislative ones. Yet the two are not unrelated. They were both characterized by a spirit of optimism and experimentation. While not confined to Germany alone, the long duration of instability in Germany—a full decade between the start of war in 1914 and the arrival of calm in 1924—intensified the desire to challenge old ideas. Some of these social and cultural innovations remain with us today. This could be seen in gender and sexual norms, which had been upset by the war. Young men had been sent off to battle for years, and women at home also faced severe hardship, but without their fathers', husbands', or brothers' supervision. By 1918, women had been tested and found more capable than many had previously assumed possible. Some women's insistence on maintaining the independence enjoyed during the war years, coupled with the loss of an estimated 2 million German men, made it inevitable that gender norms would continue shifting in the postwar period. Along with their new political rights, including the right to vote, women also benefited from new economic opportunities. Longer-term economic trends, combined with the demographic imbalance, opened job opportunities for women in the 1920s. Telephone operators, typists, and other office workers were in great demand, as were salesclerks in the growing consumer goods sector. These young female employees had little opportunity for career growth, and male bosses and customers regularly mistreated them. But white-collar jobs did pay better than most manufacturing work, and these jobs offered a certain level of prestige.

The economic independence afforded to young, single, urban women made it possible for some to defy tradition and become "oriented exclusively toward the present."[2] Social commentators and novelists took to calling them New Women. This moniker, however, did not apply to most females. Those living in rural communities and religious families saw less change to their daily lives, and women everywhere were still expected to get married and eventually leave the workforce to focus on their families, provided their husbands' salaries sufficed. For working-class women, marriage continued to mean the exhausting double burden of wage work and domestic chores. While we need to be careful not to overstate the extent of change experienced by most women living in Germany, the existence of the New Woman fostered broader discussions about female agency, sexual practices, and sexual identity. Some women found mates who committed themselves to a modern "companionate marriage" that valued the woman's contributions and her desire for sexual pleasure. Communist and social democratic doctors and activists who recognized the economic and health consequences of large families on poor mothers led public campaigns to promote access to birth control and end the criminalization of abortion.

A desire to challenge the sexual status quo was also reflected in the vibrancy of the LGBTQ community, particularly in Berlin. But this community still faced obstacles; gay men and their allies sought to overturn the criminalization of gay sex, and though they failed to achieve this goal, the policing of urban gay bars, nightclubs, and areas known for hookups decreased in these years of greater tolerance. To some extent the lasting image of Weimar Berlin as a site of sexual liberation and hedonism is a product of Nazi hyperbole. There were substantial efforts in the 1920s to challenge older gender norms and standards of sexual behavior, and there were new opportunities for self-expression and leisure activities. However, as the NSDAP grew in size and influence, the Nazis exaggerated the extent of change and blamed this "decadence" on outside influences, military defeat, and republicanism in general. Socialists, Jews, liberals, and feminists became the scapegoats for broader social change. The Weimar Republic's urban centers were hardly dens of iniquity, and change came slowly. Abortion was not legalized; female "career women" were still extremely rare; gay men and women were not in most cases "out" in public; and gay sex remained a crime, though infrequently prosecuted.

Experimentation also intensified in the arts. As with gender norms, not everything changed radically, but avant-garde artists who pushed the limits of their mediums gained widespread attention in these years. For some, art was a political tool to further the democratizing impulses of the Republic. The Bauhaus school was founded in 1919 and combined the teaching of fine and applied arts. A co-ed student body learned techniques that were not only of high aesthetic value but that also ideally could be made accessible to the masses through the use of modern materials and mass production. Although the arts and crafts studios of the Bauhaus also created innovative textiles and ceramics, furniture, and photography, the architecture associated with the school is its greatest legacy. For the Bauhaus architects, chiefly Walter Gropius and Ludwig Mies van der Rohe, the styles of Imperial Germany had died alongside the monarchy and the nationalist chauvinism that they believed had led to war in 1914. A completely new style was needed to reflect the machine age, but it also needed to be "organic" and connect human users with the natural world around them. Politically motivated, they dreamed of (and in some cases realized) modular housing and other buildings that could bring sunlight and fresh air to residents of all incomes. The new architecture eschewed exteriors with pompous ornamentation and rejected interior decoration that prized dust-collecting knickknacks and heavy furniture. This outmoded look was exchanged for an international style with clean lines and surfaces. Function and form were to be united.

While this international style in home design and interior décor did not become accessible to large numbers of Germans in the 1920s, its forward- and outward-looking perspectives were shared by other aspects of popular culture in these years. Film became a favorite past-time for many across Germany and was affordable for most (Figure 2.1). While Germany had a home-grown film industry, which supported both standard fare and cutting-edge expressionist features, Hollywood gained an early foothold and contributed to the international success of silent-era movie stars, including

FIGURE 2.1 *Full house at the "Primus" cinema, which opened on Hermannplatz in Berlin in 1928 with over 2000 seats (Bundesarchiv, Bild 183-1982-1116-502).*

Charlie Chaplin. Music, too, borrowed sounds and styles from beyond Germany's borders. American jazz and other forms of popular music became staples in the nightclubs and dance halls. Multinational consumer goods firms, like the US-based General Motors and Coca-Cola, and the German skincare firm Nivea marketed their products during the stable years in the vast illustrated press and in advertisements that blanketed Germany's urban streetscape with visions of abundance and opportunity.

Germans did not purchase durable goods like cars or household appliances at the same rates as other Europeans or Americans, but the overall trend was clear in the mid-1920s: Weimar Germany was becoming more economically and culturally entwined with its western European and transatlantic neighbors. Its political culture seemed to stabilize in these years. In addition to the legislative achievements mentioned earlier, support for the democratic process and the rights and responsibilities enshrined in the 1919 constitution grew. Political party and trade union membership remained high in these years, and voter turnout was strong at all levels of government. The courts upheld freedom of the press and other forms of expression, and tolerance of religious and other forms of difference was on the rise.

The Nazi Movement in Democratic Germany

The failed putsch attempt in 1923 offered useful lessons to the Nazi leader and his supporters, and the thirty-five-year-old Hitler spent his time in prison processing past mistakes and planning his next moves. Uncharacteristically, Hitler summed up this period of learning and camaraderie among like-minded acolytes succinctly, when he declared, "Landsberg was my state-paid university."[3] Hitler was released from jail shortly before Christmas 1924, and he discovered a different country from when he entered prison nine months earlier. The revolutionary era was over, and the NSDAP needed a new strategy for a more stable political climate. Hitler was determined to reorganize and expand his party with the aim of making inroads in local and national elections. He still desired to rid Germany of the Republic. But now he rejected the idea of a violent coup and planned instead to use to his advantage the very democratic political structures that were gaining strength. Over the next several years, Hitler and other top Nazis built a modern political machine, which enabled and rewarded mass participation across Germany, and which in time they hoped would translate into mass support for Nazi candidates.

There were some risks to this ostensibly legal, parliamentary strategy. For one, Hitler would need to ensure party unity behind his leadership. In most democratic, multi-party systems, party leadership rotates, and many perspectives inform the party message. Hitler was not interested in such dynamics. In the weeks following his release he engaged in two efforts to solidify his control. First, he finalized the manuscript for his book,

Mein Kampf (My Struggle). Part biography, part political manifesto, the book highlighted his self-understanding as the messianic future leader of Germany and drew together the racist and nationalist strands of his belief system. Second, he worked to force the NSDAP's quarreling lieutenants to put aside their differences and line up behind the one true leader. He achieved this latter aim through a series of meetings and publicly staged events. On February 27, 1925, the National Socialist German Workers Party was officially reconstituted. The parliamentary strategy got an unexpected boost later that summer when Germany's president, the Social Democrat Friedrich Ebert, died suddenly. A journeyman saddle maker by trade, Ebert embodied the pragmatic social democratic roots of the Republic since its founding, serving as chancellor during the revolutionary period before being selected by the National Assembly to serve as Germany's (provisional) first president in 1919. In that role Ebert was the first commoner head of state in the nation's history.

Although the parliamentary system limited the president's role, the position was not solely symbolic. The president had the authority to dissolve parliament and call new elections, appoint or dismiss the chancellor, and, under Article 48, issue presidential decrees during times of emergency. The first round of voting to fill the presidency after Ebert's death offered the public a wide range of candidates, and it ended with the trouncing of the former First World War hero and Beer Hall Putsch conspirator, Erich Ludendorff. This pleased Hitler, for it removed a potential rival on the far right. In the second and final round, the even bigger war hero, the elderly Field Marshal Paul von Hindenburg, bested the Catholic Center Party member Wilhelm Marx, in part because the Communist Party leader, Ernst Thälmann, chose to stand as a candidate rather than consolidating the left's chances by supporting Marx. Hindenburg's victory was a fortuitous outcome for the NSDAP as it helped move the Republic further to the right.

The critical work of expanding the Nazi Party continued. Two of the key figures in this period were Gregor Strasser and Joseph Goebbels. Both were skilled organizers who hoped to broaden the party's base socially and geographically, in part by amplifying the socialist strain in early Nazi thinking. As leader of the party's Working Group Northwest, Strasser penned a 1925 manifesto that sought to draw in working-class supporters through a promise of nationalizing industry. It also proposed an alliance with Soviet Russia as a counter to the capitalist nations that had authored the hated Versailles Treaty. Both men were shocked, however, when Hitler angrily denounced the manifesto at a meeting of the party's leaders in early 1926. Forced to retract their ambitious statement, Goebbels wondered for a time if he still had a future in the movement. Weeks later delegates at a Nazi Party conference re-confirmed Hitler's role as sole leader. The 1920 party program was declared "sacrosanct" and thereby closed to further revision. And the party unified behind the broader ideas outlined in *Mein Kampf*, which included the acquisition of so-called "living space"

(Lebensraum) on Soviet territory secured through a life-or-death struggle with Bolshevism, rather than a Soviet-German alliance against capitalism. Hitler, however, did want to keep the skilled Strasser and Goebbels on his side, and in the following months both received important new assignments. Goebbels became Gauleiter (regional leader) of Berlin, and Strasser became chief propagandist for the party and then took on the role of Organization Leader, making way for the twenty-six-year-old deputy, Heinrich Himmler, to step into the propaganda role.

These reassignments were effective. Goebbels hated Berlin because of its cosmopolitan tolerance and its well-integrated Jewish population, but he also knew the importance of "winning" the capital for Nazism. Despite complaints in his diary about "the deafening noise" and "horrendous conditions" in the city, he accepted the critical assignment as a sign of Hitler's faith in his abilities, and he dived into the new work with zeal and persistence, imagining himself as "Hercules in the Augean stables."[4] Berlin's residents had thus far shown little interest in the NSDAP, which had managed to attract only roughly 800 members in a city of 4 million. In the capital, support for the Republic, or a communist alternative, remained strongest. Goebbels was a gifted organizer, writer, and orator, and he made a quick and lasting impact on the Berlin NSDAP. Gregor Strasser also took to his new role with enthusiasm. Over the next two years, Strasser implemented a series of organizational reforms that coordinated and amplified a unified party message. Recognizing the goal was to win elections, he redrew the borders of the party's regional sections to line up with the parliament's electoral map. He also strengthened the authority of the regional chiefs, who, along with the regional propaganda leaders, would work with his office to deliver propaganda that was both up to date and in line with the aims and strategies of the national leadership.

It is important to remember that in the years following its relaunch, the NSDAP remained a marginal political force with limited influence and resources. And much of what Strasser, Goebbels, and other regional leaders built in this period at the grassroots borrowed from tried-and-true social democratic and communist tactics: the use of propaganda to advertise events and promote ideology; uniformed marches; the engagement of women and children in party activities; and staging political rallies and social events at workplaces and in homes. While these elements are essential to any political campaign today, such methods were still being pioneered in the 1920s, and even Hitler admitted that the Nazis needed to emulate the political left if their movement were to gain the mass support needed for widespread electoral success.

This propaganda strategy entailed wooing German women and teenagers, as essential to the short- and long-term success of the party. In 1926 the NSDAP founded the Hitler Youth, the first Nazi women's organization, and the Nazi Students' League, which mobilized university students. The National Socialist Factory Cell Organization (NSBO) followed in 1928 as a means of countering the strength of the SPD-aligned trade unions and factory organizations. The most important of the party's mass organizations was the stormtroopers, or *Sturmabteilung* (SA), the paramilitary wing of the party (Figure 2.2). The SA had been outlawed after the failed Beer Hall Putsch, but the government lifted the ban in 1925, and the SA once again played an influential role in rallying support to the party. Even in towns where the NSDAP did not have a large presence, local SA members held regular marches to draw attention to the party's platform, and during campaign seasons they provided protection to Nazi politicians at rallies and harassed rival parties' speakers at competing events. The SA also provided opportunities for male camaraderie through leisure activities like camping, hiking, and drinking at pubs.

Two further initiatives in the late 1920s tell us much about how the party broadened its support at the grassroots level while becoming increasingly invested in Hitler's dictatorial leadership. The first was the compulsory adoption of the "Heil Hitler" (Hail Hitler) greeting in 1926. Although it was not new, the codification of its use this year was telling. On the one hand, the NSDAP was looking to enlist and motivate a broad swath of Germans to support the movement by creating rituals that fostered a sense of belonging among its members. On the other hand, the party infrastructure was strictly hierarchical in nature, from the smallest cell in an

FIGURE 2.2 *Essen's Stormtroopers leave for the Nazi Party rally in Weimar, 1926. At center in a suit stands Josef Terboven, who would later serve as Gauleiter of Essen and Reichskommissar for Norway during the war (Bundesarchiv_Bild_119-0779/ CC-BY-SA 3.0, CC BY-SA 3.0 DE, Public Domain, via Wikimedia Commons).*

apartment block and village circles to larger town and city units, and up to the regional Gaus (districts). At each level a leader commanded those below and answered to those above, all the way to the powerful regional leaders, or Gauleiter, who reported directly to Hitler. With the ritualization of what became known as the "Hitler greeting," even non-political interactions between Nazi supporters, for example, neighbors running into each other at the market, commenced with this invocation of loyalty and obedience to their leader.

Another long-lasting innovation of 1926 was the re-introduction of what became the annual Nazi Party rally. That year's event was held on July 3 and 4 in Weimar, the adopted home of two giants of the German Enlightenment, Goethe and Schiller, and more recently the place where Germans wrote their first democratic constitution in 1919. It was also the original home of the Bauhaus, which decamped for the friendlier environs of Dessau in 1925. German nationalists were proud of Weimar's long-standing association with German culture, while Hitler saw in the birthplace of the hated Republic and home of the decadent artistic avant-garde an invitation to reclaim the city for the far right by holding his mass gathering there. After a successful rally in Weimar, which attracted an estimated 8,000 participants, about half of whom were stormtroopers, the Nazis moved the annual event to Nuremberg in 1927 because of the city's more suitable parade grounds, reliable local party base, and sympathetic police. Nazi supporters took pilgrimage-like treks from around the country to the rally site, where they engaged in several days of marching, listened to endless speeches, and participated in fun and games. The German press emphasized the enthusiasm of attendees and the dynamism of the party's leadership, especially Hitler, who attended each year. Leftist newspapers criticized the rallies as monotonous, but even their reporters were sometimes taken aback by the NSDAP's ability to mobilize support, which, as one journalist exclaimed in 1927, even included "twelve-year-old school kids marching in military uniform."[5]

Who were the men and women who boarded trains to Weimar and Nuremberg, became neighborhood block captains, disseminated Nazi literature, and signed up their sons as members of the Hitler Youth? As we have seen, the very first supporters of the party, those who joined between 1920 and the Beer Hall Putsch at the end of 1923, were mostly Bavarian men. Like others who joined a far-right group in the early years after the First World War, many of these first Nazis were veterans of the conflict, now disillusioned by defeat and disgusted by the establishment of a democratic Republic that they believed had surrendered the last vestiges of German dignity through compliance with the Versailles Treaty. Hitler and Hermann Göring, who would become one of the most important men in the Nazi regime, are examples of this group. But the NSDAP also gained early adherents among those too young to fight in the First World War. Germans born around the turn of the century grew up in a society steeped in nationalist fervor, and the war only strengthened that chauvinism. Still in their late teens at the time of defeat and in their early twenties during the economic crisis of 1923, this cohort experienced Germany's failures acutely. Their prospects for security or advancement in the mid-1920s seemed dim. Unemployment remained relatively high, and wages were low, even during the more stable part of the decade. For some born around 1900, therefore, the Nazi Party offered an alternative—a chance to right the wrongs of the past, to play one's part in history-making events, and to avenge the defeat of their fathers or brothers. As Werner Best, who went on to become a leader of the movement, put it: "not to be able to fight as my father did, as a soldier for the German victory, became the trauma of my youth …"[6] This trauma pushed the young Best to seek opportunities for action in the years that followed.

By the late 1920s, Nazi efforts to build a national following were beginning to pay off. But party membership and support for the movement were not necessarily the same thing. Women, for example, were far less likely to join the party in the 1920s than men, though plenty of wives or daughters shared their husbands' or fathers' political beliefs. Of the men who joined after Hitler's release from prison, the majority were middle-class and lower-middle-class Protestants who worked as craftsmen, shopkeepers, or small business owners. Teachers and lower-ranking civil servants also began to fill the party membership rolls. University students were also drawn to the party in large numbers, a surprising development given the Nazis' disdain for intellectual learning and reasoned debate. Nonetheless, many were attracted to the NSDAP's youthfulness and radical nationalism, which stood in contrast to the communists' anti-capitalist message that their families denounced. In the mid-1920s, two-thirds of NSDAP members were under the age of forty.

What about factory workers? The level of support for Nazism among Germany's industrial labor force has been a source of debate. Socialists and communists, at the time and in the decades after the regime's demise, have argued that fascism and its Nazi variant were a response to the inherent crises of capitalism and that Hitler was a tool of big business interests who feared a workers' revolution. Workers were believed to have recognized the capitalist interests pulling the strings and therefore rejected Hitler's appeals. In fact, some industrial workers were attracted to planks within the original Nazi Party platform, including those that called for corporate profit sharing and the end of "the slavery of interest." Workers were also not immune to antisemitism, though that prejudice does not seem to have been a leading cause for support of the movement. Those workers who were members of trade unions and active in social democratic and communist politics did not tend to abandon their beliefs for Nazism (see Plate 2). However, some skilled workers—especially those outside the major cities—felt a kinship with the lower middle classes and could find the Nazis' nationalism and language of German unity appealing. Support was also found among unskilled laborers, such as itinerant or piece-rate workers like those who sewed buttons on garments, whose precarious employment meant they had never built a strong connection to Germany's SPD-led workers' culture.

We are still missing one important social group. Even though Germany had experienced significant urbanization and industrialization over the previous fifty years, in the 1920s one in three Germans still lived in a rural area, and the vast majority of these individuals made their living through agriculture. For most of the 1920s, farmers and farm laborers had not shown much interest in the Nazi Party. But starting in 1928, the NSDAP recognized that this was a largely untapped pool of potential voters, and it began targeting these communities and their interests in the party's promotional activities. The effort paid off, especially with Protestant small farm owners and laborers, who came to believe Nazi rhetoric that called for German self-sufficiency with respect to its food supply and promised to protect the rural way of life and celebrate it as intrinsically German.

Traveling orators and party publications crafted specific appeals to farmers and agricultural laborers, but the party tailored different messages for different audiences. Small businessmen were told they were the backbone of the country, pushed aside by big business and its Jewish financiers. University students were told that their futures had been squandered by an ineffectual republican government. Women were told that their sacrifices for the nation were second to none and that in the Third Reich mothers would get the respect and support they deserved. Despite the Nazis' clever appeals to individual constituencies, the core ideological message remained: the time had come for Germany to "awaken" and recognize the nation's external and internal enemies, whom Adolf Hitler alone could defeat. Abroad, Hitler would re-establish German strength among nations, casting off the shackles of Versailles. And at home, he would establish a *Volksgemeinschaft*, a national community built on social, cultural, and racial unity, where those who carried "Aryan" blood would thrive. Liberalism was a foreign import that had enabled "non-Aryans," especially Jews, to become owners of big businesses that cheated and exploited customers and employees. When they were not "capitalists," Jews were portrayed as the opposite, as communist organizers who pitted Germans against one another and took orders from the Bolsheviks in Moscow. Once Germans defeated these forces of evil, the Nazis promised, they would begin to see the rewards long due to them. Germany would play a leading role on the world stage, enjoy an abundance of material goods, and benefit from social harmony at home. All of this was possible if Germany put its confidence in Hitler as the nation's sole leader and put aside internal divisions, whether based on class or religion. It was not that all "Aryan" Germans would be the same in this National Socialist utopia. Rather prosperity would come to all members of the national community, and Germans would appreciate one another's varied contributions to the greater good (as defined by Hitler and the party). Those perceived to be undermining this project or endangering Germany's long-term survival would be identified and removed from the *Volksgemeinschaft*.

Armed with this message, a formidable organizational structure, and a charismatic leader, the party aimed to grow rapidly. But in the regional elections of 1926 and 1927 the NSDAP made little headway, garnering less than 4 percent of the tally in all ten contests they entered, and in some—like the elections in the state of Saxony in the fall of 1926—the party received less than 2 percent of the vote. By the time the federal parliamentary elections rolled around in 1928, the economy had improved further, and the NSDAP fared even worse. After all the door knocking, speeches, and parades, the Nazi Party only carried 2.6 percent of the vote nationwide. However, as historian Thomas Childers has noted, 13.7 percent of the vote went to other fringe parties, demonstrating that even as the Weimar Republic stabilized, a substantial contingent of disaffected voters remained, mostly from within the middle classes, who looked for better options than they believed the major parties offered.[7]

The Period of Crisis

Monocausal explanations of major historical changes are never adequate. This statement holds true when investigating how Germany's first democratic Republic was swept aside after little more than a decade by what would become a genocidal dictatorship. Put another way, there is no easy answer to the question: why did Germany, one of the most educated, industrialized, and cosmopolitan countries on the planet at the end of the 1920s, overwhelmingly accept the suspension of individual rights in favor of an authoritarian regime led by a hate-filled and violent foreigner with no experience in governing?

We have already explored some of the long-term developments that fueled the radicalism of Adolf Hitler and his comrades: the humiliation of defeat in the First World War; deeply ingrained antisemitism and nationalist chauvinism; frustration with the challenges posed by parliamentary democracy; and an economy battered by war and revolution. We can also point to the rise of fascist movements across Europe, with Mussolini's earlier success in Italy inspiring Hitler. Gender historians have also seen the changing opportunities for women in the first two decades of the twentieth century as adding to the rise of misogynistic and hypermasculine politics and political violence in the 1920s. All of these factors contributed to the emergence of National Socialism, but they were not enough to bring the movement into the mainstream by 1928. Here, then, we must also look at the short-term factors that enabled Hitler's attainment of power.

After the hyperinflation of 1923 was brought under control and the Reichsmark was revalued in 1924, Germany's economy gained traction over the next five years, though much of the recovery was financed by American loans, and even with this assistance, many of the early socioeconomic promises of the Weimar Republic remained illusory. The long-desired eight-hour workday, introduced in late 1918 as part of the landmark partnership between the trade unions and industrialists, had been suspended for most workers during the economic crisis of 1922–3. Anxious employers remained wary of bringing the Stinnes-Legien Agreement back when stability returned. In May 1924 Germany's largest trade union reported that over half of its members worked forty-eight hours a week, and among them 13 percent worked fifty-four hours a week. Most workers would have to wait again until 1929, when cutbacks to production schedules occasioned by the emerging Depression resulted in shorter work weeks—for those who were still employed.

The Great Depression was a global catastrophe, but some countries were hit harder than others. Germany faced the most acute crisis in Europe. Already in 1928, some American banks were recalling loans made to Germany. After the panic selling of stocks began in New York in October 1929, many more American banks called in the loans they had made to German banks earlier in the decade, which in turn meant German banks were forced to retrieve funds from business owners across the country, leading thousands of small and large companies and farms to downscale or shutter their operations in the following months and years. Unemployment skyrocketed. The official number of registered unemployed shot up from 1.6 million in 1929 to 6.2 million in early 1932, though historians estimate that another million unemployed are missing from that tally because they no longer bothered to register their status, knowing they no longer qualified for assistance. While this widespread economic collapse had real material consequences for Germans, it would be wrong to draw a straight line from economic crisis to the Nazi dictatorship. In fact, there are two separate storylines, which we must pursue in light of the Depression. For the next two years the two stories intersected but had potentially separate outcomes: the fate of the Weimar Republic and the fate of the Nazi Party.

The Republic, emerging out of the ashes of the tremendous human losses associated with the First World War, was designed, as explained earlier, as a social welfare state. Citizens, at their most vulnerable, were to be protected by the resources of the state. Unfortunately, after 1929 this social safety net was quickly overwhelmed by the level of need. The massive public deficits that emerged stoked fears of a return to the runaway inflation of just six years prior. For the unemployed, long-term joblessness led to despair and a sense of betrayal. For some, these feelings translated into political radicalism. Even those who maintained their jobs saw desperation in their midst. Hundreds of people gathered at unemployment offices, long lines snaked in front of soup kitchens, homeless encampments sprang up in city parks, and gaunt, shoeless children skipped school to beg (Figure 2.3). Lea Grundig, a twenty-four-year-old artist in Dresden in 1930, wrote in her postwar memoir that "unemployment became a tragedy for many. Not only because of the poverty that mutely sat at their table at all times. Not working, doing nothing, producing nothing—work that not only provided food, but also, despite all the harassment and drudgery, was satisfying, developed skills, and stimulated thinking; work, a human need—it was not available; and wherever it was lacking, decay, malaise, and despair set in."[8]

Germany's many local and national newspapers reported on increasing levels of crime and the accompanying growth of radical parties on the extreme left (KPD) and right (NSDAP). Even those who had maintained faith in republicanism began to question whether the system was up to the task of solving the country's myriad problems. Some at the very highest ranks of the government themselves drew the conclusion that the Republic was fatally flawed. These included all the chancellors since 1929 and President Hindenburg, the aristocrat and former Field Marshal now in his eighties who was less accustomed to republicanism than he was to monarchy and the authoritarian structures still embraced by the Germany military. Despite the legislative role granted to the parliament in the Weimar Constitution, as president, Hindenburg wielded considerable power of his own. As noted earlier, among other important duties, the president appointed or dismissed the chancellor and could issue emergency decrees in times of crisis.

Hindenburg was the one constant in an unfolding drama. The chancellors and their cabinets did not have the same staying power, as one government after the next toppled when they failed to maintain a large enough coalition in the Reichstag to pass legislation. The Republic had always been governed by ruling coalitions, which, given the precarious state of the economy and

FIGURE 2.3 *Large crowds at an unemployment office in the workers' district of Berlin-Neukölln, 1932 (Bundesarchiv, Bild 146-1996-039-20A).*

foreign relations pressures, meant that a total of twelve men held the title of chancellor between 1919 and 1929. One political consequence of the Depression, however, was that governing coalitions became even more difficult to sustain, and they were increasingly led by those who hated the Republic.

The era of relative political stability ended in March 1930 when the last pro-republic coalition failed to secure an agreement to keep the country's unemployment insurance program afloat financially. The program faced severe deficits, and the failure of the SPD and the German People's Party (DVP), a center-right party representing business interests, to find a path forward during these early months of the Depression, helped a small number of President Hindenburg's more conservative advisors to engineer the downfall of Hermann Müller's government. Centre Party politician Heinrich Brüning was recruited by this circle of insiders, led by Reichswehr general Kurt von Schleicher, to head a new, more right-leaning cabinet, from which the SPD would be excluded. Brüning agreed to the plan, stepped in as chancellor and introduced austerity measures to reduce deficit spending. This move, which only deepened the crisis and suffering among German families, was intended to weaken the SPD, still the largest party in the Reichstag. Brüning also hoped to demonstrate to Germany's former adversaries that the country was unable to make its reparations payments. When the parliament refused to accept the austerity budget of the "Hunger Chancellor" in July 1930, Hindenburg dissolved the parliament and called for new national elections in two months' time. In the weeks leading up to the voting, Brüning's plan was put into place by presidential decree. It included cuts to wages and retirement benefits, including those for wounded veterans. Brüning also decreased the amount of funding reserved for the states, which led to a further round of cuts at the regional level, especially to education.

When the parliamentary elections called for by Hindenburg were held in September, the republican parties bore the brunt of Brüning's deeply unpopular policies and the worsening crisis. The SPD, Brüning's Center Party, the Democratic Party, and the DVP all lost several percentage points compared to the results of the previous federal election. The radical movements gained ground. The Communist Party was up 2.5 percent over the 1928 results to a new high of 13.1 percent, and the NSDAP celebrated the most remarkable victory. It went from 2.6 percent of the votes in 1928 to over 18.3 percent, or from 12 deputies to 107. The Nazi Party now enjoyed the second largest voting bloc in the Reichstag. Only the SPD held a slight lead, but its support was sinking, from 29.8 percent of the vote two years prior to 24.5 percent in September 1930, which translated into a loss of ten seats. And here is where the two stories—the fate of the Republic and the fate of the Nazi Party—become dramatically intertwined.

When the Reichstag was dissolved in July 1930, Joseph Goebbels, who had become the Nazi Party's national propaganda chief in addition to his duties as Berlin Gauleiter, set about coordinating the coming campaign. The message was almost entirely negative. The NSDAP railed against the Young Plan, a new payment schedule for reparations renegotiated the year before, and it continued its assault on the Versailles Treaty and the hated "war guilt" Paragraph 132. It also lashed out against the capitalist system and its supposed leaders, the Jews, who had demanded fulfillment of the treaty's terms and who consequently had led Germany into a depression. In short, the party had no new creative solutions to the overwhelming problems facing Germany. Rather Nazi supporters cast blame not just on Jews, capitalists, and communists, but also on "the system"—the Republic itself. They harnessed a widespread anger that accompanied a new slide into political and social chaos. While the message did not offer much in the way of policy details, there was a sustained coherence to the critique, engineered by a state-of-the-art propaganda machine. Even more important than message and optics was action. In the last four weeks of the eight-week campaign, the party hosted thousands of rallies throughout the country. Each of these events, big or small, offered the visual presence of brown-shirted stormtroopers. The uniformed SA embodied dynamism. Its members were youthful, dedicated, and ready to serve their leader. It was this promise of an "awakening," represented by SA activists, that brought people to the polls.

Hitler and Goebbels expected a good showing, but no one predicted the surge they received. The lower middle classes, especially in Protestant towns and villages, continued to answer the Nazi call, but the NSDAP was no longer a fringe party; support came from the educated middle classes, farmers, and even workers. There was enough anger and fear across the entire country, and for many the established parties were either part of the system, as Nazi campaigners charged, or were implicated in having been around for decades without creating lasting stability. Such was the case with the traditional right-wing party, the gradually weakening German National People's Party (DNVP).

Beyond the NSDAP, the only other untested alternative among the major parties was the Communist Party. Founded in 1919, as we saw in Chapter 1, it too sought revolution in Germany and an end to the Republic. The KPD also saw its fortunes rise during the Depression. Capitalism appeared to have run its course. The Communist Party, however, was hobbled by its ties to the Soviet Union and by its unwillingness to recruit from beyond the industrial working class. Given the traditional strength of the SPD with that societal segment, the KPD's increases during the Great Depression largely came from the most destitute—unskilled and unemployed laborers. Nonetheless, the KPD was a formidable presence, as the third largest party in the Reichstag following the September 1930 election, having received just over 13 percent of the vote. With significant gains on the far left (KPD) and astounding gains on the extreme right (NSDAP), forming a governing coalition in the Reichstag looked impossible for Brüning. Calling new elections again would likely bring further gains to these anti-republican parties, so the Social Democrats and other parties in the center held their noses and allowed Brüning to continue governing by emergency decree. With a third of delegates now representing two parties that declared openly their desire to overthrow the Republic—the Nazis and communists—normal parliamentary discussion was elusive. Both parties' representatives disrupted proceedings on a regular basis by shouting and singing over those who attempted to engage in serious debate. The animosity displayed inside the Reichstag was amplified on the streets, as the three largest parties—the SPD, the NSDAP, and the KPD—maintained uniformed paramilitary units. The SA and communist Red Front Fighters' League were the most aggressive and violent, but the pro-republic Reichsbanner and the later SPD-led Iron Front saw their members regularly dragged into bloody confrontations as well.

The violence was not simply a side show. Increasingly, the SA's strategy was to physically dominate a town or area of a city. If any other party sought to raise awareness for its own candidates or platform in the same area, its members risked a physical confrontation. Using such an approach, the Nazis insisted, demonstrated an action-oriented mindset and a willingness to sacrifice life and limb for the movement and the nation. Some Germans found this violence off-putting and saw the SA men as nothing but thugs. Others responded positively to the brownshirts' determination to best their rivals and accepted Nazi claims that their actions were purely in self-defense; the SA was only protecting party activists from the alleged aggressive behavior of communists. Still others weren't sure what to make of what seemed like an ominous civil war-like atmosphere. In areas where, over time, the local Nazi units could claim to have "cleaned up" the streets, by silencing communist and socialist activists, the NSDAP could end up winning over the undecided.

The violence led Brüning to seek presidential support for a decree in March 1931 that required all political meetings to be sanctioned by the police and mandated that all political leaflets and posters had to pass muster with police censors. Even though the police across Germany tended to side with the SA when assigning blame after pub brawls or street attacks, Hitler feared that the stormtroopers, or, even worse, the NSDAP, could be banned, and he sought to rein in SA behavior. Doing so precipitated a mutiny within the SA. Berlin SA leader Walter Stennes argued that the party bigwigs had no right to ask the SA to change its methods. Rather, they should be thanking the stormtroopers for their sacrifices in getting out the votes and quashing the competition. In Stennes's mind, the party would be nowhere without its brownshirts. Numbering over 100,000 men by the spring of 1931, when the conflict boiled over, a large contingent within the SA agreed with Stennes; they saw victory on the horizon and resisted any change in tactics. Hitler ultimately undercut support for Stennes, who now called for a complete break from the NSDAP, by reminding the men that there was no National Socialism—the belief system, the movement—without himself, the

one true leader, Adolf Hitler. Faced with the ultimatum, the majority of SA
men stayed loyal to Hitler and the Stennes Revolt dissolved.

Just as Hitler drew Strasser and Goebbels closer after their wayward
actions in 1926, he now sought to rein in his stormtroopers by bringing his
old friend Ernst Röhm back to the leadership of the SA. Röhm had his critics.
His homosexuality was well known within the party, and many believed
it disqualified him from being a leader in—and even a member of—the
NSDAP. But Hitler forcefully defended his friend and ensured that Röhm
remained loyal and obedient. The organization continued to grow under
Röhm, thanks to its new leader's willingness to respond to the needs of men
thrown off course by the Depression. By establishing "SA Barracks" and
providing meals for homeless men and camaraderie for all, the SA doubled
again in size and counted over a quarter million men as members in 1932.

The dramatic rise in SA membership was mirrored in the party's broader
recruitment successes. Between the September 1930 election and the end
of the calendar year, close to 100,000 Germans applied for membership in
the NSDAP. The number of names on the party rolls would double again
in 1931, and by the end of 1932 there were close to 1.5 million dues-paying
members. It seemed that the Nazis had struck upon a winning recipe: high-
intensity campaigning when an election was near and frequent opportunities
for supporters to engage with the party when there was no campaign
underway. The membership dues pouring into party headquarters funded
the building of a sophisticated organizational and propaganda apparatus.
The Nazi message spread through a vast media network. In early 1930,
forty-nine newspapers championed the Nazi line. By 1932 the number had
grown to 127, and the party's most important daily paper, the *Völkischer
Beobachter*, quadrupled its circulation between 1929 and 1931.[9]

Through 1931 the political situation remained stable. Brüning was still
chancellor, despite his inability to form a lasting coalition. Emergency decrees
became normalized, and his government survived several no-confidence
votes, thanks to the unenthusiastic tolerance of the Social Democrats. But
political violence continued, and Germans feared that a civil war was near.
The Stennes Revolt had been thwarted, but the SA's most thuggish members
proved impossible to control, despite admonitions from Röhm. Meanwhile
the Depression grew worse. Brüning was able to negotiate a twelve-month
reprieve on reparations payments, but his deflationary policies failed to
stem the economic decline. In July 1931 the Darmstadt and National Bank,
one of Germany's largest financial institutions, collapsed, contributing to a
deeper international financial crisis than in 1929. German unemployment
reached 4 million by the end of the summer and continued to climb.

Hitler faced a critical decision at the start of 1932, namely whether or
not to announce his candidacy for the presidency. Victory was unlikely, and
he would be pitting himself against the revered incumbent, Hindenburg.
But if he fared well in both rounds (as no candidate was likely to win a
majority in the first round of voting), he would have a stronger case for the

chancellorship. Hitler decided it was worth the risk. He easily made it to the second round. On April 10 Hindenburg won the run-off election with 53 percent of the vote compared to Hitler's 36.8, followed by the KPD candidate, Ernst Thälmann, with 10 percent. The Social Democrats and other pro-republican parties once again had to come to the aid of an autocratic leader, throwing their support behind the octogenarian Hindenburg to keep Hitler from becoming head of state. Although Hitler was defeated, his national campaign succeeded in showcasing his popularity. It was aided for the first time in German history by air travel, which allowed Hitler to appear at more than one rally per day. Beginning his new term, President Hindenburg asked Brüning to step down and a largely unknown conservative politician from the Center Party, Franz von Papen, was selected, on the urging of one of Hindenburg's chief advisors, General Kurt von Schleicher. Unlike his predecessor, von Papen was willing to work with the NSDAP and reached out to Hitler, who promised his support of a Papen government on two conditions. First, he demanded that Papen lift the ban on the SA and the SS (Schutzstaffel, Hitler's black-shirted security echelon), which Brüning had introduced in April because of mounting violence. Second, he demanded that a Papen government call for new elections. Papen agreed to both, thinking an election would usher in a Reichstag more supportive of his own leadership. Having lost the race for president, Hitler, however, eyed the chancellorship for himself, and now he had 400,000 SA men back on the streets to help him achieve his goal. Papen's leadership, he assumed, would be short-lived.

With temperatures rising and the restless SA set loose on its rivals, the summer of 1932 was a bloody one. The July 1932 federal elections returned another stunning victory for Hitler's party. The NSDAP took 37.4 percent of the votes cast, making it for the first time the largest bloc in the Reichstag. The communists only gained about 1.5 percent for a total share of 14.6 percent, and the SPD declined further to 21.6 percent. The Catholic Center Party remained relatively steady at 12.5 percent, but the other two republican parties, the German Democratic Party and German People's Party, had been reduced to irrelevancy, capturing just over 2 percent of the vote combined. Hitler believed the results gave him the right to be the next chancellor, but Hindenburg, who was no fan of this Austrian political novice, was unwilling to grant his desire. Indeed, the president resisted putting any Nazi in the new government, despite the NSDAP's recent electoral success. The Reichstag, however, was not willing to tolerate a new von Papen cabinet, and its passage of a no-confidence vote sent the country back to the polls yet again in November. An exhausted public voted in a fourth national election that year, and the results brought a surprise. German support for the NSDAP had *dropped* by 4.3 percent. The Nazis were still the largest party in the country, with a healthy 33.1 percent share of the total vote, but they seemed to be losing steam.

Back in April, Goebbels had feared that the NSDAP might end up "winning itself to death,"[10] by which he meant that the public might grow tired of all the campaigning—speeches and marches, rallies and rhetoric—that so far had failed to catapult the party to power on the national stage. His premonition from the spring appeared now to be materializing, and a dark cloud descended over Hitler and his deputies. The party was deep in debt, and support was slipping nationally and on the local level. The public was growing weary of a brash party that told every constituency that it could solve their problems but that never showed any results. It didn't help that not a single Nazi had ever been named to a Reich-level cabinet position, so suspicious the old conservatives were of these populist upstarts. Shaken, Joseph Goebbels confided in his diary his worries about the future:

> Every new [election] report brings a new defeat. In the end we have lost thirty-four seats. ... We have suffered a setback. ... We now face difficult struggles that will require sacrifices. The main thing is to maintain the Party. The organization must be reinforced, and its spirit must be raised. The series of mistakes and shortcomings that have crept in must be stopped. ... I am right there at hand to make sure that the depressed mood in the Party does not spread too much. ... We have overcome other crises, we shall also manage this crisis.[11]

Having gained a little breathing room in the November election, von Papen planned to use emergency decrees to finally bring an end to the Republic by altering the constitution to strengthen the executive branch at the expense of the elected parliament. Other conservatives around Hindenburg, including Schleicher, feared that such a move would lead to an uprising among communists and socialists, and so they convinced Hindenburg to remove von Papen and install the military officer Schleicher as chancellor. Betrayed, von Papen grew determined to bring down Schleicher, and he turned to Hitler for support. The two met repeatedly in secret, but with both men wishing to be chancellor in any new government, discussions stalled. The stalemate could not last, however, and Schleicher knew he would face a no confidence vote when the Reichstag came back into session in late January 1933. Schleicher rightly believed that the economic crisis would soon show tangible signs of easing and pleaded with Hindenburg to preemptively dissolve it to buy himself some time. The elderly president, however, refused to grant him his wish. Hindenburg also continued to maintain his position that a Hitler-led cabinet was not a viable solution.

With no support coming from Hindenburg and wishing to avoid the humiliation of a defeat in the Reichstag, Schleicher submitted his resignation on January 28, leaving the role of chancellor open. Von Papen stepped in once again—this time to convince Hindenburg to back a cabinet led by Hitler, as chancellor. Adolf Hitler (and his thuggish party) was not the ideal leader for Hindenburg or those who surrounded him. But von Papen argued that a Hitler cabinet would support their authoritarian wishes and weaken the left. Hitler's unpredictable nature and more radical beliefs were a concern, but they planned to surround him with Papen as vice-chancellor and non-Nazi conservatives in most other seats. This arrangement, they believed, would tame Hitler and build a parliamentary coalition with majority support, thereby averting potential unrest. As Papen infamously boasted, "In two months we'll have pushed Hitler so far into a corner that he'll squeal."

Hindenburg finally agreed. Hitler was sworn in by Hindenburg on January 30, 1933, and the SA conducted a torchlit parade past his Berlin residence in celebration that evening. The party's reporters reveled in the scene, writing in *Der Angriff* the following day that it compared to "no other event than the first days of August 1914 when an entire people stood up to the last man against a world of enemies and joyously expressed its will and resolve to fight."[12] The famed Jewish German painter, Max Liebermann, along with scores of others who had feared Nazi power, experienced the event quite differently. Watching the victorious columns of marchers, Liebermann remarked: "I couldn't possibly eat as much as I wanted to puke."[13]

The Depression did not create National Socialism, nor did it alone cause the collapse of the Weimar Republic, but it was a catalyst for rapid change in these years. By 1929, after several years of relative stability, the Republic still enjoyed limited support within the presidency, chancellery, cabinet, judiciary, and police. Without any real determination at the top to uphold the principles of the Republic, it was easy to turn a blind eye to, or actively undermine, democracy during the years of crisis that followed—and to use the economic collapse as an excuse to introduce authoritarian rule. This attack on democracy began with Heinrich Brüning in 1930, not with Hitler in 1933. It was fitting that the SA joined Hitler in the celebrations of January 30th, for no other unit or organization was more important to the movement's success. The NSDAP never secured an absolute parliamentary majority in a period of free and open elections, but the party had come to power largely through legal means, when Hindenburg rightfully asked Hitler to form a government, owing to the Nazi leader's widespread popularity and his own desire to give a National Socialist the chance to rule—or self-destruct. The "parade of collapsing governments ended with a torchlit parade" on January 30, 1933, but the violence did not.[14] It would only increase under the guise of state authority.

Notes

1   Constitution of the German Reich, August 11, 1919, Article 163, https://en.wikisource.org/wiki/Weimar_constitution

2   Elsa Hermann, "This is the New Woman" in *The Weimar Republic Sourcebook*, Anton Kaes, Martin Jay, and Edward Demindberg, eds. (Berkeley: University of California Press, 1994), 207–8.

3   Adolf Hitler quoted in Volker Ullrich, *Hitler. Volume I, Ascent*. Translated by Jefferson Chase (London: Vintage, 2016), 165.

4   Fröhlich, ed., *Die Tagebücher von Joseph Goebbels*, excerpt from November 1, 1926, 114.

5   "Hitler-Pleite in Nürnberg," *Berliner Volkszeitung* 75, no. 395 (August 22, 1927), 2.

6   Werner Best quoted in Eric D. Weitz, *Weimar Germany: Promise and Tragedy* (Princeton: Princeton University Press, 2007), 345.

7   Thomas Childers, *The Third Reich: A History of Nazi Germany* (New York: Simon & Schuster, 2017), 99–101.

8   Kurt Tucholsky, "We Nay-Sayers" in *The Weimar Republic Sourcebook*, Kaes et al. eds., 97.

9   Childers, *The Third Reich*, 134.

10 Joseph Goebbels, *Vom Kaiserhof zum Reichskanzlei: Eine historische Darstellung in Tagebuchblättern* (Munich: Zentralverlag der NSDAP, 1934), April 23, 1932, 87.

11 Joseph Goebbels, "Diary Excerpt from November 6, 1932" in *The Nazi Germany Sourcebook: An Anthology of Texts*, Roderick Stackelberg and Sally A. Winkle, eds. (London: Routledge, 2002), 119.

12 *Der Angriff* quoted in Peter Fritzsche, *Hitler's First Hundred Days. When Germans Embraced the Third Reich* (New York: Basic Books, 2020), 96.

13 Max Liebermann quoted in Fritzsche, *Hitler's First Hundred Days*, 92.

14 Melita Maschmann, *Account Rendered: A Dossier on My Former Self* (Lexington, MA: Plunkett Lake Press, 2013), 11. Maschmann, who attended the event as a girl with her parents, notes that violence erupted along the parade route and finds the heady mix of sights and sounds created an "intoxicating joy."

Additional Reading

Allen, William Sheridan. *The Nazi Seizure of Power: The Experience of a Single German Town, 1922–1945*. Revised edition. Brattleboro: Echo Point, 2014.

Balderston, Theo. *Economics and Politics in the Weimar Republic*. Cambridge: Cambridge University Press, 2002.

Childers, Thomas. *The Nazi Voter: Social Foundations of Fascism in Germany, 1919–1933*. Chapel Hill: University of North Carolina Press, 1983.

Crew, David. *Germans on Welfare: From Weimar to Hitler*. New York and Oxford: Oxford University Press, 1998.

Kolb, Eberhard. *The Weimar Republic*. London: Unwin Hyman, 1988.

Koshar, Rudy. *Social Life, Local Politics, and Nazism; Marburg, 1880–1935*. Chapel Hill: University of North Carolina Press, 1986.

Marhoefer, Laurie. *Sex and the Weimar Republic: German Homosexual Emancipation and the Rise of the Nazis*. Toronto: University of Toronto Press, 2015.

Siemens, Daniel. *Stormtroopers: A New History of Hitler's Brownshirts*. New Haven and London: Yale University Press, 2017.

Swett, Pamela E. *Neighbors and Enemies: The Culture of Radicalism in Berlin, 1929–1933*. New York: Cambridge University Press, 2004.

Turner, Henry Ashby. *Hitler's Thirty Days to Power: January 1933*. Reading, MA: Addison-Wesley, 1996.

3

Consolidating the Nazi Regime and Building a Police State

On March 14, 1934, a schoolboy in Bliesmengen, Germany, sent a handwritten letter to Adolf Hitler requesting a photo of the chancellor for his tenth birthday. Young Friedrich had "heard a lot about Hitler and read a lot about him in the newspaper," but because the Great Depression had drained his family's finances and his own piggy bank, he could not afford to purchase a portrait. An adjutant to Hitler in the Reich Chancellery office responded by sending the boy a photo of the Führer and an accompanying letter delighting in the fact that Friedrich's "wish had been happily fulfilled."[1]

On the same day, 3,700 miles away in New York City, thousands of people gathered in Madison Square Garden while others tuned in to their radios to hear a mock trial of Adolf Hitler, accused of "crimes against civilization." According to the charge, "the Nazi government in Germany has not only destroyed the foundations of the German Republic, but, under penalty of death, torture, and economic extermination, and by process of progressive strangulation, has reduced and subjugated to abject slavery all sections of its population." Speaker after speaker—from noted American jurists to politicians—made their case against Hitler, and after four hours of testimony by the prosecution and no case by the defense, the "court of humanity" proclaimed Hitler guilty in absentia.[2]

Here are two stark images on the same day a little over a year after Hitler came to power: a child excited about Germany's "rebirth," and an angry crowd of American civil libertarians, politicians, and worried Jews condemning the Nazis and standing for a moment of silence in honor of Hitler's victims. How do we account for these two profiles of Germany in 1934, one marked by youthful exuberance and the other by criminality? Historians have tried for a long time to understand the relationship between consensus, enthusiasm, and state violence under Nazism. The Third Reich has commonly been portrayed as twelve years of terror: the secret police were everywhere; arrests were constant; speaking against the regime came under penalty of death; and a police state ruled. But scholars also understand that many Germans were quite happy during the Nazi years, as jobs came back after the Great Depression and leisure opportunities abounded. Members of the citizenry who were not deemed racially inferior were invited into the *Volksgemeinschaft* and embraced Hitler and his policies. This chapter begins to address this debate—often simplified as "coercion versus consent"—by looking at Nazi rule and the construction of a state that both terrorized large parts of its population *and* enabled ten-year-olds to feel a part of something historical—the birth of a new, "thousand-year Reich" under National Socialism.

When Adolf Hitler came to power on January 30, 1933, few people predicted that he would establish a dictatorship. Originally known as the Reich Cabinet of Salvation, only three of the eleven ministers were members of the NSDAP. Aside from Hitler, Hermann Göring served the Nazi Party as minister without portfolio and acting Prussian Minister of the Interior, and the other Nazi Wilhelm Frick was Reich Minister of the Interior. The remaining cabinet members came from the conservative parties or were nonpartisan (Figure 3.1). Many Nazi critics in Germany and abroad were actually excited about this political development: Hitler would not pass "the test of power." "It is possible," wrote the French Daily, *Le Temps*, "that the new chancellor will be quickly exhausted by this exposure and his reputation as a worker of miracles will vanish."[3] Hitler's appointment and his predicted impotence as a leader would be exposed and the Nazi Party would fade in influence.

As we saw at the end of the last chapter, the conservatives, led by former Chancellor and now Vice-Chancellor Franz von Papen, were more optimistic. They themselves had put Hitler into the chancellorship, confident that with so few Nazi Party members in the government, Hitler would bend to their will. They felt that after years of political instability, they could harness Hitler's popularity to pull the country out of the Great Depression, diffuse the political power of the left, and bring Germany back to greatness. This optimism was echoed in the diary of Hamburg schoolteacher Luise Solmitz, who effused about the new government of "national concentration": "What a cabinet—one that we could only have dreamed about last July ... on each member I place a tremendous amount of hope."[4] Both enthusiasts like Solmitz and critics had little sense that Hitler would use the police, the courts, and propaganda to assault political and racial enemies and dismantle the very institutions on which the German democracy rested.

It was one thing to proclaim a "Third" Reich, or Empire (the first being the Holy Roman Empire and the second the German Empire from 1871 to 1918). It was another to lay out a plan of governance. In his first speech as chancellor, a radio address on February 1, Hitler outlined his aims (Figure 3.2). He spoke of his plan to restore a unity of "mind and will" among farmers, workers, and the middle classes. He would defend Christianity and

FIGURE 3.1 *Adolf Hitler's governmental cabinet, January 30, 1933. Sitting from left to right are Hermann Göring, Adolf Hitler, and Franz von Papen. Standing from left to right are Franz Seldte, Günther Gereke, Lutz Graf Schwerin von Krosigk, Wilhelm Frick, Werner von Blomberg, and Alfred Hugenberg (Bundesarchiv, Bild 102-14268).*

the family and spark a political and racial awakening. He railed against the poisonous influence of the left and promised that Germany would not sink into "communist anarchy." To help realize these plans, the new government asked exhausted Germans to vote again in a month. While this election was part of his original coalition deal upon assuming power, Hitler saw it as an opportunity to consolidate his rule by expanding his party's representation in the Reichstag and obtain a mandate in support of Nazi rule. To achieve this goal, he would first have to neutralize the communists and socialists, who at 37 percent had together received more votes than the NSDAP the prior November.

Hitler received an opportune chance to destroy the left when on the night of February 27, 1933, the Reichstag building where the parliament had met since 1894 went up in flames. The building's plenary chamber was gutted, and that night Marinus van der Lubbe, a former member of the Dutch Communist Party, was arrested and confessed to having started the fire to provoke German workers to rise up against fascism (Figure 3.3). Van der Lubbe was found guilty and sent to the guillotine in January of 1934. At

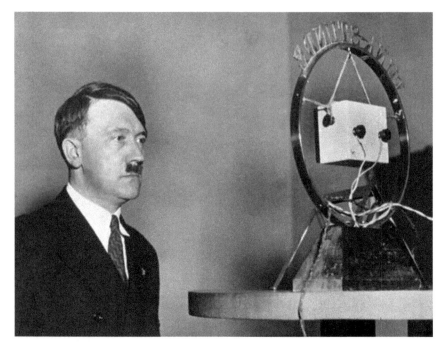

FIGURE 3.2 *Hitler's first radio address, February 1, 1933 (Bundesarchiv, Bild 183-1987-0703-506/Unknown author/CC-BY-SA 3.0, CC BY-SA 3.0 DE, via Wikimedia Commons).*

the time of the fire, observers within and beyond Germany suspected that van der Lubbe had been framed and that the Nazis had set the conflagration themselves to justify the planned assault against the left. This view has generally been debunked by historians, though recent new evidence has emerged pointing again to the Nazis themselves as possible culprits. Whatever the case, Hitler and President Hindenburg used the burning of this symbol of democracy (a system neither loved) to issue the Decree of the Reich President for the Protection of People and State, otherwise known as the Reichstag Fire Decree. This February 28 order was a significant step in undermining the legal foundations of the Weimar Republic. It nullified the civil protections embodied in the German constitution, from freedom of speech to the freedom of assembly. Noteworthy is the phrase "protection of the people." Hitler portrayed himself not as a violator of basic rights but as a savior of the very nation that could grant those rights in the first place. Hitler would protect Germany from the communists, socialists, Jews, and other "internal enemies." With this decree, some Germans bemoaned the loss of their civil liberties, but others were delighted by Hitler's decisiveness. As Luise Solmitz noted the day after the fire, "all of the thoughts and feelings of most Germans are devoted to Hitler ... His glory reaches to the stars."[5]

FIGURE 3.3 *The plenary hall of the Reichstag destroyed by fire, February 1933 (Bundesarchiv, Bild 102-04607).*

Creating a Dictatorship

The Nazis did not actually need the Fire Decrees to unleash terror against the political left. Upon Hitler's coming to power, Hermann Göring, head of the Prussian interior ministry, swore in young Nazi supporters as auxiliary policemen, who, along with the regular police, the SA, and the Gestapo (*Geheime Staatspolizei*–Secret State Police), rounded up political enemies. Headed originally by Göring, the Gestapo had its origins in the Prussian political police before 1933, and it became the most public face of the terror state, arresting people and eventually managing almost two dozen prisons across occupied Europe (Figure 3.4). On March 3, the Nazis detained KPD leader Ernst Thälmann, who had called unsuccessfully for general strikes after Hitler came to power. In preparation for Thälmann's trial, Nazi attorneys had trouble getting the prisoner to admit to any crimes. He was therefore delivered to the Gestapo on March 3, 1933, for "special handling." As he wrote later:

> They ordered me to take off my pants and then two men grabbed me by the back of the neck and placed me across a footstool. A uniformed Gestapo officer with a whip of hippopotamus hide in his hand then beat my buttocks with measured strokes. Driven wild with pain I repeatedly

FIGURE 3.4 *Gestapo and police sort through material confiscated from the Communist Party central headquarters on Bülowplatz, Berlin, February 1933 (Bundesarchiv, B 145 Bild-P056663).*

screamed at the top of my voice. Then they held my mouth shut for a while and hit me in the face, and with a whip across my chest and back. I then collapsed, rolled on the floor, always keeping face down and no longer replied to any of their questions.

Thälmann was held in solitary confinement for eleven years, until he was shot at Buchenwald concentration camp on August 18, 1944, on Adolf Hitler's orders. Other communists and socialists were not as "lucky" as Thälmann and did not survive the first months of the Nazi regime.

On March 5 Germans went to the polls for the fifth national election in less than a year. Hitler portrayed this as a referendum on his young leadership and his party. But just in case some people were wavering, the Nazis used voter intimidation and violence to ensure a parliamentary majority for the NSDAP. With the Fire Decrees, noted a German in his diary, the regime had "taken from the left socialist party every opportunity to continue the campaign to the end."[6] Hundreds of SPD and KPD activists were arrested around the country, the two parties were prohibited from staging rallies or meetings, and their newspapers were shuttered. Nonetheless, when the result came in, Hitler was devastated: at 44 percent of the popular vote, the NSDAP again did not get a majority. The parties on the left still got

30 percent of the vote, even with most of the KPD deputies incarcerated, dead, or out of the country. The Catholic Center Party followed with 11 percent of the vote.

With this result, the remaining smaller bourgeois and conservative parties were on their own rendered impotent. Yet because he did not have a parliamentary majority, Hitler still depended on them to build a coalition and pass legislation. As an end run around this, Hitler negotiated a deal with the conservatives and the Center Party to pass an Enabling Act on March 23. This gave Hitler's cabinet the power to enact legislation for four years without the approval of the parliament. The Center Party agreed to this in exchange for a promise that the new regime would protect Catholic civil and religious freedoms. With KPD leaders in jail and the SPD voting against the act, 83 percent of the other Reichstag deputies agreed to give almost absolute power to the Nazis. Hitler would renew the Enabling Act two more times, effectively consolidating his unlimited power for the remainder of his rule. Hitler could now negotiate the dissolution of the smaller parties over the next few months. The Center Party dissolved itself in exchange for a formal agreement between the Nazi regime and the Vatican (the *Reichskonkordat*) to defend the rights of German Catholics, and on July 14, the parliament, now fully controlled by the NSDAP, passed the Law against the Establishment of Parties. It stated that "the National Socialist German Workers' Party constitutes the only political party in Germany." Any attempt to establish another would result in penalties and imprisonment up to three years. Germany had become a one-party dictatorship.

In less than six months the improbable chancellor had managed to destroy democracy in Germany. While the constitution was nominally in effect for the remainder of the Nazi years, the Weimar Republic was effectively dead in the summer of 1933. Through a combination of pressure, opportunism, disdain for democracy, and a sense of resignation, the center-right parties, whose deputies once had little taste for the rabble-rouser Hitler, had taken themselves out of existence.

These early months of repression and maneuvering give a sense of how rapidly the earth shifted under the ground of German politics. Through a process known as "synchronization" (*Gleichschaltung*), the Nazis used laws and physical intimidation to bring society and politics in line with the NSDAP. From villages to large cities, non-Nazi mayors were forced into retirement or hounded out of office, to be replaced by willing Nazis. This was also true at chambers of commerce, men's and women's organizations, sports societies, school boards, chess clubs, and every other civic institution. Often a process of "self-coordination" took place, out of both opportunism and an instinct for survival. If an organization was not "nazified," it faced dissolution. Its members scrambled to kick out Jews, whose presence could jeopardize the existence of a local chapter. Associations quickly adapted their messaging to the aims of the Nazi *Volksgemeinschaft*. For example, the Rotary Clubs, since which their arrival in Germany six years earlier, had committed themselves to international service and cooperation, now shifted their message to one of hyper-nationalism, much to the distress of the Rotary International office in Chicago.

The speed with which organizations purged themselves is striking, but this "self-synchronization" combined genuine enthusiasm for the Nazi cause with fear of the Hitler government. With the Enabling Act, state parliaments were abolished, and the Nazis used violence to bring regional and local governments in line with Berlin's policies. In February, the Prussian Ministry of Interior allowed for the shooting of "enemies of the state." On May 2, one day after the Nazi-led "May Day" celebration of German workers, the regime destroyed the offices of trade unions and banished all but Nazi-led worker associations. Unions were replaced by the Nazis' German Labor Front (DAF), which was to represent all German workers, now "freed" from leftist political leadings.

In 1933 and 1934, law after law served as the building blocks of a Nazi dictatorship. On March 12, 1933, the Nazi flag with the swastika was given equal status to the flag of the German state.[7] In May of 1933, Germans were forbidden from desecrating symbols of German history or those that accompanied the "national reawakening" under Hitler.[8] In December of 1933, the NSDAP was declared "inexorably linked to the German state."[9] The same month, the regime forbade the misuse of uniforms and symbols and criminalized any critical speech that would harm the Reich and the image of the government and the Nazi Party.

The Nazis understood that a monopoly over information would be central to their attaining total power. The press and other media quickly came under the purview of Joseph Goebbels, who entered the cabinet in March in the new position of Reich Minister of Public Enlightenment and Propaganda. This office presided over a large censorship apparatus for the remainder of the Nazi years (see Chapter 6). In keeping with this, Germans witnessed what might be called the "synchronization of speech." There were new rules about proper ways to give a public lecture or make a phone call and about what words (such as "radio") were the property of the Propaganda Ministry. The regime mandated in 1936 that members of the press and foreign consulates stop citing *Mein Kampf* to justify contemporary political choices; Hitler's book was declared a "historical source" that should not be quoted without proper understanding of the context in which it was written.[10] The regime also rejected the use of written dialects in "low German," which would presumably represent a regional rather than a national mode of thought.[11]

Not all laws controlling speech and behavior were unique in substance. In the Weimar Republic and in other countries, laws existed to protect youth, to regulate the dissemination of information, and to streamline culture. But there were key differences between Germany and, for example, the United States. First, laws that discriminated against Jews and other categories of people in employment or housing, which were left up to a state or municipality in other settings, were now issued by a centralized, single party state in Germany; unlike in the United States, for example, one could not escape racist laws by moving to a more tolerant region of the country. Second, as we will see in Chapter 4, these laws targeted not just a specific act, but the supposed criminal in his or her essence—as a Jew, as an "Aryan," or as a member of an organic racial community. Third, the laws were promulgated in the context of a rapidly developing dictatorship, which relied on fear, passivity, and conformity as well as on enthusiasm.

Mechanisms of Terror

The criminalization of non-Nazi political activity in 1933 and a wave of arrests led to a massive influx of people into the judicial system. With prisons filled in the early months of 1933 and makeshift detention centers springing up around Germany, the Nazis established an overflow detention facility in March in the town of Dachau, 10 miles northwest of Munich. This would be the first purpose-built installation in what would grow into a network of thousands of concentration camps (*Konzentrationslager* or KL) (see Plate 13). These must be distinguished from death camps that would appear in the conquered territory of Poland after the outbreak of the Second World War and that would be the key sites of mass murder. Contrary to a popular belief, the early camps were not populated *en masse* by Jews, but by socialist and communist political detainees. While in "protective custody," prisoners were subjected to beatings, drill exercises, harsh labor, and minimal food (Figure 3.5). The entrance to the enclosed camp at Dachau bore the notorious sign "work sets you free." Like "protective custody" this mocking phrase barely masked the cruel intent of the camp, where 32,000 prisoners died over a twelve-year span. In this early period, KL prisoners were usually released after weeks or months of "reeducation," physically and morally defeated and under pressure to emigrate. But for others, like Oskar Müller, a communist in the Prussian federal state parliament, 1933 marked the beginning of twelve years of arrests and rearrests and imprisonment in Dachau and in penitentiaries.

In order to house the flood of political prisoners, the Nazis turned basements, docks, and warehouses into concentration camps. These ad hoc installations were the iconic expression of a rapidly emerging police state. In the mid- and late 1930s new, larger camps were built to accommodate thousands of Jews, gay men, Jehovah's Witnesses, and people on the margins who were seen as loiterers, "shirkers," and habitual criminals. The term "asocial" and "work-shy" came to represent those who did not conform to social norms. Beggars, prostitutes, alcoholics, drug addicts, psychopaths, pacifists, Seventh Day Adventists, and others were all swept into concentration camps. Over time the system grew into a vast network. The Oranienburg camp near Berlin was founded in 1933, and in 1936 it

FIGURE 3.5 *Concentration camp prisoners at Dachau engaged in forced labor, May 24, 1933 (BPK-Bildagentur 30023594).*

was moved to nearby Sachsenhausen to house mostly political prisoners. The Buchenwald camp opened in 1937 near the central town of Weimar and housed not just Jews but also Slavs, disabled people, Roma, political prisoners, and freemasons. After the annexation of Austria in 1938, Mauthausen was set up for prisoners to perform backbreaking labor in a rock quarry. And at the end of this same year, the SS opened Neuengamme in Hamburg. With eighty-five satellite camps in the region, Neuengamme put prisoners to work in a brick factory. By the end of the Second World War, by some counts, 3.5 million prisoners had been incarcerated in 44,000 KLs and other detention sites.

Concentration camps get the most attention in studies about the Nazi system of punishment; they were a sprawling bureaucracy of terror. But the regime also depended on the regular court system, led by Nazi judges or conservatives who had little sympathy for the left or for Jews. In Germany before Hitler, safeguards against arbitrary state power had been built into the penal code. Even as democracy foundered, the Weimar Constitution acknowledged equality under the law and guarded against the invasion of privacy in mail, phone, and telegraph communications. It protected freedom of assembly and speech. After Hitler came to power in 1933, however, most laws protecting the rights of innocent citizens were abrogated. The rights to privacy and the freedom of assembly were wiped away, and laws were not promulgated by an independent legislature but by executive power, with the backing of a fully nazified Reichstag. By 1934, courts had been federalized, and the independent judiciary was gone. Sentences for violations of the law were increased, with the death penalty introduced for political crimes. In the early Nazi years, most judges throughout the broader legal system did not, as such, subscribe to a National Socialist worldview. But most believed in a strong, authoritarian government that defended law and order. The regime took all political criminal cases out of regular courts and put them under the jurisdiction of a new "People's Court" and other "special courts," where only Nazi loyalists could serve as judges. Those accused of high treason entered a courtroom festooned with swastikas and images of Hitler. Here, there was no opportunity for appeal. Over the course of the Nazi dictatorship, these special courts handed down almost 40,000 death sentences. In the 1930s, next to the imperial and Weimar-era prison system and seventy KLs, there were special prisons and detention sites run by the SA and the SS. According to historian Richard Evans, between 1932 and 1937, the prison population in Germany rose from 69,000 to 122,000, an increase of over 75 percent.[12]

Why did Hitler use the courts at all? Why go through the appearance of due process? Hitler used the law to offer a pretense of legal propriety to the Germany citizenry and the international community. But this formal reliance on the "rule of law" was not simply a publicity move. A functioning judiciary lent legitimacy and order to the Nazi reign of terror. Moving through the corridors of "justice" was a frightening experience defined by often arbitrary brutality that was all the more shocking because it had legal backing.

Some scholars, drawing from an important book by political theorist Ernst Fraenkel, have referred to Nazi Germany as a "dual state," which relied on both the legal norms of the constitutional state and the extra-legal power of Hitler and his party. The civil service, the judiciary, and the governmental ministries affiliated with the office of the chancellor maintained the "normative" state that continued to function, at least on paper, until the very end of the Nazi regime. Just as the United States has a Department of State or a Department of the Interior, so too did Germany continue to have a foreign ministry and an interior ministry from 1933 to 1945. But the other part of Fraenkel's equation—the "prerogative state"—centered around the wanton authority emanating from the movement that Adolf Hitler embodied. The NSDAP, the SA stormtroopers, the SS blackshirts, and the party offices in Munich put into play National Socialism's obsessions with racial and ideological purity.

The dual state idea captures the interplay of law, ideology, and arbitrary rule in National Socialist Germany. But one must not make too much of this dichotomous model, for in the Third Reich the normative state and the prerogative state were intertwined. The courts became handmaidens of the Nazi Party, and politicians combined their work in state and party institutions. The normative *and* prerogative state played a central role in the exercise of violence. Party and state officials orchestrated boycotts, produced antisemitic placards, arrested and executed undesirables, and gave the courts the tools with which to justify these acts. Within this system there were conflicting views about the role of public violence in Germany. Lawyers and policymakers defended street justice, but some Nazis worried that vigilantism would offend bourgeois Germans' sense of propriety. With a wave of attacks on Jews as a backdrop, Nazi leaders began to denounce public, "individual actions," wishing instead to channel brutality into the more secretive and systemized world of prisons and KLs. The regime sought to control public violence—on the streets and behind barbed wire and prison bars.

The Nazi regime's desire to manage all violence was a source of frustration to Hitler's own paramilitary, the SA. After Hitler came to power, a faction of the brownshirts, led by Ernst Röhm, was eager to move to another phase of revolution which, in keeping with the 1920 party program, would take an axe to the capitalist structures of the state. As Hitler settled into governing, the SA grew restless. The troopers missed the excitement of the street fight, resented the power of the regular army (which they hoped to penetrate), and wanted to punch harder against perceived enemies. As one former SA man later reflected, "*We* created (the revolution of 1933), *we* prepared the way, why wouldn't we carry on with it?"[13] Hitler had other plans. In order to carry out a program of rearmament, he needed the support of the armed forces and industrialists without the nuisance of a restive SA. In the spring of 1934, Hitler grew convinced that his formerly loyal stormtroopers were planning a coup d'état. There is no evidence that Röhm and his men were plotting, but there *is* abundant evidence from Vice Chancellor Papen's office of a clumsily planned conservative coup, and Hitler got wind of this. Talk within the SA of a "second revolution" and a desire to exact revenge on his political enemies prompted Hitler to lash out violently. On June 30, 1934, the Nazis began a "cleansing action." The SS and the Gestapo arrested Ernst Röhm and other SA members, some of whom were known to be gay and whose capture Joseph Goebbels defended as a sweep against immorality. What has come to be known as the "Night of the Long Knives" had begun. For two weeks the Nazis took vengeance on political enemies. Two SS officers gave Röhm a pistol and ordered him to commit suicide. When the intransigent SA leader refused, they shot him dead. The regime murdered other SA leaders as well.

This blood purge, carried out under the code name Operation Hummingbird, saw eighty-five murders, with some victim estimates running considerably higher. The Nazis assassinated Kurt von Schleicher, Hitler's predecessor as German chancellor, and Gustav Ritter von Kahr, the

Bavarian governor who had suppressed Hitler's attempted coup in 1923. Both were seen as reactionaries aiding the SA. Papen, current vice chancellor and Schleicher's predecessor as chancellor, was spared, but many of his political associates were not. Nor was Gregor Strasser, who had competed with Hitler for leadership of the NSDAP in the early 1930s. The dead also included Catholic politicians and journalists like Otto Ballerstedt, an early political rival of Hitler's who was shot in the back of the neck and dumped in a forest, and Erich Klausener, former leader of the Catholic Action group who had publicly criticized Nazi violence.

This blood purge shocked Germans and the world. It looked like Hitler was embracing the very lawlessness that he decried. But he justified his crushing of the "Röhm putsch" in the name of preventing chaos, and Nazi jurists quickly devised rationales for the killing spree. Public opinion during the following weeks varied from horror to approval, as Hitler hoped to root out the street toughs who put the national renewal in a bad light. The SA shock troops who had aided Hitler in his rise to power now played a much smaller part in the Nazi movement. But the regime still unleashed them at times of its choosing—to rampage Jewish businesses, to terrorize bystanders, and during the war to serve as air raid wardens and to help "Germanize" parts of occupied eastern Europe.

The Night of the Long Knives consolidated Hitler's power, delighted the Reichswehr, and endeared the chancellor to Hindenburg, who a year before had doubted the skills of this "miserable Bohemian corporal." But the president did not have much time to savor this victory for law and order and for his armed forces. One month after the end of the purge, Hindenburg died from kidney failure. A mere two hours after the Field Marshal's passing, Hitler abolished the office of the presidency and declared himself Leader and Reich Chancellor of Germany. He claimed that it would dishonor Hindenburg's memory to maintain the presidential office (which Hindenburg had occupied for nine years), but few saw this as anything but a final step toward dictatorship. Hitler was now legally "the *Führer*" ("the leader"), a title he had already enjoyed within the NSDAP since the 1920s. The abstract, spiritual power of this office now trumped the formal trappings of the German chancellorship. In his attempt to woo the army, Hitler held a lavish funeral for Hindenburg, where expressions of mourning reflected genuine public sorrow for the loss of the "Hero of Tannenberg." Every member of the armed services henceforth swore allegiance not to the German state but to Hitler himself: "I swear by God this sacred oath: I will render unconditional obedience to Adolf Hitler, the Führer of the German Reich and people, Supreme Commander of the Armed Forces, and will be ready as a brave soldier to risk my life at any time for this oath." Minister of Defense General Werner von Blomberg agreed to refer to the chancellor no longer as "Herr Hitler" but as "Mein Führer." Soldiers, sailors, and airmen followed suit (Figure 9.5).

The Führer

On August 19, 1934, a national plebiscite brought Germans to the polls. Voters were asked to affirm that "all former powers of the President of the Reich are demised to the Führer and Chancellor of the Reich Adolf Hitler. He himself nominates his substitute." Not taking any chances, the SA and Gestapo intimidated people to cast a "yes" ballot. And they manipulated the results. With a purported 90 percent affirmative vote, Hitler now claimed popular support for a dictatorship. Any order, if it did not conform to the letter of written law, could be defended as emanating from the office of the "Führer," without parliamentary approval and without the backing of a head of state. Hitler knew, however, that this arbitrary power would be flimsy without a façade of popular democracy. In his capacity as chancellor, he forwarded his wishes to the Reichstag, now populated by Nazi deputies. They would pass laws that Hitler could either carry out as head of government or ignore in his capacity as "Führer." Prosecutors could proceed against political prisoners with the force of "legal" statutes and precedents, but Hitler could also intervene when he wanted. In defense of his country, Hitler gave himself the power to act as "supreme judge" without recourse to the courts.

Even before Hindenburg's death, the idea of Hitler as more than a mere chancellor had taken hold in the wider public. The concept of a "Führer" inspired a bureaucratic and ideological reordering of society. In all walks of life, Germans embraced the so-called leadership principle: a boss was "Führer" to his employees, and a husband was the "leader" of his wife and children. The *Führerprinzip* (Führer principle) celebrated seemingly natural hierarchies and gave force to the idea that each person had a unique place within the family, organization, or national body. In keeping with these principles, "mini-Führers" appeared throughout Nazi politics and society. Having proven their ideological zealotry and organizational skills, these party bosses headed federal and local offices and tried to anticipate Hitler's wishes and conform to the ideological precepts of the state without formal orders from the top. This process of "working toward the Führer" saw acolytes and fanatics vying to implement and radicalize Nazi politics. Nazi Gauleiters created large bureaucratic empires, competing with each other in a system where Hitler often responded to an idea floated by the most recent person he had spoken with. This "polycratic" government fostered a hierarchical chain of sycophants who were rewarded for their devotion as they climbed the ranks of power.

This loyalty had an entrepreneurial element. Nazi Germany was not only a *Volksgemeinschaft*; it was also a *Leistungsgemeinschaft* (performance community) where workplaces would be measured on productivity and cleanliness and awarded titles like "model factories" (Figure 5.3). This meant that within a rigid chain of command everyone could still be their own Führer, maintaining order and exercising their "will"—in sports, at home, and at work—in ways that would honor the nation or Volk. Gauleiters bestowed "Gau Badges" to civilians for loyalty or good work. The regime honored long-term party members and other admirable Nazis with The German Order, the Gold Party Badge, and the Coburg Badge, to name a few of the awards.

Nazi Germany celebrated itself as a meritocracy, free from class war and the egotism associated with crass American democracy or "Jewish capitalism." Much like Napoleon, whom French people saw as having risen from lowly Corsican beginnings to the emperorship, Hitler was portrayed as the ultimate expression of the "self-made man." In the early 1920s, by his own account, he had been a mere "drummer," rallying on behalf of the movement, only to rise to the heights of power through his oratorical and organizational abilities. Many Germans had already begun to see Hitler in these terms—as a man of action and will. He was deified as all powerful but also as a kind, just, and merciful father figure to all German children and to his beloved German Shepherd dogs. Paradoxically, Hitler portrayed himself as above the law and also as working *within* legal parameters. Unlike age-old views of an omniscient and omnipotent deity, however, some people felt that Hitler disapproved of or was even unaware of the brutality that suffused German society. "If the Führer only knew" was a common refrain, indicating both the unease with political violence and a belief that the good leader was ill-served by the thugs below him. Ironically, when Hitler spoke of smashing his enemies, supporters saw these threats as justified responses to non-sanctioned violence and criminality.

A cult of personality blossomed into what one scholar has termed the "Hitler myth." Whether a fanatical follower or a cautious observer, you would be hard pressed by the mid-1930s to deny Hitler the credit for pulling the economy out of its doldrums, rearming the country, and accruing foreign policy victories. This charismatic leadership resounded in the spectacles of Nazi power. The annual Nuremberg party rallies were massive displays of loyalty to Hitler, during which swastika-clad youth brigades mingled with spade-carrying laborers in uniform. Days of parades, torchlit ceremonies, speeches, flags, "Heil Hitlers," "*Sieg Heils*" ("Hail Victory" cries), and camaraderie were captured on film and disseminated to national and international audiences. Leni Riefenstahl, a former actress and celebrated director, released *Triumph of the Will*, her "documentary" of the September 1934 Nuremberg party rally, to both great praise for her innovative film techniques and a few yawns as audiences slogged through the two-hour movie.

Each annual party rally in Nuremberg had an accompanying theme relating to Nazi ideology or to the general mood of nationalism and optimism. In 1933 it was the Rally of Victory, and the next year—a few months after the SA purge—the Rally of Unity and Strength. Rallies of "Freedom" and "Honor" and a "Greater Germany" would follow in succession. Within each festivity, there were endless paeans to country and leader. The September 1938 party rally in Nuremberg lasted for a week. The first day was a Day of the Leaders, followed by Hitler Youth Day, a Day of the SA and SS, and Armed Forces Day, each replete with speeches, parades, athletic competitions, and the presentations of prizes. Such celebrations were on powerful display during the Summer Olympics in Berlin in 1936, where Hitler's cult of personality inspired the crowds at the games to scream for their "Führer."

Enthusiasm for the Führer was evident not only in choreographed public spectacles, but also in the number of people rushing to join the Nazi Party (Figure 3.6). Reasons for joining were varied, from true excitement about the Nazi "revolution," to peer pressure or the demands of a boss, to an assumption that doing so would be good for one's career and not doing so would be detrimental. Whatever the reasons, the surge of membership applications reflected genuine and widespread excitement about Hitler's first months of rule. Enthusiasm was also evident in personal letters sent to Hitler. Many were of a martial nature, congratulating the leader on having rekindled a muscular pride in Germany with his foreign policy triumphs. But others expressed a swooning, spiritual love for Hitler. Wrote a novice poet to Hitler: "My heart shatters when I call out 'my Führer' ... when I call you, oh leader, the tears pour down ... My heart lies in tatters because I am not with you."[14] Others addressed their letters to "Good Uncle Hitler," drawing on his avuncular image in newspapers and books.[15] Readers saw him holding children's hands, kissing babies, and sacrificing his own needs—including marriage and parenthood—to those of the nation. The Propaganda Ministry produced a steady flow of publications that reinforced this message. Yet Goebbels was careful to avoid cheapening the Führer through the production of kitschy devotional objects. Hitler himself would not tolerate public monuments and statues in his likeness,[16] but this did not stop the proliferation of busts and paintings of the Führer, nor the renaming of central urban squares as Adolf Hitler Plazas.

In short, Adolf Hitler and National Socialism became very popular in the 1930s. In public and private, many Germans sought to realize the *Volksgemeinschaft* through model behavior—by hanging pictures of the Führer in their homes, by playing Nazi-themed board games, by displaying lists of National Socialist "family values." They even mimicked Hitler's table settings in their own dining rooms.

The real popularity of Nazi Germany should not obscure what some Germans saw as a forced conformity in offices and factories, in written correspondences, and in schools, where Germans—not without some grumbling and pushback at first—adapted to the compulsory "Heil Hitler" salutation. Instead of "good morning" or "good afternoon," a range of robotic or exaggerated gestures to the Führer's health became a measure of how well one had adapted to the new cult of personality. In a show of goodwill, however, people with brain injuries or motor impairments were allowed to withhold the greeting.[17] Hitler controlled the police, the media,

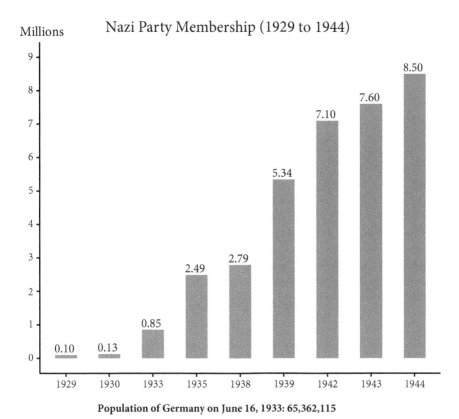

Millions   Nazi Party Membership (1929 to 1944)

Population of Germany on June 16, 1933: 65,362,115

FIGURE 3.6 *By the end of 1920, Nazi Party membership was about 2,000; by early 1922 it was 6,000; by the end of 1925, c. 27,000. Admission of new members was put on hold effective May 1, 1933, but this rule was relaxed on May 1, 1937, and admission was fully reopened on May 1, 1939 (Source: Bernd Sösemann, Propaganda (Stuttgart: Steiner, 2011), 951. Reprinted with permission of the author).*

and the courts, and demanded subservience to the state. In short, even in a popular dictatorship, an apparatus of terror tightened around German society in the 1930s.

Policing the Reich

The person charged with meting out this terror was Heinrich Himmler, who headed the SS. A former chicken farmer and agronomist obsessed with cross-breeding and genetics, Himmler took over the SS in 1929 when it was a coterie of a few hundred black-shirted bodyguards protecting Hitler. Under Himmler's leadership, the SS grew into a fiercely loyal cohort of ideologically committed "political soldiers" devoted to racial purity and the Germanic occultism that Himmler himself indulged in. In 1934, Hitler employed the SS to crush rivals and critics during the Night of Long Knives. In the months before the purge, Himmler had extended his authority over local, regional, and state police, and in 1936, under pressure from Hitler and Himmler, Interior Minister Wilhelm Frick decreed that all the police forces of the Reich were to be placed under Himmler, as Reichsführer SS. Himmler was now chief of the German police, and all officers were servants of Nazi ideology (Figure 3.7). He presided over the Kripo (Criminal Police) and the Orpo (Order Police), commanded by SS officer Karl Daluege and comprised of the regular uniformed police officers throughout the Reich. The Orpo itself was made up of city guards, motorized gendarmes, mounted police, traffic police, fire brigades, air raid police, and waterways protection police. The Nazis were also in charge of the railway police, the mining police, the post office protection service, customs officials, factory protection units, the hunting police, and the harbor police. Himmler's ideological police came to include almost a million men during the Second World War. It was a sprawling bureaucracy that would include military units, as well as "deathshead units" that operated the concentration camps and extermination camps.

After 1936 the number of offices devoted to law and order mushroomed. Within Himmler's purview was the SD, or the Security Service, which

FIGURE 3.7 *SS Reichsführer Heinrich Himmler speaks to a prisoner in a Dachau workshop, May 8, 1936 (Bundesarchiv, Bild 152-11-12 CC-BY-SA 3.0, CC BY-SA 3.0 DE, via Wikimedia Commons).*

according to Himmler was tasked with discovering "the enemies of the National Socialist concept" at home and abroad. Founded and led by the sadistic former naval officer Reinhard Heydrich, the SD became the chief spy agency and a central player in the murder of Europe's Jews. More familiar to many Germans was the Gestapo, an organization that has been the source of debate. While contemporaries and some historians once saw this organization as "omniscient, omnipotent, and omnipresent," scholars now emphasize how poorly equipped the Gestapo was. Compared to East Germany's later version of the secret police, the Stasi, the Gestapo was short on manpower. The Gestapo did not lurk on every street corner. It did rely on paid informants, but its information about individuals' attitudes and behaviors often came from voluntary denunciations. If one suspected a neighbor or coworker of having a forbidden relationship with a Jew or of criticizing the regime, one might call the Gestapo. Some have portrayed this voluntarism as a sign of how much the general public made the wheels of oppression turn in Nazi Germany. But at times the Gestapo expressed its frustrations that too many reports about petty squabbles were coming into its offices. It had no interest in adjudicating property boundary disputes and personal vendettas, which clogged the machinery of oppression against political enemies.

The regime didn't rely only on the Gestapo. It also monitored the populace with the modern tools of surveillance. In 1933 and 1939 the Nazi government carried out censuses and devised other forms of record keeping that would help them round up enemies. The Reich Office of Statistics worked with police and health officials to monitor criminality and disease. A Labor Book, a Health Pedigree Book, a Duty to Register Book, a Registry of the Populace, and personal identification numbers were all tools with which the state observed, counted, and captured citizens. These means of surveillance, however, paled in comparison to the Nazis' formal security organizations. In 1939 Himmler amalgamated and placed under himself the SD, Kripo, and the Gestapo. Heydrich was in charge of all three in a combined new office, the Reich Security Main Office (RSHA). The SS was now in control of all aspects of internal and foreign intelligence and policing, and the distinction between the formal state bureaucracy and the party's ideological apparatus all but disappeared.

This immense bureaucracy of state repression should not negate the fact that Hitler was a beloved figure in Nazi Germany. But he was also feared, admired, and despised. This diversity of views marked German society, but it also resided within individuals, who could harbor conflicting sentiments. One could look askance at Hitler's treatment of minorities but approve of his foreign policy. One could bristle at Hitler's crude attacks on the "Jewish press" but be grateful that had brought about a revitalized German nationalism. One could admire this simple Austrian who had risen to the highest office in the land but also fear his wrath. And one could secretly deride the flow of propaganda but also be happy with its message of racial unity.

How does one evaluate the balance between support for Nazism and fear of the regime? Some people spoke of the "German *Blick*" (German look) during the Nazi period in order to emphasize the compulsory nature of support for Hitler. This was a distrustful and frightened glance in an enclosed area like a subway or tram; it was a careful survey of a public space to see if one was being watched. But this cautious and fearful behavior does not mean that Hitler's speeches and Goebbels' propaganda forced the public into supporting the regime. As we will see, Germans enjoyed moments of pleasure and enjoyment in daily life; the Third Reich was a popular dictatorship. But it was also a brutal one. Prisons overflowed and capital punishment rates soared, with the guillotine serving as the regime's execution method of choice. If you had a hereditary illness, you were subject to sterilization or death. If you were a drug addict, you could be imprisoned for years. If you were a petty criminal, a prison cell or a concentration camp awaited you. If you were a union leader, a communist, a socialist, a democrat, or belonged to a Christian minority, you had a good chance of your life being ruined. If you spoke ill of the regime, listened to the wrong music, or behaved suspiciously, you were subject to arrest. If you were Jewish or Roma you were ostracized or killed. In the prophetic words of an SS newspaper in 1939, "anyone who is not basically for Germany but against Germany does not belong to us and will be eliminated. If he does not emigrate on his own initiative, then he will have to be locked up. If that does not help, then we will have to make him a head shorter."[18]

In 1933 Germany ceased to be a functioning democracy. It was a one-party regime initially fashioned after the mass movement in Italy, which railed against political divisions and established a hyper-nationalist dictatorship. According to both Hitler and Mussolini, a "national uprising" had swept away the numbing and ineffective parliamentary system. In this Germany and Italy were not unique. By the time the Second World War broke out, a form of fascism or authoritarianism also ruled in Spain, Portugal, Poland, the Soviet Union, and throughout much of the rest of eastern and southern Europe. In 1941 there were just eleven parliamentary democracies left across the globe. And yet the Nazis and other dictatorships then and now have liked to say that their system is the true expression of the people. Hitler boasted that he had built a "beautiful democracy." National Socialist Germany was the product of a "revolution from below," where, the Nazis argued, people power came to full expression in the person of Hitler, in marching SA men, and in the dazzling lights of a rally. The Führer represented the will of the people—in splendid public spectacles but also in the cell blocks and detention bunkers of Dachau, where prisoners were flogged, hung from poles, forced to stand for hours, and murdered.

Notes

1 Nikolaus F. to Hitler, March 14, 1934, in Henrik Eberle, ed., *Briefe an Hitler* (Bergisch Gladbach: Lübbe, 2007), 160–1.

2 "Hitler on Trial," https://www.aish.com/ho/i/Hitler-on-Trial.html

3 Quoted in "Sees Hitler Facing Fall," *New York Times*, February 1, 1933, 10.

4 Luise Solmitz quoted in *Bedrohung, Hoffnung, Skepsis: Vier Tagebücher des Jahres 1933*, Frank Bajohr, Beate Meyer, and Joachim Szodrynski, eds. (Wallstein: Göttingen, 2013), 152.

5 Ibid., 163.

6 Ibid., 412.

7 "Erlass des Reichspräsidenten über die vorläufige Regelung der Flaggenhissung," March 12, 1933, in *Propaganda: Medien und Öffentlichkeit in der NS-Diktatur*, vols. 1 and 2, Bernd Sösemann, ed. in conjunction with Marius Lange (Stuttgart: Steiner, 2011), 114.

8 "Gesetz zum Schutze der nationalen Symbole," May 19, 1933, in ibid., 120–1.

9 "Gesetz zur Sicherung der Einheit von Partei und Staat," December 1, 1933, in ibid., 167.

10 "Pressenanweisung: Aussenpolitische Ziele aus *Mein Kampf*," February 5, 1936, in ibid., 381.

11 "Bekanntmachung der Regeln für die plattdeutsche Rechtschreibung," July 2, 1933, in ibid., 341.

12 Richard J. Evans, "Coercion and Consent in Nazi Germany," *British Academy Review* 151, no. 10 (2007): 26–7.

13 "Reflections of an SA Man" in *Nazism: A History in Documents and Eyewitness Accounts, 1919–1945*, Vol. 1, Jeremy Noakes, and Graham Pridham, eds. (New York: Schocken, 1983), 187.

14 Horst Schrade to Angela Raubel, Hitler's sister (with a request to give it to her brother), *c.* December 10, 1936, in Eberle, ed. *Briefe an Hitler*, 225.

15 Annelene K. to Hitler, May 7, 1933, in ibid., 133.

16 "Verbot der Errichtung von Denkmälern des Führers," December 10, 1933, in Sösemann, *Propaganda,* 170.

17 Alison Owings, *Frauen: German Women Recall the Third Reich* (New Brunswick: Rutgers University Press, 1993), 236.

18 Excerpt from *Das Schwarze Korps*, January 26, 1939, in Noakes and Pridham, *Nazism*, Vol. I, 499.

Additional Reading

Broszat, Martin. *The Hitler State: The Foundation and Development of the Internal Structure of the Third Reich*. London: Longman, 1981.

Cesarani, David. *Becoming Eichmann: Rethinking the Life, Crimes, and Trial of a "Desk Murderer."* First Edition. New York: Da Capo Press, 2004.

Fritzsche, Peter. *Hitler's First Hundred Days: When Germans Embraced the Third Reich.* London: Basic Books, 2020.

Gellately, Robert. *Hitler's True Believers: How Ordinary People Became Nazis.* New York: Oxford University Press, 2020.

Kershaw, Ian. *The "Hitler Myth": Image and Reality in the Third Reich.* Oxford and New York: Oxford University Press, 1987.

Kershaw, Ian. *The Nazi Dictatorship: Problems and Perspectives of Interpretation.* Fourth Edition. London and New York: Bloomsbury, 2000.

Longerich, Peter. *Heinrich Himmler.* Translated by Jeremy Noakes and Lesley Sharpe. Oxford and New York: Oxford University Press, 2012.

Stackhouse, Ryan J. *Enemies of the People: Hitler's Critics and the Gestapo.* Cambridge: Cambridge University Press, 2021.

Wachsmann, Nikolaus. *Hitler's Prisons: Legal Terror in Nazi Germany.* New Haven and London: Yale University Press, 2004.

Wachsmann, Nikolaus. *KL: A History of the Nazi Concentration Camps.* New York: Farrar, Straus, and Giroux, 2015.

4

Racism and Biopolitics

Adolf Hitler was a racist, and his party embraced racism. For Hitler, more than any other world leader, the biological makeup of a person determined whether they could join the body politic—and eventually whether they would live or die. The lynchpin of his xenophobia was hatred of Jews, whom the Nazis saw as a racially distinct people. Point 4 of the NSDAP's Twenty-Five-Point Program from 1920 stated that "only a national comrade can be a citizen. Only someone of German blood, regardless of faith, can be a citizen. Therefore, no Jew can be a citizen." In speeches and particularly in *Mein Kampf*, Hitler also railed against Blacks and against Slavs, who populated the lands in eastern Europe into which Hitler wanted Germany to expand. But Jews were his abiding obsession.

Despite the centrality of racism in Hitler's worldview, when the Nazis came to power in January of 1933, it was not clear that it would be a primary feature of German politics. Jumpstarting the economy and reining in communism were the orders of the day. Hitler's vision of a great German awakening was unquestioningly tied to xenophobia, and he dreamed of a racially exclusive utopia. But during the Great Depression the Nazis had toned down their antisemitic rhetoric; railing against Jews and other minorities was less successful at the ballot box than projecting a broader commitment to economic stability and law and order.

As we saw in the last chapter, Hitler moved first against political rather than racial minorities. This is reflected in pastor Martin Niemöller's 1946 poetic meditation on his and his fellow Germans' tragic passivity as the Nazis widened their network of victims. First, they came for the socialists, then for the trade unionists, then for the Jews, then for him.[1] These words capture the primacy of the Nazis' assault on the left in the early years of the regime. Since German Jews were often members of the KPD and the SPD, they found themselves early targets. Werner Scholem, the brother of Jewish mysticism scholar Gershom Scholem, was a leading communist and delegate in the Reichstag in the Weimar years. He was arrested in the spring of 1933, transferred to Buchenwald in 1938, and murdered in 1940. Fellow Jewish

KPD member Georg Benjamin was arrested in April 1933 and released toward the end of year, only to die in a concentration camp in 1942.

Jews were rounded up as members of the political left. But it would be a mistake to ignore the immediate attacks on Jews *as Jews*. In March of 1933 violence against Jews broke out across Germany. Men and women were harassed on the streets if they didn't stand at attention to a passing formation of SA men, and right-wing thugs beat up people who "looked Jewish." In the last weeks of March, the SA imprisoned 124 Jews in the Bavarian city of Regensburg. Among them was industrialist Alfred Biswanger. When he asked the two SA men who pulled him from his shop the reason for his detention, he was told that they had orders to arrest "every member of the race."[2] By the end of the year, 482 cities and towns had seen attacks on Jews.

National Socialism and Race

What was it about Jews and Judaism that the Nazis found so threatening? As we saw in Chapter 1, Nazi ideologists had long spoken of Germany in terms of ethnic homogeneity. Drawing on racial theories from the prior century, Nazi "blood and soil" writers saw a link between the land and the biological strength of the people who inhabited it. Ethnic intermixing and the introduction of other "impure" elements, such as hereditary illness, threatened to weaken both race and nation and augur their downfall. Hitler and ideologues like Alfred Rosenberg, the head of the NSDAP Office of Foreign Affairs, were inspired by the writings of French aristocrat Arthur de Gobineau and the British racial theorist Houston Stewart Chamberlain. Both had claimed to have scientifically mapped and ranked the human races. The superior groups included the "Aryan" or "Nordic" types, who populated western and northern Europe and who supposedly bore less evidence of interbreeding (Figure 4.1). Jews and Africans were at the bottom of the racial hierarchy.

Not every Nazi theorist agreed with this racial categorization. Anthropologist Egon von Eickstedt at the University of Breslau, who divided humanity into the three groups of Europoid, Mongoloid, and Negroid, did not see Jews easily fitting into any of these. This was not to humanize Jews, however. If not a race, Jews were that much more dangerous since they could surreptitiously infiltrate pure populations. Hans F. K. Günther, a professor at the University of Berlin and one of the most influential racial theorists in the interwar years, also did not see Jews as a distinct race but rather as a mongrelized "anti-race," whose insinuation into the German genetic pool caused irreparable harm. Günther, who served as a mentor to SS leader Heinrich Himmler, did not, however, hesitate to promote a more colloquial reference to Jews as a race for propagandistic and practical reasons. But he felt that establishing a rigidly scientific distinction between Germans and Jews would prevent the flexibility needed to weed out the latter.

FIGURE 4.1 *Nazi racial science poster, 1938. The left two columns are labeled "German youth," and the right two are "Jewish youth" (United States Holocaust Memorial Museum Collection, Gift of David and Lucinda Pollack).*

The regime arrested Jews in the early months of the Third Reich, but some of the first legal measures concerning biological health addressed other groups, namely the intellectually and physically disabled. In devising these measures, the Nazis looked to eugenics for inspiration. Eugenicists rejected the Enlightenment view of human beings as open to improvement. Character traits, they asserted, were inheritable and uninfluenced by education or environment. In order to enhance a country's racial stock, eugenicists advocated the eradication of genetic diseases from a population through wide-ranging immigration restrictions and sterilization. Until the emergence of National Socialist Germany, the United States led the world in such "negative eugenic" measures and promoted them alongside progressive health, sanitation, urban planning, and family policies. By the beginning of the 1930s, thirty US states could legally sterilize people against their will: women and men seen as profligate, criminals of all manner, and patients in psychiatric hospitals. And from Canada to Japan, dozens of other countries also put eugenics policies into place in the 1920s and 1930s.

The Nazis studied the writings of foreign eugenicists and took part in international conferences throughout the 1930s. But Nazi Germany's program of racial discrimination went much further than any other country's. In July of 1933 the regime enacted the Law for the Prevention of Hereditarily Diseased Offspring, which called for the involuntary sterilization of those suffering from a number of purportedly genetic disorders. They included schizophrenia, bipolar disorder, intellectual disability, hereditary epilepsy, blindness, deafness, and alcoholism. Many of these illnesses were not in fact passed on from parent to child, and those targeted for sterilization often insisted that their disability had resulted from injury after birth. But that did not matter to the regime, which in any case saw severely disabled people as an "unproductive" burden on the state. Doctors at nursing homes, at health clinics and psychiatric wards, and at schools for the mentally and physically disabled referred cases to newly established hereditary health courts, which determined if a person, according to the law, "may be rendered incapable of procreation by means of a surgical operation." Some 400,000 Germans were involuntarily sterilized between 1933 and 1945.

This law indicated that the Nazis would make good on their promise to "cleanse" Germany of those elements damaging to the race. In addition to the above, gay men, the so-called "feeble minded," and people deemed insane or habitually lazy were branded dangerous. Photographs of "idiots" adorned pages of magazines and school textbooks, accompanied by exhortations to consider the costs of feeding such undesirables (Figure 4.2). One journal contrasted the healthy bodies of German boys to that of a developmentally disabled Black man; the money spent on feeding this person, the journal argued, could be better spent on these hale youths. In the late 1930s, the Nazi regime swept habitual criminals, vagrants, and beggars into concentration camps. Convicts were forced to wear a green triangle on their prisoner stripes, while the "asocial" and the "work-shy"—which included alcoholics, prostitutes, pacifists, and the mentally ill—wore a black triangle. The latter group wore an additional white armband with the word "Blöd" (stupid) on it (see Plate 3).

Nazi ideas of racial purity converged with assaults on political and social enemies. In the Buchenwald and Sachsenhausen concentration camps genetic enemies were behind the same barbed wire as religious and political prisoners. Racial and non-racial categories could overlap. If a camp prisoner

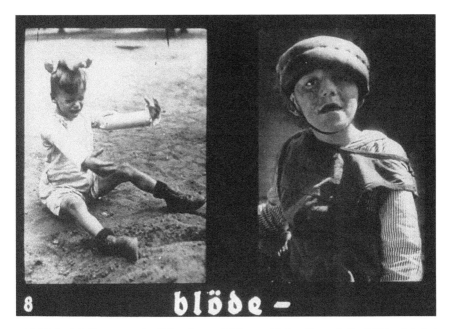

FIGURE 4.2 *Propaganda slide of two children with intellectual disabilities labeled here as "imbeciles," c. 1934 (United States Holocaust Memorial Museum, courtesy of Marion Davy).*

were, for example, Jewish and communist, a downward pointing red triangle was sewn over the yellow upward triangle to form the multicolored star of David, indicating both racial and political degeneracy. Another group that crossed categories were Sinti and Roma (formerly known pejoratively as "Gypsies"). They were seen as an itinerant group, prone to begging and other dishonest behaviors that disrupted civil society. They spoke the language Romani, based on ancient Sanskrit. For decades, governments throughout Europe had attempted to regulate this population on the margins of society. In the 1920s, German police escorted Roma as they moved from county to county to ensure they did not engage in criminality. For the Nazis the "Gypsy question" was both racial and social. Not unlike Jews, Roma were considered genetically inferior and prone to delinquency. In December 1938 Heinrich Himmler issued a circular "Combating the Gypsy Nuisance" and opened an office with the same name to collect data. All Roma over the age of six were divided into three categories: "Gypsies," "part-Gypsies," and nomadic persons behaving like "Gypsies." The regime gathered information on some 26,000 Sinti and Roma who resided in Germany in the early 1930s. The next year the Reich Interior ministry decreed their relocations from their settlements to special internment and labor camps, in addition to concentration camps (Figure 4.3). Their removal was preceded by careful genealogical study.

FIGURE 4.3 *Collection camp for Sinti and Roma in Hellerwiese (present-day Belgradplatz) in Vienna, c. 1937–41. From this gathering point, Sinti and Roma were sent to concentration and death camps (Bundesarchiv, Bild 146-1987-115-51).*

The Nazis also hoped to remove Black people from the racial pool. In 1933, there were up to 25,000 people of African ancestry in Nazi Germany. Many of their parents or grandparents had come from Germany's African colonies. The Nazis had no coherent policy toward this population, but the regime ostracized children of black-white unions, forbade sexual relations between Blacks and "Aryans," prevented Afro-Germans from attaining elite jobs, and, with some exceptions, barred them from entering the military. Some of these patterns of exclusion predated the Third Reich, but the Nazis ramped up the persecution. While Afro-Germans were not killed *en masse*, they did endure tremendous hardship in what was left of their civilian lives and in concentration camps. In particular, hundreds of so-called "Rhineland Bastards," the children of African servicemen from the French army and white German women, underwent forced sterilizations to mitigate the supposed danger of further racial intermixing.

Nazi Antisemitism

The Nazi regime cast a wide net as it rounded up its victims. But its abiding fixation was on Jews. Despite Nazis' obsession with race, anti-Jewish policy was as much about Jews as political and economic actors as it was about them as despoilers of "German blood." Just as in *Mein Kampf*, the regime drew together long-standing views of Jews as money-obsessed economic exploiters and conspiracy theories about Jews controlling the world. One of the first acts against this group had less to do with racial obsessions than with traditional views about Jews, money, and power. A persistent claim on the German right was that Jews were "overrepresented" in the country's professions. In 1933, there were approximately 523,000 Jews in a country of 67 million, representing less than 1 percent of the population. This was a successful, highly assimilated minority, widely present in law, medicine, entertainment, and business. As we saw in Chapter 1, since the early 1920s, right-wing activists had called for a diminished role for Jews in the economy and a transfer of Jewish businesses to their "rightful" non-Jewish owners. In late March 1933, Propaganda Minister Goebbels announced a nationwide boycott of Jewish-owned shops on April 1, purportedly as a commensurate response to Jewish-led boycotts of German products abroad. This was also punishment for the so-called "atrocity propaganda" in Britain and the United States, which called out the heightened antisemitism in Germany. The irony of trying to answer foreign "lies" about persecution with more persecution was apparently lost on the Nazi leadership.

On April 1 Germans headed to their favorite stores to find them either shuttered by their owners or blockaded by SA members with placards decrying the "traitorous" act of shopping at a Jewish business. These uniformed stormtroopers stood in front of Jewish-owned shops dissuading customers from entering and harassing those who chose to do so, as well as the owners and employees who tried to carry on with their work. They handed out flyers to passersby about the importance of "buying German" and plastered buildings with crude antisemitic slogans. Anti-Jewish epithets defaced shop windows, and crowds of Nazis, along with curious onlookers and would-be customers, gathered outside stores. When the day was over, the boycott was widely seen as having failed; many Germans had ignored the blockade or had condemned it. Wrote Luise Solmitz in her diary: "The mood of the people seemed depressed; most did not agree with this (boycott)."[3] A frustrated Goebbels called off the action after one day. The international backlash was severe enough that in the aftermath he feared the loss of his position in Hitler's inner circle. International investors were concerned by the blatant racism and the domestic instability the boycott seemed to portend.

The boycott was the first of many antisemitic measures promulgated in April, and they indicated again that the Nazis would at first proceed against Jews not per se as racial minorities but as visible members of Germany's economic and professional life. On April 7, the Reichstag passed the Law for the Restoration of the Professional Civil Service. It forced "non-Aryans" and political opponents out of all government jobs, from public school teacher to postal worker to local and regional politician. That same month saw Jews expelled from the legal profession, except when "consulting" for Jewish clients (Figure 4.4). Jewish doctors were next. Their practices were dropped from the national health insurance program, effectively disincentivizing non-Jewish patients from using their services. Jews were driven from their medical offices if they did not leave voluntarily. In the meantime, the presence of Jewish students in public schools and universities was sharply curtailed. No more than 5 percent of the student body at any given public school could be Jewish, and Jews were pushed into community parochial schools. The quotas applied to higher education too. If you were an incoming Jewish university student in 1933, you found yourself suddenly without prospects for a college degree. If you were a doctoral student having conducted years of research, you might find yourself without the chance to submit a dissertation, or without an advisor, who had perhaps been removed on racial grounds.

How did employers know who was Jewish and thus worthy of expulsion? In the first few years of the Nazi regime, they had few guidelines and often relied on non-racial markers: someone's last name was typically Jewish; a coworker knew his officemate's background; someone "looked

FIGURE 4.4 *Nazis march Jewish attorney Dr. Michael Siegel barefoot through Karlsplatz in Munich. On May 10, 1933, Siegel had complained to the police that one of his Jewish client's civil rights had been violated. Siegel was beaten by SA men, stripped, and humiliated. The board around his neck reads, "I am a Jew and will never complain to the police again" (Bundesarchiv, Bild 146-1971-006-02).*

Jewish." The civil service law did define a Jew as someone having at least one grandparent "of the Jewish religion," but it is doubtful that employers consulted any such written definition when they expelled their "Jewish" workers. For its part, however, the regime tried to establish who, exactly, was an "Aryan," and here biology and race reenter the picture. The Interior Ministry's racial experts clarified the above definition by crafting a so-called "Aryan paragraph." According to a first draft of the measure, Caucasians, who included Germans, Slavs, Afghans, and Indians, were counted as "Aryan." Blacks, Jews, Arabs, Berbers, and various kinds of Mongoloid or "yellow" people were not. The Interior Ministry ultimately rejected this elaborate definition since it allowed for non-Europeans to keep their jobs. It was replaced with a simpler, but no-less-clarifying assertion that one was "Aryan" if they were "tribally related to German blood." Such hair-splitting would bedevil the Nazi regime for many years. Were Slavs really "Aryans"? Would a strict definition of racial Jewishness lead to the loss of too many valued employees? As the Nazis legislated against "non-Aryans," they would need to come up with a more functional definition. But even without it, the process of social and professional isolation had begun.

What followed the Civil Service law were around 2,000 antisemitic laws on the national, regional, and local levels that sought to socially isolate Jews. Jewish actors were kicked off the stage and screen. Jewish scientists were barred from their laboratories. Jews were banned from serving as journalists and editors, except if they worked for a Jewish newspaper. Meanwhile the government shuttered, took over, or nazified most of the 4,700 newspapers in print in January of 1933. Jews were kicked out of choruses and choirs and were removed from leisure and civic organizations, from hiking clubs to Rotary Clubs. The latter provides a case study in self-coordination. The esteemed men's service club had come to Germany eight years earlier and had become a premier gathering place for businessmen, doctors, professors, and artists. After Hitler came to power, Jews were asked to showcase their organization's service ethic and "voluntarily" dismiss themselves, thereby protecting their non-Jewish clubmates from government attacks. Such was the twisted logic of coordination: Jews could be forcibly expelled from their professional and civic positions, but many departures were preceded by conversations about how Jews should "do the right thing." By stepping away, they would prevent their friends from having to associate with them.

In 1933 antisemitism had still not overtaken German society, and there was some genuine squeamishness about the Nazis proceeding against a highly assimilated and patriotic minority. Even Germany's President Hindenburg did not agree to a full-scale assault on Jews and refused to sign the civil service law until it made exceptions for Jewish veterans of the Great War or those who had lost a father or son in battle. Around half of the country's Jewish civil servants could keep their jobs by virtue of this "front fighter privilege". But it was only a matter of time before decorated soldiers would feel the effects of these laws on their professional lives. In these early years one could still say they knew "decent Jews," such as these veterans. This was hardly an expression of philosemitism, but it was less vicious than the Nazis' unrelenting Jew-hatred.

Antisemitism, some scholars argue, is rooted in envy. In interwar Germany, according to this view, non-Jews resented Jews for their success beyond their numbers and wanted what they had—their property, their jobs, their money. Whether or not this reading of collective psychology is compelling, removing Jews from German professional life did provide opportunities to "Aryans" for career advancement. Berlin had about 4,300 lawyers and jurists in 1933, with over 40 percent of them of Jewish origin. This meant that in the capital city alone, where one-third of German Jews lived, two thousand jobs in just one field opened up after Jews were disbarred. Young, often well-connected ideologues had few qualms about taking a Jewish attorney's job and practicing law in the name of the Nazi revolution. The same went for the medical professions. In 1933 there were about 5,600 Jewish doctors in Germany. By the end of the year, half had lost their livelihoods, to be replaced by "Aryans."

By the end of 1933 much of German professional life was "Jew-free." The following two years saw less legislation and even a cautious hope among Jews that Hitler had done all that he planned to do with the "Jewish Question." In 1934 Hitler devoted more energy to weeding out his political enemies, culminating in the Night of the Long Knives. But that doesn't mean that the regime had shelved its consideration of Jews' fate. In 1934 the Propaganda Ministry founded an Institute for the Study of the Jewish Question, whose eventual leader, Eberhard Tauber, combined his antisemitic and anticommunist efforts into a campaign against "Judeo-Bolshevism." In 1934 at the local level, acts of persecution continued. Walking down a street, Germans encountered antisemitic posters or frequented a kiosk selling copies of the antisemitic newspaper *Der Stürmer* ("The Attacker"). Publisher Julius Streicher filled this tabloid with the most salacious and inflammatory tropes of antisemitism. Hooked-nose Jews, greedy financiers, and rapists adorned the covers and found their way into display windows and office waiting rooms (see Plate 4). A special issue in May of 1934 was devoted to the Blood Libel, the age-old lie that Jews murdered Christian children and used their blood in their rituals. The front page had a drawing of hideous-looking Jews holding a vessel to collect the blood streaming from the naked bodies of angelic Christian children they had just murdered. According to one German looking back in later life, "We kids used to look at ("Der Stürmer") because it was wild stuff. It was pornographic, not in the sense of showing nudity or girls or something, but it was a real low-grade type of propaganda. It was the *National Enquirer* equivalent in the Nazi Party."[4]

The Nazis reached for classic antisemitic tropes to target Jews not just as a racial enemy but as politically and culturally dangerous. Within a given issue, *Neues Volk* (A New People), a magazine published by the

Nazi Office of Racial Policy, might deny Jews were being persecuted but also revel in the slow removal from Germany of the Jewish "foreign body," whose control of the international press or whose production of degenerate art was poisoning the Volk. Nazi publishing houses issued explanatory pamphlets about the importance of antisemitism and the "world historical" mission of removing Jews from the country. The regime taught teachers how to incorporate antisemitism into their lesson plans. There were even governmental decrees about how to speak about Jews. Germans were advised to avoid the term "Antisemitism" (*Antisemitismus*) altogether in writing and speaking since Arabs were also Semites and no policy was directed against them. The preferable term was "anti-Jewish" (*antijüdisch*).

Watching popular documentaries on the Nazi years, one might assume today that Germans were all seething racists who followed Hitler's obsessions about purity in lockstep. But in reality, it took time for the broader public to come around to the Nazi mission. There was no shortage of skepticism about the "Nordic" or "Aryan" idea. The ideal of the "splendid blond beast" (a name given to the square-jawed, fair-haired Heydrich) was met with the reality that most Germans had brown hair. A version of the joke popular in National Socialist Germany went that the perfect German was "blond like Hitler, slim like Göring, and beautiful (or tall) like Goebbels." Melita Maschmann, a middle-class girl and devoted member of the Hitler Youth, recounts in her memoirs how she and others made fun of the whole "Nordic racket." At a wedding she attended in a forest, the bride and groom put on all the trappings of "Aryan" piety—with bonfires and flowing robes. The bride, announced to the guests as "the fairest of women," was, according to Maschmann, "small and fat and had dark, nervous eyes." She was "no Brunhilda."[5]

These small acts of mockery did not stop Maschmann or others from embracing Nazi lessons about German superiority. There was a psychological disconnect between Maschmann's adoration of a close Jewish friend and her belief that "global Jewry" was an abstract, threatening force. Maschmann struggled with this contradiction after the war, but others who had had a more visceral response to the "Jewish problem" probably did not. These were the ones who, even in the "quiet years" of 1934 and 1935, sprayed stores with acid or smeared buildings with inscriptions like "Jew, Stinking Jew," "Out with the Jews," or simply "*Jude*." Jews were denounced for any number of violations, and vigilante justice abounded, rooted in a supposedly deep revulsion to the Jewish body and a fear of racial mixing. "Aryans" and Jews who were discovered having intimate relations with each other might be paraded through towns bearing placards revealing their status as "Race Defilers." In the absence of more aggressive directions from the top, Germans engaged in spontaneous bouts of vandalism, harassment, and assault.

Hitler had a sense that such actions were strategically unproductive. He grew irritated with both the SA's demands to unleash on Jews, and with so-called "spontaneous actions" in the streets. He most assuredly had no sympathy for Jews. But he felt that their ultimate exclusion depended on rational analysis and coherent policies. Hitler had warned against dangerous passions in one of his earliest statements on antisemitism. In a 1919 letter about the "Jewish Question" that he sent to an army soldier, Adolf Gemlich, he had written that "antisemitism as a political movement must not be, cannot be, determined by emotional criteria, but only through the recognition of facts." Hitler was referring to what he saw as the inevitable negative emotional reactions "Aryans" had to interpersonal transactions with Jews—a revulsion at Jews' supposed odors and money grubbing. Eliminating this insidious race, Hitler felt, required sober analysis of demographics and "legal" actions—not mass hysteria.

An example of this legalistic approach came on September 15, 1935, when the regime announced the Reich Citizenship Law at the annual Nazi Party rally in Nuremberg. It stated that any citizen would have to be of German "blood." Accordingly, Jews were stripped of their German nationality and made "subjects" of the Reich. They were now formally stateless, unable to vote in elections, enjoy government benefits, or get a valid passport for travel. This legislation was accompanied by the Law for the Protection of German Blood and Honor. Henceforth, under penalty of imprisonment, they could not marry non-Jews. Premarital and extra-marital sex between Jews and non-Jews was also forbidden. Jews could not hire "Aryan" housekeepers under the age of forty-five, presumably because lecherous Jewish men were unable to resist the temptations of a young German woman, and these child-bearing age women should in any case be home with their children. And Jews could not fly the German flag, now changed to the swastika. But in a cruel mockery, the laws protected a Jew's "right" to display blue and white "Jewish colors," presumably to indicate that Jews represented a separate nation.

These so-called Nuremberg Laws took away Jews' civil rights and sexual freedom. They also revoked Hindenburg's veteran exceptions to the civil service law. But the regime still struggled to define what a Jew actually was, and it took another couple of months to design and publish a formula. Some members of the regime argued that a "Jew" should be defined broadly in order to eliminate as many as possible from German society. Others felt a narrower definition would allow for some people with partial Jewish ancestry to contribute to society and even serve in the army. The latter view won out. The Nazis defined a Jew as anyone with three or four Jewish grandparents, thereby watering down the April 1933 law and overriding those pushing for a more expansive definition. New categories were created for half and quarter Jews, known as *Mischlinge*, or mixed breeds. For the moment, these Germans would not lose their citizenship, but the law allowed for some non-Jews to be pushed into the Jewish category based on religious affiliation and practice. Importantly, the Nazis had no rigorous understanding of race to draw on because it was an artificial category. The regime was making it up as it went along. By the end of 1935 those with three or four Jewish grandparents had been legally kicked out of every sphere of German life except the economy. Around this same period, the Nazis passed a number of animal-rights laws. Animals could not be used in product testing and vivisections. Jews, the regime made clear, were lower than animals.

How did Jews react to these laws? For some there was an odd sense of relief. After all the regulations and sporadic actions, they felt that the new situation, while degrading, was at least clear. Jewish Zionist and journalist Robert Weltsch had already advised his co-religionists in 1933 to "wear it with pride, the yellow badge." At this point, this appeal to wear the Jewish star was only metaphorical; to Weltsch and others, the anti-Jewish boycott in April of 1933 and now these laws indicated that Jews must band together because assimilation had failed. The National Representation of the Jews of Germany (*Reichsvertretung*, RV), which spoke for Jews in all political matters, issued a desperate accommodation to the new reality:

> The Laws decided upon by the Reichstag in Nuremberg have come as the heaviest of blows for the Jews in Germany. But they must create a basis on which a tolerable relationship becomes possible between the German and Jewish people. The Reich Representation is willing to contribute to this end with all its powers. A precondition for such a tolerable relationship is the hope that the Jews and Jewish communities of Germany will be enabled to keep a moral and economic means of existence by the halting of defamation and boycott.[6]

The RV felt it had to issue such a statement because Hitler had said the Nuremberg Laws would be the basis for future coexistence. In reality the Jewish leadership now had a strong sense that Jewish life in Germany was coming to an end. Zionist organizations indicated that the Jewish youth should seek their fortunes abroad. In the aftermath of the Nuremberg Laws there was a rush of Jews seeking advice about leaving the country, and emigration offices were overwhelmed.

The Racial Bureaucracy

With the Nuremberg Laws, the regime had the legal tools with which to proceed methodically against Jews and other racial "inferiors." The Nazis built a massive bureaucracy to enact its persecutory measures. After 1935 the number of research and policy organizations devoted to this utopian goal of cleansing the race multiplied rapidly. Hereditary health courts determined who would be sterilized. The Kaiser Wilhelm Institute for Anthropology, Heredity, and Eugenics became a premier site of racial research under the direction of renowned professors Eugen Fischer and Otmar von Verschuer. The Reich Health Office, under Dr. Leonardo Conti, had its own Racial-Hygiene and Heredity Research Center devoted to "the Gypsy question," working in tandem with the Kripo under Heydrich's command. The Kripo's Criminal Biological Institute, under Arthur Nebe, identified Jews and other "misfits." These institutes were found throughout Germany and relied on the services of professors and the police. At Jena University, Karl Astel led the Provincial Office for Racial Questions, devoting himself not only to racial science but also to engineering the model Nazi university and engaging in anti-tobacco activism (cigarettes were seen as damaging to individual and public health). The Rhineland Provincial Institute for Neuro-Psychological Eugenic Research registered racial outsiders on index cards, which would later be used to track these people down. In Giessen there was an Institute for Hereditary and Race Care. The North-East German Research Community studied Germany's Slavic ethnic minorities, as did later the Publication Office in Berlin, the Institute of German Eastern Labor in Krakow, and the Reinhard Heydrich Foundation in Prague. Two of these were headed by historians. There was a Committee of Experts for Population and Racial Policy, a department of People's Health in the Interior Ministry, and a Reich Committee for the Scientific Registration of Serious Hereditarily-and Congenitally-based Illness. And Walter Gross's Nazi Office of Racial Policy was staffed by 2,000 "educators," who were responsible for publishing *Neues Volk* and other propaganda that raised a racial awareness in the German population. It is ironic that Germany's universities and research institutions, which were among the most respected in the world, had now become the centers for pseudo-science.

This sample of the many institutions devoted to volkish health gives a sense of the often-overlapping endeavors among party and state officials and the private sector to oversee the racial reordering of Germany, and eventually Europe. Driven by an entrepreneurial spirit, these Nazi ethnocrats—administrators of racial purity—inculcated into the population what historian Claudia Koonz has called a "Nazi conscience"—a sense that biological purification was a higher moral calling. SS leader Himmler's *Ahnenerbe* (ancestral heritage) thinktank studied Germanic folklore and the presence of "Aryans" in the archeological record. But the daily lineage and kinship research fell to an army of experts who combed through church records, historical documents, museums, and family trees. Contrary to popular belief, they did not dabble in the occult or channel ancient Germanic ancestors (though Himmler himself led studies of genealogy and folklore in a castle in Wewelsberg). Rather, their lucrative jobs entailed working with the Interior Ministry's Office of Kinship Research to issue "Aryan certificates" to public sector employees who had to prove their racial pedigree in keeping with the civil service law. This latter office in turn worked with the Reich Office of Statistics, which analyzed identity papers and census records to gain a full view of the German population and relay any information about Jews to the SS Department of Jewish Affairs. In short, the persecution of Jews was a massive enterprise that created a new bureaucracy encompassing tens of thousands of participants.

To establish their positive racial credentials, average citizens had to prove "Aryan" ancestry back to 1800, while SS officers had to trace it back to 1750. This was not always easy, and some Nazis found themselves in the awkward position of having to account for their racial pedigree. The fair-haired Heydrich himself was dogged throughout his life by the suspicion that he had Jewish forebears. And Hitler himself never shook the false rumor that his paternal grandfather had been a Jew. Still today, the myth that "Hitler was Jewish" is pervasive. Others, in turn, who were practicing Christians but who had three or four non-"Aryan" grandparents were forced to make peace with the fact they were now a racial minority under law. For example, the late Columbia University professor Fritz Stern's family had converted to Christianity in the late nineteenth century, and he himself had been baptized. But the Sterns were still compelled to emigrate because they were "racially" Jewish.

The National Socialist obsession with health and ancestry and the abundance of offices devoted to their study have led some historians to refer to Nazi Germany as a "racial state." By this they mean that race fundamentally defined all policy goals and actions from 1933 to 1945, and it pervaded most aspects of daily life. Yet as we saw with the attempts to define Jewishness, Nazi leaders themselves recognized the arbitrary nature of racial classification and often applied race pragmatically. Indeed, some Nazis took pains to sever their worldview from the biological sciences. Wrote Günther Hecht, a zoologist, SA member, and racial hygienist: "National Socialism is a political movement, not a scientific one." Nazism, he felt, was not interested in questions of evolutionary biology or debates within the life sciences, but in the practical political needs of the party, "firmly rooted in reality." There was, he wrote, "no such thing as National Socialist anthropology or genetics."[7] Even the Nazi obsession with blood was only metaphorical. Serology and seroanthropology—the study of A, B, and O blood types and their diffusion among the world's populations—were of little importance to the regime precisely because the Nazis knew that actual blood was not a marker of any real human diversity. What this meant for Hecht and his cohort is that ostracizing Jews and Roma did not rely on an ironclad definition of racial perfection. Rather, it depended on using any tools at their disposal to get rid of racial, cultural, and political "enemies". While some Nazis believed that the existence of pure races was scientifically provable, others found them bogus and unnecessary.

"Racial science" was flimsy at best, but it still saturated German society. The symbolic power of biology helped mobilize Germans during the Third Reich. Advertisements taught citizens which household products were better for their racial health. Germans learned which vices—such as the use of tobacco or caffeine—threatened the national body politic. Rape, kosher slaughter, and the supposedly disgusting Jewish physicality appeared widely in Nazi propaganda. Racial scientists measured noses, and math problems in textbooks asked pupils to weigh the opportunity costs of feeding the physically and intellectually challenged. The Nazi public sphere was overrun with the language of sex, bodies, and danger. In short, Nazi racial policy toward minorities was built on the language of biological purity even if its designers knew that no such thing existed.

Stepping up the Terror

In July of 1935, the city of Dortmund banned Jews from swimming pools and sun decks. The reason was that "healthy Aryans" were supposed to feel revulsion at the sight of the Jewish body. They also needed to protect themselves from contamination in the water. Henceforth, when a Jewish-looking patron showed up, bathers chanted antisemitic slogans or pointed to the new sign reading, "Access to these facilities is forbidden to Jews." This posting became an increasingly common sight in Nazi Germany, especially as national laws followed local ones. As the 1930s progressed, Jews were forced to sit on segregated park benches; then they were banned from parks altogether. Jews were barred from restaurants and forbidden from using the "Heil Hitler" greeting (though few would want to, except to blend in). Jews could no longer buy flowers. The list of prewar anti-Jewish measures goes on and on, reflecting both the regime's increased confidence that it could solve the "Jewish Question" and the softening of the German public to these measures. In towns where no Jews resided, racist signs still went up.

The regime could be strategic about disseminating racist propaganda, especially when gauging foreign reactions. In preparation for the winter and summer Olympics in 1936, it banned signs indicating that Jews were being persecuted. Placards like "Juden sind hier unerwünscht" (Jews are unwelcome here) or *judenrein* (a declaration that a town or institution was Jew-free) had to come down. The whitewashing seems to have been effective. Wrote American journalist William Shirer in his diary: "I'm afraid the Nazis have succeeded with their propaganda. First, the Nazis have run the games on a lavish scale never before experienced, and this has appealed to the athletes. Second, the Nazis have put up a very good front for the general visitors."[8] Shirer was right. As soon as the games concluded, the signs went back up and the persecution continued.

As the decade proceeded, not every German Jew could adhere to Weltsch's admonition to take pride in their pariah status. Some turned to Zionism and tried to find a way to British-controlled Palestine. Other Jews became more religious, finding succor in the daily rituals of Judaism. Some people, not least the veterans who had fought for Germany with pride, sank into a depression, with their wives working to keep households functioning and keeping their "chin up for the children's sake."[9] Jews could also deny their Jewishness by trying to pass as "Aryan." This was easier for fair-haired Jews because they could conform more readily to this racial ideal, particularly if they could take advantage of the anonymity of the big city. Other responses included self-blame. Perhaps Jews had not been religious enough; they had tried to assimilate into Christian society, and they had abandoned their commitment to God and to their people, and this was their punishment. An opposing view held that Jews were not assimilated enough. By clinging to their religion, they had missed an opportunity to stake their claim to an increasingly secular society. Some German Jews pointed fingers at poor eastern European Jews who had emigrated to Germany in the first decades of the twentieth century, with caftans and traditional garb attracting the attention of antisemites like Hitler. Any sense of resentment toward fellow Jews, however, was trumped by anger at the majority population and despair about the loss of friendships. Non-Jews abandoned their social relationships with Jews out of ideological conviction or with the resigned sense that it was safer to distance themselves. Such people might encourage their Jewish friends to leave Germany, but in doing so out of good intentions, they were still doing the regime's bidding.

Emigration did remain an option until the onset of war, but it was not easy. When people pose the question "why didn't more Jews leave earlier?" one must acknowledge the psychological and practical barriers. Patriotism, combined with denial, could be powerful. Intellectually, one might suspect that danger lay ahead, yet this could be met with a kind of paralysis—an inability to make pragmatic plans based on these fears. As a practical matter, Jews also couldn't simply leave; countries had to take them. Those who were well connected or who had foreign relatives to sponsor their emigration had a distinct advantage. Albert Einstein was the most famous émigré. His professional connections in the United States allowed him to settle at Princeton University. Composer Arnold Schoenberg, who was on vacation in France in 1933, was warned not to return to Germany and he eventually made his way to the United States. Max Born, physicist and one of the fathers of quantum mechanics, fled to Great Britain in 1933.

At this early stage, the Nazis promoted emigration in a number of forms. In August of 1933 the Haavara Agreement between the Nazi regime and Zionist organizations allowed for the eventual emigration of 60,000 Jews to British Palestine. These Jews were allowed to take more of their wealth than others fleeing the country. By the end of 1933 around 37,000 Jews had emigrated from Nazi Germany, mostly to other countries in Europe. But the remaining had few means to leave, or they hoped to wait out the terror. "This too shall pass" was a common sentiment, paired with German Jews' unwillingness to renounce a country they called home and to which they had as much claim as non-Jews. Such views stood next to a hard reality. It rapidly became common knowledge that those who had fled into France and Holland were often without income or employment. German Jewish agencies, including those committed to Zionism, implored Jews not to leave until they had a secure employment opportunity elsewhere, and they saw Jews even returning to Germany to be with family and wait out the Nazis.

Nazi "Mercy Killing"

For much of the 1930s Jewish-Germans held out the hope of the regime miraculously collapsing, or they escaped the country outright. But they were not yet targeted *en masse* for murder. For another group of people, however, there was a different reality. This was the physically and intellectually disabled. In 1938 a German woman gave birth to a baby with one arm, one leg, severe mental disabilities, blindness, and deafness. Faced with this difficult situation, the parents wrote to Adolf Hitler seeking permission to have doctors end the child's life. Hitler granted their request, and he used this case to advance a goal he had long harbored: the elimination of what he and others deemed "lives unworthy of life" in order to purify the health of the German race. To carry out this agenda, the following year Hitler authorized his personal physician Karl Brandt and Philipp Bouhler, a high-ranking Nazi Party official, to orchestrate what would be known as the Children's "Euthanasia" Program. This program, under the codename T4 (from the address of its Berlin headquarters at Tiergartenstrasse 4), was expanded in 1939 to include adults. This was not "mercy killing" in any sense. Those chosen for murder were not terminally ill, and their families usually had no say in the matter. The process involved social workers, doctors, and nurses, who provided information on individuals institutionalized in hospitals and asylums. Teams of assessors then made the grim decision about who should live and who should die.

These assessors often failed to examine or even see the individuals they marked for death. A red plus sign on a patient's or resident's file meant a death sentence, while a blue minus sign signified the continuation of care. Some healthcare professionals refused to participate in this program, but there were many other ambitious and zealous doctors, nurses, administrators, and judges who carried it out. Patients selected for death were transported from institutions to specially designated "hospitals," where they were killed. Various methods were employed, including mobile gas vans, gas chambers, lethal injections, gradual starvation, and the use of individuals in deadly "experiments." Some victims knew what was in store for them and begged for mercy, thus attracting the attention of nearby townspeople. Yet in an attempt to keep the killings a secret, T4 personnel informed families of their loved one's murder with the euphemism of "sudden death." In total there were six major killing centers involved with the T4 program in the Reich, with others established in occupied Europe during the Second World War. By the time the regime collapsed in 1945, 200,000 Germans and Europeans had fallen victim to this mass killing program (see Plate 13). The Nazi regime used T4 to pioneer killing methods they would turn to again during the Second World War.

The persecution of minorities in National Socialist Germany was about more than an obsession with biology. The Nazis could never find any distinct racial markers for Jews or Roma or those with hereditary illnesses, and they therefore depended on common stereotypes about criminality, sexuality, and economic power. And the broader German public never became as obsessed with biology as did Hitler, Himmler, Rosenberg, and Gross. Even the anthropologists, biologists, and genealogists whose offices engaged in genetic surveillance constantly ran up against the limits of science. Bavarian Gauleiter Hans Schemm's statement that National Socialism is "applied biology" thus has to be rethought. The language of racial cleansing permeated society and informed the most terrifying of policies. And there were indeed bloodthirsty images: "When Jewish blood spurts from the knife ... " was a lyric from one of the songs Melita Maschmann had to sing in the Hitler Youth.[10] But for her and others, Jews were more of a catch-all "bogeyman" than a classification within a racial hierarchy. And for all the talk of getting rid of those with hereditary illnesses, the majority of those sterilized in the 1930s came from working-class backgrounds, indicating that power and wealth allowed exceptions to rules of biology that were supposed to transcend one's social position. In short, German nationalism in the Nazi years was less about blood than a devotion to the *Volksgemeinschaft*. Nazis referred to each other more often as *Volksgenosse*, or national comrade, than as *Rassengenosse*. And the word "Volk" was employed more as a marker for culture, language, and history than for a discrete Germanic race sanitized of Jews and other undesirables. In short, despite—or perhaps because of—the Nazis' undisciplined views of race, discrimination and murder proceeded apace for reasons often far removed from the realms of biology. But consistent or not, the language of biology pervaded the public sphere and the myriad laws that destroyed the lives of ethnic and sexual minorities and the intellectually and physically disabled.

Notes

1   In other versions of this saying, Niemöller (correctly) mentioned communists before socialists.

2   "Report by Alfred Biswanger on his arrest in March 1933," https://www.jmberlin.de/1933/en/04_11_report-by-alfred-binswanger-on-his-arrest-in-march-1933.php

3   Luise Solmitz quoted in *Bedrohung, Hoffnung, Skepsis: Vier Tagebücher des Jahres 1933*, Frank Bajohr, et al. eds. (Göttingen: Wallstein, 2013), 185.

4   Eric Johnson, *What We Knew: Terror, Mass Murder, and Everyday Life in Nazi Germany: An Oral History* (Cambridge UK: Basic Books, 2005), 148.

5   Melita Maschmann, *Account Rendered: A Dossier on my Former Self* (Lexington, MA: Plunkett Lake, 2016), 62, 63.

6   RV announcement, *Jüdische Rundschau*, no. 77 (September 24, 1935), https://www.jewishvirtuallibrary.org/german-jewish-response-to-the-nuremberg-laws

7   Günther Hecht, "Biology and National Socialism," in *The Third Reich Sourcebook*, Anson Rabinbach and Sander L. Gilman, eds. (Berkeley: University of California Press, 2013), 167–9.

8   William L. Shirer, *Berlin Diary: The Journal of a Foreign Correspondent, 1934–1941* (Boston: Little Brown, 1940), diary entry from August 16, 1936, 65.

9   Marion A. Kaplan, *Between Dignity and Despair: Jewish Life in Nazi Germany* (Oxford: Oxford University Press, 1998), 61.

10 Maschmann, *Account Rendered*, 60.

Additional Reading

Bergen, Doris. *The Twisted Cross: The German Christian Movement in the Third Reich*. Chapel Hill and London: University of North Carolina Press, 1996.

Burleigh, Michael, and Wolfgang Wippermann. *The Racial State: Germany, 1933–1945*. Cambridge: Cambridge University Press, 1991.

Friedländer, Saul. *Nazi Germany and the Jews: The Years of Persecution, 1933–1939*. Volume 1. New York: HarperCollins, 1997.

Hutton, Christopher. *Race and the Third Reich: Linguistics, Racial Anthropology, and Genetics in the Dialectic of Volk*. London: Polity Press, 2005.

Kaplan, Marion A. *Between Dignity and Despair: Jewish Life in Nazi Germany*. New York and Oxford: Oxford University Press, 1998.

Koonz, Claudia. *The Nazi Conscience*. Cambridge, MA: The Belknap Press of Harvard University Press, 2003.

Lewy, Guenter. *The Nazi Persecution of the Gypsies*. Oxford and New York: Oxford University Press, 2000.

Pendas, Devin, Mark Roseman, and Richard Wetzell. *Beyond the Racial State: Rethinking Nazi Germany*. Cambridge: Cambridge University Press, 2017.

Schleunes, Karl A. *The Twisted Road to Auschwitz: Nazi Policy toward German Jews, 1933–1939*. Urbana and Chicago: University of Illinois Press, 1990.

Wildt, Michael. *Hitler's* Volksgemeinschaft *and the Dynamics of Racial Exclusion: Violence against Jews in Provincial Germany, 1919–1939*. Translated by Bernard Heise. New York: Berghahn Books, 2012.

5

Economy and Society

When historians asked West Germans in the 1950s and 1960s what they remembered about National Socialist Germany, many offered fond memories of the prewar years. They spoke of the "good" that the Nazi regime had achieved before the war, including ending the Depression and putting Germans back to work, and they marveled at how the one-party state had ended political discord and returned law and order to German streets.

How do we reconcile this positive view of prewar Nazi Germany with the erosion of individual rights and violence discussed in the previous chapters? For true believers, even full knowledge of the Holocaust after 1945 was not enough to convince them that Hitler had presided over an evil regime. But for most Germans, the answer to this question is more complicated. This chapter addresses this puzzle by exploring economic developments and consensus building in the runup to war. The first section looks at the regime's response to the Depression and its early attempts to marginalize "non-Aryans," especially Jews, and those "Aryans" considered to be "unproductive," from economic life. It also examines the economic challenges of preparing for war, such as shortages of hard currency and natural resources in Germany, and the rebuilding of a military that had been effectively dismantled by the Versailles Treaty. The second section turns to the ways the regime mobilized the population to support its racist, expansionist aims before 1939. Social and economic policies rallied so-called "Aryans" and isolated Jewish Germans. Attempts to bring to life the long-promised *Volksgemeinschaft*, a race-based people's community, involved both exclusionary and inclusionary practices. Many Germans embraced a dictatorship that protected and empowered them, and this helps explain why so many later supported the war effort and, even after its defeat, looked back on these years fondly.

Financing Rearmament

Adolf Hitler and his supporters were ambitious. They insisted their movement, backed by the full authority of the state starting in early 1933, could right the past wrongs they believed had been carried out against Germany, address all the challenges facing their country in the present, and chart a future that would see Germany take its rightful place as one of the most powerful and prosperous country in the world. The empire the Nazis sought to build in Europe was, like all colonial empires, to be secured through theft and bloodshed and sustained through the forced labor of colonized peoples and the extraction of natural resources in the colonized lands. Realizing this imperial dream would require decisive military victories over a vast territory. However, as historian Adam Tooze has explained, "the problem was how to achieve all of this with the limited means at Germany's disposal and against the resistance of most of Europe, indeed the world. Ultimately, this was an economic as much as a military problem."[1] For this reason, the Nazi regime saw the steering of the economy and its expansion as preconditions for its imperial quest.

The regime's immediate priority was to counter the impact of the Depression, including mass unemployment. Hitler focused on the economic crisis in his first speech to the nation after being named chancellor:

"Within four years the German farmer must be saved from pauperism. Within four years unemployment must be completely overcome. Parallel with this, there emerge the prerequisites of the economy. ... The National Government will combine this gigantic project of restoring our economy with the task of putting the administration and the finances of the Reich, the state, and the communes on a sound basis."[2]

In this vein, the regime pursued policies that had a positive impact on the country's economic outlook. Increased public spending aided the recovery, though an uptick in government outlays had already begun in 1931 under the final Weimar-era administrations, and similar strategies were implemented in other countries. For example, the voluntary labor service created in Germany in 1931 to provide work to the legions of unemployed was mirrored in the Civilian Conservation Corps and other New Deal programs in the United States. Indeed, there is evidence that German recovery began in 1932 when the Depression bottomed out. Nonetheless, Hitler benefited from the fortuitous timing of his appointment and took credit for improvements. Likewise, the change in government in 1933 itself raised expectations that recovery was possible and thus helped fuel spending.[3] As it did elsewhere, unemployment started to decline that year.

While the regime's investment in work-creation programs was good policy in combating unemployment, Hitler's government already began to scale them back by the end of 1933 in favor of rearmament. Chapter 8 will explore in depth the Nazis' ideological and geo-political reasons for remilitarizing the country. For now, it is worth noting that funneling money into the rebirth of the German military not only put Germans back to work, it also hastened the day when war would be possible. As Hitler explained to his cabinet only a week after taking power, "the next five years in Germany must be devoted to the rearmament of the German people. Every publicly supported job creation scheme must be judged by the criterion of whether it is necessary from the point of view of the rearmament of the German people."[4] In the world rankings of GDP per capita in the interwar period Germany languished in eleventh place, behind all its peers in Europe and North America. While historians now know that colonial powers generally spent more to maintain their empires than they gained from them in economic riches, Hitler looked at the countries with larger GDPs than Germany—the United States, Britain, the Netherlands, Belgium, and France—and drew the conclusion, as others did at the time, that conquest, not free trade, was the only path to greatness.[5]

By spring 1933, the army had compiled a list of 2,800 companies that were ready and willing to fulfill orders from the military. Manufacturers welcomed the business because the Depression had led to dormant production facilities (Figure 5.1). Twelve months later, 17,000 aircraft had been ordered for construction by 1939, which entailed the monumental task of designing and manufacturing countless individual parts ahead of the aircrafts' assembly. While these planes would become the core of a new air force, for the time being most were described as civilian and training aircraft to avoid international scrutiny. In the summer of 1933 the arms giant Krupp began producing tanks, which it masked as "agricultural tractors," and the navy put in its orders for ships and other equipment in the fall.[6] This construction required vast numbers of laborers, but in 1933 there was still an army of unemployed workers in Germany eager for stable wages (see Plate 12).

Soldiers would also be needed for the coming war, and here too the regime's militarism helped it achieve its promise of full employment. Already in spring 1935 conscription was reintroduced. Starting on March 15, 1935, all non-Jewish males who had reached the age of eighteen and had already served six months in the Reich Labor Service (*Reichsarbeitsdienst*, RAD) were required to serve an additional year in the armed forces. The regime launched recruitment drives in 1934 to fill out the ranks of the army, navy, and the new air force, the existence of which was officially unveiled in 1935. In June of that year, the government made a six-month enlistment in the Reich Labor Service compulsory for all men between ages eighteen and twenty-five. Women could volunteer for labor service, but it was not mandatory for them until the war began. Reich Labor Servicemen were involved in construction projects in the agricultural and forestry sectors, and notably in the building of autobahn motorways, which Weimar leaders had proposed and which Hitler enthusiastically supported. By 1936, 130,000 Germans were employed directly in the building of highways, and countless others depended for their work on the building and supply services that supported highway construction. By the next year, Germany had built 1,200 miles of motorway, and by 1942, this amount had doubled.

The regime hoped the experience of national service in the RAD would foster comradeship across regional, class, and urban/rural divides. For men,

FIGURE 5.1 *Leading German industrialists give the Hitler salute at an assembly in the capital in November 1933. From right to left: Dr. Gustav Krupp von Bohlen und Halbach, leader of the Reich Estate of German Industry, Theodor von Renteln, head of the Reich Estate for German Trade and Handicrafts and President of the Federation of Chambers of Industry and Commerce, and Albert Vögler, General Director of United Steel Works (Bundesarchiv, Bild 102-16496).*

service involved living in barracks in military formations and conducting manual labor up to seventy hours per week. RAD men were not allowed to leave the camps and pay was meager. Ideologically, the service period was meant to act as a bridge between the training the Hitler Youth provided boys and the eventual military training they received after conscription. Only NSDAP literature was allowed in the barracks and social activities, including meals, were highly regimented. In addition to preparing the men for military conscription, RAD leaders sought to break down class identity by teaming working-class and middle-class men together, though at times this led to bullying, with middle class laborers receiving most of the harassment.

Some participants in the Reich Labor Service, like Melita Maschmann, reveled in the hard work and communal living as an opportunity to "get down to practice," by which she meant contributing in a tangible way to the establishment of a prosperous, unified *Volksgemeinschaft*.[7] Others, however, grew disillusioned by the harsh conditions. Harald Quandt, Joseph Goebbels' stepson, summed up his experience as "bad food, mistreatment, censored mail."[8] Men's service had to be made compulsory because as unemployment dried up, so did the interest in participation among many young people. At the height of the Depression in 1932, as many as 6 million had been out of work in Germany. By 1934, thanks in large part to secret spending on arms manufacturing, that number had already fallen to 4 million. By prioritizing heavy industry in the name of war preparation and filling the ranks of the country's armed forces, Germany achieved full employment by 1936.

Issuing armaments contracts was one thing. Paying for all this new manufacturing was another, especially given the sharp decline in Germany's gross domestic product during the Depression and with it the tax revenue that the government relied on to pay its bills. And after the trauma of the 1923 hyperinflation, printing Reichsmarks was not yet an acceptable option. As late as 1938, the nation's tax revenue still only covered slightly more than half of state expenditures. A key figure in Germany's preparations for war, then, was the Reichsbank President and Minister of Economics from 1934 to 1937, Hjalmar Schacht, whom Hitler entrusted in March 1933 to find a way to finance his military buildup. Governments regularly raise capital from international lenders, but Hitler's government did not want to draw attention to the arms production, which ignored the Versailles Treaty's limits on the size of the German armed forces. To circumvent the Treaty, Schacht created a shell corporation, known as the Metallurgical Research Institute (MEFO, for short), which issued MEFO-bills to pay for arms contracts. Defense companies could in turn exchange these bills for Reichsmarks. By 1935, however, a conflict had emerged between Schacht, on one side, and Hitler and the Wehrmacht on the other over the best strategy for readying the nation for war. The economics minister worried about inflation and insisted that hard currency should be sought via export markets, while the nation continued to decrease imports. He predicted Germany would not be able to finance a war until 1942. Hitler, however, believed Germany could be ready for an expansionist war by 1940, if the reins on deficit spending were loosened. He saw Schacht's warnings as overly pessimistic, and in the summer of 1936, Hitler changed course. As Schacht later reported, his plan "did not suit either Hitler's mentality or his intentions. Everything had to be bigger and to be done quicker. Rearmament must be sped up and increased."[9] While Schacht remained Minister of Economics until late 1937, his authority was usurped by someone willing to meet the Führer's timeline. That person was Hermann Göring, who, along with his position as commander of the new German air force or Luftwaffe, was put at the helm of the ad hoc Office of the Four-Year Plan in 1936. Göring famously called his rival Schacht on his first day in the new role to taunt: "I am now sitting in your chair!"[10] The new office's mandate was captured in its name—to ready the nation for war in four years.

With Göring's appointment, preparation of the economy for war intensified. In 1936 expenditures on the military amounted to 11 percent of GDP. By 1939 it had risen to roughly 23 percent of national income, significantly greater than the UK at 15 percent, France at 9 percent, and the United States at 1 percent.[11] Only Japan was close with a military burden of 22 percent in 1939. A closer look at individual resources critical to the German war economy shows a massive rise in productivity in these years: coal production increased by 18 percent in the first two years of the new plan; aluminum production rose by 70 percent; petroleum production advanced by 63 percent among other impressive gains.[12] Yet the economic problems Schacht had identified remained. Production still failed to meet the gargantuan demands of building an armed forces capable of defeating allied European powers in the near future. The goal was to raise an army of 3.6 million men with 102 divisions and at least 5,000 tanks. Hitler also intended to construct a wholly new air force and launch a massive new naval fleet, something dubbed the "Z Plan." More troubling, much of the necessary production still relied on key imports, despite measures to bolster autarky, and these imports continued to deplete foreign currency reserves. For example, aluminum production had risen by 70 percent, but the plants used for processing it still relied on raw materials purchased abroad. Exports that could bring in foreign currency were far outpaced by imports. For Nazi Germany's leaders, the only way around this was to have a war sooner rather than later. Hitler's quest for *Lebensraum*, or living space, secured through expansionist military victory in Poland and the Soviet Union, would be critical to capturing the needed natural resources that would sustain the dreamed-of Nazi empire. Göring himself summed up the situation perfectly: "The struggle which we are approaching demands a colossal measure of productive ability. No end to the rearmament is in sight. The only deciding point in this case is victory or destruction. If we win, then the economy will be sufficiently compensated."[13]

On November 5, 1937, Hitler called a meeting with the heads of the armed forces to convince them that war was necessary by 1940. Whether he was looking for confirmation of a specific plan or simply laying out his thinking about the importance of securing *Lebensraum*, the military chiefs left the meeting concerned about a premature assault. Hitler must have sensed their hesitation. In the following weeks, as explained in greater detail in Chapter 8, he dismissed his Minister of War and Commander in Chief of the German Army and relieved fourteen other generals of their posts. He created a new title for himself, Commander of the Armed Forces, and promoted others who were less likely to question his directives. A similarly motivated purge was undertaken in the Foreign Ministry around the same time.

The Nazi regime's direction of the economy toward self-sufficiency and its focus on rearmament and related industries needed for war, like mining and chemical manufacturing, has led some to wonder if the German economy should be viewed as a command economy rather than a capitalist one in these years. As with many sectors of German society, after 1945 West German industrial leaders sought to distance themselves from the crimes of the Nazi period, by emphasizing state control of the economy under the Nazi dictatorship. But in fact business leaders retained a substantial amount of freedom in their day-to-day decision making. The Nazi regime continued to recognize private property (except when it belonged to racial and political "enemies"), and the negotiation of contracts continued largely as before. In short, the Nazi economy maintained the basic structures and behaviors of capitalism, albeit with increasing government intervention and the top-down setting of production and investment priorities. Despite the rationing of raw materials, companies regularly ordered more than they needed to fill contracts to keep supplies from competitors. Some firms ignored calls to abandon manufacturing consumer goods to maintain brand recognition among shoppers for a future postwar era. Others kept Jewish employees or Jewish clients longer than basic government directives allowed, as they relied on these individuals or deemed these relationships critical for their company's success. Even simple commands like retooling advertising to meet the standards set by the Propaganda Ministry were routinely ignored or only half-heartedly adhered to in the name of commercial competitiveness. These business decisions were not examples of resistance to the regime or its ideological principles, as some industrialists claimed after 1945. Rather, the Nazi state and economic leaders found ways to work together: business owners were reassured that Hitler planned no radical economic restructuring and thus tolerated greater state intervention in some sectors, and the regime in turn allowed for some independence for business owners. Capitalism, in other words, adapted to the new order, and the government, the party's leaders and members, and many business owners found ways to profit from the new relationship.

Class Structure in the Prewar Years

Did full employment by 1936 allow Hitler to achieve his goal of creating a *Volksgemeinschaft*, or national community? The Nazis saw the *Volksgemeinschaft* not only as a group of racially homogenous and ideologically like-minded people, but also as a "classless" community. The Nazis believed that racial solidarity could overcome the disunity caused by socioeconomic stratification, which they felt had crippled the Weimar Republic. But they rejected the Marxist belief that class difference always led to competition and conflict. In contrast, all productive "Aryans" would now have a role to play in the country's rebirth, and while those roles differed by age, gender, and employment category, all Germans, the Nazis promised, would be respected for their contributions to the nation.

This promise to replace conflict between socioeconomic groups with racial solidarity did not require fundamental changes to the distribution of wealth and property among "Aryans." Wealthy non-Jewish Germans continued to enjoy luxuries and privilege into the war years, and most lower income

Germans continued to follow the career paths of their forebears. Some individuals were able to take advantage of opportunities for upward mobility via the expanding state and party bureaucracies or new technical fields, but in general the class structures held firm. There is also a misconception that during the Nazi period women did not work outside the home—that their duty to the race began and ended with their roles as mothers and wives. While Nazi propaganda prioritized a domestic image of womanhood, and the regime introduced policies to encourage married women to stay home, about half of all German families could not make ends meet on one salary. In those cases, as we will see in Chapter 6, married women continued to seek wage labor to supplement the family income. Single women, whose numbers were elevated by the losses of men during the First World War, also returned to the workforce as the Depression waned, especially as white-collar office workers in the growing bureaucracies that supported all levels of government, the complicated party structure, including the many mass organizations tied to the party, and the private sector (Figure 5.2).

The focus on rearmament meant that the employment situation for male and female industrial workers remained positive throughout the prewar years. One thing that had changed dramatically was that the new government had dissolved the powerful German trade unions on May 2, 1933, and their leaders were some of the first to be imprisoned in the nascent concentration

FIGURE 5.2 *Typist for the German Labor Front, 1938 (Bundesarchiv, Bild 183-H02370CC-BY-SA 3.0, CC BY-SA 3.0 DE, Public Domain via Wikimedia Commons).*

camp system. The regime despised the social democratic trade unions, but even the conservative trade unions were disbanded, as a potential source of opposition to state authority through strikes and other worker actions. In their place, the Nazis established the German Labor Front (DAF) on May 10, 1933. The DAF claimed to champion the needs of all employees, manual laborers as well as white-collar workers and professionals. While such rhetoric was meant to demonstrate respect for all forms of labor—farmers to engineers, office managers to factory employees—the DAF was nothing more than a voice of the NSDAP within the workplace.

Keen to build support among Germany's workforce, the German Labor Front set out to build programs meant to woo workers to the side of National Socialism. The DAF's Strength through Joy (*Kraft durch Freude*, KdF) program promoted affordable recreational activities, which will be discussed later in this chapter. One of KdF's subsidiary programs, Beauty of Labor (*Schönheit der Arbeit*), was intended to coordinate the beautification of German worksites and improve working conditions. In addition to making sure the grounds around factories were planted with flowers and exteriors were given a new coat of paint, the Beauty of Labor office monitored such elements as lighting, air quality, and temperature on the factory floor (see Plate 5). It also oversaw the efficiency of plant layout and workstations as well as hygiene and other important qualities that affected worker satisfaction and productivity, such as the availability and quality of changing rooms, cafeterias, and childcare facilities. By the end of 1935, 12,000 German companies had beautified their work sites.[14] Company owners were expected to cover the costs of renovations or other enhancements. Many factors motivated company owners to get on the bandwagon. Some felt pressured to fall in line and show support for the regime's programs; others were happy to comply if doing so convinced workers that the dissolution of the trade unions had been for the best; and still others may have simply sought to improve conditions for their employees. As one proponent cheered, "people can produce more in clean, airy, and bright workplaces. ... "[15] In some cases, the costs of renovations were passed down to the workforce. In one example from a cardboard factory in Saxony, the workers were each required to give up 1.5 hours of pay to fund the purchase of a radio for the common room to comply with Beauty of Labor standards.[16] Not surprisingly, some workers grumbled at the idea of self-financing workplace enhancements.

It is important to remember that despite introducing programs that had some benefits for workers, the DAF and therefore its members had no collective bargaining rights, and strikes were outlawed. As a result, especially in the second half of the 1930s, as the government intensified the production of war materials and suppressed wages, and excess labor no longer existed, employment conditions worsened. Despite job security, which had been hard to find during the Weimar Republic, long hours and high demands to meet the goals set for war-readiness led to discontent about wages and the speed of production in some industrial sectors (Figure 5.3). Industrial wages did not regain the levels achieved in early 1929 until 1938 at the earliest. If one factors in the compulsory fees and "voluntary" dues paid to the nazified economic and political associations, workers did not take home as much as they did in 1929 until the first full year of the war, 1940.

FIGURE 5.3 *Miner with his pit lamp, c. 1935. Workers like this one were critical to the regime's rearmament plans (Bundesarchiv, Bild 183-2010-0408-503).*

Those who owned the factories that received the government orders related to re-armament were largely supportive of these developments. Increases to corporate tax rates in these years were a small price to pay for vastly higher profits and the disappearance of social democratic union organizers on factory floors. The KPD had not had as much of a presence as the SPD among employed laborers in the Weimar Republic, but its goal of nationalizing industry along the Soviet model meant that the regime's mass arrests of communist leaders in early 1933 was met with approval within the business community. While most German industrialists were skeptical about funding Hitler's movement before 1933, almost all were happy to keep their heads down and reap the benefits of government investment.

While the regime prioritized heavy industry in the mid-1930s, it also paid attention to the large agricultural sector. Food shortages during the First World War had damaged morale and productivity and had led to malnourishment and a spike in infectious diseases among Germans by the latter years of the conflict. Knowing this, Hitler's government sought to wean the country off its dependence on imported foods and bolster its own farming sector. Protectionist measures to support domestic produce and livestock had increased during the Depression, which meant Germans were already used to regulation in this sector. However, when Reich Minister for Food and Agriculture Richard Walter Darré set out to regulate all imports and fix prices for all home-grown agricultural products under the newly established Reich Food Estate in 1933, some farmers grew concerned about the new limits on their independence. And, yet, when they compared these interventions with the news of mass death associated with the collectivization of agricultural land in the Soviet Union in the 1930s, they considered themselves lucky. Indeed, as has been observed, some of the structures put in place to control production, distribution, and consumption of the German food supply in these years laid the groundwork for the heavily state-controlled European agriculture sector today.[17] By the onset of war in 1939, the Reich Food Estate's policies had achieved considerable success. Germany had made itself self-sufficient in the cultivation and production of bread, potatoes, meat, and sugar, and some other staples, but only through strict rationing. Even then, 15 percent of the nation's food supply continued to be imported, and intermittent shortages of certain favorites led to muted grumbling among consumers. Autarky, or economic self-sufficiency, was a goal that could only be achieved by predatory extraction from what the Nazis defined as "the East," comprising largely Polish and Soviet territory.

As with the working class, the German middle class also included a diverse set of people and employment categories. The economic prospects for university-educated professionals remained strong in the 1930s, though for lawyers, doctors, and academics, there was increasing pressure to fall into line with the regime. As the young attorney, Sebastian Haffner, admitted years later about his response to the early changes that came to the judiciary, "I frightened my parents with wild proposals: I would leave the law courts; I would emigrate .... But it went no further than the expression of these intentions. ... Perhaps it was best to hold steady and let things pass over me."[18] Among middle-ranking civil servants, opportunities grew in conjunction with the increasingly sophisticated state apparatus. To some extent this expansion of white-collar employment reflected trends seen in democracies in these years that correlated with the growth of state-supported social services and governmental planning. Thriving in these positions in Nazi Germany, however, for example as municipal officials or schoolteachers, required some acceptance of or ability to tolerate the exclusionary practices of the regime.

For members of the "old middle class," especially retail shop owners and craftsmen, the outlook remained poor. Members of this group were among the early supporters of Nazism. They saw the expansion of chain retailers, department stores, and mass production in the 1920s as undercutting their livelihoods, and they found in the NSDAP a party they believed would defend their interests. From its founding in 1920, the Nazi Party claimed it would protect German artisans and small business owners from "Jewish competition" and other economic rivals. Despite these promises and the tactics targeting Jewish retailers and craftsmen (discussed below), the long-term outlook for so-called "Aryan" German shop owners and craftsmen remained shaky, even as the Depression waned. Preparation for modern war left little room for artisans and small shops to thrive. Most of these small businesses served individual consumer needs and desires, while the Nazi state moved to prioritize heavy industry, offering large firms incentives to become more efficient. As a result, some companies moved away from consumer goods production altogether after 1933. Simultaneously, the state suppressed individual consumption by artificially restraining workers' wages, meaning purchasing power remained low, which kept customers from patronizing local shops. Imports, too, were restricted to encourage self-sufficiency. As a result, artisans struggled to find and afford the raw materials needed to produce their wares, and retailers had little ability to import finished goods for their store shelves. These measures and others dampened the prospects of small business owners throughout the 1930s, and once war came many more closed permanently.

Economic Persecution of German Jews

As we saw in previous chapters, the NSDAP had always portrayed Germany's Jews as predators or parasites, who lived off and weakened the nation. But the range and contradictory nature of the racist metaphors reserved for the relationship between German Jews and the economy was remarkable. At times Jews were fat cat capitalists, who mistreated workers and pushed smaller manufacturers out of business with their cheap goods and underhanded sales practices. At other times, they were radical Marxists who sought the end of private property in favor of a Soviet-style revolution. Jews were targeted as lazy landlords and financiers, who got rich despite being "unproductive," while also being criticized as "over-represented" in the professions—as doctors, lawyers, and professors. At times they were the string pullers of the press and parliament; in other contexts, they were vilified as poor rag men and peddlers.

Despite this confused messaging, or perhaps because such confusion allowed people to pick out which claims about Jews seemed most salient in any given context, the Nazi regime was successful in its efforts to use legislation and rouse public sentiment in ways that undermined the ability

FIGURE 5.4 *"Germans! Shop only in German stores!" Flyers like this one were meant to demonize Jewish-owned department stores like Tietz and discount stores like the German branch of the American Woolworth brand (Wohlwert) with its uniform pricing (Ehape), c. 1933 (Bundesarchiv, Plak 002-036-009).*

of Jews in Germany to participate in the economy. The 1933 Law for the Restoration of the Professional Civil Service, as we saw, excluded Jews from working as government officials, professors, schoolteachers, police officers, or any other public sector jobs. Certain business models were targeted as "Jewish," "foreign," and "anti-German," including department stores and chain stores, and regulations were passed that made it difficult for these businesses to stay afloat (Figure 5.4). In the private sector, the exclusion of Jews was slower. That did not change the fact that for many German Jews, state-sanctioned antisemitism was often first experienced in economic terms: Jews were let go from employment, or lost customers or clients, or faced prejudiced decisions in the courts when it came to business contracts, tax assessments, or tenancy agreements.

As evidence of the new government's commitment to "defending" German business owners, Nazi leaders organized a nation-wide boycott of Jewish-owned business ahead of the Easter holiday in 1933. For Germany's Jews, the April 1, 1933, blockade discussed in the last chapter was chilling. Kurt Rosenberg, a lawyer based in Hamburg, worried about the future and began planning to send his wife and children abroad. Despite the support the family received from friends and neighbors, it was impossible to ignore the ways the country was changing. He wrote on the second day of the boycott, April 2, 1933, "We are receiving flowers and cards from our Christian friends, who want to show us their attitude [toward the boycott]. With every gesture like this, we are thankful, because it restores our belief in mankind, if not in people per se."[19] Some German shoppers were disgusted by the harassment of the SA; others were simply annoyed by the inconvenience of not getting into their favorite shops ahead of their Easter celebrations. One young non-Jewish woman's experience was not uncommon, and it captures the process by which a gulf opened between so-called "Aryan" and Jewish Germans. Returning from a skiing trip, Liselotte Otting found herself in Munich in the midst of the boycott. She and her friends were "infuriated," she said, "but we did not … We thought, stay out of it. And of course, it started, how can I say it? That [you] thanked God you were not a Jew."[20]

After the official boycott was lifted, businesses were still expected to prove they were "Aryan-owned and controlled." Receiving a certificate to that effect from the local branch of the NSDAP meant the company (big or small) could avoid harassment and future boycotts, though a reputation as a Jewish-owned firm could be hard to shake. Business rivals sometimes used the public memory of a company as Jewish to try and convince customers to switch brands, as was the case with the parent company of Nivea skincare products. Despite removing five Jewish members from its management board in spring 1933 and receiving official recognition as an "Aryan firm" from the government, competitors continued to circulate flyers and ads that labeled Nivea products as "Jewish skin cream" throughout the mid-1930s. As in the case of Nivea's parent company, the need to prove "Aryan-ownership" and leadership led to the layoffs of many Jews who had run companies effectively for decades. It also meant that businesses owned by Jews had to be sold. As a result, through the mid-1930s, Jewish owners were forced to sell their business of all sizes or close them. Pressure from officials and local antisemitism meant the vast majority were sold far below market value.

The Nazis referred to the process by which businesses and other property, including homes and valuable personal effects, were effectively stolen from Jews as "Aryanization." But this euphemism doesn't really capture the brutality of a process that we would be better to call dispossession. The theft could be based on the outright seizure of a Jewish-owned business, or it could be incremental, beginning perhaps with the loss of customers, followed by a landlord who refused to renew a shop lease. Soon the only avenue to avoid complete financial ruin was to sell the business, but here too local "Aryan" competitors conspired with officials to purchase the business far below what it was worth. "Aryanization" played a significant role in the process by which Germany's Jews were excluded from society and left vulnerable to further antisemitic legislation and violence. It also meant that, in addition to the state, individual non-Jewish Germans profited off the theft of their own neighbors and business partners, as it was often current "Aryan" employees or owners of competitor firms who snapped up these businesses.

Losing their ability to earn a living pushed some German Jews to emigrate. Others hoped that conditions would improve and struggled to stay afloat financially amid the persecution. Still others desperately wished to leave but could not afford the travel documents, moving costs, and confiscatory taxes imposed on émigrés by the Nazis. While the regime officially supported Jewish emigration, the state drained fleeing Jews of their savings. Those who remained saw their incomes steadily decline, leaving Jewish families little or no means with which to emigrate. As we will see in Chapter 10, this persecution, by which Germany's Jews were methodically pushed out of the economy, culminated in early November 1938 when the regime coordinated the violent attack on those Jewish businesses that had remained open (along with synagogues and Jewish residences). In the aftermath of the November Pogrom, Hermann Göring declared the economy "Jew-free," insisting that any German Jew still engaged in economic activity in the country would be forced to cease work immediately.

Consumers and the People's Economy

Coming out of the Great Depression, Germans longed for the financial security that came with steady employment, and they also wanted to enjoy life in ways that seemed increasingly available to those living in neighboring countries. Just as the Nazis promised to put Germans back to work, the party had also promised to close the gap in living standards that had begun

to widen in the 1920s between the First World War's victorious nations (the
UK, France, and the United States in particular) on one side and Germany
on the other. Given the suppression of wages and the continued persistence
of class difference, which meant upward social mobility remained relatively
limited, it is clear the regime did not deliver on its promise to create material
abundance for all. This is not surprising, because the great prosperity that
Hitler planned was expected to be financed through the domination and
colonization of Europe, particularly the lands to Germany's east including
Poland and the Soviet Union. And yet much like other countries, Germany
did remain on the path toward the development of a mass consumer society
in the prewar years, one that had begun in the stable middle years of the
Weimar Republic.

Despite prioritizing rearmament and heavy industry, the regime's leaders
wanted so-called "Aryan" Germans to be happy and fulfilled. From 1933 to
well into the war years, Hitler's government encouraged "Aryan" Germans
to see themselves as capable and deserving of the good life. After all, if
"Aryans" were superior, it stood to reason that they should have access to
life's bounty at least as much as those in "degenerate," multicultural societies
like the United States. This is not to say that hard work was not expected
for Germany to achieve its potential. The ideal Nazi was a "man of action"
and sacrifice. Germans were implored to participate in the remaking of their
country, whether through long hours in a factory or agricultural fields, or
in collecting donations for the Winter Relief, a Nazi Party initiative that
had begun during the Depression years to collect funds and disseminate
household goods and clothing to the needy and grew to become a massive
annual campaign to support the poorest members of the *Volk*. But this
dedication to the project of remaking Germany was also to be rewarded,
and the economic stability that arrived in the mid-1930s bred confidence
among Germans and greater desire for material goods.

Hitler's government sought to balance the affirmation of these desires
with a realism that reflected the prioritization of war and the belief that
material abundance would follow victory. The regime also sought to balance
a recognition of individuality with the importance of community solidarity
within the *Volksgemeinschaft*. One historian has argued that we should
think of Germany in the 1930s as an era in which "virtual consumption"
was promoted.[21] By this he meant that dreams of enjoying mass-produced
consumer goods, especially the newest technology, were cultivated by the
regime even if the vast majority of people did not have access to time-saving
appliances or other durable goods, like personal automobiles, until well after
the Nazi regime was gone. This forward-looking message about individual
consumption was promoted and managed by the state in several ways.

One strategy was to manufacture *Volksprodukte*—people's products
that were intended to be affordable by all. Household products like the
Volksstaubsauger, or "People's vacuum cleaner," were intended to bring
modern technology and efficiency to German homes. The two most famous,

the *Volksempfänger* (people's radio) and the *Volkswagen* (people's car or KdF-car), tell us much about the ambitions and limits of the German economy in these years. Radio was an essential mass communications technology in the interwar period, and household ownership of radios had skyrocketed in the United States and parts of western Europe in the 1920s. Sales of radios to individuals in Germany, however, lagged, owing primarily to economic instability. People listened in community centers, workplace cafeterias, and other common areas, but most families did not own their own wireless set. In 1933 the newly appointed Propaganda Minister, Joseph Goebbels, called for the creation of the People's Radio. When the basic set went on the market at 76 RM, it wasn't the cheapest radio available in Europe, but its affordability and the propaganda surrounding it did increase the number of families who made a purchase (see Plate 8). There wasn't a single "People's Radio." There was a range of sets at different price points, and private firms continued to sell fancier models. In other words, differences in price and taste that reflected class status and other variables remained. More information on the political and cultural importance of radio is provided in the chapter on art and culture.

At the other end of the price scale, the *Volkswagen* was a pet project of the Führer, who recognized that Germany was being outpaced by its rivals in car ownership. The cost of ownership, which included high registration fees as well as gasoline that carried high import taxes, meant that only the wealthiest Germans could afford their own cars. Hitler challenged the nation's automakers at the German Auto Show of 1934 to produce a car with a selling price of 1,000 RM, which was about half the cost of the cheapest vehicles on the market at the time. It would take three years for the designers at Porsche Motor Corporation to present their prototype to Hitler, but despite its unassuming looks the "beetle" could not be produced anywhere near the price the Nazi leader had called for. Nonetheless, 300,000 Germans began saving for the day when the beetle would roll off the assembly line. They did this by depositing 5 RM a week into specially designed KdF-Car savings accounts. Each deposit was marked with a stamp to illustrate progress toward the goal of car ownership. The program was popular, because it connected citizens to the national project of "motorizing Germany," while also seeming to support their individual dreams of getting behind the wheel of an automobile (see Plate 6). The Social Democratic Party in exile was frustrated by the enthusiasm this project garnered among the population. Their underground supporters within Germany reported:

> For a large number of Germans the announcement of the *Volkswagen* [People's Car] came as a pleasant surprise. There developed a real KdF-Car psychosis. For a long time the KdF Car was a big talking point among all classes of populations … With the KdF car, the leadership of the Third Reich has killed several birds with one stone. In the first place it removes for a period of several years, money from the German consumer that he

would otherwise spend on goods that cannot be supplied. Secondly, and this is the most important thing, they have achieved a clever diversionary tactic in the sphere of domestic politics.[22]

Despite the popularity of the People's Car savings plan and "the Volk's faith in the Führer and in the Labor Front's" promises to deliver, no Volkswagen beetles made into the hands of German consumers during the Nazi era.[23] Two years after the prototype was splashed across the pages of illustrated magazines throughout the country, Hitler presented a model ready for production and gave one to his partner, Eva Braun, for her birthday. But later that year, the war began, and all facilities were outfitted for the production of military vehicles, including the Volkswagen plant at Wolfsburg, which had opened the year before. In 1937 only about one out of every sixty-one Germans owned a car, a level that had been surpassed in France and Britain a decade prior, and a staggering one in five Americans owned a car. Widespread car ownership would not come to (West) Germany until the 1950s.

Although the Volkswagen must be considered an example of "virtual consumption," the regime's interest in "motorization" was part of a larger strategy to modernize Germany in ways that would bolster its self-sufficiency in advance of war, while instilling pride and optimism among Germans that the nation was moving in the right direction after years of instability. Central to the motorization plan was the establishment of a network of dual-carriage motorways linking the country's main cities. A fan of car travel, Hitler had seen the state of the country's road systems during the electoral campaigns of the early 1930s, and he declared his plans for the new network just months after coming to power. Fritz Todt, a civil engineer and long-time NSDAP supporter, was put in charge of the project. The expansive network was not yet complete when war broke out, but 3,500 km had been constructed and are still used today. The autobahn was lauded by regime supporters as more than a means to get from point A to point B; it was a "cultural monument."[24] The building project demonstrated the technical knowhow of German engineers backed by the state; it created jobs and provided enjoyment to Germans by making travel quicker and more comfortable, and it supported the movement of troops and military vehicles before and during the war. Planners sought out scenic routes for the various branches of the autobahn to showcase the natural beauty of the countryside and foster pride in the German landscape. Hitler himself liked to review and approve the architectural drawings for bridges and rest stops along the routes. Some observers have wondered whether these decisions show a respect for the natural environment that should be viewed as a forerunner to the environmental movement of recent decades. It is true that Nazi leaders were enamored of the countryside, but this did not keep them from believing that technology should master the environment, and the autobahn planners were not averse to tunneling through mountainsides or razing forests to make way for the new highways.

While the majority of Germans did not have the purchasing power to own an automobile, they did increase their travel by bus and rail in these years. The fact that consumer goods production declined, owing to the prioritization of heavy industry, meant that many Germans had expendable income by the second half of the decade and looked to purchase pleasurable experiences in place of material goods. Germans were supported in their desire for fun ways to spend their leisure time and holidays by the launch of the German Labor Front's program Strength through Joy (KdF). KdF offered package tours—from local and regional day trips to a historic site, cultural event, or sporting venue, to longer trips within Germany and even international cruises by ocean steamer. Buying in bulk, KdF could pass along the savings to its patrons, and the program was praised in the international press for offering middle- and working-class Germans exciting new opportunities. As the *Washington Post* reported in early 1939, "more and more luxurious are the 'strength through joy' ships, on which German workers are taken on pleasure cruises at minimal cost."[25]

It is easy to see the benefits of the program for the country's leaders. Enabling tourism within Germany (and most trips were domestic) deepened patriotism and goodwill toward the government among those who participated and among the business owners who received KdF contracts. Inns, restaurants, and other tourism-related service industries had been hard hit by the Depression. Strength through Joy organizers booked hotels and inns in depressed regions of the country to pump money into the local economies. States like Spain and Portugal were selected as international destinations, because they were cheaper and more likely to leave Germans feeling good about the level of prosperity back home, and they had Nazi-friendly governments. Norway was popular because it represented Nazi ideals of Nordic beauty. And program brochures made it clear that all workers—from industrial laborers to professionals—were welcome. Together travelers would form a microcosm of the *Volksgemeinschaft*, creating ready-made propaganda opportunities to extoll the successes of National Socialist consensus building.

That KdF tours did not routinely visit top attractions (at home or abroad), given the costs of visiting sought-after sites, especially in high season, left some travelers disappointed.[26] However, the program was a great success overall. Historians have reviewed letters and diaries describing the trips and found positive memories, and attendance at KdF events remained high throughout the prewar years. Nazi leaders agreed it was a hit, and the amount of money invested in the program grew over time. The German Labor Front spent 8 million RM on KdF in 1934, and that sum jumped to 29 million RM in 1937, reaching 33 million in 1939.[27] Between 1934 and 1939, Germans booked 43 million KPD trips—a hefty number for a total population of roughly 65 million, even if some individuals traveled more than once. Even though most of these participants were enjoying short adventures of one to three days within Germany, rather than long-distance domestic or international holidays, participation rates were still remarkable.

One publication about the German Labor Front went so far as to claim that "it is no exaggeration to say that for millions of Germans KdF has made the world beautiful again and life worth living again."[28]

There are important qualifiers to this praise. While the trips were available to all, the longer trips to far away destinations remained beyond the means of most travelers. Middle-class adventurers were more likely to sign up for a cruise to Madeira and were overrepresented in the more elaborate domestic holidays as well. In addition to the cost of the longer trips, few industrial laborers received enough vacation days to participate in lengthy travel. Moreover, class, religious, and regional prejudices were frequently replicated on board the ship or among those staying at a resort. For example, all attendees from one city might dine together, while ignoring those from other cities or regions. Catholic town residents were reported at times to show little enthusiasm for tour buses full of Protestant out-of-town visitors. Class differences, reflected in dress and speech, could also lead to separate groupings among the revelers, or complaints about the behavior of tourists deemed less sophisticated. None of this should come as a surprise. These societal divides were not new, and most participants still enjoyed themselves and were grateful to Strength through Joy and the Nazi Party for making the travel possible. These tensions do illustrate, however, that while the program was a success because it was popular and gave the regime ample opportunity to instill in Germans a belief in the Nazis' vision of community, the state's ultimate goal of crafting a unified society based on racial solidarity was less successful than might be presumed.

Throughout the prewar period Hitler and his inner circle continued to believe in the *Dolchstoßlegende*, or stab-in-the-back myth, which claimed that deprivation on the homefront during the First World War had led those at home to abandon the country's soldiers and sailors in 1917 by supporting strikes and protests for peace. Women, Jews, and leftist activists were identified as the ones truly responsible for defeat in 1918. Belief in this "stab in the back" influenced domestic planning throughout the Nazi dictatorship. It provided part of the rationale for the German Labor Front and activities like the Strength through Joy travel program. Nazi leaders were also motivated to avoid a repeat of wartime deprivation by achieving economic autarky and preparing people sooner for unavoidable shortages. Rationing of some goods began as early as 1934, and certain imports like rubber, coffee, and cotton cloth were periodically in short supply throughout the prewar years, leading to hoarding by retailers and some individuals who remembered how valuable items like bicycle tires had become during the last war. And yet the regime's concern about public opinion never disappeared completely, meaning the importation of desirable food stuffs and finished goods never ended entirely, even though propaganda campaigns in the mid- and late 1930s sought to promote locally available products like North Sea fish and brown bread over preferred menu items that included imported ingredients.

The Four-Year Plan had a direct impact on daily life in Germany. On the one hand, it confirmed for many the closeness of another war. While support for Hitler's leadership had grown substantially by the end of 1936 thanks to the political and economic stability that had emerged and Hitler's ease on the world stage, which had included the successful hosting of the Olympic Games that summer (as we will see in Chapter 8), most Germans were not interested in another large-scale conflict. The Four-Year Plan also meant that living standards remained relatively low in Germany, despite full employment. Durable consumer goods like washing machines and refrigerators remained luxury items in Germany, while they became more commonplace in other western European countries and in the United States. Clothing and food prices also remained high, owing to restrictions on importations of cotton and wool. The housing shortage that had existed for decades remained unsolved, because investment in construction focused on military preparations, such as the erection of military barracks to house the growing armed forces. Most Germans continued to live in small rental units with limited modern amenities. As Hitler's 1940 deadline for war approached, working conditions became increasingly high-pressure and in some cases dangerous. Workers who spent long hours on the factory floor began to grumble, and Hitler may have worried that discontent at home would grow unless their attention was diverted. Moreover, the longer he waited to launch a war, the better prepared his enemies would be.

Notes

1   Adam Tooze, "The Economic History of the Nazi Regime" in *Nazi Germany*, Jane Caplan, ed. (Oxford: Oxford University Press, 2008), 169.

2   Adolf Hitler, "Proclamation of the Reich Government to the German People," February 1, 1933, https://ghdi.ghi-dc.org/sub_document.cfm?document_id=3940

3   Richard Overy, *Göring: Hitler's Iron Knight* (London: IB Taurus, 2012), 25–6.

4   Richard J. Evans, *The Third Reich in Power* (New York: Penguin, 2005), 337.

5   "Hossbach Memorandum," November 10, 1937, https://avalon.law.yale.edu/imt/hossbach.asp

6   Evans, *The Third Reich in Power*, 339.

7   Melita Maschmann, *Account Rendered: A Dossier on my Former Self* (Lexington, MA: Plunkett Lake, 2013), 31–2.

8   Joseph Goebbels quoted in Peter Fritzsche, *Life and Death in the Third Reich* (Cambridge, MA: Belknap, 2008), 100.

9   Hjalmar Schacht, *Account Settled* (London: Weidenfeld & Nicolson, 1949), 90.

10 Overy, *Göring*, 68.

11 Data for the Soviet Union isn't available for 1939, but its military burden in 1940 was 17 percent. Mark Harrison, "The Economics of World War II: an overview" in *The Economics of World War II: Six Great Powers in International Comparison*, Mark Harrison, ed. (Cambridge UK: Cambridge University Press, 1998), 21.

12 Evans, *Third Reich in Power*, 362.

13 Overy, *Göring*, 50.

14 Shelley Baranowski, *Strength through Joy: Consumerism and Mass Tourism in the Third Reich* (Cambridge UK: Cambridge University Press, 2004), 110.

15 G. Starcke, *Die Deutsche Arbeitsfront (1940)* in *Nazism, 1919–1945*, Vol. 2, Jeremy Noakes and Graham Pridham, eds. (Exeter: University of Exeter Press, 1995), 349–50.

16 Baranowski, *Strength through Joy*, 115.

17 Tooze, "The Economic History of the Nazi State" in *Nazi Germany*, 176.

18 Sebastian Haffner, *Defying Hitler. A Memoir*. Translated by Oliver Pretzel (New York: Picador, 2000), 138–9.

19 Kurt Rosenberg quoted in *Bedrohung, Hoffnung, Skepsis. Vier Tagebücher des Jahres 1933*, Frank Bajohr, Beate Meyer, and Joachim Szodrynski, eds. (Göttingen: Wallstein Verlag, 2013), diary entry for April 2, 1933, 40.

20 Alison Owings, *Frauen: German Women Recall the Third Reich* (New Brunswick, NJ: Rutgers University Press, 1993), 71.

21 Hartmut Berghoff, "Methoden der Verbrauchslenkung im Nationalsozialismus" in Dieter Gossewinkel, ed. Wirtschaftskontrolle und Recht in der nationalsozialistische Diktatur (Frankfurt, a. M: Klostermann, 2005), 281–316.

22 SOPADE report (1939) in *Third Reich Sourcebook*, Anson Rabinbach and Sander Gilman, eds. (Berkeley: University of California Press, 2013), 668.

23 Anonymous, "Five Years of Strength through Joy" in Rabinbach and Gilman, eds., *Third Reich Sourcebook*, 678–9.

24 Friedrich Tamms, "The Reichsautobahn as All-Encompassing Architectural Marvel" in Rabinbach and Gilman, eds., *The Third Reich Sourcebook*, 675–7.

25 "Nazi Vacation Ship Luxurious, Cheap" in *The Washington Post*, March 12, 1939.

26 Kristin Semmens, *Seeing Hitler's Germany. Tourism in the Third Reich* (Basingstoke: Palgrave, 2005), 114–15.

27 Baranowski, *Strength through Joy*, 54.

28 Starcke, *Die Deutsche Arbeitsfront (1940) in Nazism*, Noakes and Pridham, eds., 350.

Additional Reading

Baranowski, Shelley. *Strength through Joy: Consumerism and Mass Tourism in the Third Reich*. Cambridge: Cambridge University Press, 2004.

Barkai, Avraham. *From Boycott to Annihilation: The Economic Struggle of German Jews, 1933–1943*. Hanover, NH: Brandeis University Press, 1989.

Gregor, Neil. *Daimler Benz in the Third Reich*. New Haven and London: Yale University Press, 1998.

Herbert, Ulrich. *Hitler's Foreign Workers: Enforced Foreign Labor in Germany under the Third Reich*. Translated by William Templer. Cambridge: Cambridge University Press, 1997.

James, Harold. *The Nazi Dictatorship and the Deutsche Bank*. Cambridge: Cambridge University Press, 2004.

Kreutzmüller, Christopher. *Final Sale in Berlin: The Destruction of Jewish Commercial Activity, 1930–1945*. Translated by Jane Paulick and Jefferson Chase. New York: Berghahn Books, 2015.

Overy, Richard. *War and Economy in the Third Reich*. Oxford: Clarendon Press, 1994.

Swett, Pamela E. *Selling under the Swastika: Advertising and Commercial Culture in Nazi Germany*. Stanford: Stanford University Press, 2014.

Tooze, Adam. *The Wages of Destruction: The Making and Breaking of the Nazi Economy*. London: Penguin Books, 2007.

Wiesen, S. Jonathan. *Creating the Nazi Marketplace: Commerce and Consumption in the Third Reich*. Cambridge: Cambridge University Press, 2011.

6

Arts and Culture

Hitler's government made it clear that a future war would demand loyalty and sacrifice. But loyalty to what? It was not only to their country and to the Nazi movement but to a renewed idea of Germany rooted in cultural greatness. The country's new leaders hoped to fuse martial values with a sense of pride in Germany's rich artistic and literary traditions in ways that prior regimes, they claimed, had not. In this chapter we will examine how the visual arts, music, radio and film, and architecture were used toward these ideological ends. As we will see, the idea that all art created in National Socialist Germany was strictly policed and conformed to a narrow Nazi aesthetic is mistaken. In fact, the regime and party ideologues never talked about "Nazi art" or the "nazification" of the arts. Rather they claimed to be revitalizing "*German* art,"[1] which they saw as an integrative force at home and as a means to improve Germany's reputation abroad. Debates about the definition of German art persisted through the 1930s, and some scholars have referred to what emerged as "contained plurality,"[2] meaning that there was no single perspective or style that drowned out all the others, despite policies to exclude Jews and those critical of the regime and promote an artistic vision that furthered ideological goals.

Nazi culture is often contrasted to that of the Weimar Republic and its embrace of experimentation. But in 1920s Germany avant-garde art shared the performance stages, galleries, and cinemas with objects and productions that followed more traditional forms and styles. Germany's new Nazi government chose to ignore this reality and condemn Weimar culture as uniformly decadent and indicative of the internal crises besieging the nation. Weimar, the Nazis argued, did not represent "German values" like nationalism and the romantic ideals of heroism and beauty. The Nazis thus aimed to coordinate the arts to promote cultural producers and artistic outcomes that would both unite the *Volksgemeinschaft* and lift Germany's reputation abroad.

There are two points worth emphasizing here. First, Germans wanted to be entertained as well as inspired. This led to some experimentation in cultural policy, with certain aspects of coordination stalling or being abandoned entirely to maintain public support. Second, no society is completely uniform in its beliefs or tastes, and no two individuals experience art the same way. Even where repression against "un-German" artists was swift, some Germans found ways to continue enjoying the works of targeted artists and musicians they admired. The regime pursued a challenging path between release and control, encouraging and enticing "Aryan" Germans to create and sustain a cultural vision shaped by National Socialism.

The Propaganda Ministry

Hitler and his chief propagandist, Joseph Goebbels, were long-time adherents of the belief that emotional stimulation was an important political tool. Hitler first rose to prominence in the newly created National Socialist movement not as a grand thinker or strategist, but as a powerful speaker, a "drummer" of men, who could energize and win over those who came to hear his theatrical public performances. What's more, Hitler fancied himself an artist and at age eighteen had applied for admission to Vienna's Academy of Fine Arts, only to be disappointed by rejection. Fifteen years later, as he sat in Landsberg prison planning his return to politics after the failed Beer Hall Putsch, he dictated a whole chapter of *Mein Kampf* about the importance of propaganda as essential to generating the mass support that would lead to his chancellorship. But in many ways, the early Nazis were playing catch-up, mimicking the bold graphics and passion-laden language of their enemies in the 1920s. Germany's social democrats and communists had adopted with great effect the propaganda stylings and strategies of the international workers' movement and the Russian Revolution in the 1920s, and it was to the left that the Nazis looked for inspiration as they sought a mass following.

It should not surprise us, then, that the new Nazi government was quick to devote resources to the establishment of the Ministry for People's Enlightenment and Propaganda, which was launched by decree on March 13, 1933, just six weeks after the Nazis took power. Joseph Goebbels had led the NSDAP's propaganda efforts since 1930, so it made some sense that he would be handed this larger portfolio. Goebbels saw his task as the "mobilization of the mind" in support of the National Socialist revolution. He went so far as to suggest the mandate he had been given was "possibly even more important" than the task given to the Defense Ministry to protect the nation. In the First World War, he explained, the German military was prepared materially as no other country had been, but Germany was defeated because "the weapons of our minds did not fire."[3] Goebbels vowed to avoid repeating that mistake.

We can think of the work of the ministry as falling under three main areas that corresponded to the three titles Goebbels carried simultaneously. As

Reich Minister of Propaganda, he led the spiritual education of the nation; as President of the Reich Chamber of Culture, he coordinated and regulated all aspects of Germany's culture industries; and as Director of the Central Propaganda Office of the NSDAP, he oversaw messaging about the party and ensured the consistency of education within the party's mass organizations. This chapter focuses on the second role, the coordination and regulation of the arts via the work of the Reich Chamber of Culture, though other examples of the Propaganda Ministry's work and Goebbels' influence are found throughout this book.

The Reich Chamber of Culture (*Reichskulturkammer*, RKK), launched in September 1933, had seven branches. They were radio, press, theater, film, visual arts, music, and literature. The concept behind such a structure was not new. For decades, many artists in Germany had been calling for a system that brought oversight and consistency to wages, training, and benefits in these fields. Given that many artists, musicians, actors, and writers had been in favor of reform for some time, many were cautiously optimistic about the potential of the RKK when its establishment was announced. Supporters looked forward to greater professional legitimacy and were thankful for the financial resources that the Propaganda Ministry contributed to the German arts industries, especially after years of economic depression.

One reform was a requirement that all those who worked in any of these sectors had to be registered as a member of the RKK. Outspoken critics of the regime were targeted immediately, like the non-Jewish writer Heinrich Mann and the artist Käthe Kollwitz, who were both forced to resign from the Prussian Academy of Arts in early 1933 and excluded from the RKK. Other famous artists, Jews and non-Jews, could see the writing on the wall and fled the country in 1933, including Erich Maria Remarque, Alfred Döblin, Heinrich Mann and his more famous brother, Thomas Mann, the communist playwright Bertolt Brecht and the Jewish composer with whom he worked closely, Kurt Weill. Separately, the passage of the Law for the Restoration of the Professional Civil Service in April 1933 led to the dismissal of many in the arts from public sector positions, including professors of music and art disciplines and state museum and orchestra employees. Even radio stations were publicly held entities, which meant that Jewish employees and socialist and communists were fired.

It took longer to purge those practitioners who weren't famous and those working in the private sector. The language that covered RKK membership eligibility was vague at first and only made more explicit that Jews were ineligible in 1935. A wave of expulsions followed. Once excluded, many Jewish German writers, actors, musicians, and visual artists joined the Cultural Association of German Jews. A handful of Jewish academics, artists, and community leaders had first formed what became known later as the Jewish Culture League in the summer of 1933. Eventually eighty-two cities and towns opened branches of the League, which staged concerts, plays, and exhibits. The League also offered arts training and presented lectures on cultural topics with the goal of providing artists and audience members, as one ad declared, "contact with elation, consolation and joy!"[4] Schocken Press continued to publish books by Jewish authors and themes until it was shuttered by the authorities in 1939. The press's namesake Salman Schocken had emigrated to Palestine in 1934, but his employees kept printing books for another five years, bringing enjoyment and education to their readers.[5] The Culture League's membership stabilized around 18,500, with those leaving Germany replaced by new members until its dissolution by the Gestapo in 1941, the same year deportations of German Jews to "the East" began.

Although mandating RKK membership to work in any artistic field had a tremendous impact on individuals working in the arts and media in Germany, it does not mean all content was cleansed of the influence of great artists now unable to participate in Germany's cultural world. The long-term goal of the RKK was to achieve consensus on the definitions of artistic beauty and value, making censorship unnecessary.[6] But this aim was never achieved. The onset of war meant tighter restrictions, and, in the war's latter years, fewer resources and less accessibility to the arts. True uniformity was also undermined by the strength of some national and international artistic trends and by the vastness of artistic production, which meant rooting out offending works was a mammoth, perhaps impossible, exercise.

Those who attained RKK membership often engaged in self-censorship in response to the fear of expulsion and professional ruin. Coercing artists to censor themselves saved the regime from much of the "micro-managerial headaches of censorship," but Goebbels' ministry also put in place some important restrictions.[7] Art and entertainment that explicitly or implicitly criticized the government, the NSDAP, or Germany was suppressed, as were depictions of criminality and artistic expressions considered lewd. German film producers had faced censors since 1930, so submitting content for review before release was not new to them, nor was the practice particular to Germany. Many countries, including the United States, policed content in these years. Musical compositions of some famous avant-garde composers, like Arnold Schoenberg, were prohibited quickly. The regime banned jazz and other so-called "Negro music" in 1935, though it never completely disappeared from Germany in these years. More than other forms of art, music was particularly tricky because of the wide range of styles and the diverse venues and forms in which music appeared. The nation's premier concert halls could be monitored to some extent, along with radio broadcasting, but small concert venues and recorded music played publicly or in private homes were nearly impossible to control. There were also film scores and even advertisement jingles that in theory needed oversight.

The role of print media in education and the communication of local, national, and international news made its control a priority of the regime.

Most of the vast number of daily and weekly newspapers in Germany were closed or reoriented toward a Nazi perspective in the first weeks of the regime. The Reichstag Fire Decree, issued at the end of February 1933, effectively banned all social democratic and communist newspapers. Two important dailies, the *Berliner Tageblatt* and *Frankfurter Zeitung*, remained relatively independent until they were forcibly closed in 1939 and 1943 respectively. Local Nazi officials and their supporters, especially university students, organized book burnings in May 1933 to demonstrate their newfound power to determine what could be read in the "new Germany," but an official comprehensive list of banned books by Jewish and other targeted authors did not appear until 1935 (Figure 6.1). A small number of editors continued to support persecuted writers. The Rowohlt press published the works of well-known Jewish writers until it was taken over by the NSDAP in 1938. Another publishing house, S. Fischer, continued to defy the regime until its non-Jewish owner and editor Peter Suhrkamp was arrested by the Gestapo in 1944. "Aryan" Germans' private collections of books remained private, and even banned books were still read in some homes. Translations of some foreign titles, like *Gone with the Wind*, remained popular, despite the emphasis on "German" culture. Like the editors of the *Berliner Tageblatt* and *Frankfurter Zeitung*, some directors of major arts institutions held on to their positions, owing to their celebrity or personal relationships with the country's new leaders. For example, the famed actor Gustav Gründgens continued to lead the Staatstheater in Berlin, despite being a gay man and choosing to stage plays that had fallen out of favor with the regime. And the Berlin Philharmonic remained under the direction of Wilhelm Furtwängler, who, despite his own antisemitism and support for the regime, continued to arrange concert programs that included the works of banned artists. At minor provincial theaters, banned playwrights or composers continued to be performed on occasion simply because of the lack of oversight.

We need to remember, then, that despite the myths of an all-powerful Propaganda Ministry, the coordination of the arts and media was often haphazard and at times contradictory. With little to point to as a coherent cultural policy, internal rivalries and ambitions, public opinion, and the strength of some contemporary trends in the arts meant the cultural realm remained more diverse than is commonly understood.

Painting, Sculpture, and Architecture

When it came to painting and sculpture, Nazi officials and those who supported the regime were torn. German Expressionism, which had developed over the previous two decades, had garnered worldwide acclaim. German expressionists and other modernists in the early twentieth century rejected the idea that the goal of the artist was to recreate reality to the best of their ability. Rather, the expressionists focused on giving shape

FIGURE 6.1 *University students preparing to burn "un-German" writings and books at Berlin's Opernplatz, May 10, 1933 (Bundesarchiv, Bild 102-14598/CC-BY-SA 3.0, CC BY-SA 3.0 DE, via Wikimedia Commons).*

to their emotions and inner life through the creative use of color and form, including abstraction. Between 1933 and 1936 some art gallery and museum directors continued to show modern art, including those by famous non-Germans like Vincent van Gogh and Jewish German painters like the impressionist Max Liebermann. And some within the party hoped German Expressionism could be reconciled with the new era. They argued that the style was uniquely German. Jewish artists should still be banned, and abstract images were irredeemable, but once those changes had been made, they hoped German Expressionism would be worthy of praise and state support as a native modern style, just as Italian Futurism had been embraced by Benito Mussolini's regime. This group argued that the *völkisch* art that was emerging as the favored style of the regime was kitschy and emotionally stunted.

For a while Joseph Goebbels favored salvaging German Expressionism, but he was also wary of his position in Hitler's inner circle in relation to others like Bernhard Rust, Minister of Education and Goebbels' chief rival, and the anti-modernist Alfred Rosenberg, whose main task for the Führer was the ideological training of party members. Both men were outspoken critics of all modernist art and design, and both vocally supported the purging of modernist works from public collections as well as the mocking display of such art to illustrate the dangers of so-called "Cultural Bolshevism." The debate required Hitler's intervention. At the 1934 NSDAP party rally in Nuremberg, Hitler seemed to criticize both sides, attacking modernist art and "backward-looking" art that did not equal the revolutionary moment. In 1935 at the same venue, he came out more strongly on the side of Rosenberg, though his earlier comments on the limits of *völkisch* art should not be ignored. Thereafter, to protect himself Goebbels sought a more rigid path against Jewish artists and non-Jewish modernist artists.

This process began in late 1936. On November 26, Goebbels banned art criticism, which meant newspaper journalists were limited to observational descriptions of art shows, rather than qualitative assessments. Antisemitism was at play in this decree. Nazis believed Jews controlled the press and the art market. Art critics who praised "crap" in illustrated magazines and newspapers, as Goebbels had crudely argued, did so in order for Jewish art collectors to reap huge profits. Again, it is not clear that all artists saw this restriction negatively. Some undoubtedly felt that critics had too much power to make or break an artist's career and supported this attempt at reining in their influence. Around the same time Goebbels also tasked Arthur Ziegler, president of the Reich Chamber of Visual Arts, with the confiscation of artworks from museums known as the *Entartete Kunst Aktion* (Degenerate Art Action) of 1937. The confiscated works were then assembled into an exhibit of the same name, which included 730 pieces by 112 artists. It opened to the public in July of that year, starting in Munich and traveling throughout the country. Confiscations continued, and by the fall roughly 17,000 paintings and graphic artworks had been taken from 101 museums and galleries. Some Nazi officials wanted the confiscations to include art from private collections as well, but that did not happen at the time. Private collections owned by Jews, however, were "Aryanized" as Jews left the country through emigration before 1939 or through deportation thereafter.

The so-called "degenerate" art was modernist art by "non-Aryans" and "Aryans" alike. The works were targeted for their abstract imagery or unrealistic color palettes, for their frightening (and implicitly pacifist) portrayals of war, and their probing depictions of sexuality, violence, and poverty. Even the works of Nazi sympathizer Emil Nolde and the expressionist art of German soldiers who died in the First World War, August Macke and Franz Marc, were ridiculed as degenerate. Artworks were disrespectfully displayed amid slogans and captions that disparaged them as talentless, lewd and "demented." Visitors to the exhibition were expected to conclude that corrupting "international" and "Jewish" influences had created such "trash." The Munich exhibition was the most widely traveled and publicized of the "degenerate art" shows, but it was not the only one. In total thirty German cities hosted such exhibits, many welcomed more than one such event.

The Munich exhibit of degenerate art opened the day after the nearby House of German Art launched its first annual show of state-approved art. The degenerate art attracted 20,000 visitors per day for a total of over 2 million in Munich alone, before spending two years moving around the country and opening to equally excited crowds. The state-sponsored art received little attention in comparison. It presented German landscapes and images of romanticized pastoral life. Paintings and sculptures that captured the heroism of sport, war, and industrial or agricultural labor were richly featured. Nudes were common as well, symbolizing the beauty of nature and womanhood and the strength and bravery of the masculine spirit. Hitler helped select works for the House of German Art launch and attended the festivities, which were repeated annually.

While the state-sanctioned art did not enjoy huge crowds, Goebbels chose to focus on the popularity of his anti-modernist exhibit as a sign of success. Most attendees of the Degenerate Art exhibit in Munich and elsewhere did get on board, declaring the paintings ugly or disgusting. But there is also evidence that some visitors made their way through the exhibit quietly as if in mourning, and others entered with an open mind and drew conclusions that did not line up with Goebbels' intentions. The diarist Franz Göll visited the show in 1938 in the capital, where he lived. Göll's reaction to Otto Dix's painting *Der Krieg* (The War) painted in the last years of the Republic demonstrates that some ordinary Germans could see through the lies. Yes, Göll agreed, *Der Krieg* was "horror-inducing," but not because of the artist's lack of skill: "The picture is not a bloody-minded depiction of the degenerate, war is."[8]

While the two exhibits were presented to the public as opposites in every way, there were some gray areas, which demonstrate how nebulous a concept such as "German" art really was. Some artists who had their work displayed in the Degenerate Art exhibit had also been invited to submit works for the House of German Art's launch. And others who were included in the House of German Art's inaugural exhibition had had works confiscated as degenerate. A small number of painters had samples of their work appear in both the Degenerate Art Exhibit and the House of German Art.

In the end, the regime confiscated as many as 20,000 artworks from museums across the country. Some of the foreign-owned works were returned to the museums that had lent them to German institutions, but many others were sold off for personal gain by corrupt Nazi officials or by the state to procure badly needed foreign currency. Some revenue was put aside so Hitler could build his own art collection. Like the Führer, several of the highest-ranking Nazi officials amassed astounding personal art collections, including Hermann Göring, Joseph Goebbels, and Hitler Youth leader Baldur von Schirach, all of whom lived lavish lifestyles. Thousands of "degenerate" art pieces confiscated from museums, however, could not be sold, because by flooding the market with available works, prices had collapsed. Anxiety about an impending war also made shipment of expensive art works too risky for some investors. With few alternatives and a belief that the art was intrinsically worthless, close to 5,000 paintings, drawings, and other fine art pieces were discarded on a bonfire in Berlin in March 1939.

The shift to a more rigid stance toward modern art, beginning in 1936, left artists in a difficult position. The regime called for an art based on racial criteria that had to be timeless and yet meet international standards. The most popular form was the landscape, notably the work of nineteenth-century romanticist Caspar David Friedrich and the early-twentieth-century *Heimat* style perfected by Julius Paul Junghanns and others, whereas cityscapes, a staple of 1920s realism, largely disappeared. Peasant life, family and individual portraits, and labor scenes were idealized. Even in a society that was building highways and modern factories, peasant life was believed to reflect an authentic, honorable German experience of racial unity and social harmony. Mother and child portraits mirrored long-standing religious motifs, but nude women also became increasingly common. One favored artist was Arthur Ziegler, who had helped orchestrate the confiscation of "degenerate art" in his role as president of the Reich Chamber of Visual Arts. His most famous work, "Four Elements" (1937), hung in Hitler's residence. It depicted four female nudes reclining on a stone plinth representing fire, earth, water, and air and captures well the preferred style of the regime.

Sculpture played a far larger role than painting in Nazi-era public projects. It was used to adorn bombastic new buildings and public squares. Its solidity, according to the regime's leaders, was meant to match the new era's military might, devotion to the Führer, and party solidarity. Granite and limestone were popular materials, given their natural, timeless heft, but after 1937 bronze took over as the most appropriate material to embody the regime's virtues: courage, loyalty, and readiness. Sculptor Arno Breker trained at the Düsseldorf Academy and then in Paris in the 1920s. The son of a stone cutter, his early career developed along "a distinctly modernist track," and he even incorporated some elements of abstraction into his works.[9] After 1933 he disagreed openly with the concept of "degenerate art," but he would also become one of the regime's most highly touted and richly rewarded artists. He produced sculptures for the Berlin Olympics and was included regularly in the annual "Great German Art" exhibits in Munich, and his sculptures representing "The Party" and "The Army" were placed at the entrance to the new Reich Chancellery in 1939 (Figure 6.2). Breker was rewarded handsomely for his efforts to integrate classicism and modernism. He received extensive media attention and was given a huge studio and a villa in Germany. Hitler himself gifted Breker on his fortieth birthday a country estate that was originally built for Frederick the Great. He earned extremely high commissions for his sculptures, and his works were exhibited in the French capital, where he lived during its occupation by the Germans in an "Aryanized" luxury apartment when he wasn't at the Ritz.[10] Joining the NSDAP only in 1937, Breker was even given an artificially low party membership number by Hitler, so he appeared to be an "Old Fighter."

FIGURE 6.2 *Arno Breker's monumental statue "The Party," which, along with "The Armed Forces," flanked the entrance of the new Reich Chancellery in Berlin, designed by Albert Speer and opened in 1939. This photograph was taken in 1942. (Bundesarchiv, Bild 183-H27141 CC-BY-SA 3.0, CC BY-SA 3.0 DE, via Wikimedia Commons).*

Sculptures like Breker's were intended to work in concert with a new architecture to create a lasting, public expression of the greatness of the times: "The word in stone." Hitler had dreamed of becoming an architect and took personal interest in the most ambitious architectural projects advanced after 1933. The style the regime favored for official buildings was not very original, replicating neoclassical motifs that could be found in similar buildings elsewhere in Europe and North America: the use of white limestone, columns, and colonnades, to signify solidity, timelessness, and power. But as with fine arts, the story is more complicated and the styles and building practices employed after 1933 were more varied than a singular focus on neoclassicism would suggest.

Like other art forms, modernist architecture had also gained attention during the Weimar Republic, as architects sought to combine modern building methods with a style that broke away from designs tainted by the imperial era, war, and defeat. The new architecture eschewed exteriors with pompous ornamentation and rejected interior decoration that prized dust-collecting knickknacks and heavy furniture. This outmoded look was exchanged for an international style with clean lines and surfaces and was promoted among others by the architects teaching at the Bauhaus arts school. As the political right gained steam in the 1920s, the Bauhaus had been forced to move from Weimar to Dessau in 1925 and again to Berlin in 1932. Each time the school's director sought a more supportive location, where the school and its designs would not be pilloried in the local right-wing press. In one *Völkischer Beobachter* article during the November 1932 campaign, the diatribe drew on a confused mix of Jewish and east Asian references: "The Bauhaus—that was 'the Cathedral of Marxism,' a cathedral, however, which damned well looked like a Synagogue. To the "inspiration" of this 'model school' we owe not least those oriental boxes which we have described before, [and] which are repugnant to good taste."[11] Facing financial crisis and harassment by the Gestapo, the last Director Ludwig Mies van der Rohe closed the school permanently in August 1933.

As we saw with painting, however, not all modernist elements were rejected in architecture, and the Nazi building program included a wide range of styles. Paul Ludwig Troost was tapped by Hitler first to lead the regime's construction projects. He died in 1934, but the buildings that were constructed according to his plans combined the traditional with the contemporary, and neoclassicism with specifically German styles. While this generated a conservative look, Troost did not shy away from using modern building techniques, including steel reinforcements. His most famous completed complex was the monument to the Beer Hall Putsch dead, flanked by party headquarters and the Führer's House in Munich. He also designed the House of German Art discussed above. Creating a permanent home for the annual rallies in Nuremberg became the work of Troost's successor, Albert Speer. Speer planned a large complex, including arenas, the world's largest sports stadium, and a grand parade route, though only some elements were finished before the war. The central parade ground with seating for spectators and a speaker's dais at the Zeppelin Field was completed and provided an impressive backdrop for the films and photos that marked the annual occasion (Figure 6.3). The complex borrowed from both Greek and Roman styles to emphasize the Germans' racial lineage and connections to empire. While Speer also relied on Roman construction techniques, his reasoning for selecting granite and brick was not tied to a disdain for modern methods. Rather steel and iron were prioritized for the rearmament program.[12] Only thirty years old in 1935, for Speer "the modernist element was paramount" despite his "hybrid approach."[13] As the new chief architect, Speer recruited a number of other young architects, who like him had been trained during the Weimar Republic and could easily adopt his pared down, modern take on classicism.

The searchlights used at the Zeppelin Field to create a "cathedral of light" reaching to the heavens during night-time events is another good example of Speer's (and the regime's) willingness to integrate modern technology and techniques into their building plans and aesthetic style. The choreography employed at official events with their intricate formations of marching supporters also relied on modernist preference for geometric symmetry. In 1938 Speer began to lead the design work for what would have been a totally new capital, Germania, to replace Berlin and a reimagining of Hitler's Austrian birth town, Linz, as the focal point of a Hitler cult. Little of Germania was ever completed beyond Hitler's new Reich Chancellery, which opened in early 1939, thanks to the work of forced laborers commanded by the SS to provide the necessary stone. Once the war interceded, little further building took place, and even less survived to 1945.

Scholars have emphasized the bombastic, even megalomaniacal, nature of the Germania plans, but looking at most of what was built before the war, one recognizes significant similarities between the Nazis' designs for public buildings and those for new state buildings in Washington, DC and other capitals in the same era. The stadium designed for the

FIGURE 6.3 *The "Cathedral of Light," a dramatic effect meant to awe visitors to the Nazi Party rally grounds in Nuremberg on September 8, 1936 (Bundesarchiv, Bild 183-1982-1130-502/CC-BY-SA 3.0, CC BY-SA 3.0 DE, via Wikimedia Commons).*

Olympic Games held in Berlin in August 1936 is another example. The first architect selected to design the stadium had produced a glass and steel structure that was considered too modern for the timeless virtues of competition and heroism embodied by the Olympics. Speer replaced the glass with natural stone to great acclaim, and once the flags and swastikas were removed after 1945, it looked like many other sports stadiums, dating back to the Roman Colloseum. It is still used today for athletic comptitions and concerts.

Other examples push the argument further. Plans to update the Hamburg harbor to showcase Germany's commercial strength included a suspension bridge over the Elbe that would have reminded visitors of the Golden Gate Bridge that opened in San Francisco in 1937.[14] While that bridge was never erected, others were built along the first stretches of the autobahn in the mid-1930s. These projects, alongside the sleek, modern filling stations that dotted the new dual carriageway reflect an international, minimalist aesthetic, even while the autobahn's patrons, including Hitler, saw the highway system as a chance to highlight Germany's natural wonders and connect Germans to their homeland. Former Bauhaus Director Mies van der Rohe submitted his own designs for these sites and others, believing his vision to be compatible with the goals of the project; he chose to emigrate only in 1938. Other modernist architects who were most at home in the Weimar Republic also found ways to continue working in the Nazi era, including Speer's mentor, Heinrich Tessenow, who remained skeptical of National Socialism. Modernist inflected designs could be found in surprising places. Communist prisoner Franz Ehrlich, trained at the Bauhaus, was commanded to design several structures at Buchenwald concentration camp, along with the infamous "*Jedem das Seine*" ("To each his own") iron gates, which are lauded today for their artistry and modernist typography. While some historians have speculated that the camp's SS commanders never noticed the "degenerate" styling of the lettering, a number of Ehrlich's interior designs for offices at Buchenwald also included modernist elements.

About 2,000 artists across all disciplines emigrated from Germany after 1933. Given the expense and the desirability of having an invitation of employment, almost all of these were artists with international reputations. Those who remained led quiet lives. The regime did not target "degenerate" artists with violence, as long as they were "Aryan" and had not been outspoken left-wingers or liberals before 1933. The writer Erich Kästner, whose novels were tossed on the bonfire in 1933, remained in Germany. So did Dadaist Hannah Höch, who was prohibited from exhibiting her paintings. She continued to make new works privately and was even granted admission to the Visual Arts Chamber in 1942, where she had access to scarce arts materials.[15] A means of self-preservation, remaining in Germany, should not be confused with resistance to the regime.

Music and Film

Many at the time believed German music to be the nation's greatest cultural contribution to the world: Mozart, Beethoven, Bach, Haydn, Schubert, and other renowned classical composers were all German speaking. When Goebbels and other officials thought about building pride and unity among Germans through the arts, these names quickly came to mind. When they looked to promote German culture abroad, as evidence of the respect (and even superior status) they felt the nation was due, music stood at the pinnacle of German cultural achievement, long recognized for its "universal greatness."[16] What mattered most, however, was that music more than any other art form was believed to offer the greatest opportunity for a shared experience. For decades observers had insisted that those who came together to perform, conduct, and listen to German music in concert halls around the country were together giving life to the idea of the nation. And yet, starting in the Weimar Republic and continuing into the Nazi period, the shared experience of the concert hall appeared on the decline—undermined by private listening on the radio or gramophone, the growth of popular music, and the economic crises that dampened ticket sales. National Socialists hoped in part to reverse this trend. It was in the concert hall that the national community, the *Volksgemeinschaft*, could be forged and embodied.[17] These special qualities of German music meant that it also deserved special protection as Germany's most valuable cultural inheritance.

The Reich Music Chamber (RMK) led these efforts. On the one hand, the RMK sought to coordinate the work between the various music institutions in each city and the local authorities and NSDAP mass organizations. The regime also worked to remove Jewish musicians and conductors from German stages, though this took some time, and the same goes for excluding Jewish audience members. In some cases, Jewish patrons of the art were sorely missed as subscription holders. In Frankfurt, the exclusion of Jews in 1934 led to a 40 percent drop in ticket sales, belying the claim that a visit to the philharmonic had been a particularly non-Jewish, German experience.[18] The works of "racially Jewish" composers, Nazis insisted, including those with international reputations like Gustav Mahler or Felix Mendelssohn-Bartholdy, would also need to be eliminated from programming. Despite their popularity with German audiences, antisemitic commentators and officials claimed Jewish composers only offered poor imitations of the German musical tradition, an argument first championed by the revered German composer Richard Wagner in 1869. As with other artists and academics, many Jewish musicians joined the Jewish Culture League to continue plying their craft and earning a living as best they could. The League's musical offerings were quite varied, combining both non-Jewish German and Jewish traditions. The League branches outside the major cities in Bavaria, for example, were more regularly composed of female members and focused more on Jewish folk and liturgical music.[19] So-called "Gypsy" musicians were not expelled in the mid-1930s alongside Jews. In these years, Roma were considered "asocials" along with vagrants and prostitutes and did not receive much scrutiny at the RKK. Only after Himmler signaled that he intended to purge the "Gypsy menace" from Germany in 1939 did Roma musicians face expulsion from the Music Chamber.[20] The RMK also did not expel members suspected of being queer. According to the Propaganda Ministry's own internal instructions, those men convicted for homosexuality under Paragraph 175 were only given a warning, unless their sentences were six months or longer. One opera singer who received a nine-month sentence under Paragraph 175, for example, kept his Theater Chamber membership, though he was prohibited from performing for German troops, reflecting the regime's misplaced concern about the "spread" of homosexuality in male-only environments.[21]

Even before the Nazis came to power, increasing support for the far right in the late 1920s meant that booing, heckling, and even violent protest became common at performances of Jewish and Black musical artists. Reviewers in the Nazi Party press were quick to pan concerts in which a "non-Aryan" was asked to perform or conduct one of the German greats, using racist and antisemitic language. For early Nazis and others on the right, it was "bad enough" for German concert halls to host Black jazz musicians, but what really angered them was that "now the public was willing to consume their own [German] music performed by members of a primitive race." After 1933, Black international performers stayed away from Germany. Despite the interest in hearing them that remained among fans, Marian Anderson, Duke Ellington, and other American greats were legally prohibited from taking the stage. Black German musicians, like Jews and others newly defined as outsiders in their own nation, suffered social and economic isolation. It wasn't just that their racism kept Nazis from appreciating their talent. Black or Jewish singers performing German *Lieder* was "akin to racial mixing," which threatened to dilute and destroy the greatness of the music.[22]

Although for Nazis it was less dangerous for Black musicians to play jazz, this modern music was rejected as "degenerate" regardless of who played it. In the 1920s jazz had found a welcome home in the music and dancehalls of Germany's cities. Even if racism shaped how stars like Josephine Baker were presented, reviewed, and enjoyed, jazz performers had found a receptive audience and made legions of new fans. Just as Black classical music artists had seen the climate grow increasingly dark by the end of the Weimar Republic, jazz music also became a flashpoint before 1933. Jazz was decried for a variety of reasons based on racist-laden assumptions. Its roots in Africa and the United States meant it was inherently inferior to music that originated in Europe. Evidence for this assertion was found in the music's syncopated rhythms, despite their use by some respected German composers, and the use of non-orchestral instruments like the saxophone. Nazis denounced the way jazz musicians played the reed instrument and insisted that playing, listening to, and especially dancing to jazz music encouraged sexual promiscuity, which could lead to the so-called racial mixing between "Aryans" and others that Nazis most feared. And, yet, jazz remained popular among its young fanbase, supported by jazz clubs in the major German cities where white German musicians continued to perform live. American popular music, including big band swing, was also featured regularly in the Hollywood films that continued to draw large audiences in prewar Nazi Germany—Fred Astaire and Eleanor Powell dance routines were even admired by Hitler.[23]

Jazz was most closely associated with Black musicians, but American and European Jews were also targeted as complicit, as fans, musicians, lyricists, managers, and record producers. Both threats—Jews and Blacks—were combined in the infamous poster (see Plate 7) advertising the Degenerate Music exhibition that followed on the heels of the successful Degenerate Art exhibition and opened first in Düsseldorf in May 1938. A monkey-like, sax-playing cartoon figure is depicted on the poster wearing a yellow Star of David on his lapel, symbolizing the alleged role of Jewish forces in the spread of cosmopolitanism and other perceived attacks on German culture. Degenerate Music included more than jazz. Compositions by Jews and "'Aryan'-composed" modernist music that veered away from classic tonality or rhythms were also declared degenerate. Unlike the Degenerate Art exhibit, this one failed to attract much interest and it was closed in June, only traveling to three other cities. The exhibit even elicited muted criticism from within official circles. As in the visual arts, there was no way to fully separate "German music" from all modernist stylistic influences or from the achievements of those now viewed as non-German on racial grounds.

Despite being a celebrated contemporary composer and conductor, Arnold Schoenberg was easy to cast aside as both Jewish and the "father of atonal music." Other composers who worked in a more traditional style and had great popularity, like Walter Braunfels, who was Catholic but had one Jewish parent, were also excluded along racial criteria. The Austrian Alban Berg, Schoenberg's former student, was one of the most famous non-Jewish composers labeled degenerate. But not all composers were easy to label. Paul Hindemith had composed for left-wing artists like the playwright Bertolt Brecht and the Bauhaus artist, Oskar Schlemmer, and employed atonal and also Dada-ist elements in the 1920s. By the 1930s, however, Hindemith had found ways to integrate some of his modernist impulses with more classical harmonic and melodic idioms. His music became more accessible to the average listener, and he expected he would find favor in the new Germany not just as a composer but also as a teacher. He hoped to increase opportunities for musical education throughout Germany as a way of strengthening and enhancing German culture.

Hindemith gained approval within the NSDAP's Fighting League for German Culture before 1933 and was even given a post within the Reich Chamber of Music in early 1934. But leading Nazis were reluctant to embrace his compositions. The director of the Berlin Philharmonic, the world-renowned Wilhelm Furtwängler, made his support for Hindemith public, angering Hitler and Goebbels, who felt challenged by Furtwängler's defense of the composer. Furtwängler resigned his positions as a result of the dispute. He was eventually reinstated, not least because hundreds of concertgoers gave up their subscriptions to the Philharmonic in his absence.[24] Middle-class arts patrons were not necessarily showing support for Hindemith by canceling their subscriptions. Many were not fans of modernism in music or the visual arts, but they were heavily invested in arts institutions, as embodiments of their values and social status, and in this example did not appreciate the regime's attempts to undermine Furtwängler's authority.

Mindful of public opinion, Goebbels made peace with Furtwängler, despite the latter's pronouncements that the best German musicians should be employed in Germany regardless of racial background. Furtwängler's fame enabled him to be outspoken, though Hindemith remained shut out, and Jewish musicians were lucky if they found a route to emigration. With the exclusion of so many stars of the music scene, as well as many of its avid concertgoers, the Music Chamber focused on the promotion of the German masters, and attendance at most of the country's major symphonies rose substantially as economic stability arrived in the mid-1930s. Where that did not happen, the drop-offs in attendance had less to do with the exclusion of Jewish artists or modernist music than they did with the lingering impact of the Depression and the competition for attention posed by other forms of listening.

Recorded music—phonographs played on gramophones—had been growing in popularity since the turn of the century, especially among the middle classes, despite debates about commercially successful popular music eroding the preference for German classical music and live concerts. But the regime paid little attention to controlling this sector. Listening to records was largely a private pastime, causing little concern for the dictatorship. The propaganda value of records was also minimal, given the very nature of recording events as opposed to the impact of a live broadcast. Instead, the new regime pinned great hopes on the radio, which Goebbels referred to in 1933 as the "most modern and the most important instrument of mass influence that exists anywhere."[25] Listening became, "'a national duty,' quite literally a prerequisite for participation in public life."[26] Lacking the intimacy of the concert hall, where audience members could see each other and feel a sense of belonging along with those to their left and right, the radio was to create a *Volksgemeinschaft* virtually through shared listening (see Plate 8). Goebbels intended that "no important political or historical events" would happen without the nation's participation. In today's globally connected era of around-the-clock instant news, such a statement sounds less than revolutionary. But at the time, news was delivered in print once or twice a day. People learned of major events after the fact and therefore without a sense of being there. Radio would change that.

The first step was to encourage mass ownership of radios. Goebbels succeeded by supporting the production and promotion of the affordable People's Radio, or *Volksempfänger* (VE). The first model was introduced in August 1933. Germany had lagged behind western Europe and North America when it came to installing radios at home. In the 1920s only about 10 percent of the population was part of the listening public (about 6 million), and more than 40 percent of those were in the cities. Cost was the biggest roadblock, which officials sought to remedy with the introduction of the VE. More expensive and better-quality sets continued to be available, but the VE was priced and promoted in a way to attract rural Germans and unskilled workers in the cities, who had not yet purchased a set. The launch of the VE was accompanied by a large advertising campaign and a traveling exhibition that reached 1 million Germans in 1936 with the aim of convincing them of the value of radio ownership and listening. The campaign was largely successful, even if the set's performance was limited to local stations and the one long-range German station, though the claim that these limitations were intentional is false. Germans could purchase upgrades to extend the reach of the VE and many others could access foreign radio stations through more powerful receivers. By 1938, there were about 38 million listeners—or about half the population—and the percentage of owners continued to climb into the war years (though Germany was only catching up to its neighbors in terms of radio's reach). Factory cafeterias, public meeting halls, schools, and other gathering spaces were also outfitted with radios and loudspeakers so that Germans would always be connected to the nation's leaders and its historic events. Of course, "non-Aryan" retailers were not allowed to sell the People's Radio in their shops.

The second goal was to make sure the scheduled programming engaged the listening public. This task proved to be more challenging than expected, even though officials were aided by the fact that radio broadcasting was already largely in the hands of the state when the Nazis came to power. Decision-making authority sat largely with a twenty-nine-year-old, former auto mechanic named Eugen Hadamovsky, whose authority over personnel decisions within the Reich Broadcasting Corporation led to the termination of 13 percent of all employees in the first six months of the regime. Hadamovsky's active purge of employees may be why the Reich Radio Chamber was deemed unnecessary and dissolved in 1939.[27]

Charting a successful National Socialist radio schedule remained challenging. At first the new government flooded the airwaves with explicit political content. Throughout the first months of Nazi rule, nightly programming presented speeches by the new chancellor. Even on holidays, programming did not vary. May 1 had been celebrated as international workers' day throughout the Weimar Republic. In 1933 the new regime rebranded the holiday as the National Day of Labor, but still saw it as an occasion to attract workers to the Nazi cause. And, yet, throughout the day the radio broadcast speech after speech, with no musical or otherwise non-overtly political interludes. Not only was this lineup incredibly tedious, but it replaced the music, comedy, and drama that the listening public had grown used to during their leisure time.

In response to negative feedback, in 1934 officials cut back on political oratory and increased the number of hours devoted to classical German culture. Substantial programming, including both lectures and performances, was devoted to Beethoven, Bach, and Handel. Wagner's operas were broadcast, as were readings from literary greats like Friedrich Schiller. Even with these changes, however, the lineup of shows was still failing to capture the wide audiences the RMVP desired. Educational programming in the form of political messaging and high-brow German classics had limited appeal. Thereafter, programmers made a shift away from seeing radio only as a teaching tool. Instead, greater attention was shown to the wishes of listeners. Not all serious music and lectures were dropped, but they were now outnumbered on the airwaves by dance music, entertaining concerts, and variety shows—especially in prime time (8:00 p.m. to 10:00 p.m.). With few other distractions, 80 percent of listeners now turned on their sets after the evening meal.[28] The move to variety shows, in particular, created a relaxing and entertaining leisure period before bed. We should not conclude that this shift in programming meant that the regime had failed to achieve its aims. Rather, the RMVP came to recognize that providing citizens what they wanted—in this case, pleasurable evening listening—also had the power to build cohesion and community among Germans and goodwill toward the government. It also meant they were sitting by the receiver when the overtly political content began.

As noted at the outset, film censorship existed in Germany before 1933, and the RMVP did release films that are recognized today as explicit political propaganda, including the two fictional dramatizations of the Nazi rise to power *Hitlerjunge Quex* and *Hans Westmar*, both released in 1933, and the monumental artistic film that covered the Nuremberg Party Rally of 1934 by Leni Riefenstahl, *Triumph of the Will* (1935), which was followed by her sweeping *Olympia* in 1938 as a celebration of the successful Berlin Games two years earlier. Some point to Riefenstahl as the most influential woman in the regime, given Hitler's support for these films. It is also important not to forget the newsreels that highlighted each of Hitler's international "successes" as well as the growth of the domestic economy and his popular support throughout the prewar years. And, finally, the onset of war was accompanied by the release of virulently antisemitic films seen by millions in 1940; *Süss the Jew* was wildly popular. *The Eternal Jew* was not a box office hit but was screened regularly by Hitler Youth, SS and other party organizations and officials (see Plate 4). These films deserve our attention, because they helped cast Hitler and the Nazi regime in a triumphant light for a mass audience. They promoted the regime's gendered worldview that helped prepare boys and young men to see themselves as soldiers, and girls and young women to accept their supporting roles in the new society. These movies also reinforced the "Aryan" population's antisemitism on the eve of their Jewish neighbors' deportations.

However, what is surprising is how little the bulk of film production changed. If we look at the entire body of films produced in the Nazi years, it becomes clear that the film industry continued to produce the sorts of films people wanted to see. There may have been less social critique than had been present in the Weimar Republic, but it was replaced with an increasing number of high budget lavish dramas and comedies. In other words, German cinema did not diverge significantly from the path taken in the previous decade, nor did it look that different from the film industries in other countries, except, as was true throughout the creative industries, in the expulsion over time of Jewish actors, writers, producers, and others.

The vast majority of German films were not unlike the love stories, historical dramas, adventures, musicals, and comedies Hollywood produced in the 1930s. Indeed, one of Hitler's favorite movies was *Gone with the Wind* (1939). If there was an overarching message to the films made in these years, it would be that personal fulfillment and social harmony can coexist. Overtly political films were rare and remained so even during the war years. Even those commissioned directly by the state, which was less than 10 percent of the total films made in these years, were largely entertainment films. There were clear commercial and artistic risks to churning out overt propaganda: *Triumph of the Will* only ran for three days in Berlin. Even SPD informants, who wanted to see the regime in as terrible a light as possible to foster resistance, noted that "anything one could speak of as a new worldview [in film] is entirely absent."[29] After Jews were prohibited from mainstream cinemas' in 1938, the Jewish-only cinemas' governing body found two-thirds of mass-marketed German films to be acceptable for showing their audiences.

Germans also continued to produce films abroad and import American films, both points which seem to counter their xenophobic attitude. Most of the best Hollywood films made their way to Germany in these years as they had during the 1920s silent era, and American stars, like the comedy duo Laurel and Hardy, were big draws, as was Charlie Chaplin before them. In addition to being high quality in terms of their artistic and production value, which many German filmmakers tried to imitate, Hollywood's scripts were also considered the gold standard, because the Americans had succeeded in creating the integrative "film for all" that the Germans sought. It isn't surprising, then, that *Glückskinder*, one of the decade's most popular German-made feature films, was in fact a remake of the 1934 Clark Gable romantic comedy, *It Happened One Night* (Figure 6.4). Movies that had mass appeal—usually ones with happy endings—held out the promise of transcending class and regional divisions and bolstering German unity. A film's widespread popularity also meant commercial success, which remained vital to the industry, because the advent of talking pictures and other cinematic innovations had substantially increased production costs.

FIGURE 6.4 Glückskinder (Lucky Kids) *film poster, 1936 (Unknown author, Public domain, via Wikimedia Commons).*

That Jewish American studio owners, directors, and writers had contributed mightily to many of the Hollywood hits that the regime's leaders enjoyed was a fact that Hitler's inner circle chose to ignore.

During the war years, as elsewhere in Europe, cultural events diminished and explicit propaganda supporting the war effort increased in Germany. Artwork and architectural marvels were destroyed amid the fighting. And yet theaters and concert halls, cinemas and radio broadcasters continued to offer cultural experiences to the public to the extent that was possible even in the last months of the conflict. In some ways, as we will see, the German public's need for pleasure and distraction only increased during the war, and keeping civilians content remained a priority of the regime's cultural programming. Despite emigration, propaganda, and violence, the cultural scene in Germany remained complex, and there was never a singular Nazi vision for the arts.

Notes

1   Pamel M. Potter, *The Art of Suppression: Confronting the Nazi Past in Histories of the Visual and Performing Arts* (Oakland: University of California Press, 2016), 9.

2   Martina Steber, "Regions and National Socialist Ideology: Reflections on Contained Plurality" in Claus-Christian Szejnmann and Maiken Umbach, eds. *Heimat, Region, and Empire. The Holocaust and Its Contexts* (London: Palgrave Macmillan, 2012), 25–42.

3   Joseph Goebbels, "Address to Representatives of Radio," March 25, 1933, in *The Third Reich: Politics and Propaganda*, David Welch, ed. (Florence: Routledge, 1994), 183–4.

4   "Activities of the Cultural Association of German Jews," June 19, 1934, Appendix E in *The Arts in Nazi Germany*, Jonathan Heuner and Francis R. Nicosia, eds. (New York: Berghahn Books, 2007), 179–80.

5   Moritz Föllmer, *Culture in the Third Reich* (Oxford: Oxford University Press, 2020), 158.

6   Welch, *The Third Reich*, 33.

7   Corey Ross, *Media and the Making of Modern Germany: Mass Communications, Society, and Politics from the Empire to the Third Reich* (Oxford: Oxford University Press, 2008), 269.

8   Franz Göll quoted in Peter Fritzsche, *The Turbulent World of Franz Göll: An Ordinary Berliner Writes the Twentieth Century* (Cambridge, MA: Harvard University Press), 163.

9   Jonathan Petropoulos, *The Faustian Bargain: The Art World in Nazi Germany* (Oxford: Oxford University Press, 1999), 265–66.

10 Petropoulos, *The Faustian Bargain*, 231–3.

11 *Völkischer Beobachter* article quoted in Barbara Miller Lane, *Architecture and Politics in Germany, 1918–1945* (Cambridge, MA: Harvard University Press, 1985), 162–3.

12 Paul Jaskot, "Heinrich Himmler and the Nuremberg Party Rally Grounds: The Interest of the SS in the Germany Building Economy" in *Art, Culture, and Media in the Third Reich*, Richard Etlin, ed. (Chicago: University of Chicago Press, 2002), 238.

13 Jonathan Petropoulos, *Artists under Hitler: Collaboration and Survival in Nazi Germany* (New Haven: Yale University, 2014), 282.

14 Föllmer, *Culture in the Third Reich*, 135.

15 Alan Steinweis, *Art, Ideology, and Economics in Nazi Germany: The Reich Chambers of Music, Theatre, and the Visual Arts* (Chapel Hill: University of North Carolina Press, 1996), 127.

16 Kira Thurman, *Singing Like Germans: Black Musicians in the Land of Bach, Beethoven, and Brahms* (Ithaca: University of Cornell Press, 2021), 5–9 and throughout.

17 Hansjakob Ziemer, "The German in the Concert Hall: Concertgoing and National Belonging in the Early Twentieth Century" in *Dreams of Germany: Musical Imaginaries from the Concert Hall to the Dance Floor*, Neil Gregor and Thomas Irvine, eds. (New York: Berghahn Books, 2020), 33–5.

18 Hansjakob Ziemer, *Die Moderne hören: Das Konzert als urbanes Forum, 1890–1940* (Frankfurt a.M: Campus Verlag, 2008), 342.

19 Dana Smith, "Female Musicians and 'Jewish' Music in the Jewish *Kulturbund* in Bavaria, 1934–1938" in *Dreams of Germany*, Gregor and Irvine, eds., 123–44.

20 Steinweis, *Art, Ideology and Economics*, 126–7.

21 Ibid., 130.

22 Thurman, *Singing Like Germans*, 161.

23 Michael H. Kater, "The Impact of American Popular Culture on German Youth" in *The Arts in Nazi Germany*, Huener and Nicosia, eds., 38.

24 Petropoulos, *Artists under Hitler*, 101.

25 Joseph Goebbels quoted in Ross, *Media*, 281.

26 Ibid., 330.

27 Ibid., 283.

28 Ibid., 338.

29 Ibid., 312–13.

Additional Reading

Föllmer, Moritz. *Culture in the Third Reich*. Translated by Jeremy Noakes and Lesley Sharpe. Oxford: Oxford University Press, 2020.

Gregor, Neil. *The Symphony Concert in Nazi Germany*. Chicago: University of Chicago Press, 2024.

Hagen, Joshua, and Robert C. Ostergren. *Building Nazi Germany: Place, Space, Architecture, and Ideology*. London: Rowman & Littlefield, 2020.

Kater, Michael. *Different Drummers: Jazz in the Culture of Nazi Germany*. Oxford: Oxford University Press, 1992.

Miller Lane, Barbara. *Architecture and Politics in Germany, 1918–1945*. Cambridge, MA: Harvard University Press, 1968.

Petropoulos, John. *Art as Politics in the Third Reich*. Chapel Hill and London: University of North Carolina Press, 1996.

Potter, Pamela. *Art of Suppression: Confronting the Nazi Past in Histories of the Visual and Performing Arts*. Oakland: University of California Press, 2016.

Rentschler, Eric. *The Ministry of Illusion: Nazi Cinema and Its Afterlife*. Cambridge, MA: Harvard University Press, 1996.

Ross, Corey. *Media and the Making of Modern Germany: Mass Communications, Society, and Politics from the Empire to the Third Reich*. Oxford: Oxford University Press, 2008.

Thurman, Kira. *Singing Like Germans: Black Musicians in the Land of Bach, Beethoven, and Brahms*. Ithaca and London: Cornell University Press, 2021.

Uekoetter, Frank. *The Brown and the Green: A History of Conservation in Nazi Germany*. Cambridge UK: Cambridge University Press, 2006.

Welch, David. *The Third Reich: Politics and Propaganda*. Second Edition. London: Routledge, 2002.

7

Youth, Gender, and Sexuality

This chapter begins with an exploration of what it was like for "Aryan" children to grow up in Nazi Germany and how life differed for Jewish children and others not welcomed into the *Volksgemeinschaft*. The regime educated children in the Nazi worldview and prepared them to lead Germany into the future. This training, which extended to adult men and women, was based on a particular anti-feminist gendered hierarchy. Nazis emphasized gender difference and the complementarity between femininity and masculinity. But these concepts can only be understood within the context of Nazism's racist framework. Racial purity was the goal, and men and women were called on to help achieve that goal through the adoption of gender-specific roles and behaviors. In this chapter, we will also explore some of the ways the state attempted to shape individual beliefs and behavior beyond childhood, including sexual identity and family life. However, as we will see, there were limits to what the regime could accomplish. Words like "brainwashing" and "indoctrination" do not reflect the range of individual experiences in Nazi Germany, nor do they capture the importance of what historians have called "self-mobilization," which refers to some Germans' active and voluntary embrace of the regime's agenda.[1]

Children and Youth

It is hard to know how many children in the Weimar Republic took notice of Hitler's victory on January 30, 1933. Some may have overheard their parents talking about the political crisis over the previous months or years or may themselves have been involved in politicized youth organizations. Jewish children may have been more aware of their parents' anxieties about the future, though mothers and fathers are skilled at hiding such emotions from their children. Some older boys and girls later recalled seeing the headline in the newspaper; others remember pro-Hitler teachers who were caught up in the excitement giving them the following day off from school. Fifteen-year-old Melita Maschmann was "overcome with a burning desire to belong"[2] to the movement after witnessing the first night's torchlit parade. But many children and teenagers were surely content to ignore the appointment of yet another chancellor in Berlin. As one ten-year-old boy in 1932 admitted decades later: "I knew about politics almost as much as a fish [knew] about flying."[3] The emerging Nazi regime, however, was interested in this boy and in all young people. National Socialism was a movement that prided itself on its future-looking attitude that would propel its "1,000-year reign." It is not surprising, therefore, that its leaders were interested in harnessing the energy and imagination of the country's young people.

Schooling

Germany had done more than most countries in the early twentieth century to extend formal education to the masses. By 1933 most German children attended school until the age of fourteen. Still only a small minority went on to secondary school and even fewer attended university. The regime moved quickly to "coordinate" the education system. The Law for the Restoration of the Professional Civil Service covered all public-school teachers, which meant that Jewish and socialist teachers were purged from classrooms in 1933 and 1934. The law applied to university professors as well. As many as 1,600 of Germany's 5,000 university professors and instructors were forced out in the first year of the regime, only to have their roles filled by those willing to support the dictatorship. The NSDAP also established the *NS-Lehrerbund* (National Socialist Teachers' League) early on and enrolled 90 percent of teachers by 1934. As in any mass organization, membership in the *NS-Lehrerbund* did not require full ideological commitment, but it did mean the regime had the means to influence and police teachers. The Teachers' League organized courses to share updates and provide educators with training in a new, National Socialist curriculum.

Nazi education was not a complete departure from Imperial and Weimar-era pedagogy. Love of country and respect for the military and other authorities were already deeply ingrained in German education. New guidelines for the teaching of history in 1934 reminded teachers that they should present to students the "German nation's essence and greatness." What was new, however, was a mandate to teach the nation's history through the lens of biological determinism by highlighting the "hereditary characteristics" that served as the permanent motor of history. While the guidelines explained that "the powerless and insignificant have no history," German students were encouraged to see themselves as part of their nation's story—to feel the weight of its past and the responsibility of contributing to its future success.[4] Alongside history, other subjects that were seen as fundamentally German were also given priority, especially language and literature. And two new subjects, genetics and race science, were first introduced in Prussia in 1933, and could be found in other parts of the country by 1935. Even so, the country's economic woes meant that republican-era textbooks were not replaced with nazified ones for several years in certain regions.

Where pre-1933 textbooks remained, Nazi propaganda and rituals shaped school ceremonies and daily routines. School children were required to gather to listen to Hitler's speeches on the radio and celebrate a variety of nazified festivals, and school libraries were purged of books deemed dangerous to the Reich. Beyond the time spent in classrooms, sport and physical fitness were given high priority at state schools. Young bodies needed to be fit to fulfill their fundamental duties to the nation: girls were prepared to be attractive mates and mothers, and boys would grow into soldiers.

Not all children attended state schools. Both Catholic and Protestant-run schools were common in Germany, with over 40,000 in Prussia alone, though increasingly parents were exhorted to enroll their students in the secular school system. The regime worked to convert religious schools into state-run schools over time, seeing the worldview professed in those institutions as ultimately incompatible with obedience to National Socialism. In the late 1930s, Catholic schools in Bavaria were sites of tension, as school administrators and parents pushed back at requirements to replace the crucifixes which traditionally hung in classrooms with portraits of the Führer. Jewish private academies also existed in Germany before 1933, though only a small percentage of Germany's well-integrated Jewish minority chose to send their children to these religious schools.

Already in 1933 officials limited the numbers of Jewish students in state-run schools, and those Jewish students permitted to remain were regularly targeted for ill-treatment (Figure 7.1). Oral histories from the era indicate that classroom experiences varied, depending primarily on the political stance of the teacher. Ardent Nazis openly ridiculed Jewish students and encouraged bullying by non-Jewish classmates, while a few teachers did their best to maintain an open and tolerant classroom, despite the pressures on them and on administrators to conform. Students sometimes weren't sure whether their teachers were true believers or just paying lip-service to Nazi ideals to hold on to their jobs. Non-conforming instructors who didn't support the dictatorship had to be careful, lest parents report them to the authorities. Nor was it uncommon for teachers to denounce parents if a student's mother and father were seen as undermining National Socialist teachings at home.

Over time Jewish students were driven out of the public system. Of the 15,000 Jewish boys and girls enrolled in Prussian state schools (including the more tolerant capital, Berlin) in 1932, only about 27 percent of them remained in 1936. It is easy to see why. Even in classrooms led by teachers who sought to minimize bullying, Jewish students were forbidden to travel on class outings or write essays on topics associated with German history or National Socialism. They were seated separately in class and purposely

FIGURE 7.1 *Integrated school class in Berlin, 1933. There are three Jewish girls in this image. All were expelled from the school in the years following, including Marion Sauerbrunn to the right of the teacher in the second row. The photo belonged to her (United States Holocaust Memorial Museum, courtesy of Marion House).*

given lower marks than "Aryan" students. At one school, when students gathered to sing in celebration of Mother's Day, the Jewish students were not allowed to join in. When one asked why they were excluded, the teacher replied: "I know you have a mother ... but she is only a Jewish mother."[5] The last Jewish students who had withstood the torment and remained in state schools through 1938 were removed by decree after the November Pogrom. The 1933 sterilization law had also made it possible for school administrators to move disabled students to special schools (*Hilfsschulen*), many of which were led by supporters of the regime's sterilization policies and its "euthanasia" of severely disabled children.

A small number of boys (and even fewer girls) attended newly established Nazi elite schools. The first National Political Institute of Education (Napola) opened in 1933 to honor Hitler's forty-fourth birthday (Figure 7.2). Additional Napola, Order Castles, and Adolf Hitler Schools followed later in the decade. Intended as training grounds for future party leaders, Hitler insisted that these schools be run by the party, and as such they were administered by SA and SS officers rather than professional educators. Some of these elite boarding schools were opened after 1939 in the occupied territories to educate a new generation of leaders for the empire. Criteria for admission included superior physical and racial fitness and character, judged through competitive sport. To some extent these schools provided working-class boys opportunities for upward mobility. Physical fitness was the only entrance requirement at the Adolf Hitler schools, and about one-fifth of all students were from working-class backgrounds. The education standards were low at these "elite" schools, reflecting the anti-intellectual stance of the regime. While some party leaders hailed the decision to prioritize character development (loyalty to Hitler and the national community and a will to action and sacrifice) over attainment of knowledge, others complained that graduates were nowhere near prepared to take on positions of responsibility in the state or party apparatus. The regime's willingness to downplay the importance of intellectual development also provided the nation's leaders with the rationale for shortening schooling by one year in the late 1930s to make way for mandatory labor service.

Fewer students were therefore prepared to enter university, and fewer were motivated to do so, given the attacks on higher learning. On Germany's world-renowned university campuses, members of the National Socialist German Students' League (*NS Deutscher Studentenbund, NSDStB*) harassed the remaining non-member students and non-conforming professors. The number of German women attending university dropped precipitously,

FIGURE 7.2 *Napola classroom, no date. Forty of these elite Nazi boarding schools were opened between 1933 and 1945, including four for girls (Bundesarchiv, Bild 146-1978-013-07/CC-BY-SA 3.0, CC BY-SA 3.0 DE, via Wikimedia Commons).*

thanks to restrictions on women in the professions and Nazi educational reform that increasingly prioritized home economics for girls. Male students also grew less interested in university degrees. The regime closed some of the university preparatory high schools (*Gymnasiums*) and stepped up its criticism of higher education and the professions that required advanced degrees, like teaching, law, and science. This led to a decline in total university enrollment from 104,000 in 1931 to 41,000 in 1939. Only the numbers studying medicine increased dramatically in these years, thanks to the status of racial hygiene in Nazi Germany.[6] Of the 41,000 remaining university students on the eve of war in 1939, just about all of them were members of the National Socialist German Students' League.

The Hitler Youth

One reason the regime diluted schooling in the prewar years was because its leaders put more faith in the education of young Germans through the party's mass organization, the Hitler Youth (HJ). Founded in 1926, the organization remained small like the NSDAP in the 1920s. There were many German youth organizations, dating back to the late nineteenth century, which offered boys and girls camaraderie, mentorship, and recreational activity. As the NSDAP gained a mass following in the early 1930s, however, so did the HJ. By 1932 the organization counted a little over 100,000 members, and by the end of 1933 there were over 2 million members, due in part to the forced integration of the older youth clubs. The Protestant Church alone had organized 600,000 young people, who now found themselves members of the HJ. Nazi leaders wished to get all youth enrolled and introduced State Youth Day the following year. Saturdays were thus turned over to the HJ for sporting competition, and children who were not members had to attend separate, mandatory Saturday schooling along with Jewish students.

By the end of 1935 still fewer than half of all ten- to eighteen-year-olds were in the HJ. There were fewer total girls than boys enrolled, but the rate of growth among girls was higher. On December 1, 1936, the first Law of the Hitler Youth dissolved the last independent youth organization—one led by the Catholic Church—and declared that the HJ "encompassed all German youth." By 1938, 82 percent of Germany's eligible youngsters were members. Boys aged ten to thirteen were organized in the *Deutsches Jungvolk*, while similarly aged girls joined the *Jundgmädelbund*. At fourteen boys transitioned to the Hitler Youth, and girls moved on to the League of German Girls (*Bund Deutscher Mädel*, BDM). Even then, HJ leader Baldur von Schirach, who had joined the NSDAP as an eighteen-year-old himself in 1925, was not satisfied. Determined to see 100 percent of eligible boys and girls involved in the HJ, a second law was introduced in 1939 that conscripted those who remained outside the organization. Parents who continued to keep their sons and daughters from participating drew the unwanted attention of authorities and could be fined. At seventeen, young people participated in the Labor Service year. Party membership was available to those eighteen and older, as were mass party organizations, nazified professional associations, and the armed forces. This meant that all "Aryan" Germans could engage with National Socialism throughout their entire lives.

Some youngsters loved their time in the HJ and BDM: the camping and hiking, the uniforms and songs, the competitions and national pride (Figure 7.3). Helmut Becker-Floris's Catholic parents were against the regime and the idea of their son joining the HJ, but they eventually permitted his participation in the *Jungvolk* "so he wouldn't have trouble at school." That was good enough for young Helmut, who enjoyed the sports and the camaraderie of the expeditions. For a while he also played music in an HJ band and later had the opportunity to learn how to ride a horse.[7] These activities, suffused with nationalist rhetoric, were not dissimilar to those found in other youth organizations like the Boy Scouts or the nineteenth-century German *Wandervogel* movement. As the boys got older and the war approached, however, HJ activities became increasingly militarized. They included marksmanship, map reading, and mock military maneuvers. As Kurt Elfering reported, "since we were to become soldiers, we also certainly had to learn the foundations of being a soldier. We had to learn to assemble in rows of three, turn left and also right. Stand at attention, 'forward march',

FIGURE 7.3 *War games made fun. Boys from the Deutsches Jungvolk, the section of the Hitler Youth for boys between ages ten and thirteen, compete in a tug-of-war while wearing gas masks, 1933 (Bundesarchiv, Bild 133-393. Unknown author CC-BY-SA 3.0, CC BY-SA 3.0 DE, via Wikimedia Commons).*

'division halt', and all the rest."[8] HJ youth were also involved in antisemitic actions: physical attacks on passersby, breaking windows of Jewish-owned shops and homes, desecrating Jewish cemeteries, and killing Jewish-owned livestock were common behaviors throughout the country.[9]

Another thing that distinguished the HJ and BDM from other youth organizations is that leaders encouraged their young charges to rebel against non-Nazi forms of authority, taking advantage of the fact that teenagers are already defiant. The HJ leaders were adolescents themselves, and to the younger boys and girls they could seem more like trusted older siblings. In comparison, parents, pastors, and other traditional authority figures seemed old-fashioned and out of touch with the new Germany. The regime and its affiliated organizations encouraged youngsters to see themselves as willing servants and as future leaders. As Baldur von Schirach explained in 1933, Hitler Youth members learned "camaraderie" and "loyalty," "pride" and "obligation" ... "but they have also been trained to become the future."[10] Instilled with confidence and loyalty to the Führer, HJ members were told not to shy away from rejecting those who refused to support the new order. In one of the era's early propaganda films, the young *Hitlerjunge Quex* does just this. He turns his back on his communist father and the local KPD youth organization in favor of the order and discipline he discovers after stumbling upon an HJ gathering.

As with any large organization, local experiences varied. The intensity of military drills and racist instruction about the glories of war, for example, depended on the level of fanaticism of a given Hitler Youth leader. BDM units also varied in this respect, with some more focused than others on eugenics and the role of "Aryan" women in propagating the race. But oral histories of former BDM members indicate that their activities were in general less overtly political and militaristic than programming in the boys' organizations (Figure 7.4). At first Melita Maschmann found her BDM meetings filled with "tedium" and yearned for more political discussion. She formed an "elite" reading group with other students at her secondary school, but she was reprimanded by local BDM leaders when they learned of her initiative. Forced to disband, Maschmann went back to group meetings filled with singing, telling folk stories, and arts and crafts, though she was given the task of handling the unit's press communications to keep her occupied (and perhaps to give her superiors opportunities to mentor and monitor her behavior). Some girls were particularly attracted to the BDM for the opportunity, which was still rare at the time, to engage in sport. This author recalls meeting a female retiree in Heidelberg in the early 1990s, who denounced the dictatorship but still reminisced proudly about her BDM athletic victories. She showed off track medals and photos from a Hitler Youth sports festival she had attended in the mid-1930s.

While some youngsters were highly motivated by HJ programming, others were turned off by the militarism and domineering style of some local leaders. Most kids probably fell somewhere in between. They were

FIGURE 7.4 *Girls from the Jungmädelbund, the section of the League of German Girls for those between ages ten and thirteen, hang posters encouraging others to join, no date (Bundesarchiv, Bild 133-130 CC-BY-SA 3.0, CC BY-SA 3.0 DE, via Wikimedia Commons).*

not overcome with adoration for the Führer and the racist dogma expressed during HJ meetings, but they were willing to put up with the aspects they found less attractive in order to have fun with their friends in the countryside or to attend a sports festival instead of school. Others enjoyed the sense of belonging and status that came with wearing the uniform. Jewish children were, of course, barred from participation. And while no Jewish parent would want to send their child on an HJ outing, some Jews who grew up in Germany in the 1930s later recalled a desire to belong as a youngster, when neighbors or classmates went on expeditions or wore uniforms to school events, leaving them isolated, in some cases ashamed, and vulnerable to bullying and physical violence. We should also not forget that class differences continued to shape society. Working-class kids left school at fourteen for the labor force. While they were expected to be enrolled as HJ members after the 1936 law, they were far less likely to participate in its activities, given their work commitments. And when they did participate, they were more likely to have other interests competing for their energy and attention. Mandating membership also meant that HJ meetings increasingly had young people present who did not want to be there, which in some locations bred dissent or apathy within the unit.

Excluded from these activities, Jewish teenagers increasingly stuck together after 1933 and tried to enjoy the same things as non-Jewish teenagers: hanging out in cafes, attending the movies, or going on their first romantic dates. Social outings, however, caused great anxiety, especially for their parents, because there was always a chance that a group of Jewish teens might be refused service, taunted by non-Jewish passersby, or even physically attacked. Given these realistic concerns, Jewish pre-teens and teens increasingly spent time at activities coordinated by Jewish youth groups. Such organizations had existed before 1933, but just as we saw with the school system, during the Weimar Republic most Jewish families had preferred to integrate their children into non-sectarian social clubs rather than Jewish-only organizations. By 1936, however, about 60 percent of all Jews aged twelve to twenty-five had joined Jewish associations, roughly double the percentage involved before the Nazi rise to power. Members met in private homes and offices to avoid prejudicial remarks in public, or worse. After German hostels no longer accepted "non-Aryan" travelers, the Jewish community raised funds to establish Haus Bertha (1934–7), which provided hundreds of Jewish youngsters a safe and fun holiday getaway over the next three years. But turmoil and fear were never far away. Local membership rolls fluctuated as new people arrived and others left the country. As Marion Kaplan notes, one thing all young Jews had in common was that they had recently been rejected by close friends.[11]

The Jewish youth organizations were varied, but the largest emerged in 1934 after the consolidation of the Jewish Pathfinders and the Zionist Maccabi Hazair. The Zionists trained young people for the agricultural life that awaited them in Palestine and deepened, refreshed, or even introduced their members to Judaism and Jewish history. Participation in the Zionist association in some cases intensified generational tensions between young people and their parents. Young Zionists found it possible to imagine and commit to the idea of life outside Germany, while many of their parents had a harder time accepting that they no longer had a future in Germany. Some parents even disapproved of their children's newfound political beliefs and Jewish identity. Young people considered *Mischlinge* by the regime, because they had partial Jewish heritage, could be excluded from all youth groups. Prohibited from the HJ and BDM as "non-Aryan," but unable to join many Jewish groups because they had been baptized as Catholics or Protestants, these youngsters were among the most isolated in the years before the war.

Gender and the *Volksgemeinschaft*

When we look at what impressed Germans about the Nazi movement in the period before the party came to power, and especially in the years following Hitler's appointment as chancellor, contemporaries used words like dynamism, charisma, and unity. In part, of course, the dynamism and unity of the movement were staged. Goebbels' ministry created a glittering façade that masked the assault on individual rights and individual bodies.

Hitler's charismatic engagement with the public was highly orchestrated. His personal photographer was always at his side producing images that showed the candidate, later chancellor and then Führer, as approachable and laser-focused, as both a regular guy and the only person capable of rescuing Germany from its trials and tribulations. The Nuremberg rallies were choreographed and filmed; the strategic use of uniforms, flags, and parades in German towns and cities of all sizes was meant to create an atmosphere that enacted revolution. All "Aryan" Germans were expected to play a part in Germany's rebirth. Just as children were required to enroll in the HJ to train their bodies and minds for war and a future in which Germany held dominion over Europe, adults were also called on to support the Reich and take an active role in its regeneration. Not everyone wanted to participate. Some found the activism a bother, and others felt acutely the loss of political rights and diversity of thought. But for those who answered the call to build a powerful, united Germany, there were many opportunities.

Participation was gendered. Party membership was open to men and women, but from the start the NSDAP idealized hypermasculine paramilitary-style activism. As noted earlier, the NSDAP's first members were demobilized soldiers and those who had joined the Free Corps movement after the armistice. The party retained its military ethic and aesthetic until the collapse of the dictatorship. The men who had joined the party before 1933 were considered "old fighters." They helped the movement come to power and retained an honored status. Those men who had died supporting the cause before 1933 were venerated as martyrs. Their sacrifices to the movement were celebrated in song and films and commemorated with plaques and statues. There were no female Nazis celebrated this way. The ideal Nazi was a man of action, disciplined and fit, ready to follow those above him and lead those below. These attributes were taught early in the Hitler Youth. Boys were to be tough, and hazing and aggressive behavior were regularly praised.

Ideal femininity was complementary, nurturing, and supportive. Girls and women were taught to embrace concepts like duty and sacrifice, but they were not allowed to be decision-makers (Figure 7.5). Final authority was always to rest with a man. Ideal Nazi females were expected to reject artifice; the pronounced use of makeup and hair dye was seen as unnatural and un-German. Traditional German styles, like dirndl dresses and long braided hair, were promoted as reflective of "Aryan" beauty standards. But in reality, urban middle-class women continued to shop for modern dresses and suits. The wealthy still looked to Paris for the newest trends, while agricultural and industrial female workers sought the most functional and affordable styles, including short hair and trousers for work. Uninterested in most areas of domestic policy, Hitler chose not to set up an office of women's affairs in 1933, disappointing his female followers. And while such lack of interest was not uncommon among male politicians of the era, the level of anti-feminism within the new government was radical.

FIGURE 7.5 *SS photograph depicting the ideal family in wartime, February, 1943.*
Father is absent, but everyone smiles, as the focus turns to the son wearing his Hitler
Youth uniform (Bundesarchiv, Bild 146-1973-010-31 CC-BY-SA 3.0, CC BY-SA 3.0
DE, via Wikimedia Commons).

Hitler's cabinet was quick to restrict women's involvement in the economy
and government. Just about all women who held governmental roles at the
local, regional, or federal level before 1933 were removed from their posts
after the arrival of the new regime. Married female doctors were prohibited
from practice, and by 1935 unmarried female medical doctors were no
longer allowed to receive payment from the state health insurance system,
which was also the case for all Jewish doctors. After 1936 women could no

longer serve as judges or public prosecutors, and the small number of female lawyers were harassed by male colleagues and other officials. Women were no longer permitted to sit on juries because the state claimed their inability to reason adequately rendered them ineligible. Women who worked in the private sector were offered incentives to leave their jobs, and employers were told not to hire married women, known as "double earners."

These exclusionary practices raise the question: why did large numbers of women support the Nazi Party and Hitler's government after 1933? There are many answers—just as there are for male supporters—and many line up with men's decisions. Women too were nationalists, believed Germany had been mistreated and needed to stand up for itself, and insisted Jews and socialists were weakening the country. If asked why they would support an anti-feminist government, female Nazis might say that the liberation the parties of the Republic had offered women in the 1920s had failed to materialize or had led to undesirable outcomes. For these women greater opportunities and responsibilities in education, the economy, and the public sphere had come without any decrease in responsibility in the home, leaving them feeling exhausted rather than liberated. Older women may not themselves have experienced the changes associated with the "New Woman," but hearing about Germany's falling birth rate convinced some of them that feminism had gone too far. Young and old, then, were drawn to what the Nazis appeared to be offering: a newfound respect for family life in which the wife and mother was honored and given pride of place. These women were also drawn to the charismatic Hitler, who didn't drink alcohol or smoke, who praised German mothers, and who promised a future of unity and prosperity for their children.

The women and men who believed that Hitler's government would re-establish a mythical nineteenth-century "traditional" family, however, were disappointed. In many ways the Nazi regime undermined the family unit, which was weakened by a dictatorship that demanded all loyalty and obedience to the Führer, even if that meant rejecting familial relations or other forms of belonging. Just as children were encouraged to reject their parents in favor of their Hitler Youth leaders, adults were similarly instructed to prioritize the needs of the Reich over their family's needs. For adults, this meant attendance at regular meetings and events held by the SA, the party, the Women's League, or countless other Nazi organizations and professional associations. Participation meant that on many evenings and weekends family members were apart from one another, each attending their own gender and age-specific events.

Women did have a role to play in the new Germany. And while it was not wholly limited to motherhood and marriage, it began there. They were expected to pass on their "valuable," "Aryan" genetic endowment to a new generation, and to nurture their children so that they grew up healthy and aware of their "racial responsibilities." "Aryan" females were taught to protect the sanctity of the race, which meant first and foremost picking a suitable ("Aryan") mate. Starting in June 1933, "Aryan" newlyweds were offered state loans to help with the costs of setting up a new home, and the conditions of the loan improved if the wife gave up her employment and had children. The marriage loan scheme was popular, arriving while the Depression still limited people's income and savings. From 1936 all newlyweds received a copy of Hitler's *Mein Kampf* along with reading material about the *Ahnenpass*, or racial passport. The National Socialist People's Welfare (NSV) and women's organizations invested great time and money setting up various training courses for young women on how to be better mothers and homemakers, including education in first aid, hygiene, and nutrition. This was coupled with misinformation about heredity and the dangers of so-called racial mixing.

Hegemonic masculinity under the Nazis emphasized military virtues. For the individual strength, discipline, and self-control were critical, but just as important was the focus on comradeship. Based on an idealized memory of First World War combat, Nazis believed that the success of their movement depended on the strength of the bonds between men who served together in the struggle—bonds that were forged by each man's willingness to support his comrades and sacrifice his own comfort or safety for others. While all men were expected to participate in the SA or military, elite status was granted to those in the SS based on its members' deeper ideological commitment and racial purity. SS men were expected to set the standard for others in their level of commitment to Hitler and National Socialism and in their personal lives, marrying young and fathering a large brood. Their wives also had to commit to the role, not just as spouses and mothers, but as vanguard members of a new society based on racist principles and a will to violence. And the SS was not as small a unit as its elite status might indicate; over 800,000 men joined between 1931 and 1945.[12]

While most men were not members of the SS, all adults were expected to contribute to the greater cause of remaking Germany. Although wage work was frowned upon in general for married women, those who needed to make ends meet could retain their jobs. Single women who had chosen careers in suitably feminine roles maintained those, and there was some expansion of roles deemed acceptable as the state and party bureaucracies and technical careers grew. In addition to supporting their family members' participation in party activities, women themselves were also expected to participate in the many party-run activities geared toward them. They helped collect funds and donated goods to the annual Winter Relief Aid campaign, which began during the Depression and continued to grow throughout the decade, supporting ("Aryan") Germans of lesser means. Roughly 1 million party members, assisted by the HJ and BDM, raised funds yearly under the slogan "A People Helps Itself."[13] One initiative asked German families (as well as owners of restaurants and inns) to replace the traditional Sunday midday meal once per month with a "one pot" (*Eintopf*) stew. Volunteers were tasked with visiting homes and eating establishments to collect the money saved on ingredients—and to make sure housewives and cooks were following the directive. This demonstration of community, however, was unpopular, and many families maintained their own Sunday traditions.

After 1936 calls to sacrifice for the collective good became increasingly common, with women playing a vital role in helping Germany adapt to the autarkic goals laid out in the Four-Year Plan. Housewives learned to cook without preferred ingredients; they were given primers on how to keep clothes clean without high-fat content cleaning agents; and they were told to serve fish instead of meat and to collect metal scraps. Not all women appreciated this advice. Some insisted they knew more about cooking and cleaning than male bureaucrats or domineering Women's League leaders. Others worried about impending war and wished their children and husbands could spend more time together. But many believed in Nazi goals. They basked in newfound respect as stewards of the race and enjoyed some status as leaders in the organizations and associations that catered to women and families.

All this activity was intended to teach Germans to prioritize the collective over the individual—*Gemeinnutz geht vor Eigennutz*—as the basis of a united and strong *Volksgemeinschaft*. In addition to this work that women and men were asked to undertake in their homes and communities, thousands of new camps were established to educate members of the *Volk*. By the late 1930s about 400,000 young people were living communally in the Reich Labor Service, SA, and SS training camps. Another 600,000 went to kids' summer camps. About 500,000 attended the Nuremberg Party rally every fall, setting up tents on the grounds and in the vicinity. In addition, many professional groups required training sessions that took place at these campsites, including over 200,000 state schoolteachers. Some adults who attended these training camps did so to get along or to protect and perhaps advance their career aspirations. However, even among those who felt "forcibly volunteered,"[14] the vast majority got used to the new normal.

As the primary danger to the *Volksgemeinschaft*, Nazi propaganda and so-called racial science portrayed Jewish masculinity as the opposite of the Nazi male ideal. Jewish men were represented as weak and effeminate, and also as selfish, scheming, hypersexual, and animalistic. In most cases, Jewish men (like "Aryan" men) were the family breadwinners, and their identities were tightly bound to their professions or careers. When they lost the ability to work in their chosen professions, either in 1933 with the removal of Jews from the civil service or later in the decade through various Nazi licensing schemes and the "Aryanization" of the private sector economy, Jewish men were deeply wounded by their inability to care for their families and contribute to society. Some men found ways to work illegally for a time. Erich Bloch, a Jewish adman, for example, continued to submit designs as a freelancer after he was refused the official advertisers' license by the Reich Chamber of Culture. Looking back on these years, one attorney's son recalled: "We had no way of comprehending how utterly devastated my father felt at this destruction of his world."[15]

The importance of their work identities also made it more difficult for some Jewish men to consider emigration, which in the best-case scenario would require recertification or the rebuilding of networks on arrival in a new country. For many others emigration would mean a completely different (and unwanted) future, for example, as an agricultural laborer in Palestine. That said, many male Jews were quite able to redirect their energy toward gaining a new skill that might be easily transferable and in demand in a new homeland. Despite an established career in business, Salo Rosenthal reasoned that training as a tailor would allow him to keep his family afloat—first by working "under the table" in Germany and then abroad.[16]

Jewish women did not appear in Nazi propaganda to the same extent as Jewish men. When they were featured, they were most often depicted as tempting sirens, who seduced "Aryan" men into sexual liaisons, or as androgynous degenerates incapable of and uninterested in motherhood. In reality, Jewish women lived a wide range of lifestyles, depending on their income, religiosity, education, and marital status, just as "Aryan" women did. After 1933, Jewish women's lives, however, also changed dramatically. With newly unemployed husbands, some middle-class Jewish women were forced to take on wage labor for the first time—mending, washing, and tutoring. Jewish women were the main caregivers in their families and were kept busy navigating the expanding restrictions on daily life. They took it upon themselves to protect their children from the increasing animosity in German society as much as possible, stretching family resources to make ends meet and maintaining family rituals like holiday celebrations and birthdays. Some Jewish women pushed for emigration and readied their families for departure by learning new languages or beginning the arduous bureaucratic process to leave the country.

Sex and Sexuality

Historian Dagmar Herzog has referred to National Socialist Germany as an "immense venture in reproductive engineering."[17] What Herzog was getting at was the extent to which the regime marshaled resources to shape sexual behavior in ways its leaders believed supported and enhanced the nation's racial profile. This meant, on the one hand, restricting the reproductive ability and sexual practices of those whom they believed undermined the health of the nation: chiefly, Jews, Roma and other minorities, "Aryans" with mental or physical disabilities, and gay men. Efforts included the demonization of sex within these groups. Nazi propaganda targeted Jews especially as sexual predators, who intentionally sought to seduce and defile "Aryans." Jews and other members of persecuted groups also faced sterilization, incarceration, or murder. On the other hand, resources were showered on so-called "healthy 'Aryans'" to encourage them to reproduce and to find joy in heterosexual relations, including sex outside of marriage.

Many European nations in the 1920s had concerns about population decline (Figure 7.6). Long-term trends of decreasing family size had been magnified by emigration and the losses suffered during the First World War and the influenza epidemic that followed. Policies to increase birth rates and to seek ways to "improve" the population through eugenic measures were common throughout Europe and North America. The declining German birth rate was one symptom of racial crisis for the Nazi regime. Nazis worried that the "Aryan" race would die off entirely if important measures were not put in place, including the expulsion of Jews and the sterilization of "Aryans" who were not considered fit enough.

State and party leaders also wanted to ensure "Aryans" understood the importance of procreation. Women of childbearing age were given training by midwives and others about the importance of motherhood and healthy pregnancy practices, like abstaining from alcohol. The policing of abortion also intensified. Abortion had been illegal throughout the 1920s, despite a campaign by feminists and medical personnel to overturn Paragraph 218, which outlawed the procedure, but the Nazis prosecuted women who sought abortions and doctors who provided them far more aggressively than their Weimar predecessors. Birth control advice became increasingly difficult to get, especially in working-class districts, because reproductive health centers formerly run by the SPD and KPD had been shuttered. Middle-class Germans had more options, but with military casualties mounting after 1939, the sale of birth control was made illegal in 1941.

Despite all the propaganda and attempts to limit access to birth control, couples continued to make decisions based on their family's needs. The birth rate in Germany did climb after 1933, but that was relative only to the deep dip in births during the Depression years. Even with economic stability and years of propaganda and education, Germans continued to follow western European trends of limiting family size to around two children. Most women who won the nation's highly publicized "Honor Cross of the German Mother" (first awarded in 1938 to "Aryan" mothers of at least four "valuable" children) were middle-aged or elderly, meaning their children were born well before 1933 when larger families were common, and not as a result of Nazi propaganda.[18]

For many Nazis male homosexuality was a danger to society not unlike abortion. In both cases, according to Nazi thinking, "Aryan" Germans were actively and selfishly rejecting their duty to procreate. The desired outcome of sexual relations was racially healthy offspring. Nazis also feared contamination. Gay men, they claimed erroneously, could turn other males, especially young men and boys, toward homosexuality. And the same selfishness, according to Nazi ideologues, that led a woman to choose her own health or happiness over a pregnancy could also infect a society. It had, they argued, during the Weimar Republic, and further education and

Marriages and live and illegitimate births,
1900, 1905, 1910 and 1913-41

Year	Per 1,000 of the population		Live births per 1,000 women of childbearing age	Illegitimate births per 1,000 births
	Marriages	Live Births		
1900	8.5	35.6	*	8.7
1905	8.1	32.9	*	8.5
1910	7.7	29.8	128.0	9.1
1913	7.7	27.5	*	9.7
1914	6.8	26.8	*	9.8
1915	4.1	20.4	*	11.2
1916	4.1	15.2	*	11.1
1917	4.7	13.9	*	11.5
1918	5.4	14.3	*	13.1
1919	13.4	20.0	*	11.2
1920	14.5	25.9	*	11.4
1921	11.9	25.3	*	10.7
1922	11.2	23.0	90.0	10.7
1923	9.4	21.2	82.3	10.4
1924	7.1	20.6	79.8	10.5
1925	7.7	20.8	80.2	11.9
1926	7.7	19.6	75.4	12.5
1927	8.5	18.4	70.6	12.3
1928	9.2	18.6	71.3	12.3
1929	9.2	18.0	68.7	12.1
1930	8.8	17.6	67.3	12.0
1931	8.0	16.0	62.0	11.8
1932	7.9	15.1	59.5	11.6
1933	9.7	14.7	58.9	10.7
1934	11.1	18.0	73.3	8.6
1935	9.7	18.9	77.2	7.8
1936	9.1	19.0	77.6	7.8
1937	9.1	18.8	77.1	7.7
1938	9.4	19.6	80.9	7.7
1939	11.2	20.4	84.8	7.8
1940	8.8	20.0	84.2	*
1941	7.2	18.6	*	*
1942	7.4	14.9	*	*
1943	7.3	16.0	*	*

* not recorded for 1910/11
(Statistisches Jahrbuch des Deutschen Reiches: 1938:47; 1941/42:77; 1952:36)

FIGURE 7.6 *Source: Women in Nazi Germany, Jill Stephenson, Copyright 2001 and Imprint. Reproduced by permission of Taylor & Francis Group.*

surveillance was needed to make sure women understood that all racially healthy pregnancies were to be supported. SS leader Himmler even linked homosexuality and abortion together in his 1936 plans for one office to combat both, arguing that

> ... the relatively high number of abortions still being performed today that are a major violation of the ideological tenets of the National Socialist worldview, as well as homosexual activities on the part of a not insignificant segment of the population, which pose one of the greatest threats to our youth, requires more effective measures for combating these public menaces to society than have thus far been implemented.[19]

Lesbian sex was never criminalized, and while stories of persecution, arrests, and even violence exist, these relationships do not appear to have raised the same level of alarm among Nazi leaders as those between men. As one medical official reported in 1937:

> In our view, the danger to the nation's survival is here not at all as great as in the case of gay men. First, it should not be forgotten that in Germany we have always had more females than males; second, that we lost 2 million men in the war; and third, that of the available men several more million do not count because they are homosexuals.

In other words, Nazi ideologues believed that the nation could more easily "tolerate" women who did not contribute reproductively. Their understanding of lesbianism also led them to believe a significant number of young gay women would return to heterosexuality later in their lives to have children.

In addition to this fear that the health of the nation could ill-afford men who did not reproduce, the attack on male homosexuality was also fueled by the fact that the Nazi project relied on a vision of "true German men" as hypermasculine soldiers who would redeem Germany. The existence of gay German men was a fundamental threat to that vision. In most Nazis' minds, gay men were by definition not soldierly and therefore unsuited for this work. And yet, National Socialism also glorified the camaraderie of male-only military units, which led several commentators to speak and write about gay men as ideally suited for military life. Ernst Röhm, Hitler's long-time friend and co-conspirator in the 1923 Beer Hall Putsch, was gay, and while he was forced to keep his sexual identity "masked" to avoid criminal prosecution throughout his life, his homosexuality was well known. This fact did not keep Hitler from calling on Röhm to lead the SA in 1931, and Röhm's own memoir railed against German society for ostracizing gay men as unfit for service during the First World War, leading in some cases to suicide. For Röhm, one goal of National Socialism was to reject this "false morality" and accept "natural instincts" that only deepened soldierly comradeship. What mattered most to Röhm were a man's skills on the battlefield.[20] Despite the existence of this perspective, homophobic beliefs that gay men were weak and vulnerable to blackmail, and that they had the seductive powers to "turn" others gay, remained prevalent. Given the homosocial world created by the party, the SA, the SS, the HJ, and the armed forces, if homosexuality could "spread," it surely would within these male-only environments. For all these reasons, most Nazi leaders believed it was critical to stamp out male homosexuality, or as Himmler declared, "our Volk will fall to ruin as the result of this scourge."[21]

Gay bars and other hangouts, along with periodicals aimed at queer audiences, were forced to close in the first weeks of the regime (Figure 7.7). As one publisher of a gay magazine wrote in November 1933:

FIGURE 7.7 *Before closing down the famed El Dorado gay and trans nightclub in Berlin, the police used surveillance photos of patrons coming and going to arrest individuals on suspicion of having sexual relations with other men (thus violating Paragraph 175). After the club's forced closure, the ruling party flaunted its power by covering the boarded-up windows with swastikas ahead of the federal elections in March, 1933 (Landesarchiv Berlin, F Rep. 290 (03) Nr. II6938/Foto: k. A.I).*

I am completely cleaned out by these five confiscations: I have nothing left to sell and am now ruined from a business point of view. I do not even know what I and my dependents will live on in the future. For my whole life's work is destroyed. Most of my followers do not even have the courage to write me a letter, and certainly not to give any financial support for my work.[22]

On the morning of May 6, 1933, students threatened the female custodial staff until they gained entrance to the locked offices of Dr. Magnus Hirschfeld, founder of the Institute for Sexual Science in Berlin. A Jewish medical doctor and gay rights activist, Hirschfeld had campaigned against Paragraph 175 and had done much to champion the idea that homosexuality was innate. The youth destroyed Hirschfeld's large library, medical archive, and extensive correspondence, hauling away many of the books to the infamous book burning on the Opernplatz, a central square on Berlin's university campus (Figure 6.1). At the time of the attack, Hirschfeld was abroad—a lucky coincidence, given the thugs' declaration that they wished to "hang him or burn him to death." He would never return to Germany.[23]

Most of those convicted of breaking the long-standing law against gay sex were sent to prison. Paragraph 175, which had been on the books since 1871, used a very narrow definition of sex, which meant that many men evaded prosecution before the Nazi rise to power. Not satisfied with the existing legislation, the Nazis amended Paragraph 175 in 1935, making it much easier to prove guilt. The revision led to a wave of arrests in the years that followed. An estimated 100,000 men were convicted across the life of the regime. About 10 percent of convicted men ended up in concentration camps, where they were identified by a downward pointing pink triangle sewn on their uniforms. Purportedly incarcerated to be re-educated and returned to heterosexuality, they were targeted by camp and prison guards for degrading, at times sadistic, treatment. The homophobia of the regime was also used to target the Catholic Church and the pockets of resistance that existed in that institution. While surely homosexuality existed among priests and monks, and pedophilia was shamefully ignored by Church leaders, the regime sensationalized both matters to demonize all Catholic priests and brothers, weaken faith in the Church, and arrest large numbers of clergy.

For heterosexual "Aryan" men and women, the message was clear that procreation was the priority, but research in the last decade indicates that heterosexual pleasure was also considered desirable and even promoted among privileged groups in the Reich. For decades after 1945, Nazi society was considered a prudish one in which sex was considered solely as a means to an end—procreation between an "Aryan" husband and wife. It remains the case that when Nazi ideologues were writing for or speaking to audiences of Christian conservatives either before or after 1933, they tended to stress this limited view of sexuality. But we now understand that many Nazis also prized sex for pleasure, including premarital and extramarital sex. Sex was also thought to have health benefits, relieve stress, and increase labor productivity.

To some extent this pro-sex attitude replicated the arguments made by 1920s German sex reformers, many of whom like Magnus Hirschfeld were Jewish and/or members of the SPD or KPD. However, as we have seen, the Nazis viewed matters of gender difference and sexual behavior within the framework of an exclusive national community. Sex among Jews was therefore viewed as dirty or lascivious, and gay sex was considered perverted and policed. Sex between Jews and non-Jews was banned in 1935 as part of the Nuremberg Laws, and those arrested for breaking the law (or denounced on suspicion for having done so) were often humiliated publicly by SA men or other zealots. What we have added to the picture is that sex for fun was encouraged as another benefit of being "superior." Advertisements for hormonal therapies to improve sexual performance were included in mainstream magazines, and sexual pleasure rather than procreation was the explicit promise of an effective treatment. Divorce was made more accessible under Nazi leadership, reflecting the growing acceptance that couples should not be forced to stay together if the relationship was no longer sexually or otherwise satisfying.

As a result of this more permissive environment, teen pregnancies and sexually transmitted infections were on the rise among BDM and HJ members. One Nazi doctor reported that less than 5 percent of those individuals preparing for marriage he interviewed were still virgins, and many had had several partners, beginning their active sex lives in their late teens.[24] Pregnancies out of wedlock were tolerated by the NSDAP as long as the offspring was deemed "racially valuable" and healthy. In these cases, expectant mothers could receive assistance from party agencies. Some women were cared for in SS-run *Lebensborn* (Font of Life) houses where they stayed until delivery, after which the agency arranged adoption. *Lebensborn* homes also welcomed those children who were thought to have been fathered by elite SS men. By 1945, almost 10,000 children came out of these *Lebensborn* facilities, which comprised six maternity hospitals in Germany and eleven more in occupied Europe. That increasing numbers of Germans no longer viewed sex as shameful or sinful reflects trends seen elsewhere in the interwar period, but the regime's attack on parental and religious authorities, its glorification of youth, and its desire to see the population grow also persuaded Germans that members of the *Volk* could and should enjoy sex.

The fact that most Nazi leaders did not embody the ideals of "Aryan" masculinity has befuddled students of the movement since the 1920s. As we noted in Chapter 3, the fact that Hitler was not blond and did not father any children, that Goebbels had a birth defect, that Göring was decadent in his tastes and not physically fit, and that Ernst Röhm was gay, to cite but a few examples, puzzled observers then and today. But this last example is emblematic. After selecting Röhm in 1931 to quell dissent in the SA, Hitler defended the leader of the stormtroopers against those who saw his homosexuality as incompatible with the movement. At least he did so until Röhm was no longer useful. At that point, in the summer of 1934, Hitler used Röhm's homosexuality as part of the explanation for why he had become a liability to the regime and why he had to be murdered. In this case and in the others above, leaders whose behaviors or appearances did not conform to the Nazi ideals of masculinity or racial health still demonstrated a deep commitment to National Socialism and had talents that were valuable to their Führer. What matters in an unjust society is who holds the power to determine value. These were people whom Hitler trusted and made use of, and that was enough—at least until they were deemed expendable.

Notes

1   For example, see Lutz Raphael, "Radikales Ordnungsdenken und
    die Organisation totalitärer Herrschaft: Weltanschauungseliten

und Humanwissenschaftler im NS-Regime," *Geschichte und Gesellschaft* 27, no. 1 (2001): 5–40.

2   Melita Maschmann, *Account Rendered: A Dossier on my Former Self* (Lexington, MA: Plunkett Lake Press, 2013), 12.

3   Konrad Jarausch, *Broken Lives: How Ordinary Germans Experienced the Twentieth Century* (Princeton: Princeton University Press, 2018), 65.

4   "Guidelines for Teaching History" (1938), https://ghdi.ghi-dc.org/sub_document.cfm?document_id=1568

5   Marion A. Kaplan, *Between Dignity and Despair: Jewish Life in Nazi Germany* (New York: Oxford University Press, 1985), 95.

6   Richard J. Evans, *The Third Reich in Power* (New York: Penguin, 2006), 295.

7   Helmut Becker-Floris, "Aus meinem Leben im Dritten Reich (1935–9)," LebendigesMuseum Online, https://www.dhm.de/lemo/zeitzeugen/helmut-becker-floris-aus-meinem-leben-im-dritten-reich-1935-1939.html

8   Kurt Elfering, "In der Hitler-Jugend," Lebendiges Museum Online, https://www.dhm.de/lemo/zeitzeugen/kurt-elfering-in-der-hitler-jugend.html

9   Armin Nolzen, "Der Streifendienst der Hitler-Jugend (HJ) und die 'Überwachung der Jugend,' 1934–1945" in *Durchschnittstäter. Handeln und Motivation*, Christoph Dieckmann, Christian Gerlach, and Wolf Gruner, eds. (Berlin: Schwarze Risse, 2000), 36–7.

10 Baldur von Schirach, "The National Socialist Youth Movement" (1933) in *The Third Reich Sourcebook*, Anson Rabinbach and Sander Gilman, eds. (Berkeley: University of California Press, 2013), 254–55.

11 Kaplan, *Between Dignity and Despair*, 110.

12 Peter Fritzsche, *Life and Death in the Third Reich* (Cambridge, MA: Belknap, 2008), 106.

13 Ibid., 53.

14 Ibid., 55.

15 Sebastian Huebel, *Fighter, Worker, Family Man: German-Jewish Men and Their Gendered Experiences in Nazi Germany, 1933–1941* (Toronto: University of Toronto Press, 2022), 80.

16 Ibid., 84.

17 Dagmar Herzog, *Sex after Fascism: Memory and Morality in Twentieth-Century Germany* (Princeton: Princeton University Press, 2007), 10.

18 Jill Stephenson, "Inclusion: Building the National Community in Propaganda and Practice" in *Nazi Germany*, Jane Caplan, ed. (Oxford: Oxford University Press), 106.

19 Heinrich Himmler, "On Homosexuality and Abortion" (1936) in *The Third Reich Sourcebook*, Rabinbach and Gilman, eds., 375–6.

20 Jason Crouthamel, "Homosexuality and Comradeship: Destabilizing the Hegemonic Masculine Ideal in Nazi Germany" *Central European History* 51, no. 3 (2018): 419–39, here 425.

21 Heinrich Himmler, "Speech to SS Group Leaders" (1937) in *The Third Reich Sourcebook*, Rabinbach and Gilman, eds., 376.

22 Adolf Brand letter (1933) quoted in *Hidden Holocaust? Gay and Lesbian Persecution in Nazi Germany, 1933–1945*, Günter Grau, ed. (London: Routledge, 1995), 34–6.

23 Anonymous, "How Magnus Hirschfeld's Institute for Sexual Science was Demolished and Destroyed" (1933) in *The Third Reich Sourcebook*, Rabinbach and Gilman, eds., 367–9.

24 Herzog, *Sex after Fascism*, 29.

Additional Reading

Heineman, Elizabeth D. *What Difference Does a Husband Make? Marital Status in Nazi and Postwar Germany*. Berkeley: University of California Press, 1999.

Herzog, Dagmar. *Sex after Fascism: Memory and Morality in Twentieth-Century Germany*. Princeton and Oxford: Princeton University Press, 2005.

Kater, Michael. *Hitler Youth*. Cambridge, MA: Harvard University Press, 2004.

Koonz, Claudia. *Mothers in the Fatherland: Women, the Family, and Nazi Politics*. London and New York: Routledge, 1987.

Plant, Richard. *The Pink Triangle: The Nazi War against Homosexuals*. New York: H. Holt, 1986.

Reagin, Nancy R. *Sweeping the German Nation: Domesticity and National Identity in Germany, 1870–1945*. Cambridge, UK: Cambridge University Press, 2007.

Reese, Dagmar. *Growing up Female in Nazi Germany*. Translated by William Templer. Ann Arbor: University of Michigan Press, 2006.

Roche, Helen. *The Third Reich's Elite Schools: A History of the Napolas*. Oxford: Oxford University Press, 2021.

Stephenson, Jill. *Women in Nazi Germany*. London and New York: Routledge, 2013. First printed in 2001.

8

Nazi Germany and the World

We can begin our look at Nazi foreign relations by considering the first lines of the German national anthem. "Germany above all, above all else in the world," was written by progressive nineteenth-century poet Heinrich Hoffmann. It reflected a romantic-era desire to put love of Germany above partisan interests. Before Hitler, this opening stanza was followed by others that honored justice, brotherly love, and "wine and song." But in 1933 the Nazis stripped away these pacifist stanzas and paired the new version with a "co-national anthem," the *Horst Wessel Lied*. This song was about swastikas, flags, brown battalions, and a passion for violence. Horst Wessel, an SA man who penned the lyrics, had died fighting communists in 1930 and became a martyr to the Nazi cause. This symbolic pairing of "Germany above all" and militarized stormtroopers seemed to capture the essence of a regime that trampled the nations of Europe and waged a new war. But the path to the Second World War was not simply one of hyper-nationalist belligerence. If we are to understand how, two decades after the end of the Great War, Hitler plunged Europe into a new conflict, we must consider the Nazis' aggressive foreign policy alongside its "normal" engagement with the world. From 1933 to 1939, German foreign relations involved treaty violations, alliance building among fascist and non-fascist countries, and plans to racially purify Europe. But they also entailed trade agreements, cultural diplomacy, and showing off the "new Germany" to the world. Regardless of this Nazi internationalism, Hitler never wavered from his goal of bringing Germans outside the country's borders "back home to the Reich" and expanding the country at the risk—and hope—of a racial war of conquest.

Hitler's Foreign Policy Aims

Because Nazi foreign relations ended in a genocidal war, historians have debated how central racism was to Hitler's foreign policy. Was he a radical ideologue whose decisions reflected his hateful obsession with biological purity? Or was he a power-politician who tried to expand his country in an era when all countries were vying for global influence and clinging to their empires? The answer is "both." Hitler was committed to making room for the "Aryan" race by expelling or destroying other populations in Europe, but he was also a pragmatic tactician who could alter his plans. He cut deals and wooed allies and enemies, but he was also a radical bent on global power. He was a risk taker and a keen predictor of international responses to his geopolitical moves, and he relied on his intuitive ability to understand the calculations of political and military leaders until that intuition failed him.

Whatever else we are to call him, Hitler was a militarist. From the beginning of his public life in the 1920s, he spoke of a new war and the securing of "world domination for centuries." In his *Second Book*, dictated in 1928 and unpublished until long after the Second World War, Hitler offered a stage-by-stage plan for achieving this aim. Germany would rearm, destroy neighboring states, conquer the Soviet Union, and eventually take on the United States in a show-down for global hegemony. This future war with America would be a far-off event. Within Hitler's lifetime, the USSR was the ultimate prize. That country was, in the Nazi leader's mind, "not a state but an ideology." It was the bastion of "Jewish" communism or "Judeo-Bolshevism" that needed to be eradicated. Hitler saw the Russian Revolution as led by radical Jews committed to exporting communist revolts around the world, including to Germany. In the immediate aftermath of the First World War, when communists faced off against right-wing paramilitaries and, in some cases, took over city governments, Hitler became obsessed with what he saw as an existential danger to Germany.

Hitler also focused on the geographical location and racial makeup of the Soviet Union. Bolshevism, according to Nazi ideologue Alfred Rosenberg, was not a political system. It was a "revolt of Jewish, Slavic, and Mongolian races" against the "German elements" in the Soviet Union—people who had settled there in the seventeenth and eighteenth centuries who Rosenberg felt were responsible for Russia's greatest accomplishments. Hitler and many before him bemoaned Germany's confinement to the center of Europe, with a threatening France to the west and the Slavic countries, made up of racially lesser people, to the east. Hitler dreamed of finding *Lebensraum* or "living space" for Germans. The Nazis drew this geopolitical concept, in part, from the work of geographer and Munich Professor Karl Haushofer, who had popularized an expansionist, biological understanding of foreign policy. In this view, Germany's survival necessitated a Darwinian struggle among races and nations for resources and territory. As Hitler would proclaim to his generals in 1937, Germany comprised over 85 million people and was a "tightly packed racial core" that as such had a "right to greater living space than in the case of other people." In this respect, the Nazis saw themselves as leading one of many national liberation movements to free their people and assure their survival.

This vision merged economics and ethnicity. Hitler hoped to realize a long-standing goal from the prior century of establishing economic control of central Europe. Germany would enrich itself and provide a counterweight to the United States, whose financial and political power and its conquering of "living space" and resources through westward expansion (at the expense of Native Americans) preoccupied him. In Hitler's mind, Germany would no longer be confined to "Middle Europe." The Reich, as a major exporter, needed resources and markets. It would have to secure the oil fields of the Caucasus mountains and the wheat fields of Ukraine, which would feed settlements of Germans who would displace Slavs and, of course, Jews. The future of Germany as a racially pure, self-sufficient, mass production and consumption economy lay in the east. Hitler envisioned the USSR's vast expanse of territory, stretching from Europe to the Pacific Ocean, as the future place for ethnic Germans to settle, reproduce, and work. Only a victorious war with the Soviet Union could help realize this dream.

Belligerence and Pragmatism

The success of this plan depended on the destruction of the Treaty of Versailles. Since the signing of this peace agreement in 1919, most German politicians had called for the end to what they saw as a humiliating, shameful settlement. This "disgraceful dictate" had reduced the country's armed forces to 100,000 troops and its navy to six ships, and it had forbidden an air force. Germany had to stop producing offensive weapons, give up large swaths of territory to Poland, submit itself to military occupation, pay billions of marks in cash and material reparations, and take the blame for starting the war. Even non-Germans felt that this had been a harsh punishment, and Hitler's efforts to undo the treaty gained a measure of support in Britain and the United States.

After coming to power, the Nazis spent the next six years violating the terms of the treaty and protesting what they saw as the unequal treatment of their country. In October of 1933, Germany withdrew from the League of Nations and the disarmament conference held in Geneva that month. The regime's stated reason was that the western nations had refused to grant military parity to the Reich. In fact, as we saw in Chapter 5, Germany had already begun to rearm illegally during the Weimar years, and Hitler made clear that his aim of eastern conquest depended on the immediate rebuilding of the military and armaments programs. In the summer of 1933, the government made plans to devote 5–10 percent of the country's GDP to the military, a large figure by most historical standards and one that continued to climb (see Plate 12). Accordingly, millions of rifles, mortars, and ammunition rounds rolled off the assembly lines of German factories in the coming years. Around the same time, in 1934, Hitler declared a moratorium on the payment of its foreign debts. It was not lost upon the country's creditors that this money was going to weapons.

Despite this early rearmament and his rejection of international treaties, Hitler proved to have a pragmatic streak that involved making deals with other countries. Germany's path to Russia depended on subduing eastern Europe, but Hitler needed to move cautiously. As part of its "peace politics" aimed at gaining international legitimacy, Germany secured a ten-year non-aggression pact with Poland in January of 1934. The two countries recognized each other's borders and agreed to settle conflicts through negotiations. The British, who looked favorably on this "statesmanlike" agreement, also engaged in their own diplomacy with Hitler. Unlike the French, who bristled at any suggestion of a normalized and rearmed Germany, the British were amenable to revisions of Versailles if it prevented the total diplomatic isolation of Hitler. In June 1935 the two countries signed the Anglo-German Naval Agreement, according to which Germany agreed to keep the total tonnage of its navy to 35 percent of Britain's. For his part, Hitler saw Britain as a natural ally, one that would eventually align with Germany to maintain a balance of power against France. He had spoken of his regret that Germany and Britain had not allied during the First World War. As Nazi propaganda pointed out, both countries were "Aryan" and like Germany, Britain was "plagued" by the presence of Jewish financiers. In addition, the Nazis admired Britain's ability to rule over a vast empire of Black and Brown people, who could be utilized in labor and the military. For their part, many British elites looked favorably on Hitler's fight against Bolshevism and his ability to instill pride in his people.

Foreign Responses and Foreign Relations

The British attitude to Hitler captures the complex range of responses to the new German government. To be sure, many global leaders saw Hitler as a dangerous racist and nationalist who had seized power. In response to Hitler's Jewish policies, politicians and activists around the world launched protest campaigns and multiyear boycotts of German goods (Figure 8.1). The American League for the Defense of Jewish Rights pressured stores to remove imported German products from their shelves. Thousands of people in London's East End marched to the German embassy carrying placards reading "Buy no German goods," and "Boycott goods made by Nazi bloodstained hands." The Nazis disingenuously portrayed their blockade of Jewish stores on April 1, 1933, as a justified response to this foreign boycott movement and what they called the "atrocity propaganda" being used to unfairly malign Germany on the world stage. It apparently did not dawn on the Nazi regime that responding to "false claims" of Jewish mistreatment with a very public assault on Jews would open it up to more international scrutiny.

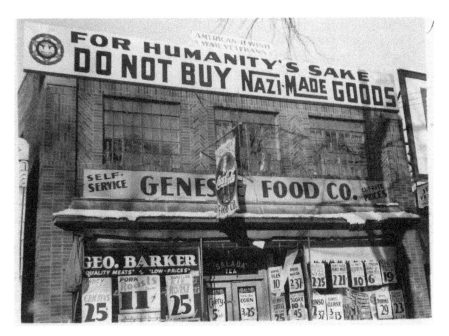

FIGURE 8.1 *Boycott of German goods by an American-Jewish veterans organization, 1930s (Public Domain; Records of the Office of Alien Property, Record Group 131; National Archives at College Park, College Park, MD).*

Over the course of the 1930s foreign correspondents in Germany and consular officials increasingly depicted Nazi antisemitism as a frightening "break in civilization." So did African American writer W. E. B. Du Bois, who spent part of 1936 on a fellowship in Berlin. He wrote that "there has been no tragedy in modern times equal in its awful effects to the fight on the Jew in Germany."[1] Du Bois had fallen in love with the country as an exchange student in Berlin in the 1890s. Now shaken by Nazi brutality, he compared Jewish persecution to the transatlantic slave trade and argued that Nazi antisemitism had "set civilization back a hundred years." The Danish envoy to Berlin Herluf Zahle had already reported in 1933 that Nazi violence was "worse than the Middle Ages."[2] American pastor C. R. Clinchy, director of the National Council of Jews and Christians, declared that the Nazi persecution of Jews "is an admission to the civilized world that humanitarianism in Germany, one of our most cultured countries, has not far progressed beyond the point of the Huguenot Massacres and the Spanish Inquisition."[3] In 1935, British author Virginia Woolf and her Jewish husband drove across Germany and wrote an unflattering portrait of a crowd of "native savages" who carried antisemitic placards and rapturously awaited a visit by Göring.[4] American author Thomas Wolfe came to Germany in 1935 and again in 1936 and documented his growing disillusionment with the country he once loved. In his final visit, he reflected on the "good" and increasingly the "evils" of fascism.[5]

Despite foreign disapproval, the Nazis recognized that many individuals abroad ignored or even embraced Hitler's authoritarian rule, his anticommunism, and his ethno-nationalism. In the late 1930s there was a wave of right-wing populism, ultra-nationalism, and fascism across the globe: Eoin O'Duffy's "blueshirts" in Ireland, Sir Oswald Mosley's "blackshirts" in Britain, the "goldshirts" of Mexico, and the "brownshirts" of South Africa. These movements embraced antisemitism to varying degrees, often drawing upon their own home-grown strains of cultural, economic, and religious hostility toward Jews as "capitalists" and "Bolsheviks" rather than the biological racism of the Nazi regime. The Falangists in Spain, for example, had little interest in racial antisemitism and felt that the "Jewish problem" could be solved through conversion to Christianity. Regardless, many populist regimes and movements expressed admiration for National Socialism and mimicked features of its anti-Jewish language and policies. And Hitler sought to reach out to them. The Foreign Office, the Propaganda Ministry, and the German Foreign Institute, which studied race and "ethnic Germanness" abroad, compiled bulky files of newspaper clippings on every aspect of racial theory and antisemitism throughout the world—from Australia to the United States to Scandinavia. These collections helped the regime craft press releases that celebrated anti-Jewish actions across the globe. Their contents also capture Germans' eagerness to engage in transnational dialogues about the "Jewish problem." The NSDAP's "Foreign Organization" office worked directly with Nazi Party affiliates in Latin America, Africa, and Sweden. In South Africa, fascists not only identified themselves as "national socialist," but members of the Afrikaner Nationalist Party also expressed a cultural and linguistic affinity with Germany. D. F. Malan, leader of the Purified National Party and later prime minister of South Africa after the Second World War, referred to Jews in a 1934 speech as "parasites" that had to be "removed." Closer to home, Anton Mussert's National Socialist Movement in the Netherlands spearheaded an antisemitic campaign in 1935, receiving almost 8 percent of the national vote that year. Finally, in the United States, numerous academics, politicians, and public figures admired the Nazis' authoritarianism and antisemitism. Christian fundamentalist writer William Dudley Pelly's Silver Legion of America went well beyond the fascist German-American Bund, a movement of German Americans that sponsored pro-Nazi rallies and Hitler-youth like summer camps. The 15,000-member Silver Shirts called for the elimination—indeed the murder—of American Jews.

The Nazis also looked to the Muslim world for support of their antisemitism. In 1938, the National Socialist press translated into German one of the Grand Mufti's tirades against Jews, and the regime prepared an antisemitic propaganda blitz in the Arab world. A Persian language pro-National Socialist paper called *The New World* celebrated a global order being paved by National Socialism. In addition, German Radio programs were disseminated throughout the Persianate world.

Germany's international engagement did not only center on racial policy and anticommunism. Hitler admired President Mustafa Kemal Atatürk's nationalism and one-man rule in Turkey, and the Nazis even classified Turks as "Aryans" under the Nuremberg Laws. And during the Second World War, he welcomed to Berlin nationalist Arabs, Indians, and Central Asians, who saw the Nazi war against their colonial overlords as opening a path to their own countries' independence. These and other foreigners' interest in Germany went beyond antisemitism. Early in the Nazi years, economic and academic leaders had a practical interest in maintaining ties to the Reich. Trade representatives from South America to Australia to Canada toured factories and made business deals with industrialists. Administrators and professors at American universities, some of whom were antisemites, maintained scholarly relations and student exchange programs with their German counterparts. The Nazi regime recognized the economic importance of cultivating these relations. Coming out of the Great Depression, Germany experienced a steady export slump, thus necessitating these continued cultural and economic contacts. Germany needed the income to pay for the increased imports of raw materials for its war buildup. It also needed imported food and finished goods for the populace and cash to service its debts. Goodwill from abroad and celebrations of the regime's openness (as opposed to Jewish "cosmopolitanism") could have only positive results.

Not only lay people but also celebrities flocked to Germany. The Duke of Windsor, who had recently abdicated the British throne and who made no secret of his admiration for Hitler, traveled with his American wife Wallis Simpson to the Reich in 1937. They dined with Goebbels, Göring, and other Nazi dignitaries, responded with warmth to Nazi salutes, and toured factories producing weapons soon to be used against the Duke and Duchess's home countries. Of more strategic importance was Mussolini's visit in 1937, which celebrated a new military alliance between the two fascist states. In a highly choreographed event, the *Führer* and the *Duce* (Leader) presented the "Rome-Berlin Axis" as an alluring, masculine alternative to a weak and unheroic liberal internationalism (Figure 8.2). One admirer from afar, US automaker Henry Ford, made no secret of his attraction to fascism. In 1938 the German consulate in Detroit repaid his adoration of Hitler with the Grand Cross of the German Eagle, the highest honor the Nazis could bestow upon a foreigner. Ford and Hitler's mutual admiration rested not only on their shared hatred of Jews, but also on Hitler's dream of creating a mobile society, with Volkswagens—inspired by Ford's Model T—moving Germans across the autobahns of an economically bustling Reich.

Nazi Germany hosted some unexpected visitors to the Reich, namely African Americans, who were well attuned to the experience of racial segregation. Everyday discrimination and rules about proper sexual relations already targeted Afro-Germans in 1933, but Black Americans—at least for

FIGURE 8.2 *Benito Mussolini and Adolf Hitler. The Italian dictator, whom Germany's Führer greatly admired, came to Berlin for a state visit in 1937, to the Munich Conference in 1938, and early in the war again to Munich, as depicted in this photo from June 1940 (https://creativecommons.org/licenses/by-sa/4.0, via Wikimedia Commons).*

a short time—continued to enjoy Germany's cultural offerings. The capital city remained a site of vibrant exchange. Mollie Lewis, a visiting African American student at the University of Berlin, finished her German stay in December 1933 with only positive things to say about her host country. In August 1934 forty-one African Americans traveled to Berlin for the World Baptist Congress, where they were by all accounts treated graciously. J. Raymond Henderson, an Atlanta pastor, reported "if there exist(ed) any race feeling as concerns the Negroes, it was conspicuous for its absence during the time we were there."[6] Thomas W. Patrick, scion of an elite Black family in New England, completed a five-year study of medicine at University of Berlin in 1936. He returned to Boston with a white German bride and some pointed observations about the dignity the Nazis accorded him, in contrast to the prejudice he encountered in the United States. But as Hitler consolidated his dictatorship and ramped up his attacks on minorities, these transatlantic connections were severed. As we have seen, the Nazis banned "Black music," namely jazz, and the great African American contralto Marian Anderson was declared unwelcome in National Socialist Germany, having dared to sing German *Lieder*.

Why were foreign observers fascinated by the Third Reich? Everyone liked a good success story. A "new Germany" seemed to have risen from the Great Depression like a phoenix from the ashes. Before breaking with Germany, novelist Wolfe wrote that "a dictatorship at full strength has an impressive aura of glittering success."[7] For some, it was not the monumentalism but the everyday enjoyments of a "normal" Germany. In the summer of 1937, a young John F. Kennedy traveled through the Reich, where the future US president took in the allures of Munich's famed Hofbräu beer house and the city's magnificent science and technology museum. He then admired the castles along the Rhine during a boat tour. During his stay, he even watched the Hollywood movie *Swing High, Swing Low*, which featured American bars, night clubs, music, and romance. Kennedy noted the popularity of Hitler, which he attributed to massive propaganda. But the regime's ability to manipulate the public did not put a damper on the American's trip.

Here was a country that defied all labels. National Socialist Germany was a dictatorship whose popularity was at once real and manufactured. It was a popular "democracy" (in the sense that on paper, the people approved of Hitler in plebiscites); it was a quasi-monarchy; it was a cult of personality. Scholars, journalists, and foreign officers tried to understand this unique experiment: Was the Nazi regime a chaotic government or a stable autocracy? Was racism central to its core, or did anti-Jewish persecution represent a passing phase? Whatever their answers, the Hitler regime provoked international discussions about the strengths and weaknesses of fascism and National Socialism as governing systems and social experiments.

The March to War

In its first five years, the Third Reich presented itself as a global citizen. But all the while, Hitler was preparing for war. As part of his plan, the Nazis hoped to install friendly regimes beyond Germany's borders. In 1934 they unleashed their followers in Austria, who constituted an illegal party in Hitler's home country, to conduct an ultimately failed coup that resulted in the murder of the fascist but anti-Nazi Chancellor Engelbert Dollfuss. When Hitler realized that Italy, which bordered Austria, and the western powers saw this as a threat to stability, he denied knowledge of the plan and disavowed the July Putsch. Hitler also intervened in the Spanish Civil War (1936–9) on the side of General Francisco Franco, who led a group of conservatives, nationalists, and monarchists against the left-leaning Republican government. Hitler would not tolerate the possibility of a "communist" Spain, which could then export its depraved ideology into France and encircle Germany in the west and east. Germany provided Franco's falangist rebels with weapons and air support.

In 1935 Hitler embarked on a series of gambles that, he hoped, would allow him to meet his economic, diplomatic, and ideological goals. The

mixed foreign response to National Socialism outlined above gave him a
sense that even with warnings not to violate the status quo, the world was
weary of containing Germany. Even before the naval treaty, Hitler signed
a secret decree in February 1935 authorizing the rebuilding of the German
air force alongside the army and the navy. The following month he ordered
universal male military conscription in the name of Germany's "protection,"
with updated plans to establish an army of 480,000 soldiers and 36 divisions.
The proclamation did not formally renounce the Treaty of Versailles, but the
12,000 people at Berlin's Sports Palace who listened joyously to Goebbels'
emotional reading of the order had little doubt that the "shameful peace"
ushered in by Versailles was tottering.

As Hitler embarked on this massive rearmament, he was encouraged to
see that the international arrangements put in place at the end of the First
World War to stop a resurgent Germany were foundering. Notable was
the League of Nations. Reflecting the isolationism of the postwar years,
the United States had never joined this organization, depriving it of the most
powerful political and economic force in the world. Moreover, the Nazis
watched in 1935 as Mussolini—inspired by Germany's forceful foreign
policy—invaded Abyssinia and launched a victorious war in Ethiopia. Hitler
congratulated the *Duce* on Italy's rebuilding of a new Roman Empire in
Africa. The League of Nations condemned Mussolini's move and imposed
economic sanctions, but Italy was undeterred, and without an international
oil embargo on the country, Italy could withstand the patchy arms, loan,
and import embargoes. Indeed, Germany provided munitions to the Italians
and, in a pragmatic move unbeknownst to Mussolini, also to its opponents
in Africa. With the invasion, so ended the "Stresa Front" of Britain, France,
and Italy, united for just a few months in 1935 by a loose promise to resist
further violations of the Treaty of Versailles.

That same year Hitler prepared for a League of Nations-sponsored
referendum in the French border region of Saarland, which had been under
international control since the war. Saarlanders headed to the polls in March
to decide whether to be part of France or Germany. Over 90 percent of
voters chose to reunite with Germany, thus unleashing a nationalist wave
of support for Hitler and his revanchist policies. In a letter to Hitler, two
sisters expressed their gratitude that their homeland would once again be
part of Germany. "With overflowing hearts we would like to thank you
for having restored its honor and freedom to our beloved Fatherland. May
heaven bless you and your work, esteemed Führer, so that you can lead our
German Fatherland to greater heights."[8] This outpouring of joy even led
expatriate Saarlanders from throughout the world to travel to the Reich to
take part in the celebrations.

In 1935 things were very much going Hitler's way as the League of
Nations had proven itself toothless. Danish Ambassador Zahle mused that
Hitler was a "fantastically lucky" man. The Saar plebiscite only consolidated
a view—unjustified, in the ambassador's mind—that this was a victory for

the entire National Socialist system. Hitler could revel in his country being "stronger internationally and even stronger at home."[9] Germany began to notch win after win and, with hindsight, we can begin to trace the march to war. Even through the following year, Hitler's aggressive moves could be seen as somehow legitimate and in keeping with postwar international commitments to national self-determination. Saarlanders *wanted* to be part of Germany. But so did the people in the territory west of the Rhine River, an area of Germany along the French border that the Great War victors had occupied after 1918. They too were Germans, who felt they deserved the Wehrmacht's protective presence. In 1930 the French ended their military occupation, which, in accordance with the Treaty of Versailles, they replaced with a demilitarization of the Rhineland. This area, 30 miles wide and now devoid of troops, served as a buffer along the French, Belgian, and Dutch borders and was designed to prevent a German invasion. Any takeover of the territory would be a violation of law.

In 1936, to the distress of his more cautious generals, Hitler drafted plans to send troops into the Rhineland demilitarized zone. He framed such a move as a legitimate response to a Franco-Soviet Treaty of Mutual Assistance of that year, which aimed to envelop Germany diplomatically. On March 7, 1936, a nervous Hitler sent 3,000 Wehrmacht troops into Cologne, Düsseldorf, Frankfurt, and other cities in the demilitarized zone. When he heard that French troops were gathering at the border of Germany, he considered withdrawing, duly noting his generals' pleas to back down. But Hitler carried through, while an unprepared and intimidated Britain and France flinched. This was a humiliating display of weakness on the part of the west. But it had avoided war and took comfort in the knowledge that the Maginot Line, a strip of fortifications along the French borders with Italy, Germany, Switzerland, and Luxembourg, would surely prove impenetrable should Germany try to invade as it had in 1914.

Germans' jubilant response to the remilitarization of the Rhineland echoed the reaction to the Saar plebiscite. This success was significant for two reasons. First, with this move, the west lost its upper hand vis-à-vis Nazi Germany. Thereafter an empowered Hitler felt that he could revise Europe's borders with impunity. Second, this victory consolidated Hitler's popularity at home and began to bring the people along with him toward ever-greater belligerence and criminality. The "Hitler myth" exalted the leader. With almost divine protection, Hitler could do no wrong. He had pulled the economy out of the Depression, he had rebuilt German pride, and he had repossessed the country's lost territories. Whatever qualms Germans might have had about racial violence, they could revel in the belief that they had reclaimed a proud place in the world. This did not mean that Germans wanted war. But it did mean that they—in their own telling—no longer needed to suffer as eternal victims.

After the reoccupation of the Rhineland, the Western powers had little doubt Hitler was determined to take more territory. Neither did the Nazi government and military. Indeed, in his "Four-Year Plan Memorandum" of August of 1936, which laid out a plan for economic autarky, Hitler "prophesied" that war was coming soon. Again, we see a combination of ideological and practical aims. He argued that since the French Revolution, which the Nazis saw as inaugurating a dangerous era of liberal individualism, the world had inevitably been moving toward a showdown with Bolshevism and "worldwide Jewry" that it seemingly represented. This war would eventually reach Germany, and in a proactive posture, the Reich would have to "protect itself"—materially and militarily—or be annihilated. With this memo, Hitler again demonstrated a consistent linking of economics and foreign policy with his core ideological obsessions—Jews and communism. He also brought to fore the sense of victimization that would define much of Hitler's rhetoric until his death. Any war Germany involved itself in would be a *defensive* one, launched by Jews and forced upon Germany as a life-or-death struggle.

The obsession with Judeo-Bolshevism was on further display in November when Germany and Japan (later joined by Italy and Spain) signed an "anti-Comintern pact." Japan was waging a brutal war of occupation in China and across Asia, and this agreement shored up each state's anti-communist credentials and provided military cover in the far east. The countries' respective ambassadors promised that Germany and Japan would ally themselves in any future attack against the USSR and would remain neutral in the case of a Soviet attack on one of them. They also agreed not to conclude any separate treaties with Moscow. Despite its name ("Comintern" was the organization representing the global communist movement), this agreement had less to do with the abstract horrors of Bolshevism than an attempt to maintain spheres of influence around the globe. Japan would control the Pacific, Germany would dominate Europe, and Italy would have at least a small foothold in Africa. The year 1936 marked a turn to a more aggressive foreign policy, driven by ideological obsessions, Hitler's massive popularity and increasing confidence, and the quest for natural resources like iron ore and oil that rearmament demanded. The Nazi regime still held out hope that Britain would ally with Germany, but this could no longer be taken for granted by the end of 1936.

A Peaceful Interlude

The memorandum accompanying the Four-Year Plan clearly indicated Hitler's bellicose intentions. But a growing anxiety abroad was tempered when the world descended on Berlin for the 1936 Summer Olympics. After Hitler came to power, the American Jewish Congress had worked to deny Germany the winter games in Garmisch-Partenkirchen and the summer games in Berlin, which had been determined in 1931. In response to attempts to pull the games, the Nazis promised that the competition would be conducted in the "Olympic Spirit" and that Jews would not be discriminated against. Germany's efforts were supported by the president of the US Olympic Committee Avery Brundage, who denounced the boycott as a "Jewish-Communist conspiracy." The International Olympic Committee (IOC) also took the regime at its word. By the times the summer games opened, Hitler had built or retrofitted twenty-one arenas, erected training facilities, and constructed a new stadium in the capital that could hold 100,000 spectators. Nazi monumentalism was on full display, but in keeping with its promise to the IOC, antisemitism was not. During the sixteen days of the summer Olympics, from August 1 to August 16, the regime removed racist signage in Berlin, and the domestic and foreign press played down the persecution of Jews. The Nazis' cynical gesture of goodwill belied the fact that they had prevented German Jews from participating in the games and had made it clear that foreign Jewish athletes were unwelcome (though some came anyway). Despite any qualms about going to "Hitler Germany," almost 4,000 athletes representing thirty-nine countries competed. Germany won the most medals, to the Nazis a supposed victory for the "Aryan" race. But the German public also fell in love with African American star Jesse Owens, who won four gold medals in track and field (Figure 8.3). While some Nazi journalists portrayed this as a shameful defeat of the white race to a Black man—and the US press hyped up Hitler's supposed snub of the star from Alabama—Owens recalled only hospitality, in marked contrast to his treatment back in the US South.

The 1936 Olympics was Nazi Germany's moment in the sun. During the games, civic associations, factories, museums, and cinemas welcomed guests from abroad. These foreigners were greeted with speeches about global harmony and international cooperation. At the summer games, Joseph Goebbels delivered a speech about the "resonating power of personal relationships between individuals from country to country." Members of the Rotary Club in Bielefeld remarked with excitement that the Propaganda Minister's speech had embodied the very goals of their movement. They saw themselves as ambassadors of goodwill who gave Nazi Germany a welcoming face to the rest of the world. For a moment in the summer of 1936, one could indulge in the illusion that Hitler was a cosmopolitan statesman and Nazi Germany was a "normal" country.

The Nazis built on the success of the Olympics at the following's year's Paris World's Fair. The German pavilion, which Hitler's architect Albert Speer designed as a monument to "German Pride and Achievement," drew 31 million visitors. Nazi architect Josef Thorak's bronze sculptures of muscular males graced the pavilion entrance. Depending on how one interpreted the artwork's name, "Comradeship," these statues embodied either "Aryan" racial unity or international solidarity. Either way, they beckoned tourists to enter the pavilion and survey the fruits of German industriousness and unity—technology, machinery, music, and Leni Riefenstahl's film, *Triumph of the Will*.

FIGURE 8.3 *Medal ceremony for the long jump at the Berlin Olympics, August 11, 1936. Athletes from left to right, Naoto Tajima (Japan, bronze), Jesse Owens (the United States, gold); Carl Ludwig "Luz" Long (Germany, silver) (Bundesarchiv, Bild 183-G00630/Unknown author/CC-BY-SA 3.0, CC BY-SA 3.0 DE, via Wikimedia Commons).*

The German pavilion stood as a metaphor for the country's relationship with the world in 1937: an invitation to experience the sights and sounds of a "new" Germany; an ambiguous gesture of global unity and racial exclusivity; and a statement of German industrial might. In a foreshadowing of a coming war, bright spotlights were trained on the muscular bodies in front of the pavilion, showcasing Germanic physical strength in the Parisian night sky. In another representative move, the Expo planners intentionally placed the German pavilion directly across from the Soviet one in a symbolic showdown between fascism and communism. By 1938, these "world views" had adherents around the globe, and pundits debated the merits of each system. Which provided more creature comforts? Which was more economically efficient, future oriented, and socially egalitarian? Visitors in Paris could debate these questions as they moved between the two pavilions. But in Spain 500 miles south, the competition was anything but symbolic. Shortly before the World Fair's opening, German and Italian planes had bombed the Basque town of Guernica, killing hundreds of civilians and shoring up Franco's positions against Soviet-backed Republicans. The aerial bombardment inspired Pablo Picasso's famous oil canvas, which depicted the dying screams and dismemberment of the town's citizens. Historians have seen the Spanish Civil War as a rehearsal for the Second World War—fascism assaulting the forces of democracy and freedom. In October, President Roosevelt condemned the "Nazi-fascist" aggressors in Spain, where 3,000 American members in the Lincoln Brigade fought alongside Soviet volunteers and other foreign nationals in the name of anti-fascism. In November of 1937, as the final visitors moved through the Paris Expo and the two sides were stalemated on the Spanish battlefields, Hitler was meeting with his generals to plan his next moves.

Nazi Aggression

In November of 1937 Adolf Hitler held a secret meeting with his German military and foreign policy leadership. The so-called Hossbach Memorandum, named for the adjutant colonel who took notes, documents the words of a confident leader determined to realize his ideological goals. In the Reich Chancellery building, the Führer once again offered thoughts of war, now with a timetable in mind. Depending on Germany's economic and military readiness, the war to create "living space" could begin as early as the following year but no later than 1943. Hitler went over a list of areas where Germany could be economically self-sufficient (in coal production and synthetic textile manufacturing) and where it had to rely on trade or conquest. Copper, tin, and most importantly, food depended on Germany's move outward, starting with Austria and Czechoslovakia. Japan and Italy were re-establishing empires, and with the exhaustion of German soil, the country needed its own. It must find resources, or, so Nazi leaders argued, Germany faced extinction.

Hitler's loose blueprint for war in the early years of the dictatorship had now become more solid. Pushed by economic pressures and his own ideological obsessions, he hoped to choose the time and place of this war. What kind of war did Hitler foresee? He envisioned not a global conflagration but localized wars of plunder and annexation that would allow him to feed and arm his country, prepare it for future conflicts, and maintain a high standard of living. As long as Britain controlled the seas, Germany would have to be proactive in finding resources to the east. An annexation of Austria and Czechoslovakia, Hitler noted, could provide "foodstuffs for 5 to 6 million people." At the meeting, Hitler tested out a variety of scenarios that would follow German military moves. He assessed the number of French and British army divisions, the effectiveness of Czech fortifications, how Poland might react to an invasion of its neighbors, and whether its actions in the east might provoke a civil war in a stunned and politically divided France. During the meeting, Hitler vented his anger at France and the United Kingdom, these "hate-inspired antagonists." For a man who still dreamed of a racial and political alliance with Britain, this was a sober assessment. Striking in the Hossbach Memorandum are phrases that came to define the actual course of events in the next few years. Attacks would happen at "lightning speed." The British and the French would "write off" the Czechs. "Surprise" and "swiftness" would be the keys to military success. Hitler did not predict immediate conflicts with France and Britain. But he had to plan for any eventuality.

The November gathering at the Reich Chancellery shows Hitler on a path to war. It left his generals shaken. During the meeting, an anxious Colonel General Werner von Fritsch, Commander in Chief of the army, and War minister Field Marshal Werner von Blomberg "repeatedly emphasized the necessity that Britain and France must not appear in the role of our enemies."[10] After the summit, both men, along with Foreign Minister Konstantin von Neurath, worried openly that Hitler overestimated the political instability of France and the likelihood that—according to one of Hitler's ideas—the Spanish Civil War might lead to diversionary battles in the Mediterranean that would pull western attention away from Czechoslovakia. They feared that Hitler also underestimated the potential for the western powers to act should Germany move east. In preparation for any war in the west, they felt, Germany needed more time to rearm.

Hitler reacted to his generals' squeamishness with a defiant purge of the Reich's military and political leadership. In February of 1938, he replaced Foreign Minister Neurath with Joachim von Ribbentrop, a dyed-in-the-wool Nazi who had negotiated the anti-Comintern pact and who would not question Hitler's aggressive plans. He also ousted Fritsch, under the pretense that the general was gay (a male prostitute was paid to testify against him) and that he was planning a coup against Hitler. The SS doctored a file to conflate Fritsch with a cavalry captain named Frisch, who had in fact been found engaging in compromising acts. That left Blomberg. To smear him, the Nazis drew attention to the fact that the woman he had recently married had been a prostitute and had posed for pornographic photos. This gave Hitler "evidence" that Blomberg was likewise unfit for office. The general resigned his post in disgrace, and Hitler took personal command of the military. He made himself Supreme Commander of the Wehrmacht, abolished the Ministry of War, and transferred its duties to a new organization, the Supreme Command of the Armed Forces under Wilhelm Keitel. Gone were many of the old aristocratic elites, and in their place were committed Nazis who would follow Hitler into battle.

Supported by loyalists, Hitler moved on to his long sought-after prize, his home country of Austria. When the disparate German-speaking kingdoms and duchies unified in 1871, some had hoped to see Austria as part of the new Reich. Prussian premier Otto von Bismarck, who saw Austria as a Catholic, anti-Prussian irritant, orchestrated a "small Germany" solution that left out this neighbor to the South. But the dream of absorbing Austria into a "greater German" nation-state never faded, and after 1933, with Hitler, an Austrian, in charge of the Reich government, talk of an *Anschluss*, or an adjoining, grew louder. Hitler made no secret of his desire for this unification, and activists on the ground in Austria began pressing for such a move.

At the beginning of 1938 tensions in Europe were growing, and Hitler's territorial moves would greatly depend on how Britain might respond. On a visit to Germany two years earlier, former UK Prime Minister David Lloyd George, who had negotiated the Treaty of Versailles in 1919, professed a change of heart about Britain's former foe. He declared that "Chancellor Adolf Hitler is one of the greatest of the many great men I have ever met." He went on: "I have never seen a happier people than the Germans," with their "universal adoration" of Hitler throughout the Reich. The Nazi system, he asserted, is "a great achievement."[11] That was 1936. But what did the British think now? Current Prime Minister Chamberlain may not have waxed enthusiastic like Lloyd George, but his foreign policy rested on the appeasement of Germany in the name of European stability. At the time appeasement was a widely accepted understanding of politics that entailed overlooking one country's violation of treaties in order to forge policies that could benefit multiple countries and maintain peace. Indeed, after the Rhineland crisis, Chamberlain not only accepted Hitler's violation of the Treaty of Versailles but even raised the idea of returning to Germany the African colonies it had lost after the First World War. Overseas recolonization was not a high priority for the Nazis, despite pressure from some lobbyists, but Chamberlain's suggestion reveals an overzealousness to offer concessions. The prime minister seemed to be looking at German imperialism from a British perspective, where overseas territories were important for raw materials. Unlike the island nation of Britain, which depended on far-flung colonies, Germans' imperial ambitions lay, for the time being, on the European continent and entailed a racial war of attrition.

In February of 1938, as Hitler was reorganizing his military, Chamberlain approached the Austrian government to sell them on the idea of unification with Germany. Austrian Nazis had already been bullying Chancellor Kurt Schuschnigg to assent to a union with Germany. As tensions increased, Hitler invited Schuschnigg to his alpine retreat in Berchtesgaden, near the Austrian border, where imposing SS men stood at attention as Hitler berated the Austrian chancellor. The Führer presented Schuschnigg with a list of demands, including putting Nazis in key positions of power in Vienna. An intimidated Austrian chancellor left the meeting even more intent on saving his country, and after granting concessions to his political opponents and expanding voter eligibility in order to attract more anti-Nazis, Schuschnigg called for a March referendum on Austrian national independence that he assumed he would win. When an infuriated Hitler learned of the upcoming vote, he demanded that the plebiscite be canceled and that Schuschnigg step down and give all power to the Nazis or risk invasion. This ultimatum expired at noon on March 11 without action by Schuschnigg. The next morning, Germany entered Austria. Citizens greeted the invading soldiers with cheers, flowers, and cries of "Heil Hitler." Later that day, Hitler entered his hometown of Braunau-am-Inn to a rapturous crowd. A month later the Nazis held a referendum in Austria to rubber stamp this *Anschluss*. With a voter turnout of over 99 percent, Austrians voted 99.73 percent in favor of unification. Their former country, now renamed Ostmark (Eastern Marches), joined a "Greater German Reich." The *New York Times* wrote that "Adolf Hitler's Germanic Empire" had received a "baptism of ballots." Kurt Schuschnigg spent the rest of the Nazi years in concentration camps.

Hitler now stood at the zenith of his popularity. Catholic Germans and Austrians celebrated with music, dancing, delirious displays of patriotism, and the constant singing of the two German national anthems. Letters arrived in Hitler's mailbox from as far away as Argentina, where a group of Austrian ex-patriots expressed their delight and made sure to write: "Ein Volk, ein Reich, ein Führer" on the envelope.[12] In contrast, wrote a *New York Times* staff reporter, Berliners up north took in the *Anschluss* with "phlegmatic calm." Despite the diversity of responses, joyful congratulations poured into the Reich Chancellery, many in the form of poems pledging eternal loyalty to Hitler and marveling at his "godlike power." Reactions outside Germany were mixed. Anti-appeasers in Britain, like Winston Churchill, felt that forceful diplomacy should have been tried. Others watched in horror as the euphoria in Vienna led to the torment and humiliation of Jews. Soldiers and smiling SS men and Hitler Youth members cut the beards of Jewish men and tormented them by forcing them to clean public toilets and streets on their hands and knees (Figure 10.1). Wrote William Shirer: "The lucky ones get off with merely cleaning cars—the thousands of automobiles which have been stolen from the Jews and 'enemies' of the regime."[13] But many Europeans who followed Chamberlain's appeasement strategy saw little reason to protest this move; Austrians were German-speaking brethren who "chose" to be in the Reich. Like the Saar vote in 1935 and the retaking of the Rhineland in 1936, this was fundamentally about unity with willing citizens. The United States, for its part, followed this line of thinking, recognizing the *Anschluss* even before the referendum and dissolving all Austrian consulates. There was no need for an embassy, according to a US diplomatic cable to Vienna, because Austria "ceased to exist as an independent nation." Meanwhile, Neville Chamberlain announced to the British House of Commons that "nothing could have arrested what has happened—unless this country and other countries had been prepared to use force." Within a week, William Shirer noted in his journal, Austria had been "completely nazified."[14]

Immediately after the *Anschluss*, Hitler and General Keitel turned their focus to "Case Green," a code name for a planned invasion of Czechoslovakia. Following the First World War, the Peace of Paris divided the former Austro-Hungarian Empire into a number of smaller nations based (in theory) on common nationality, including an independent Czechoslovak state, consisting of the lands of the Bohemian kingdom and some areas belonging to the Kingdom of Hungary. In reality, this new state, like the other postwar creations, was multiethnic, with 3 million German-speaking people living in the westernmost regions of Czechoslovakia, particularly the Sudetenland. To nationalists in Germany, notably the pan-Germanists who called for the amalgamation of all German-speaking peoples, this continued separation of Sudeten Germans from their cultural roots was unacceptable. It became a matter of policy for greater German nationalists to advocate for the annexation of the Sudetenland to the Nazi Reich.

With Case Green, the regime planned different invasion scenarios and set about blanketing German-speaking territories in Czechoslovakia with pro-Nazi leaflets encouraging Sudeten Nazis, under the leadership of Konrad Henlein, to destabilize the country through pro-annexation activism. German propaganda newsreels showed "proof" of atrocities meted out against the German minority. Sudeten mothers clutched babies as they attested to their molestation by "Czech beasts." France and Britain grew nervous about developments in Czechoslovakia, along with the increasing persecution of Jews in Austria and Germany. But a look at Hitler's public schedule reveals a country and leader at their most confident, seemingly oblivious to the anxiety abroad. In late April Hitler sent birthday wishes to the Japanese emperor, rallied Germany's youth at Berlin's Olympic Stadium with celebrations of racial unity, and went to Rome to meet with Mussolini and the Italian king. In his speeches that spring and summer, Hitler reveled in the glorious age in which proud Germans now lived. The Führer himself was on regular display. He dedicated a new subway system in Munich and laid the cornerstone for a new Volkswagen factory, at both events presenting his dream of mass motorization for the German people. He also followed the progress of building projects, like the House of German Tourism in Berlin, the cornerstone of which he had laid in 1938. The building was part of Albert Speer's planned redesign of the capital with grandiose neoclassical buildings and broad thoroughfares. The city, as we saw in Chapter 6, was to be renamed Germania, and it would be filled with new government buildings and museums, with fast trains taking Germans from their new suburban houses to the city center to witness, in Hitler's words, "the mighty structures we are erecting." More important, Hitler enthused, this urban redesign would lead to "an immense increase in foreigners visiting Germany."[15]

One could well imagine any other leader pausing his war plans in 1938 and basking in his domestic and foreign policy accomplishments. But Hitler, the programmatic thinker, moved ahead. His generals—at least the old-timers who had survived the purge earlier that year—were anything but enthusiastic. Chief of Staff General Ludwig Beck felt the army was unprepared for conflict. When his military staff told Hitler that German forces in the west were not strong enough to push back the French, the Führer responded with rage. Beck resigned, pointedly noting his inability to support Hitler's policy of aggression. As we will see later, Beck would be involved in plots to bring down Hitler. The Sudeten Germans in the meantime issued demands that they be annexed by the Reich, and Hitler repeated his claim that these people, stuck in the wrong country, had a right to self-determination. Chamberlain, who generally agreed with this stance, met Hitler three times in September to try to hash out a deal, all the while imploring the Czech government to accept Hitler's demands. With the Nazis' continual threats to invade, France ordered a partial mobilization of its army, and Czechoslovakia put its troops on full alert. Across the continent Europeans, including Germans, grew depressed at the prospect of a war over a tiny strip of land few had heard of before.

With an uprising of Sudeten Germans and German cross-border incursions as the backdrop, Hitler, Chamberlain, Mussolini, and French Prime Minister Édouard Daladier met at Munich's Führerbau (Führer building) on September 30 and hammered out a deal. Notably absent were the Czech representatives, who were forced to wait in a Munich hotel to learn the outcome. Germany, according to the Munich Agreement, could annex the Sudetenland if it consented to submit any remaining territorial claims and disagreements to mutual consultation with the west (Figure 8.4). Chamberlain delighted in a sense of accomplishment. The day before the conference, he and Daladier were ready to go to war. But now conflict was avoided because, Chamberlain felt, Hitler had shown weakness. The Führer himself agreed with this assessment, and notwithstanding the fact that he had gained the Sudetenland, he regretted even after his willingness to compromise. This betrayal of Czechoslovakia seemed to bother few people outside of Prague, and Europeans breathed a sigh of relief. Most people had fresh memories of the First World War, and the appeasement of Hitler was based on a widespread desire to avoid another war at all costs. To be sure, Germans—if not Hitler at first—saw the agreement as a victory. On the train from Munich to Berlin, German correspondents reporting on the conference swigged champagne and gloated, and the people of Munich, according to the diary of anti-Nazi Ruth Andreas-Friedrich, were "wild with enthusiasm."[16] But most Germans simply felt relief. They were surely more excited when, according to the Munich Agreement, the Wehrmacht entered Germany's newly claimed territory on October 10 to the by-now familiar sight of euphoric crowds. In his diary, twenty-four-year-old soldier Herbert Wetzig noted the presence of "flowers, flowers, and ever more flowers" as he marched across the border. "The streets are full of people," he effused. "They have certainly waited a long time for this. So long. But the time has come. Now they wave to us, and the children grab our hands and walk with us."[17] Four years later, Wetzig died in battle.

Hitler had again disproven his naysayers, but he felt cheated out of the war he had spent so much time planning. Neville Chamberlain basked in the apparent success of his appeasement policy, proudly declaring that he had achieved "peace for our time." Sadly for him, this phrase has become one of the most notorious of the twentieth century, disdained and mocked as a symbol of naïveté and wishful thinking. The Munich Agreement, or as some called it upon its conclusion, The Munich Betrayal, collapsed in March of

FIGURE 8.4 *Hitler signs the Munich Agreement, September 30, 1938 (Bundesarchiv, Bild 146-1976-033-06/CC-BY-SA 3.0, CC BY-SA 3.0 DE, via Wikimedia Commons).*

1939 when Hitler invaded the rest of Czechoslovakia. The Nazis occupied the Czech lands of Bohemia and Moravia, creating a protectorate there with its capital in Prague. They also set up a loyal puppet state in Slovakia. Hitler now had access to armaments, textile factories, industrial minerals, and other raw materials key to his quest for living space. Appeasement was dead and so was Chamberlain's premiership (and reputation) the following year. For the first time, Hitler now ruled over a population—7 million Czechs— who had no desire to be under German control. This was no longer a case of the Reich "rounding out its borders." And for the first time, Hitler could no longer plausibly play the victim card, which had allowed him a few months earlier to argue that Sudeten Germans were being persecuted. Hitler argued instead that Bohemia and Moravia had long been a part of German *Lebensraum* and were destined to be so again.

And yet, Hitler still protested that the world was surrounding his country and denying it a "right to life." With the end of appeasement as a policy, most observers felt it was only a matter of time before Hitler turned his attention to Poland. But Hitler insisted that he was a man of peace and that his territorial readjustments were complete. In a January 1939 speech, he had already outlined the prior year's successes and their fundamentally defensive nature. Hitler had been "asked" to send troops into Austria "to prevent unpredictable turmoil." It was Czech President Benes who had turned his country "into the exponent of all hostile foreign intentions toward the Reich" and who had provoked Germany with mobilization, thereby damaging "the reputation of the German Reich abroad." This anti-Nazi campaign, Hitler argued, resulted in a misperception of Germany as aggressor. "If certain newspapers and politicians in the rest of the world now allege that Germany thus threatened other nations with military blackmail, this can only be based on a crude distortion of the facts."[18] Hitler also presented a litany of slights his country had supposedly suffered. In the course of history Germany had been burdened by debts, plundered by the rest of the world, stripped of its colonies, and forced to suffer with overpopulation and no room to expand. In the First World War, the United States had repaid the service of Germans to the American Revolution and to the US Civil War with a declaration of war against them in 1917. And later, the Entente had starved Germany, tormented its POWs, and humiliated it through a dictated peace. But now, six years into the Nazi rule, Germany stood tall.

Few people believed Adolf Hitler's protestations of peace, neither in January of 1939 nor, certainly, after his further invasion of Czechoslovakia in March. Hermann Rauschning, former Nazi president of the Danzig Senate and now an opponent of Hitler, warned of German attempts at "world domination." The Nazis, he argued, saw France as a "dying nation" and Britain as having lost the "imperial spirit." Young Germany would therefore seek to take up the "White Man's Burden" from the "senile" Brits. This Nazi "nihilism," he asserted, threatened to destroy all European values.[19]

Europe was on a war footing. In response to the dismemberment of Czechoslovakia, Roosevelt set tariffs on German goods, and international protests against Hitler's grew louder. The British, humiliated by the failure of appeasement, had little choice but to promise assistance to Poland should Germany invade. The government declared, "In the event of any action which clearly threatened Polish independence, and which the Polish Government accordingly considered it vital to resist with their national forces, His Majesty's Government would feel themselves bound at once to lend the Polish Government all support in their power."[20] A more formal Anglo-Polish military agreement followed and was later extended to defending Romania and Greece. This move stunned Hitler, who—despite his regular fuming—still had dreams of unity with Britain. The Führer felt compelled to remind his population that while both countries were strong in their shared Nordic stock, Germany was more courageous and more ready for battle.

Such rhetoric did little to excite the German people. By all accounts, they were depressed by the events in Prague and what they saw as their leader's reckless adventurism. This time, in March of 1939, they did not feel a sense of accomplishment. The regime's relationship to the outside world also grew increasingly fractured. Among authoritarian regimes, National Socialism remained popular—or at least palatable—as an economic and military ally. In Spain, the year began with Franco's victory in the Civil War, and the new leader built up trade relations with Germany. Japan and Germany continued to celebrate their alliance through cultural exchanges and cheery diplomatic dispatches, and Nazi scholars looked beyond the German nation-state to study indigenous peoples, world empires, and Indo-

Aryan civilizational similarities across the globe. And as the regime stepped up its war plans, as we will see, Jewish persecution increased. The regime was encouraged by the reality of widespread antisemitism abroad—from North America to eastern Europe to the Middle East to South Africa—which was proof to the Nazis that their movement was on the march in many other places. In historian David Motadel's words, the 1930s and early 1940s were a "global authoritarian moment," when populism, anticommunism, and antisemitism converged and gave Nazi policies an international resonance.[21] But where it mattered, in Europe, Hitler faced the reality that the next steps toward *Lebensraum* would spell war. It didn't help that the United States was now getting involved. Franklin Roosevelt raised US defense spending and indicated in a speech that he would use any means necessary "short of war" to stop German "lawlessness." The year 1939 saw Germany clinging to what it could—dreams of mass motorization, celebrations of racial unity, a secret buildup of its navy, and complaints about the international campaign against the Reich and other "totalitarian countries."

On April 30, 1939, the last World's Fair until after the war opened in New York City. The United Kingdom, France, the Netherlands, and smaller democracies took part. So did fascist and authoritarian countries. The Italian pavilion fused classical and modern architectural styles in celebration of ancient Roman glory and fascist futurism. Visitors saw a bronze effigy of Mussolini, a statue of the goddess Roma, and a map of Italy's new "empire" in Africa and Albania, the small Balkan country that the *Duce* had invaded a few weeks earlier. Taking a less bellicose approach, Japan presented a Shinto shrine, a Japanese garden, and a photomontage framed by the words "Dedicated to Eternal Peace and Friendship between America and Japan." The Soviet pavilion was devoted to the socialist "world of tomorrow." Reliefs of Stalin and Lenin graced the entrance, and the halls displayed sketches of future garden cities and depictions of factory workers, farmers, writers, scientists, and artists who were building a communist utopia. At the pavilion's grand opening in May, the Soviet ambassador paid homage to the goodwill between the USSR and the United States but warned that his country would deal a "double blow" to any "instigators of war who attempted to violate the Soviet border."

Noticeably absent from the 1939 Expo was Germany. The country had originally planned to take part, but when New York City Mayor Fiorello La Guardia, whom the Nazi press labeled, among other slurs, "a dirty Talmud Jew," announced its participation, Jewish leaders called for a boycott of the World's Fair. A final American decision on German participation was preempted by the Reich's own choice to pull out. Hitler ostensibly objected to the costs, but the Nazis had already sunk $1,000,000 into the pavilion, funds which the United States now distributed to smaller European and Latin American countries that were participating. German emigres in the United States drew up alternate plans to build an anti-Nazi "Freedom Pavilion." But that fell through too.

Other countries were also absent from the 1939 World's Fair. When Franco won the Civil War earlier that year, he scuttled the Republicans' pre-defeat pavilion plans. The Czech pavilion also remained unfinished due to the country's dismemberment. But the absence of Germany was the most telling. It symbolized the growing breach between National Socialist Germany and much of the international community. If the Hitler regime hoped to impress the world, it was going about it the wrong way. On the day the Expo opened, the Nazis promulgated the Law Concerning Jewish Tenants. Municipal authorities were given permission to restrict Jews to specific houses or neighborhoods, and "Aryan" landlords could now freely evict Jewish tenants, provided the displaced could find a new home with Jewish landlords. The following day, Hitler addressed 100,000 Hitler Youth members at the Olympic Stadium as part of the annual Day of National Labor holiday (formerly May Day, which had not been an official German holiday before 1933). Ever the victim, he exhorted his audience to be prepared to fight. "Should the hour come in which an outside world believes it can reach out for the freedom of Germany, a cry of millions will shatter the air ... And should the outside world threaten us and thunder against us, they shall not succeed for the very reason they have never yet succeeded: German unity!"[22]

Notes

1 Clarence Lusane, *Hitler's Black Victims: The Historical Experiences of Afro-Germans, European Blacks, Africans, and African Americans in the Nazi Era* (New York: Routledge, 2003), 126.

2 Herluf Zahle, "Dispatch to Copenhagen," May 17, 1933, in *Fremde Blicke auf das "Dritte Reich": Berichte ausländischer Diplomaten über Herrschaft und Gesellschaft in Deutschland, 1933–1945*, Frank Bajohr and Christoph Strupp, eds. (Göttingen: Wallstein, 2012), 376.

3 "Nazi Outrages Deplored," *New York Times*, October 25, 1935, 10.

4 Oliver Lubrich, ed., *Travels in the Reich: 1933–1945: Foreign Authors Report from Germany* (Chicago: University of Chicago Press), 74.

5 Ibid., 92–134.

6 "Treated Well in Germany, Visitors Say," *Norfolk New Journal and Guide*, September 1, 1934, 3; and, e.g., "Nazis Kindly Pastor Finds," *New York Amsterdam News*, August 25, 1934, 15.

7 Robert Leigh-Pemberton, "Remembering the Nazi Games," *Irish Independent*, March 25, 2018.

8 Klara and Elly Walterhöfer to Hitler, March 8, 1936, in *Briefe in Hitler*, Henrik Eberle, ed. (Bergisch Gladbach: Lübbe, 2007), 226.

9 Zahle, "Dispatch to Copenhagen," March 25, 1935, in *Fremde Blicke*, Bajohr and Struppe, eds., 424.

10 "Hossbach Memorandum," November 10, 1937, https://avalon.law.yale.edu/imt/hossbach.asp

11 David Lloyd George, "I Talked to Hitler" (1936), https://alphahistory.com/nazigermany/lloyd-george-meets-hitler-1936/

12 Eberle, ed., *Briefe an Hitler*, 239.

13 William L. Shirer, *Berlin Diary: The Journal of a Foreign Correspondent, 1934–1941* (Boston: Little Brown, 1940), 111.

14 Ibid., 110.

15 Hitler speech on June 14, 1938, in *Hitler: Speeches and Proclamations, 1932–1945*, Vol. III, Max Domarus, ed. (Wauconda, IL: Bochazy-Carducci, 1997), 1121–2.

16 Ruth Andreas-Friedrich, *Berlin Underground: 1938–1945* (New York: Paragon, 1989), diary entry from September 30, 1938, 8.

17 Aufzeichnungen aus dem Tagebuch des Wehrmachtssoldaten Herbert Wetzig (1914–42), https://www.dhm.de/lemo/zeitzeugen/herbert-wetzig-der-einmarsch-ins-sudetenland-1938

18 Hitler speech before the first "Greater German Reichstag" (January 30, 1939), https://ghdi.ghi-dc.org/docpage.cfm?docpage_id=2913

19 Jewish Telegraphic Agency, "Book by Ex-nazi Official, Now Hitler Foe, Sees Nazism Aiming at World Domination," November 6, 1938, https://www.jta.org/archive/book-by-ex-nazi-official-now-hitler-foe-sees-nazism-aiming-at-world-domination

20 Statement by Prime Minister Neville Chamberlain in the House of Commons on March 31, 1939, https://avalon.law.yale.edu/wwii/blbk17.asp

21 David Motadel, "The Global Authoritarian Moment and the Revolt against Empire," *American Historical Review* 124, no. 3 (June 2019): 843–77.

22 Hitler speech on May 1, 1939, in *Hitler: Speeches and Proclamations*, Domarus, ed., 1599–1606.

Additional Reading

Bajohr, Frank, and Dieter Pohl, eds. *Right-wing Politics and the Rise of Antisemitism in Europe, 1935–1941*. Göttingen: Wallstein Verlag, 2019.

Blackbourn, David. *Germany in the World: A Global History, 1500–2000*. London: Liveright, 2023.

Boyd, Julia. *Travelers in the Third Reich. The Rise of Fascism, 1919–1945*. London: Simon & Schuster, 2018.

Chu, Winson. *The German Minority in Interwar Poland*. Cambridge: Cambridge University Press, 2012.

Ferenczi, Thomas. *The Foreign Policy of the Third Reich, 1933–1939*. Stroud: Fonthill, 2021.

Hart, Bradley. *Hitler's American Friends. The Third Reich's Supporters in the United States*. New York: Thomas Dunne Books, 2018.

Kühl, Stefan. *The Nazi Connection: Eugenics, American Racism, and German National Socialism*. New York and Oxford: Oxford University Press, 1994.

Leitz, Christian. *Nazi Foreign Policy, 1933–1941: The Road to Global War*. London and New York: Routledge, 2004.

Nagorski, Andrew. *Hitlerland: American Eyewitnesses to the Nazi Rise to Power*. New York: Simon & Schuster, 2012.

Phayer, Michael. *The Catholic Church and the Holocaust, 1930–1965*. Bloomington: Indiana University Press, 2000.

Weinberg, Gerhard. *Hitler's Foreign Policy, 1933–1939: The Road to World War II*. New York: Enigma Books, 2005.

Whitman, James Q. *Hitler's American Model: The United States and the Making of Nazi Race Law*. Princeton, NJ and Oxford: Princeton University Press, 2017.

PLATE 1 *Poster encouraging Germans to purchase war bonds, March 1918. The text reads: "The final blow is the 8th War Bond" (Bundesarchiv, Plak 001-005-044).*

PLATE 2 *Anti-Nazi election poster, 1932. The text reads: "The fate of the worker under swastika rule. Vote for the Social Democrats on List 1" (Unknown artist, Public domain, via Wikimedia Commons).*

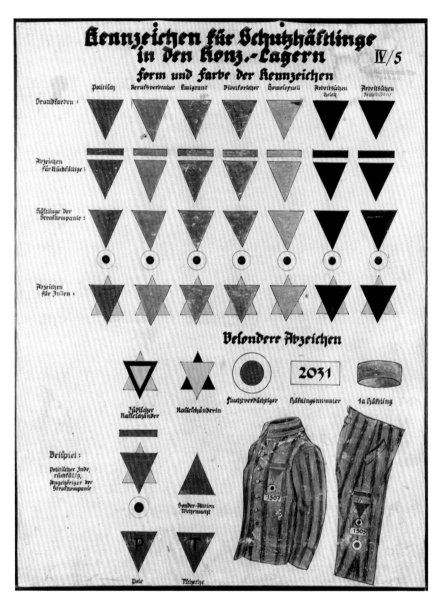

PLATE 3 *Badges placed on concentration camp inmates' clothing according to their "category" of imprisonment, 1936–1944: red for political prisoners; green for convicts and criminals; blue for emigrants and foreign forced laborers; purple for Jehovah's Witnesses and other religious minorities; pink for gay men and "sexual offenders"; black for "asocials," "work-shy," and Roma; yellow for Jews. Note the combining of categories into six pointed stars for Jews (Bundesarchiv, Bild 146-1993-051-07).*

PLATE 4 *Postcard advertising the Nazi-sponsored traveling antisemitic exhibit "The Eternal Jew" in Munich, November 8, 1937 to January 31, 1938. The exhibit's antisemitic caricatures, myths, and conspiracy theories were aimed at fomenting fear and hatred of Jews. Images like this appeared throughout* Der Stürmer. *(United States Holocaust Memorial Museum Collection, Gift of the Katz Family).*

PLATE 5 *The German Labor Front's "Beauty of Labor" program promoted improvements to working conditions to increase productivity and workers' support for the regime, following the forced dissolution of the trade unions. This 1934 poster reads: "This ... not this. Beautiful working conditions – greater joy at work" (Bundesarchiv, Plak 003-018-035).*

PLATE 6 *Promotional advertisement for the Volkswagen savings plan, 1938. The text reads: "You must save 5 RM per week if you want to drive a car!" The ad was released by the Strength through Joy office for the region of Munich-Upper Bavaria (Bundesarchiv, Plak 003-018-058).*

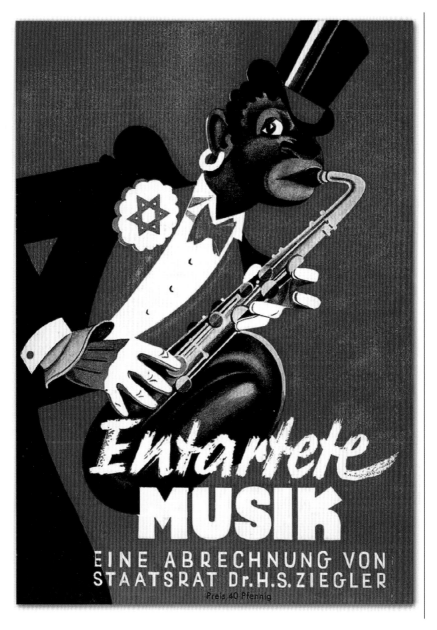

PLATE 7 *Racist and antisemitic poster for the "Degenerate Music" exhibition in Düsseldorf, 1938 (Ludwig Tersch, artist, Public domain, via Wikimedia Commons).*

PLATE 8 *"All of Germany listens to the Führer with the People's Radio," radio promotion from 1936 (Bundesarchiv, Plak 003-022-025).*

PLATE 9 *"Hamster, shame on you." Housewives were expected to manage shortages and conserve available goods during the war. Those who hoarded or traded on the black market were vilified, as in this December 1939 poster (Bundesarchiv, Plak 003-023-077).*

PLATE 10 *Cover of the Nazi women's magazine,* Die NS-Frauen-Warte, *depicting "Comrades" in 1942. The artist, Ernst Kretschmann, died on the eastern front in 1941 (Ernst Kretschmann (artist), Public domain, via Wikimedia Commons).*

PLATE 11 *Nazi war propaganda "Victory or Bolshevism," 1943 (Unknown artist, Public domain, via Wikimedia Commons).*

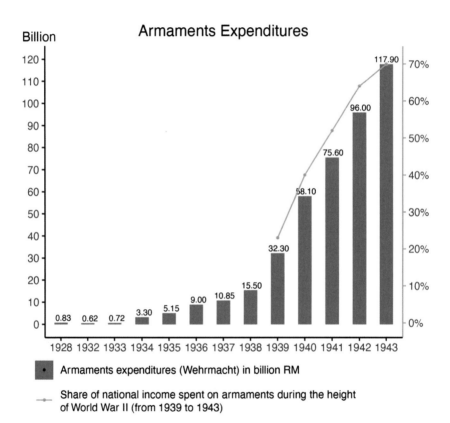

PLATE 12 *German armaments expenditures, 1928–43 (Source: Bernd Sösemann, Propaganda (Stuttgart: Steiner, 2011), 552. Reprinted with permission of the author).*

PLATE 13 *Concentration and extermination camps, and major "euthanasia" centers, from Jeremy Noakes, ed.,* Nazism, 1919–1945, Vol. 3: Foreign Policy, War, and Racial Extermination. *Exeter: University of Exeter Press, 1998, p. 645. Original cartography by Cherie Norton/Mapping Solutions. Revised cartography by Gabriel Moss, 2021.*

PLATE 14 *Europe at the beginning of December 1941, from* Germany and the Second World War, *edited by the Research Institute for Military History, Potsdam, Germany. Volume IV,* The Attack on the Soviet Union, *by Horst Boog, Jürgen Förster, Joachim Hoffmann, Ernst Klink, Rolf-Dieter Müller, and Gerd R. Ueberschär. Clarendon Press: Oxford, 1998. Original cartography by Cherie Norton/Mapping Solutions. Revised cartography by Gabriel Moss, 2021.*

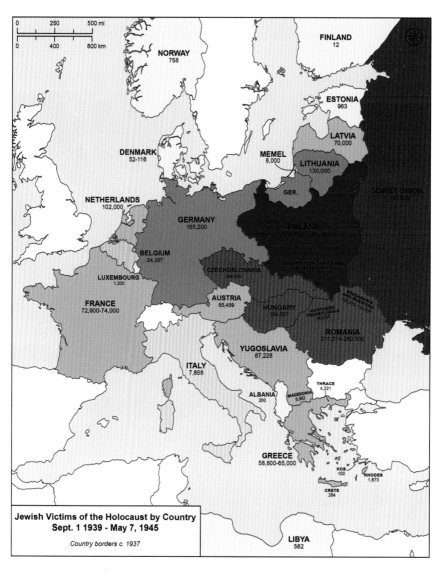

PLATE 15 *Jewish victims of the Holocaust by country, September 1, 1939–May 7, 1945 from Martin Gilbert, ed.,* The Routledge Atlas of the Holocaust, 4th edition *(London/New York, 2009); updated figures based on: USHMM,* Holocaust Encyclopedia, *https://encyclopedia.ushmm.org/en. Cartography by Gabriel Moss, 2022–2023.*

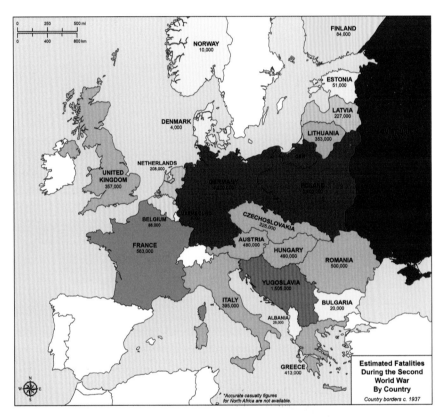

PLATE 16 *Estimated fatalities during the Second World War by country, from J. Noakes and G. Pridham, eds.,* Nazism: A History in Documents and Eyewitness Accounts, 1919–1945, Vol. 2 *(New York, 1988), p. 874, with revised figures based on additional research by Jonathan Wiesen and Pamela Swett, 2022. Cartography by Gabriel Moss, 2022–2023.*

9

War and Empire, 1939–42

The appeasement of Hitler, famously championed by the British and French during the Sudetenland crisis, failed in March 1939 when the Wehrmacht invaded what remained of Czechoslovakia. Fears of future German aggression and talk of a European war dominated the late spring and summer of 1939. To those outside Germany, it was clear the Nazis had Poland in sight, and the British committed to defending Polish sovereignty should the country be invaded. Britain and France both increased armaments spending after the dismemberment of Czechoslovakia, while Hitler worked to position Germany as a non-aggressor. He announced the upcoming annual Nuremberg Nazi Party rally would be held under the banner "Rally for Peace," though in the end it was canceled when the war erupted. Simultaneously, the government's press briefings intensified the stream of news that exaggerated and invented stories of violence by Poles against German residents in the Free City of Danzig and the Polish Corridor. Germany also engaged in diplomacy to optimize its economic and military-strategic position. This included non-aggression pacts with Latvia, Estonia, and Denmark, as well as raw materials agreements with Sweden, Norway, and Romania. Many Germans believed their leader's claims that he only sought the "acceptable and modest," peaceful incorporation of Danzig into the German Reich.[1] As one official report about popular sentiment expressed, "the answer to the question of how the problem 'Danzig and the Corridor' is to be solved is still the same among the general public: incorporation in the Reich? Yes. Through war? No."[2]

On August 23, 1939, Hitler achieved his most important diplomatic success in the form of an agreement with Joseph Stalin. The German leader knew that the Soviet Union, on its own or with Great Britain and France, could threaten his plans for a war against Poland. For their part the Soviets wanted to ensure that any German invasion would be limited to Polish territory. After weeks of negotiations in August, the deeply anticommunist Foreign Minister Joachim von Ribbentrop and the antifascist Soviet Foreign Minister Vyacheslav Molotov announced the German-Soviet

FIGURE 9.1 *Signing of the German-Soviet Non-Aggression Pact in Moscow, August 23, 1939. The image shows German Foreign Minister, Joachim von Ribbentrop, signing. Joseph Stalin smiles behind him, and to Stalin's right stands Soviet Foreign Minister Vyacheslav Molotov (Bundesarchiv, Bild 183-S52480 CC-BY-SA 3.0, CC BY-SA 3.0 DE, via Wikimedia Commons).*

Non-Aggression Pact (Figure 9.1). This agreement shocked the international community, not least those socialists and communists who had suffered under Hitler. Likewise, Germans who for six years had learned from Nazi propaganda to hate Soviet Russia were amazed at this agreement with the Bolshevik foe. The ideological archenemies Hitler and Stalin now committed themselves for the next ten years to neutrality in the event of war. The two sides also promised the peaceful resolution of conflicts and the expansion of trade relationships. In a supplementary protocol signed on the same day but kept secret from the public, they also agreed to divide Poland into German and Soviet spheres of influence. The USSR would also take the Baltic states, Finland, and Bessarabia.

War Begins: Poland and Western Europe, 1939–41

Hitler now felt secure that his plans to attack Poland would not meet any Soviet resistance. The invasion began in the early morning hours of September 1, prompted by what was reported as a Polish military assault on a

German broadcasting station near the border. In reality, the SS had disguised concentration camp inmates as Polish military personnel to manufacture an incident to which they could respond with force. German press reports announced that Wehrmacht troops were "returning fire," and skirmishes broke out in a number of locations in the Polish Corridor. Before dawn a German battleship began shelling a munitions depot near Danzig. The same day, Hitler went out on the balcony of his Berlin residence, announcing the German "counter offensive" to what he assumed would be a cheering crowd awaiting him. Finding none he went back inside to avoid embarrassment. It had been only two decades since the last war. Still mourning lost loved ones from that conflict, few Germans were eager for a new one. As one German woman recalled, "the war did not begin as it had in the summer of 1914 with jubilation and cheers. For a little while we hoped a world war could be avoided, but on September 3 these hopes were dashed. England declared war on Germany," as did France.[3]

Despite misgivings in Germany, these first eruptions of violence were quickly overshadowed by the full force of German military might. The nation's newly minted Luftwaffe advanced over Polish territory ahead of fifteen tank divisions and 3,600 armored vehicles. The tactic of a rapid deployment of air power to clear the way for armored units, known as *Blitzkrieg* or "lightning war," overwhelmed Poland's one tank division and 750 armored vehicles. Seventy thousand Poles died in this initial campaign compared to roughly 11,000 German soldiers. In keeping with the Non-Aggression Pact, Stalin and Hitler divided up Poland into spheres of influence. The Soviet Union invaded Poland from the east and incorporated the Baltic States of Estonia, Latvia, and Lithuania into its sphere and eventually annexed them into the USSR. Stalin's army also invaded Finland in November, where it fought until the spring of 1940. Soviet forces suffered heavy casualties in three months of battle, and the USSR was expelled from the League of Nations for its aggression. Although the Soviets gained territory in the settlement that followed, the Red Army's struggle to subdue the smaller nation left Hitler confident that the Wehrmacht would overcome Soviet forces easily when the time came. The western parts of Poland were incorporated into the German Reich as two new *Reichsgaue* (administrative areas) called the Warthegau and Danzig-Westpreussen. Under the terms of the pact, Germany also acquired parts of central and southern Poland. This area was governed like a colony under the brutal rule of lawyer and fanatical Nazi Hans Frank. The remaining eastern districts of Poland, amounting to 60 percent of the country, were annexed by the USSR.

The German invaders had a vision for the people and land they now occupied. Planning documents reveal that Germans would be released from heavy labor that would be borne by Slavs in the future. But the Nazis were not prepared for the large number of individuals from so-called "inferior races"—especially the 3.3 million Jews—who fell into their hands. As an interim measure, the Nazi warlords decided to herd them into ghettos across Poland, while they figured out what to do with them next. Some Poles were judged as having enough "German blood" that they could be "Germanized"; others were deported to the General Government and left to fend for themselves. In addition to the casualties associated with the military conquest and the population transfers that followed, an estimated 500,000 Jews and members of the Catholic clergy and Polish intelligentsia were murdered in the first two and half years of the war.

Rounding up Jews and clearing whole towns of Poles, the SS, Wehrmacht and police made way for ethnic Germans repatriated from Soviet territory in the northern Baltic and from the south around the Black Sea in present-day Romania. Families within the prewar borders of Germany, now known as the "Old Reich," were also encouraged to move east. By the end of 1940, 500,000 had been brought into the region. The number would top 1 million by 1944. Female volunteers from the BDM and Labor Service were instrumental in readying expropriated Polish and Jewish homes for the new settlers, who sometimes arrived just hours after the forced departure of the previous residents: cleaning the house, decorating the table with fresh flowers, and making a dinner to greet the new family. BDM girls were then sent back periodically to make sure the new residents were acting like Germans, removing kitschy decorations or replacing portraits of saints with those of Hitler. They also tended children or helped out on the farm. It was tough going for many of the new arrivals, some of whom had little agricultural experience. As one female volunteer reported, having observed a young family she was assigned to support: "The move seemed to have stunned them like a body blow."[4]

The central Polish city of Lodz offers an example of the regime's commitment to "Germanization" and the population exchanges meant to further that goal. In 1931 the city had 604,000 residents (59 percent Poles, 32 percent Jews, 9 percent Germans, and the rest a mix of other ethnicities). After the war began, the Nazis undertook a radical demographic reconfiguration. Some of the Poles were shipped further east. Others were pushed out of the city center but allowed to resettle in the suburbs to work for the Germans. A third contingent of Polish residents were shipped back to Germany as forced laborers in the war economy, and close to 200,000 Jews from the area were forced to relocate to the city's newly established Jewish ghetto. One newspaper boasted: "Two thousand keys are waiting for Germans to come and open the doors to their new homes."[5] Despite the growing military needs, the Nazi government invested heavily in city-wide renovations. No longer called Lodz, the city was renamed Litzmannstadt (after the First World War general Karl Litzmann), and its new overlords built theaters, schools, and hospitals to attract German residents. The Nazis removed Polish and Yiddish signage and renamed streets to reflect German culture (Cinderella Street, Little Red Riding Hood Street), and they renovated buildings to provide housing for municipal officials. By 1944, successive waves of Jews had been deported from the city's ghetto and murdered in the extermination camps discussed in the next chapter. A film crew was sent to Litzmannstadt in 1941 to film the progress of "Germanization" for posterity.

While such measures to expand the Reich were carried out on former Polish territory, the Western powers, despite their declarations of war, did nothing to aid Poland. These first months of relative quiet after German victory over Poland were known as the "phony war," as the British and French rushed to prepare militarily, and civilians waited to learn where the next shots would be fired. Despite their leader's confidence, Hitler's generals convinced the Führer to hold off launching an offensive in western Europe until after the winter weather had passed. By this time they hoped to have a plan to overcome the formidable French defenses known as the Maginot Line. This was a series of seemingly impregnable fortifications along the Franco-German border meant to deter Germany from ever invading. Although the French defenses did little to stymie the Führer's intentions in France, Hitler believed Britain might be persuaded to sue for peace. His vision for western Europe was never as radical or destructive as his fantasies in the east. He considered western and northern Europeans—notably Britons and Scandinavians—more racially valuable populations that could be junior partners to "Aryans" once their countries were "freed" from Jewish influence. An invasion of the British Isles was also a tall order militarily, making peace with Great Britain especially attractive. Hitler thus turned first to Denmark on April 9, 1940, where a Wehrmacht invasion force faced almost no resistance. Germany established a military occupation, under which the racially acceptable Danes maintained the greatest degree of independence among all countries occupied by the Germans. The Wehrmacht moved on to Norway next and defeated that nation by June. Securing coastal territory was key for the coming naval war and to ensure access to neutral Sweden's iron ore.

On May 10 German forces began the long-awaited attack on France. Nazi military leaders reasoned that the French would expect the Germans to avoid the Maginot defenses by coming through northern Belgium. Consequently, the Wehrmacht took a different and surprising route, cutting through the treacherous terrain of the Ardennes forest across southern Belgium and Luxembourg and into France. German Panzer divisions, whose men were hopped on methamphetamines to fight for days without sleeping, maneuvered through the forest more easily than the French expected. When they emerged, French and British soldiers were caught flat footed, having positioned themselves at the northern passage, where Germany had sent some troops as a distraction. Meanwhile, in the neighboring Netherlands, German bombers leveled the Dutch city of Rotterdam on May 14 in a gesture to intimidate the Allies. Hundreds of citizens died, and the city's destruction provided further evidence that the war would surpass all previous conflicts in its disregard for civilian lives. The Netherlands capitulated three days later, May 17, and Belgium followed suit on May 28.

German successes in France were equally stunning. By May 25 the British Expeditionary Force and some of the remaining French and Belgian troops had retreated to the northern port of Dunkirk only to find themselves trapped between the advancing Wehrmacht and the English Channel. Around 340,000 servicemen made it safely to the town, but back in London it was expected they would be lost, especially after the Belgians surrendered on the 28th. In what became known as the "deliverance of Dunkirk," given its almost miraculous outcome, just about all the men successfully escaped to Britain despite days of Luftwaffe aerial attack, owing to the combined efforts of hundreds of military transports as well as civilian and commercial vessels that rescued servicemen waiting in the harbor and on the shore. For the western Allies, there was little other good news to celebrate. The Wehrmacht entered Paris on June 14. The French surrendered just eight days later, leaving Hitler's enemies in Europe and North America shocked and painfully aware of how hard it would now be to roll back German gains. As one Jewish girl living in Warsaw recalled, "when Paris fell, people wept in the streets."[6] For his part, Hitler traveled to Paris on June 28, taking in the sights of the Eiffel Tower and the Opera with his chief architect Albert Speer and favorite sculptor, Arno Breker. He also made a point of visiting the train car in which the German delegation had signed the armistice in 1918. The sight-seeing tour was a personal highpoint for Hitler. Back in Germany, the French victory unleashed "celebration without limits," recalled one woman. "Hitler was glorified more than ever. The 'final victory' seemed close at hand."[7]

The Germans carried their racist ideology into every country they occupied. In France, the Wehrmacht separated thousands of captured French west African soldiers from white French soldiers and targeted them for particularly brutal treatment in contravention of international law. The torture and murder of as many as 3,000 Black French soldiers reveals the linked aims of military conquest and racial purity. The German army occupied the northern half of France, including the former capital, Paris. As many as 6–8 million French citizens fled their homes in this northern-occupied sector. In the south, the Nazis established a collaborationist state controlled by the revered First World War French general Philippe Pétain. It was known as the Vichy regime because its headquarters were based in the city of the same name. Between 1933 and 1939, France had been a haven for German Jewish refugees, as well as communists and other supporters of the Spanish republic who had fled to France after Franco won the civil war in the spring of 1939. Jews from other European countries had also sought safety in France as the Wehrmacht overran their hometowns elsewhere. All these refugees were now vulnerable. Arrests were common throughout France, and further escape routes, indeed in some cases back to Spain, were cut off. The Jewish German philosopher Walter Benjamin had fled Germany for France and secured a visa to the United States, which he was hoping to reach through neutral Spain and Portugal. Having learned that Spanish authorities planned to send refugees back to France, however, Benjamin died by suicide rather than being handed to German authorities in occupied France. In an additionally tragic turn for Benjamin, the Spaniards did allow entry to the rest of the philosopher's traveling party the following day. Looking ahead, Nazi leaders weighed a variety of options for a defeated France, some of which included versions of the "Germanization" program already underway in Poland. All of the ideas circulating among German officials aimed to keep France from ever posing a challenge to German hegemony again.

Germany's ally, fascist Italy, also declared war on France in 1940, and it was after Germany's triumph in June that Italy's leaders may have first fully realized that Mussolini and his regime were not considered equal partners to Hitler's expanding Reich. The Italians had expected to gain French territory on the continent and in North Africa and even acquire a presence in the Middle East—all to shore up fascist Italy's own claims to a Mediterranean empire. But Berlin rebuffed Italian Foreign Minister Galeazzo Ciano, and Mussolini's government came to realize that it had little if any power to ensure that Germany lived up to its promises of a postwar division of spoils among the two Axis powers. For its part, Germany also dreamed of extending the Nazi empire into Africa. But the Italians were incapable of securing territory on their own, and while the initial attempts by General Erwin Rommel's Afrika Korps to support Italian efforts in Libya succeeded, this momentum could not be maintained. The German fleet remained ill-equipped to counter a British defense of its African colonies, and after Hitler invaded the USSR in June 1941, German resources were increasingly needed in that theater. Hitler and his inner circle had expected the other fascist power, Spain, to join forces with the Germans and Italians in the Mediterranean, but Franco recognized long before Mussolini that his nation was better off remaining neutral than entering the war on the side of the Germans. The Axis would never be a partnership among equals while Hitler ruled, and other actual or potential allies of Hitler—Turkey, Portugal, Vichy France—also came to doubt whether German hegemony would be good for anyone besides the Germans.

Britons felt relieved by the safe return of their soldiers from Dunkirk in June 1940. But fears of a Nazi invasion only intensified in the summer and fall, in part because the country's chief ally, the United States, remained steadfast in its neutrality. Hitler hoped the British—whom the Nazis saw as Germans' Anglo-Saxon racial kin—would choose to avoid conflict with the Reich and negotiate for peace. However, Churchill's government refused, to the relief of most British subjects, as well as members of the Polish, Norwegian, and Dutch governments, who had taken refuge in London. Behind closed doors, German naval leadership was not confident that an assault on Britain would be successful, but German landing crafts were readied in June, and the Luftwaffe prepared to launch an aerial attack meant to knock out British defenses.

Starting in July 1940 British naval targets, coastal ports, and air defense infrastructure came under massive attack by Reich Marshal Göring's Luftwaffe. Göring had predicted that the Royal Air Force (RAF) would prove no match for his planes and airmen, but the RAF's Spitfires and Hurricanes were fast and nimble, and their pilots were aided by radar and a network of coastal observers, who warned them of arriving German bombers and fighters. Germany switched its focus to British industrial and transportation targets in August. Attacks on London commenced on September 7, but it was soon clear that the German air force could not get the job done, and the planned Nazi land invasion, Operation Sealion, which was to have been made possible by a successful air assault, was called off. The bombing campaign, or the Blitz as it was known in Britain, continued into 1941. Germany's rationale for continuing the air attack was to weaken morale and force Britain to sue for peace. That never happened, despite the loss of about 40,000 British civilians. Eventually, in May 1941 the Nazis scaled back the assault to focus resources elsewhere.

Victory in the Balkans and the Invasion of the Soviet Union, 1941

Facing disappointment in Britain, Germany turned to the Balkans in early 1941. The Nazis found plenty of allies in the region and others who were successfully bullied into supporting the growing German empire. The territory was crucial because of its native oil supply and its access to the Mediterranean and Black Seas. Romania became a close ally, and Yugoslavia was one in name, but Serbian officers were reluctant to support the Germans and staged a successful coup against the Yugoslav regent Prince Paul on March 27, 1941. Keeping Yugoslavia on its side was important to the Nazis because the Italians were not faring well militarily in neighboring Greece, a country they had invaded in October 1940. Mussolini's troops had encountered unexpectedly stiff resistance from the Greeks, who enjoyed British support, and the Italians called on German aid. Incensed by the thought of losing Yugoslav support, Göring ordered the Luftwaffe to attack Belgrade, the Yugoslav capital, on April 6, 1941; this was followed by the arrival of Wehrmacht tank divisions and infantry. The Yugoslavian army was forced to capitulate just eleven days later; its young king, Peter II, and his government fled to safety in Britain.

With Yugoslavia back under control, the Germans could now make their way to Greece in support of Italian forces, taking the capital, Athens, in April. Without adequate aerial defense, the remaining British troops were trapped along with the Greek king, George II, his government, and his army. During the fierce fighting that followed, more than 10,000 British troops were captured and thousands more killed. The Nazis installed a puppet government in Athens, with Wehrmacht troops keeping watch over key strategic sites and the Italian military occupying the rest of the country. Over the next year, however, conditions worsened in Greece after the German military and industrial firms began requisitioning supplies and the Allies erected a blockade at sea, leaving civilians without work and food. As many as 300,000 starved to death in what the Greeks termed the Great Famine.

Following Yugoslavia's capitulation, the German occupation adopted a strategy of divide and conquer by pitting local ethnic groups against one another. The Nazis allowed a Croatian state to be set up with a friendly government, led by Ante Pavelić and backed by his Ustasha fascist movement. Pavelić immediately declared war on the Allies and, in turn, was allowed to rule with impunity. He established martial law, which (along with Ustasha-led concentration camps, forced labor, and random acts of violence) was meant to drive out or kill all non-Croats, including 2 million Serbs and about 75,000 Jews and Roma. By 1943, Pavelić's regime had largely succeeded. Some of the Serbs who escaped into German-occupied Serbia joined underground resistance bands known as Chetniks. These fighters mounted the first rebellion against the German occupiers in June 1941, though many were motivated by anti-Croatian sentiment more than by anti-German feelings. Communist rebels, led by Josip Broz Tito, also mobilized, seeking to unite all those looking to oust the German and Croat criminals. In response, the Wehrmacht employed a vicious policy of reprisal for any partisan actions on Yugoslav territory. Just one German soldier's death, or even rumors of partisan activity in a town or village, could mean the deaths of 50 or 100 civilians as retribution, coordinated by the army in concert with SS and police. Jews, Gypsies, and Serbs were chosen first, but Croats and Bosnians were not free from all danger. Most of the Jews and Roma were wiped out, and estimates put Serb casualties at 300,000.

After Germany suppressed the Serb and communist insurgents in the Balkans, Britain and the United States expected the Wehrmacht to turn its attention to the Middle East and North Africa, but instead Hitler chose to direct his next assault on the Soviet Union. On June 22, 1941, the Nazis launched Operation Barbarossa. No one should have been too surprised by the Führer's invasion of the USSR. Hitler always made clear his demand for new agricultural and "living space" for Germans in the east and the destruction of what he understood to be the forces of Judeo-Bolshevism to get it. Just days before signing the Non-Aggression Pact in August of 1939, Hitler had commented to the Swiss Commissioner of the League of Nations: "Everything that I undertake is directed against Russia. If those in the West are too stupid, too blind to understand this, then I shall be forced to come to an understanding with the Russians to beat the West, and then, after its defeat, turn with all my concerted force against the Soviet Union."[8]

In the two years since its signing, the Non-Aggression Pact had substantially aided Hitler's long-term goal of defeating the USSR. It had allowed for easy victory in Poland. It presented the Germans with two

years during which they were able to subdue western Europe without the
fear of a second front opening in the east. It had bought the German arms
industry precious time to ramp up production and prepare for the expanded
military effort it would take to defeat the USSR. It had also paved the way
for several trade agreements with the Soviets between 1939 and 1941, which
sent much needed raw materials to the Reich in exchange for manufactured
goods in short supply in the USSR. Soviet trains loaded with supplies were
still on their way to Germany on the first day of the attack.

Given the success the Germans had enjoyed thus far, Hitler and the
Wehrmacht were supremely confident on the eve of Operation Barbarossa.
They felt the Red Army was composed of "inferior" Slavic soldiers and
outfitted by an economically backward state led by cowardly Jews. They
expected the Soviet army—indeed the entire Soviet system—would fall
quickly to the Nazi war machine and predicted victory before winter. The
Wehrmacht attacked in the early hours on a Sunday, and Stalin's forces and
his government were caught completely off-guard.

The Soviet leader's distrust of the Western nations, and his desire not to
provoke Hitler's government, had led him to discount British and American
warnings of an impending German attack. With the invasion of the Soviet
Union, however, Churchill and Roosevelt gained a new ally in the war
against Hitler, even if the communist dictator, Joseph Stalin, was a strange
bedfellow. The British prime minister and the American president did not
hold out much hope for a Soviet victory against the invading Wehrmacht,
which had proven itself unstoppable on land to date, but they were happy
that the Germans had opened a second front in Europe and were grateful
for any additional time before the Germans returned to the idea of invading
the British Isles.

The invading force of 3 million German soldiers and 600,000 soldiers
from allied countries faced a Red Army of 2.9 million. Outnumbered at
the start, the Soviets were well equipped. The Red Army possessed 15,000
tanks, and some models were far superior to the paltry 3,648 German
tanks the Wehrmacht assigned to the operation. The Soviets also had almost
four times as many aircraft as their opponents. Despite some advantages
in materiel, the Red Army was poorly positioned to repel the German
invasion, and the Wehrmacht took vast expanses of land in the initial stages,
covering more than 400 miles within three weeks of combat. It looked to
be a complete disaster for the Red Army. For those Soviet soldiers captured
by the Germans in the first weeks of the assault, the outlook was bleak
(Figure 9.2). Prisoners of war faced execution or tremendous suffering
under inhumane conditions in hastily established camps, which were at
times little more than fenced-in fields. The Germans had no intention of
caring for the vast numbers of POWs who fell into their hands, and as
many as 300,000 Red Army prisoners died each month in the fall of 1941.
Starvation, hypothermia, and disease took most, but thousands more were
shot or beaten by guards. Locals were prohibited from bringing food to

the prisoners, and incidents of cannibalism among prisoners were reported. By the end of 1941 German leaders realized that prisoners could be put to use as laborers on farms and in factories to support the Nazi war effort—but only if they were kept alive. While as many as 3 million Soviet POWs would succumb to malnourishment, disease, or violence from guards by war's end, the rate at which they perished began to decline somewhat starting in 1942.

In the Soviet Union the Nazis intended to seize land and enslave local inhabitants. This was the cornerstone of what Hitler's regime openly called the "Nazi new order in Europe." The day before the launch of Operation Barbarossa, Himmler commissioned the writing of a plan for the spatial reordering of Soviet territory after German victory. What became known as the "General Plan for the East" centered around the forced deportation, not counting Jews, of over 31 million individuals—the majority of Poles, Ukrainians, and Belarussians—to western Siberia, where they would undoubtedly perish. The minority permitted to remain would be subject to "Germanization," much as we saw in Poland, while Germans from the Reich would be resettled in the rich lands left empty by their removal. All east central Europe would come under German control, and the German border would move roughly 1,000 kilometers to the east. Hitler envisioned this vast swath of territory would be developed into modernized farmland and dotted with industrial cities. The entire region would be well connected

FIGURE 9.2 *Soviet POWs are transported in open cargo containers, September 21, 1941 (Bundesarchiv, Bild 101I-267-0124-20A Vorpahl CC-BY-SA 3.0, CC BY-SA 3.0 DE, via Wikimedia Commons).*

via new rail and highway networks. Most importantly, it would be German and all traces of the Slavic and Jewish cultures that had existed would be gone. According to Ian Kershaw, this "territorial solution" to the perceived problem of *Lebensraum* was "plainly genocidal."[9] But the idea of murdering all the Jews of Europe through mass shooting or by gassing in a network of industrialized death camps—the Final Solution detailed in Chapter 10—had not yet emerged in June 1941.

Already at the start of the invasion of the USSR in June, the violence took on an even more brutal shape than it had in Poland. Germans had judged Poles undeserving of sympathy; over time they would disappear as a people via "Germanization" or deportation and starvation. Local leaders—intellectuals, priests, and others held in high esteem—were thus targeted in 1939 and 1940 to undercut any building of a resistance movement. But Hitler was even more hostile to Soviet peoples. These Slavs were deemed racially inferior like Poles, but they were led by a far more sinister force, according to the German leader. The Judeo-Bolshevik cabal controlled the USSR, and according to Nazi propaganda, its sole aim was the destruction of Germany and Germans. Nazi leaders thus portrayed the war against the USSR as existential; Germany would either be victorious, or it would be annihilated. To make sure the latter did not happen, extra brutal measures were needed for Operation Barbarossa. This is revealed in Wehrmacht Field Marshal Wilhelm Keitel's Commissar Order on June 6, 1941: "When fighting Bolshevism, one ca<u>nnot</u> count on the enemy acting in accordance with the principles of humanity or International Law. In particular, it must be expected that the treatment of our prisoners by the political commissars of all types who are the true pillars of resistance, will be cruel, inhuman and dictated by hate." German troops must realize, the directive went on to add, that "it is wrong to trust such elements with clemency and consideration in accordance with International Law." The Soviet commissars were the "originators of Asiatic-barbaric methods of fighting," and if they were taken prisoner they were to be "shot immediately."[10] None of the generals involved in Operation Barbarossa raised concerns about the order, which was clearly a criminal directive to execute non-combatants upon capture, and only a very small number chose not to pass along the order to the men below them.

An infamous example of this barbarity was the use of killing squads. These *Einsatzgruppen*, or mobile killing units, were under the leadership of the Reich Security Main Office (RSHA) and were comprised of men from the SS, SD, Order Police, Criminal Police, and Gestapo, though they were attached to regular Wehrmacht units as they moved eastward first into Polish territory in 1939 and then into the Soviet Union in 1941. Each was made up of between 500 and 1,000 men, many of them well educated. They had specific instructions (issued in early July by Reinhard Heydrich) to kill Jews, communists, Roma, and anyone suspected of being a resister. In the following weeks they took as their primary job the murder of all Jews, including children and the elderly. Each "action" also involved the assistance of local collaborators. Everywhere the Germans went, the new overlords exacerbated existing prejudice and age-old conflicts, encouraging groups to fight among themselves.

The Wehrmacht and SS relied on local Ukrainians, Latvians, ethnic Germans, Russians, Belarussians, and others who actively supported the invading force in formal and informal capacities. The German leadership encouraged unprecedented measures to root out their enemies, especially Jews, but also others who resisted Nazi rule. Some locals received the promises of privileges or bribes; alcohol was sometimes enough. Locals were very useful for identifying Jewish neighbors and organizing the plunder of Jewish property and personal items. The *Einsatzgruppen*, working with Order Police and Wehrmacht soldiers, did most of the work carrying out the mass murder of Jewish civilians (Figure 10.5). The practice became routinized across a vast swath of Soviet territory: Jews were rounded up and forced to dig large pits in a nearby forest or field. These civilians— men, women, and children of all ages—were ordered to undress and then were shot into what became mass graves. Following this basic method, the *Einsatzgruppen* and their local collaborators killed around 1 million individuals as the Red Army retreated in disarray through the summer and fall of 1941 (see Plate 14).

The rapid territorial gains made in these weeks appeared to confirm what the Germans had predicted—that victory in the east would be swift. But the Soviet Union had three things in its favor: time, space, and resources, including 14 million men in reserve. Already in August 1941 the Germans saw worrisome signs. Despite the Wehrmacht's advances, the army had suffered 410,000 casualties and could only mobilize 232,000 replacements. Hitler's generals believed they could not sustain the three prongs of the invasion—to Leningrad in the north, to Moscow in the center, and to Kyiv in the south. They proposed that the next stage of attack should concentrate on the capital, Moscow, to knock out Stalin's government and undermine morale. Hitler disagreed. He believed that the Red Army would never pose a real threat to German victory, and he ordered the diversion of some center group troops to support the capture of Leningrad and others to strengthen the attempt to secure the Ukrainian "breadbasket." At first Hitler's single-mindedness seemed to pay off. The Wehrmacht took most of central and eastern Ukraine by early fall, and on November 21, 1941, it occupied the city of Rostov-on-Don, and along with it the region's industrial sites and the oil pipelines that fed the Soviet war economy. Troops could now be returned to the center group and resume the attack on Moscow. But in the intervening weeks Stalin had rethought his strategy for protecting the capital. Among other changes, he named General Georgi Zhukov on October 10 to lead the defense of Moscow. Aided by tremendous rainstorms that slowed the German advance for three weeks, Zhukov had time to reinforce his 900,000 men with another 400,000. By mid-November, the Wehrmacht had reached the outskirts of Moscow, but the temperatures soon dropped to –40 degrees Celsius, and soldiers started dying of cold in their summer uniforms (Figure 9.3). On December 5 the Soviets launched their counteroffensive, and on the 8th the Germans began a chaotic retreat. On the same day, the Americans officially entered the war against Germany's ally, Japan, which had destroyed the US naval base at Pearl Harbor, Hawaii on the previous day in its bid to dominate the Pacific theater. Three days later Hitler declared war on the United States. Historians still debate the exact reasons why he did so, but at the very least he was honoring his country's military alliance with Japan. Doing so also allowed Germany to attack US-flagged ships, which for some time had been delivering supplies to Germany's foes, without violating international law. The Germans also assumed that the Americans would enter the European conflict at some point, though not before getting bogged down in the Pacific theater. Whatever motivated Hitler's decision, the US Congress responded with its own declaration of war. Hitler was now at war with the two powers, the United States and the USSR, that he had spent so many years obsessing about and railing against, and this was not good news for his regime.

Unable to deliver a knockout punch against the Red Army, the Wehrmacht also faced several challenges of its own making in the areas it held. The Germans had expected to be aided by their ability to live off the land; the

FIGURE 9.3 *Soviet women dig anti-tank trenches to defend Moscow, October-November, 1941. A force of more than 100,000 civilians completed 100 miles of defenses around the Soviet capital (United States Information Agency, Public domain, via Wikimedia Commons).*

new *Lebensraum* would sustain the troops as the ethnocrats and female support staff began to implement the vast resettlement scheme tied to the General Plan for the East. The key figure in the military for the exploitation of Soviet land was General Eduard Wagner, who was responsible for supplying the Wehrmacht and the *Einsatzgruppen* and managing POWs. He worked closely with Göring's Office of the Four-Year Plan, as well as with Heydrich and the RSHA. There were also 19,000 civilians within the Economic Staff East, which managed the exploitation of resources in the Soviet Union. Despite this large bureaucratic infrastructure, a willingness to use violence, and the support of tens of thousands of local collaborators, the German occupiers had a terrible time controlling such a vast area. Curfews, police raids, conscription of locals for labor battalions, and draconian punishments never achieved much in the way of order. Undisciplined Wehrmacht troops looted homes and businesses, farms and offices, across the Soviet Union, destroying or stealing anything of value for their own use or for sale on the black market, and instilling resentment and hatred among the surviving population. Sexual assault, including rape, and other forms of physical violence against civilians were common.

In turn, Soviet men and women responded to calls from Stalin to defend the country from invaders as soldiers or members of partisan bands that became increasingly sophisticated and dangerous to the German occupiers. As a result, the Wehrmacht never succeeded in gathering enough food for its men. The Germans emptied whole cities of their inhabitants and set them to work in the fields, but the Red Army regularly destroyed crops and agricultural machinery as they fell back, taking tools and fuel with them. The Wehrmacht's army group center in Belarus, for example, was expected to live off the land, but the men needed 1,200 head of cattle per day to do so. The vast destruction of the agricultural sector left little fodder for livestock. As cattle grew thinner, the number needed to sustain Germany's hungry soldiers more than doubled.[11] Partisan raids on food stores didn't help either, and German-occupied Soviet cities were soon desperate for food. Nazi antisemitism was also self-defeating from a military standpoint. In Belarus 80 percent of the skilled craftsmen were Jewish, and they were all killed, wiping out the vast majority of those necessary to support the daily needs of the military occupation as metal workers, tailors, butchers, and shoemakers.

According to the General Plan for the East, over 30 million Soviet citizens would meet their deaths through mass shootings, starvation, and the elements in the first year after the invasion. But before long the plan's obvious dangers became clear: disease would follow mass starvation, and the Wehrmacht's own soldiers and German civilian officials would be at risk. As a consequence, Heydrich ordered some Jewish doctors and others be kept alive. The Nazis put a framework for food rations in place across occupied Soviet territory: 1,200 calories per day for civilian workers, 850 for non-workers, and 450 for surviving Jews. That more did not starve was largely due to smuggling and black marketeering. And while Wehrmacht soldiers were protected from mass disease, surviving civilian populations were filled with anti-German hate and a desire for vengeance.

Other long-term problems also remained. In many ways, the Germans faced the same challenges they did in the First World War—a lack of men and material in comparison to the size of the Allied forces and the combined resources at their disposal. By late March 1942, the Wehrmacht could count over 1 million casualties, including about 300,000 dead and missing, only half of whom could be replaced. As many as 8,000 Luftwaffe aircraft had been downed, and about 75,000 ground vehicles had been destroyed. Ahead of a planned summer 1942 offensive along the southern front in the Soviet Union, participating Wehrmacht divisions could only muster about half of the men required, with infantry divisions lacking on average 2,400 men each.[12] The minister of munitions Fritz Todt, and the commander of the reserve army General Friedrich Fromm, who were closest to these realities, believed the war was lost and begged Hitler to make peace with the Soviets. By the end of the first year of combat in the USSR, 40 percent of the entire German army on the eastern front (*Ostheer*) had been lost.

Manpower shortages hurt not only on the battlefield; they also hampered production of munitions and other supplies. In contrast, the Nazi regime's opponents were producing resources for the war at breakneck speed. In addition to American and British manufacturing, the Soviets—despite the heavy losses and destruction on their territory—were manufacturing at remarkable rates. When the Red Army stopped the German advance in December 1941, the Soviets dismantled and shipped production facilities further east to safety behind the Ural Mountains—a feat many people thought impossible. Doing so kept the machinery safe for the rest of the war, because the Germans did not have long-range bombers capable of making that flight. A siege of Leningrad the Nazis had begun on September 8, 1941, also showed no signs of ending. In the first winter, an estimated 1 million of the city's 3 million residents died of starvation, disease, and bitter cold. But the city held, despite hundreds of bombing raids by the Germans. Survivors used the warmer summer months to plant and store food for when the cold would return.

Increasingly short on men and fuel, Hitler decided to postpone another attempt to take Moscow in favor of launching a summer 1942 offensive to the south. Securing Soviet oil fields in the Caucuses would also mean cutting off the Red Army from a major fuel source. After intense fighting, the Wehrmacht took Sevastopol, but when they arrived at the oil fields of Maykop, they found the refineries had been destroyed by retreating Red Army units. Stiff resistance from the Soviets, coupled with spring mud that trapped the German tanks followed by soaring summer temperatures, kept the Wehrmacht also from securing the ultimate prize in the region, the oil fields at Baku. By the end of 1942 an estimated 1.5 million troops had perished or had been injured or taken prisoner, and the Nazi regime was no closer to defeating the Soviets than it had been at the start of Operation Barbarossa. Something had to be done, and soon, warned several high-ranking German generals in the summer. They recognized that the Allies were quickly gaining the upper hand in terms of military production and supply. The Germans turned their attention to Stalingrad, a city of industrial and symbolic importance, and arrived at the outskirts on August 23, 1942. Perhaps, here, the Germans would finally deliver a decisive blow to Soviet morale and manufacturing capacity. However, gambling on crushing the Soviets' fighting spirit at Stalingrad entailed significant risk. Failure there too might sow doubt among the German forces or those at home that there was no route to victory.

Germans on the Homefront and at War, 1939–42

German soldiers greeted the success in Poland and on the western front in 1939 and 1940 with euphoria. Attitudes on the homefront were similar. Most Germans had been anxious when the war began; memories of the First World War were still raw. But as their sons, brothers, and husbands triumphed and losses remained low in 1940, many Germans on the homefront were swept up in the excitement. The invasion of the Soviet Union again provoked worry. Some Germans feared that by opening a second front in the east, the regime risked losing its hard-fought gains. Others worried about an extension of the war, even if they believed that the security of Germany's new European empire demanded a confrontation with the USSR sooner or later. German public opinion swung again toward optimism when initial summer victories in the Soviet Union seemed to confirm the campaign would be short. In the summer of 1941 propagandists declared that "unprecedented prosperity" was on the horizon. Germany's day in the sun appeared finally in reach.

As we will see, the victory needed to achieve the envisioned Nazi "utopia" never came to pass, but this did not stop racially acceptable Germans from leading relatively comfortable lives, at least through 1942. The regime pursued a strategy that sought to minimize the impact of the war on daily life, still believing the chief reason for the loss in 1918 was that civilian defeatism had undermined the nation's will to victory. Rationing of food and household items went into effect at the start of the Second World War, but the prewar policies of the Four-Year Plan had already led to periodic shortages of many consumer items, thus preparing Germans for some of the changes after 1939. Even so, German civilians enjoyed better food rations than anyone else on the continent, and these remained steady until spring 1942. Heavy laborers received the highest allotment of 4,652 calories per day, followed by soldiers at 3,600, and remaining civilians at

2,570.[13] Though at times it was difficult to find the quantity of meat or fat allocated under the plan, significant cuts to the ration system arrived only at the very end of the war. Ersatz products, like synthetic textile fibers that did not hold up well, caused grumbling among the population, but most families were able to reuse and repurpose clothing and linens to avoid the replacement products. Soldiers' pay was raised during 1940, and initial limits on packages sent home were dropped (Göring's Schlepp Decree) so that men could supplement their loved one's larders with items they had either bought or stolen while abroad (Figure 9.4). They did so at a rate of 3 million packages per month. Before he became the Nobel Prize-winning novelist, the young Heinrich Böll, stationed in France, sent home "butter, writing-paper, eggs, ladies' shoes, onions, and much more." Even a half suckling pig made its way to Böll's family in Cologne.[14]

Böll's success finding goods prized by his loved ones in Germany reflected the relatively comfortable experience of many Wehrmacht soldiers stationed in France and the Lowlands during the occupation. The quick military victories in the region left the economies of these countries largely intact, and the Germans set about exploiting them to their benefit. The Wehrmacht requisitioned machinery, raw goods, foodstuffs, and finished goods on a massive scale throughout western Europe. Most of it was "paid for" by a system of credit; in other words, the German central bank owed billions of Reichmarks to the French, Dutch, Belgians, and others by the end of the war. Some mid-sized firms were purchased outright by German companies, or state-sponsored firms like the Hermann-Göring Works, which procured significant mining operations in Alsace Lorraine. Some "Aryanization" of Jewish firms also took place in western Europe, as within Germany. Most of the largest western European companies, however, remained in the hands of their owners. Private property was not expropriated as in the east, because their national governments and legal systems remained largely in place. The western European nations, though under occupation, were seen by the Nazi dictatorship as junior partners in the establishment of a new order on the continent that could challenge Anglo-American power once victory over the Soviet Union was secured.

Despite efforts to harness the economies of occupied Europe, the German war machine was still far underperforming the Allies in early 1942. Responding to the situation became even more of a challenge when Fritz Todt, chief of Armaments, died in an unexplained plane crash on February 8. To the surprise of many, especially Hermann Göring, who as head of the Office of the Four-Year Plan had hoped that Todt's portfolio would be folded into his own, Hitler appointed the young architect Albert Speer as Armaments minister. The German leader then bestowed even more power on Speer, signing a decree on March 21 that set arms production as the highest priority of all economic decision making. In the coming months, as Reich Minister for Armaments and War Production, Speer oversaw the rationalization of many manufacturing sectors—from the assembly of tanks

FIGURE 9.4 *Wehrmacht soldiers buying cake from street vendors near Notre Dame Cathedral in Paris, June 21, 1940 (Bundesarchiv, Bild 1011-129-0480-05A/ Boesig, Heinz/CC-BY-SA, CC BY-SA 3.0 DE, via Wikimedia Commons).*

and submarines to the production of tiny glass lenses used in rifle sights and the massive equipment required for forging steel—all of which led to a more efficient use of resources and increased rates of production. Although most of his efforts capitalized on earlier initiatives, Speer was happy to take credit for doubling arms production in his first year in office. Whether it would be enough remained in doubt, as the Allied nations continued to outpace the Axis powers.

Rationalization was one thing; finding the workers to run the factories at full capacity was another. Labor needs escalated dramatically in 1942, because the losses faced on Soviet territory had meant that many more men had to be called up for military service than in the first phase of the war. In order to maintain output while preserving as much of a sense of normalcy for German civilians as possible, the regime began to rely increasingly on forced foreign laborers on German soil and throughout the occupied territories.

The enlistment of Jewish prisoners was a major topic of conversation at the Wannsee Conference at the start of 1942, as we will see in the next chapter. Its participants concluded that working Jews to death made good sense for the war economy and the regime's goal of ridding Europe of its Jews. In addition to Jews and others imprisoned in Germany's vast network of concentration camps, in spring 1942 Fritz Sauckel was given the task of "recruiting" laborers, by force in most cases, for Germany's war economy. He found 150,000 skilled workers in France, though as with other aspects of occupation policy the full power and brutality of the regime's demands were made in the east. Seasonal workers from Poland had long supported the farming communities of eastern Germany, but already in 1940 new orders targeted them for greater surveillance and poorer treatment. They were required to wear badges noting their status as Poles, and fraternization with Germans was prohibited.

After the invasion of the Soviet Union, POWs were also used as laborers, and marketing campaigns attracted some young Russians looking for work. But these "*Ostarbeiter*" (workers from the east/USSR) were treated even more harshly than the Poles, and with labor needs still growing, men, women, and children of entire villages were conscripted into war work and shipped to German territory. They lived in terrible conditions and received starvation rations and wages. In many cases, they became too ill or weak to work, prompting some Nazi officials to call for better treatment in spring 1942. Hitler consented to slightly better conditions to increase productivity, but he remained adamant that if any Russian worker posed a security threat, they were to be punished by death.

Foreign female forced laborers within Germany and female civilians in the occupied countries were also frequently subject to sexual advances from German soldiers or other German men who felt entitled to sexual relations with powerless women. Military leaders have always found ways for their servicemen to enjoy sex—with prostitutes, in romantic liaisons outside of marriage, and through sexual slavery and rape. The Nazi regime was no different. It established brothels throughout the occupied territories, but unsanctioned liaisons and sexual violence remained common everywhere. The Wehrmacht's leaders provided regulated sexual recreation for their men because they feared homosexuality among the troops, and by monitoring the health and off-hour activities of sex workers in Wehrmacht brothels, there was less risk soldiers would be exposed to sexually transmitted diseases or fall prey to partisans and spies.

The women who were selected to perform sex acts in the military brothels were forced laborers like others across the Nazi empire but were doubly stigmatized after the war for having engaged in taboo sex work and for what many judged to be fraternizing with the Nazi enemy. Nazi leaders also believed that labor productivity was connected to sexual satisfaction, and with this in mind the SS even established brothels in some of its concentration camps in the early 1940s. All told, the Nazi regime benefited from the forced labor of nearly 12 million foreign workers. Relying on unpaid labor meant that wages stayed in government coffers, which could then be used to maintain social assistance programs for Germans during the war. Taxes could be kept low on the middle classes and were eliminated for working-class Germans. The regime established generous allowances for soldiers and their families, and married German women were not recruited into the labor force to the same extent as in other nations during the war. In sum, that German civilians remained relatively content until the latter stage of the war was due to the human resources as well as the material and natural resources extracted from the occupied territories.

The regime never utilized female labor to its full extent, and this likely had negative consequences for the nation's industrial output. The Labor Ministry estimated that there were 3.5 million women in Germany without wage labor or dependents in their care. But Hitler and his advisors had limited views of what they believed women were capable of, and they also worried about public opinion. While some high-ranking officials, like Albert Speer, called for the conscription of women into the labor force, Hitler and others maintained that requiring women, especially married women, to undertake wage work would undermine the regime's prioritization of the domestic sphere as the rightful domain of mothers and wives. The regime's unwillingness to abandon its goal of sheltering the non-Jewish civilian population from the realities of war as much as possible does not mean women were not asked to support the war effort or sacrifice for the cause. German women still made important contributions via their paid and unpaid work, especially in agriculture, their emotional and physical support of husbands, sons, and brothers serving in the military, and as volunteers in many roles within Germany and in the occupied territories. As many as 500,000 women, for example, served as "helpers" to the Wehrmacht by 1945, as typists, telephone operators, nurses, and other roles (see Plate 10).

Teens and youth were also put to work. During the war, the regime expanded its "Relocation to the Countryside" (*Kinderlandverschickung*, KLV) program. Begun in peacetime to provide outdoor recreation and ideological training for youth, during the war the program took on the purpose of protecting children from air raids and employing them away from cities. Working with the Nazi welfare authorities and the Hitler Youth, pregnant women and mothers of young children could accompany their sons and daughters to thousands of "camps" set up in schoolhouses, private homes, and youth hostels. Older children went on their own. In addition to receiving political education, older children also often performed some sort of labor. Teenagers stayed back and were increasingly mobilized for agriculture and other forms of work, such as tutoring newly arrived ethnic Germans in the language and customs their ancestors had "lost." Teens who stayed in their hometowns also assisted soldiers home on furlough or due to disability. Older boys helped build fortifications. Young people acted as air raid wardens and fought fires. And boys were even conscripted into fighting units in the latter stages of the war.

Germans of all ages joined the Reich Air Defense League, which had 12 million members in 1939. Similar leagues emerged in many European countries in the interwar years, as the prospect of military bombing campaigns grew. As in other nations, a large proportion of the membership in Germany was female, and its size continued to climb throughout the war. The League's aims were to educate civilians and support local safety plans. The ranks of the Air Raid Protection Squads were also often filled by women, who protected public buildings like schools and hospitals and private homes. In the countryside, air defense was less critical, though women all across the country, including in rural villages, found volunteer work as members of the two mass organizations: the National Socialist Women's League and the German Women's Corp within the National Socialist People's Welfare. Over 10 million women joined the two organizations during the war years. Members repaired uniforms and created knitted goods for soldiers, sailors, and airmen. Volunteers also ran the distribution centers for those whose homes had suffered damage or destruction in air raids. They collected and distributed clothing and linens, food and water, and other necessities to families in need. Female volunteers also ran support stations in railway terminals to assist those fleeing to safer locations, offering a warm meal and some conversation to keep spirits up.[15]

Women's motivations for volunteering in these roles varied. For some, patriotism was a driving force. They believed in what Germany was fighting for, and they wished to support the regime and its aspirations. For some women this patriotism was founded on a deep ideological commitment to National Socialism. For others, defending Germany was important enough on its own, regardless of the nation's leadership. The fact that their male loved ones were at the front was also a motivating factor for many. If their husbands and sons were risking their lives, they wanted to do what they could to help. In other cases, these volunteer positions had more immediate, tangible benefits. Some women used their volunteer experiences to start or further careers in the party or public sector. Others used them to ensure their families' access to resources, especially in the last months of the war when conditions at home deteriorated.

Women also played a critical role in their homes, stretching resources and maintaining a level of domestic comfort for their children and other family members, which bolstered morale and optimism. But the regime's efforts to shape women's work in the private sphere also created tension. Some women resented being compelled to donate household items like metal goods that could be melted down for munitions and food waste, such as used coffee grounds, from which fat, wax, resin, and cellulose could be extracted and reused in industrial production. They also resented the regime's efforts to instruct them in raising children and housekeeping, given their own expertise (see Plate 9).

Another way the regime sought to protect "Aryan" women (and uphold its understanding of rightful gender roles) was by increasing soldiers' wages so that fewer wives would find it necessary to enter paid labor during the conflict. The Nazis also increased benefits to the families of soldiers killed in action. In addition to the wives and children of these servicemen, the parents of the deceased and even fiancées were eligible for these payments. Beyond financial support, the regime offered grieving family members assistance with housing and planning for memorial services. The expansion of benefits was also intended to reassure soldiers that their families would be well cared for if they did not make it home. The regime's framing of the casualties of war as patriotic sacrifices that should occasion pride as well as grief is not surprising, but its attempt to wrest the pastoral care of mourning families from the Christian Churches led to some conflict between the state and these older institutions. Most non-Jewish Germans who grieved lost loved ones continued to turn to their local priests and ministers for spiritual guidance and comfort.

What do we know about the men who led the Wehrmacht, and the men who served under them? Historically, the German army had been an elite force filled with the sons of nobility and wealthy family. Hitler's Wehrmacht was a veritable people's army. Thirteen million men spent at least some time on the eastern front, as witnesses to and participants in the mass killings and unprecedented destruction of Operation Barbarossa. For a long time after 1945, Germans believed there had been two wars. One fought by a brave and professional Wehrmacht, made up of their brothers, sons, and fathers. They were soldiers who had respected time-honored rules of military engagement and had fought and died honorably. The other war was the criminal campaign waged by a small number of fanatical SS men, who ordered the mass civilian casualties mostly on the eastern front, manned the offices that planned the industrial killings of the Holocaust, and ran the camps where the murders occurred. This idea of an innocent Wehrmacht has been proved false over the last several decades by extensive archival work and ground-breaking oral histories with aging soldiers.

Scholars have asked how the professional officer corps became so willing to engage in the sort of criminal behavior that is discussed here and in the following chapters. The officer corps of the former military, the Reichswehr, did not think much of Hitler in 1933. And, yet, just six years later it was willing to support him in an expansionist war that included support for and collaboration with the *Einsatzgruppen* in their work of murdering Jews and other civilians in Poland and the USSR, the mistreatment and murder of millions of Soviet POWs, the brutal execution of suspected partisans, and support for the SS in the management of the genocidal camp system.

The story began with the Night of the Long Knives in June and July 1934, during which Hitler ordered the murder of Ernst Röhm and dozens of others. Killing the leader of the SA, the party's paramilitary wing, removed that mass organization as a rival to the nation's armed forces. The military's generals were grateful to Hitler for eliminating this challenger and for approving the massive expansion of the armed forces in the years leading up to the war. Hitler encouraged them to dream of a German empire and gave them the resources to do it. The army enjoyed spectacular early successes that fed their arrogance and sense of invincibility. The nation's military leaders also shared some of Hitler's beliefs about the geopolitical situation: they too believed that Germany needed *Lebensraum* and that self-sufficiency was critical to the country's survival, and they shared Hitler's hatred of Marxism. Like Hitler they also mistakenly believed that defeating the Soviet Union would be easy. Antisemitism was common among the officer corps, though the murderous fanaticism professed by leading Nazis was less common in these circles before the war.

The officer corps, however, also changed dramatically *during* the war. The Wehrmacht had 90,000 officers in 1939, but that figure had doubled by the midpoint of the Second World War. This rapid growth was made possible by Hitler's directive that performance in battle—as opposed to seniority, education, or family connections—should determine who received commissions and promotions. Those who seized the new opportunities to rise through the ranks remained deeply loyal to Hitler. The result was a dramatic change in the social composition of the officer corps. As many as 90 percent of officer cadets in 1941 had passed the rigorous *Abitur* university entrance test. That soon dropped to 50 percent. An increasing number of officers had only an elementary education, and some generals were even promoted from among the enlisted men. The point is not that less educated men were more likely to engage in criminal behavior. Rather, the Wehrmacht became a fighting force in which men were recognized primarily for their willingness to do whatever was required to achieve the regime's radical aims. Arguably, once the first atrocities were committed in Poland at the start of the war, the Wehrmacht's officer corps was bound to the regime. Their own complicity strengthened their loyalty.

But what about the 20 million men who would serve at some point in the Wehrmacht's rank-and-file? Most were ideologically committed to National Socialism and to Hitler, even though they distanced themselves from the party apparatus. From 1934 onward all soldiers were called upon to swear a personal oath of allegiance to Hitler (Figure 9.5). Most men were convinced that they were fighting a justified and necessary war against racial and political enemies. How did this happen? Those between the ages of six and eleven in 1933 would have spent six full years within the Hitler Youth before the war began, and most of that cohort would have seen some fighting by 1945. Unlike adults whose support for the regime was tempered by region, political affiliation, or religion, kids who grew up in the rebellious Hitler Youth before enlisting in the Wehrmacht did not share this hesitancy toward the regime. They were eager to show their mettle on the battlefield. As one former soldier recounted, "we wanted to avenge our fathers, those who had lost the heroes' battle from 1914 to 1918, despite having fought in the war so victoriously ... as we had been told in school. The Fatherland and the Führer needed us, the German youth, of that we were certain—that was our firm belief."[16]

FIGURE 9.5 *Reichswehr soldiers swear an oath of loyalty to the Führer, Adolf Hitler, shortly after President Hindenburg's death on August 2, 1934. During the republican period, soldiers swore an oath to the constitution. After 1933, the oath was made to the country. When Hitler became Führer and Reich Chancellor in 1934, he solidified his dictatorship. Soldiers, thereafter, were required to swear their allegiance directly to him (Bundesarchiv, Bild 102-16108/CC-BY-SA 3.0, CC BY-SA 3.0 DE, via Wikimedia Commons).*

Notes

1   Wilm Hosenfeld quoted in Nicholas Stargardt, *The German War: A Nation under Arms, 1939–1945* (London: Basic Books, 2016), 28.

2   SD report from Upper Franconia quoted in ibid., 33.

3   Dorothea Guenther, "Der Krieg 1939/40," https://www.dhm.de/lemo/zeitzeugen/dorothea-guenther-der-krieg-193940.html

4   Melita Maschmann, *Account Rendered. A Dossier on My Former Self* (Lexington, MA: Plunkett Lake, 2013), 97–8.

5   "Eine moderne Volkerwanderung," *Der Neue Tag* (Prague), May 27, 1940, quoted in Peter Fritzsche, *Life and Death in the Third Reich* (Cambridge, MA: Belknap, 2008), 174, from the original, Hans Adler, *Verwaltete Mensch: Studien zur Deportation der Juden aus Deutschland* (Tübingen: J. C. B. Mohr, 1974), 171.

6   Mark Mazower, *Hitler's Empire: How the Nazis Ruled Europe* (London: Penguin, 2008), 108.

7   Guenther, "Der Krieg 1939/40."

8   Adolf Hitler quoted in Ian Kershaw, *Fateful Choices: Ten Choices That Changed the World, 1940–1941* (London: Penguin, 2008), 63.

9   Ian Kershaw, *Hitler: Nemesis, 1936–1945* (New York: Norton, 2001), 463.

10 "Directives for the Treatment of Political Commissars" (Commissar Order), June 6, 1941, https://ghdi.ghi-dc.org/sub_document.cfm?document_id=1548

11 Martin Kitchen, *The Third Reich: Charisma and Continuity* (London: Routledge: 2014), 346.

12 Omer Bartov, *Hitler's Army: Soldiers, Nazis, and War in the Third Reich* (New York: Oxford University Press, 1992), 43.

13 Richard J. Evans, *The Third Reich at War* (New York: Penguin, 2009), 427.

14 Ibid., 335.

15 Nicole Kramer, "Volksgenossinnen on the German Homefront: An Insight into Nazi Wartime Society" in *Visions of Community in Nazi German: Social Engineering and Private Lives*, Martina Streber and Bernhard Gotto, eds. (Oxford: Oxford University Press, 2014), 171–86.

16 Werner Mork, "Kriegsbeginn am 01. September 1939," https://www.dhm.de/lemo/zeitzeugen/werner-mork-kriegsbeginn-am-22-september-1939.html

Additional Reading

Bartov, Omer. *Hitler's Army: Soldiers, Nazis, and War in the Third Reich*. New York and Oxford: Oxford University Press, 1992.

Browning, Christopher. *Ordinary Men: Reserve Police Battalion 101 and the Final Solution in Poland*. New York: HarperCollins, 1992.

Harvey, Elizabeth. *Women and the Nazi East: Agents and Witnesses of Germanization*. New Haven and London: Yale University Press, 2003.

Mazower, Mark. *Hitler's Empire: How the Nazis Ruled Europe*. London: Penguin Books, 2009.

Overy, Richard. *Blood and Ruins: The Last Imperial War, 1931–1945*. London: Viking, 2021.

Snyder, Timothy. *Bloodlands: Europe between Hitler and Stalin*. New York: Basic Books, 2010.

Stahel, David. *Operation Barbarossa and Germany's Defeat in the East*. Cambridge: Cambridge University Press, 2009.

Stargardt, Nicholas. *The German War: A Nation under Arms, 1933–1945*. New York: Basic Books, 2015.

Weinberg, Gerhard. *A World at Arms: A Global History of World War II*. Cambridge: Cambridge University Press, 1994.

10

The Holocaust

To understand the genocide of Europe's Jews during the Second World War, it is important to circle back to the two years preceding the Nazi invasion of Poland. From the earliest days of his political career Hitler was determined to conquer "living space" for the German race. This would require war, he knew, and he hoped to remove Jews, whom he saw as enemy saboteurs, from the Reich before any such hostilities began. Not accidentally, 1938 saw the regime emboldened in pursuing these twin aims. The economy had already achieved full employment by 1936—something other countries recovering from the Great Depression could not boast of—and rearmament was moving ahead. As we saw in Chapter 8, Hitler marched into his home country of Austria in March 1938, fulfilling one of the goals of far-right nationalists and pan-Germans since 1870 to bring the German-speaking country "back home to the Reich." The irony is that the more of the map Hitler conquered, the more Jews he would have to deal with. But in turn, the more Jews under his control, the more opportunities he had to experiment with radical solutions to the "Jewish Question." Such was the case with Hitler's home country. The annexation of Austria brought 192,000 Jews into the Reich, and the following year, the invasion and control of Czechoslovakia would add 120,000 Jews.

Jewish Policy in the Late 1930s

The March invasion of Austria was shockingly violent. Jews were beaten up, had their beards cut off, or were forced to clean streets and public fixtures on their hands and knees (Figure 10.1). The humiliation and torment were the handiwork of local Nazis, who acted with impunity in the absence of a functioning central government. To lend order to the process of persecution, the Nazis turned to Adolf Eichmann, head of the Security Service (SD) branch of the SS in Vienna, who himself had just led an attack on the Jewish Cultural Community offices in the Austrian capital. Eichmann had grown up in Vienna and in 1932 had joined the Nazi Party and the SS. He served in the SD's Jewish department and became, in his mind certainly, an expert on all things Jewish. He learned a little Hebrew and Yiddish and took an interest in Zionism. In the aftermath of the *Anschluss*, he was placed in charge of ridding Austria of Jews. What was still a "voluntary" process of emigration in Germany proper was a coercive one in Austria. In six months, 50,000 Jews, one-quarter of the country's Jewish population, was driven out. They often had no place to go; some were forced onto boats that wandered along the Danube River looking for a place to dock. In late April, the Jewish Telegraphic Agency reported that 12,000 Austrian Jews had been arrested and 2,000 had committed suicide. In the year following the *Anschluss*, a total of almost 3,000 Austrian Jews took their own lives.

The success of the Jewish purge in Austria encouraged the Nazis to ratchet up the terror in the "Old Reich" of Germany. Here the regime tried to balance the wish to remove Jews by hastening their emigration with that of turning them into international pariahs, making their ability to find a new country *more* difficult. In July, the regime declared that any Jew over the age of three months would have to carry at all times a special identity card, which they had to produce on the demand of an "official agency" or when transacting business. The same month, the Nazis decreed that by January 1,

FIGURE 10.1 *Hitler Youth guard Jews forced to clean streets in Vienna, directly after Austria's annexation to the German Reich, March 1938 (World History Archive, Alamy).*

1939, Jews bearing a first name of "non-Jewish" origin had to add "Israel" or "Sara" to their given names on identity papers. They were forbidden from changing their names to skirt the new regulation. And henceforth, non-Jewish Germans could only christen their newborns with "German" names, though biblical names like Joseph (as in Joseph Goebbels) were considered sufficiently "Germanized." "Aryans" who felt their names were too "Jewish" would be given priority in changing them if they had no "Jewish blood." In the early nineteenth century, Jews had taken up surnames as part of their emancipation from ghettos and their gaining of civil rights. But now they were being figuratively forced back into the ghetto, without the identities that had brought them some measure of social and political security in the prior century.

The new laws kept coming. On October 5, 1938, all passports held by Jews had to be returned; new ones issued had the letter "J" on it. Jews were also subject to a "flight tax" that made it harder to leave. The law was originally introduced in 1931 to protect against the wealthy whisking their assets out of the country during the Depression, and it effectively levied a fine amounting to 40 percent of a person's fortune over $80,000. Over the course of the decade, the percentage of forfeiture increased steadily, in part in response to the lack of hard currency in the country on account of diminished global trade and the depletion of the country's gold reserves. In June of 1938, the flight taxes amounted to 90 percent of one's assets. Desperate Jews were forced to choose between staying in the country that had disowned them and forfeiting their wealth to leave Germany, with no guarantee of achieving asylum abroad.

Here the contradictions in Nazi thinking were apparent. Hitler wanted Jews to flee Germany, but the desire to expropriate Jewish wealth made it less likely that Jews would escape and abandon their savings. For a similar reason, until 1938 the economic sphere, which was so connected with antisemitism, was still populated by Jews. Grocers, cobblers, clothing store owners, and other small stores were already hurt by Nazi blockades, but they were allowed to stay in business to provide tax revenue to the state and to service the increasingly impoverished Jewish community. Of about 100,000 Jewish-owned businesses in 1933, 39,552 were still left at the beginning of 1938. As many as 60,000 had closed or had been sold at cut-rate prices as their owners scrambled to leave the country. Nazi newspapers complained that "Aryan" retailers were still buying from Jewish manufacturers, especially in the textile industry. "Aryans" were encouraged to shop only from stores bearing the sign "Adefa" (Working Group of German-Aryan Manufacturers) near their goods, indicating that they were made by racially pure citizens. In 1938 Hitler decided to scoop up these shops and other assets. Jews were forced to register all their property and holdings at home and abroad. This included works of art, jewelry, and all types of social benefits. Any change of business or a purchase in the amount of US$2,000 or more would have to be authorized. Meanwhile "voluntary" dispossession continued, with Jews dumping their businesses at fire sale prices, receiving 30–60 percent of their value. The Law Excluding Jews from Commercial Businesses ultimately barred Jews from owning any business. As of January 1, 1939, the German economy was officially *judenrein.*

The violence also increased in 1938, as Jews were now racial and social pariahs. In the summer, "asocial Jews" were rounded up and sent to Dachau, Sachsenhausen, and Buchenwald. In most cases their "crimes"—such as illegal parking, failure to make a rent payment on time, unemployment— were a mere pretense. One might be released if one promised to sell a business or emigrate. In 1938, 282 Jews were convicted for having had sexual relations with "Aryans." In October, the SS deported 1,000 Jews with Polish citizenship, even as the government of Poland tried to block their return. Entire families were sent in sealed railway cars to the Polish border. They were expelled into a "no-man's land" as Poles tried to drive them back into Germany. They eventually found shelter in warehouses, stables, and train stations, while Jews in Poland gave them food and blankets before the Polish government finally accepted them.

One of the families deported was that of Herschel Grynzspan. As an act of revenge, this seventeen-year-old Polish Jew living in Paris walked into the German Embassy and shot a low-ranking official, Ernst vom Rath, on November 7. Ostensibly as a reprisal for this assassination, the Nazis organized the most brutal attack on Jews to date. Reinhard Heydrich drew up a list of those to be arrested, and on the night of November 9 to 10, 1938, a wave of violence overtook Germany. Planned on the same date as the German ceasefire in 1918 and the failed Hitler's putsch in 1923, this pogrom was brazen in its violence. In what the regime euphemistically called "Kristallnacht," or "the Night of Broken Glass," over 7,000 Jewish-owned businesses were looted, and almost 400 synagogues were set on fire, with 150 totally destroyed. Torah scrolls and other religious items were thrown from the buildings and defaced or burnt. Fire fighters were ordered to stand back and douse the flames only if adjoining buildings were threatened. Jews were attacked and beaten, with thousands injured, over 100 killed, and 30,000 arrested and sent to Dachau, Buchenwald, and Sachsenhausen, where some were tortured for weeks. There were 680 suicides. Shops were destroyed and looted, and broken windowpanes lined the streets (Figure 10.2).

It was not just stores and synagogues. In Austria and Germany, upon Goebbels' orders, apartments were raided, smashed, and looted. Only recently have historians begun to focus on what Wolf Gruner has called the "forgotten mass destruction of Jewish homes." Nuremberg saw the wrecking of 236 Jewish apartments, and Düsseldorf had almost double that. In Mannheim and Rostock, almost every Jewish apartment was wrecked. This was not just the handiwork of radical Nazi stormtroopers. In Vienna, the SD reported that crowds had broken through barriers and assaulted Jews, yelling "Beat them to death, the dogs!"[1] Those who did not engage

FIGURE 10.2 *Destroyed Jewish shop in Magdeburg during the November Pogrom, 1938 (Bundesarchiv, Bild 146-1970-083-42 CC-BY-SA 3.0, CC BY-SA 3.0 DE, via Wikimedia Commons).*

in violence cheered it on, proclaiming that Jews were getting what was due to them. When all was done, Hermann Göring blamed the violence on the Jews, the regime billed the Jewish community $1 billion as an "atonement tax" to pay for all the damages, and property insurance companies refused to honor their policies for Jewish clients. The remaining Jewish political organizations like the National Representation were reorganized and replaced with Nazi-run bodies, and the last Jewish newspapers were banned. All said, in 1938 attacks on Jews took place in 1,315 cities and towns, up from 98 locales in 1937.

In their final months of publication, Jewish newspapers reflected a foreboding mood. The readers of *The Jewish Handworker*, a trade publication in Berlin, could learn about the products and services still available to them from Jewish vendors: glasses at Platzmann optical, cameras at Bernstein photography supplies, and radio and refrigerator repair at Rolf Feder's shop on the Kurfürstendamm.[2] The business-as-usual look of these advertisements increasingly belied the restrained panic of the adjacent articles. The last page of the paper's final issue in October 1938 reveals both the hope and the resignation that marked the Jewish communities of Germany on the eve of the November Pogrom. Ads for Jewish restaurants and coffee shops, one for a jewelry repair store, and one for a fashion trade school give way to a sketch of a moving van and a passenger ship labeled "Abroad." The last and largest spot on the page is a banner ad for the soon-to-be "Aryanized" Nathan Israel department store in Berlin. For those who were staying in Germany, the emporium offered a "wide selection of wallpaper and upholstery." For those leaving there were "supplies for emigration."[3]

Who would take in these fleeing Jews? In July of 1938 the United States and thirty-one other countries sponsored a conference on the Jewish refugee crisis in Evian, France. Country after country expressed their sorrow about the persecution of Jews, but they refused to raise their immigration quotas for fear of being overwhelmed by refugees during a period of economic recovery. Nor did leaders want to be accused of welcoming Jews into their midst, thereby stirring up latent antisemitism in the public or displaying their own. Only the Dominican Republic accepted Jews beyond their existing quotas; it would eventually take 700 Jews, whom dictator Rafael Trujillo hoped would ethnically "whiten" the country while also clearing its jungles for agriculture.

It didn't help that Jewish passports now bore a "J" for *Jude*, permanently marking Jews as alien and making it harder for them to go about their lives in anonymity or passing as "Aryan." Some countries did step up boycotts of German goods and condemn the Nazis in the aftermath of the November Pogrom. But this was not the same as asylum, and to Hitler these protests confirmed the myth that there was an international Jewish conspiracy against Germany. Clearly this "conspiracy" did not amount to much if countries were rejecting Jews. Even for those countries that agreed to take more Jews, applicants still could experience a bureaucratic nightmare, with written appeals going unprocessed or with extra demands for proof that one could be gainfully employed. In the autumn of 1938, France and the Netherlands declared that they would take no more refugees. The doors were swinging shut on German Jews. Up until this point the Nazis encouraged Zionist activities in Germany in preparation for expected departures to British Palestine. Zionist youth had studied Hebrew, learned Jewish history, and engaged in athletics and agricultural training. But now Britain was closing off entry to Palestine. By the end of the year, the SS assumed control of Jewish emigration. In January of 1939, Heydrich opened the Reich Central Office for Jewish Emigration in Berlin, which henceforth coordinated all attempts to force Jews to leave their homeland.

On January 30, 1939, Adolf Hitler celebrated six years in power. In a speech to the Reichstag, he touted his accomplishments, reasserted his need for resource-rich colonies, and insisted that his territorial acquisitions were a response to centuries of German mistreatment. Toward the end of his address, Hitler offered his most infamous example of Germany-as-victim rhetoric. He boasted of his prophetic skills, citing his prediction during the Weimar years that he would one day become Germany's leader, and he cleverly mapped the story of his personal journey as a lonely truth-teller onto the story of Germany being an unfairly treated international outcast.

He lashed out at the Jews who had "laughed" at his ambition, and he then offered "another prophecy": "If the international Jewish financiers in and outside Europe should again succeed in plunging the nations into a world war, the result will not be the bolshevization of the globe and thus victory for Jewry but the annihilation of the Jewish race in Europe."[4]

Seven months before the outbreak of the Second World War, Hitler was thus stating openly that the coming war would end in the destruction of European Jewry. He did not have a specific plan in place in 1939, but he thought the annihilation of Jews would come about as a result of struggles against "Jewish" capitalism, which meant Britain and the United States—countries with which tensions had risen since the November Pogrom—and "Judeo-Bolshevism," which meant the USSR. The speech condensed other key elements of Hitler's antisemitic worldview: the link between communism and Jewishness; the obsession with Jewry and finance; Jews as warmongers; Jews as a race rather than a religion; and Hitler's being laughed at as a metaphor for the shaming of Germany. Whatever tragedy befell Jews in the next "world war," Hitler warned, would be a result of this people's own misdeeds. The January 30 address reveals how much war and the persecution of Jews were entwined in the Nazi vision. Over the next six years, the event that has come to be known as the Holocaust—the mass murder of up to 6 million Jews and millions of other Europeans—was inseparable from military conquest. The conflagration that consumed much of the continent allowed Hitler to pursue millions of Jews living under German occupation.

Jewish Persecution and the Run-Up to the Second World War

In the final two years before the German invasion of Poland, Hitler's territorial aggression coincided with a ramping up of Jewish persecution. After the close of the Olympics, the Nazis increasingly abandoned any concessions to international outrage. The November Pogrom was the most visible and terrifying example of the regime prioritizing racial persecution over international goodwill. In 1938 and 1939 the ostracizing of German Jews became ever more brutal, open, and bizarre. Every economic woe or governmental misstep was portrayed as the fault of the Jews. When the stock market fell in July of 1938, the Nazis attributed it to "Jewish maneuvers." In May of 1938, the Nazi press blamed Jews for a shortage of onions. Jewish speculation purportedly led to Jews cornering the vegetable market and depriving the "Aryan" *Hausfrau* of a basic staple for her family's meals. In April of 1939, the Reich barred the import of oranges from Palestine if they were grown and picked by Jews. Henceforth, the Nazis would only accept fruit harvested by Christians, whether European settlers or Arabs, who despite being racially "semitic" were considered "Aryan" for this purpose. As the Jewish Telegraphic Agency sardonically put it, "Germany has now extended racial discrimination to the vegetable kingdom."[5] Sarcasm aside, this mandate indicates how the Nazis tried to stir up a physical repulsion toward Jews. They encouraged Germans to purchase "Aryan" products and warned of the deleterious effects of consuming "Jewish" ones, especially foodstuffs. According to a placard seen as early as the 1933 boycott, "Whoever eats Jewish products will die from them." In keeping with this message, the regime shuttered Jewish-owned grocery stores and pubs, in addition to kosher establishments, and by the time the war broke out, irrational fears of contamination were channeled into a general anxiety that Jews might taint food by their very proximity to it.

Many Germans after 1945 would claim that they had not followed these seemingly trivial mandates or had not witnessed the impact of new regulations on their neighbors. But newspapers and wire services documented every Nazi utterance and every new policy. By 1938, the flow of information was steady. Telling Germans about anti-Jewish measures was a key to the Nazis' building a national antisemitic consensus while inspiring fear and awe in a police state. In 1936 a glossy Nazi magazine featured a photo spread devoted to Dachau, along with an article about how the well-run and clean camp was no longer filled with political prisoners. It was now a place for "asocials" and "Jewish parasites on the nation."[6] As we saw in Chapter 8, the regime eagerly promoted its anti-Jewish measures abroad as well. The Reich Ministry of Propaganda worked with local right-wing movements to distribute Nazi literature. In Switzerland, pro-Nazi leaflets were widespread in the German-speaking cantons in the late 1930s. And in the United States, Hitler's policies had vocal supporters. In June 1938, retired US General George Van Horn Moseley, in testimony before the House Committee on Un-American Activities, praised the Nazis for solving "the racial problem." Meanwhile Nazi organizations—even small ones like the German Agricultural League—compiled notes and articles on "Antisemitism and the Jewish Question at home and abroad." Wire services, like the Jewish Telegraphic Agency, issued a constant flow of alarming stories about Nazi actions, large and small.

Escaping Germany

If the world knew so much, what did it do to help the Jews before and after the November Pogrom? The July 1938 Evian Conference, which addressed the Jewish refugee crisis, had shown that the international community had little appetite to take in many immigrants. And this response emboldened the Nazi regime. Evian, wrote a Nazi intelligence staff member, had proved "an extensive aversion to a significant flow of emigrants either out of social considerations or out of an unexpressed racial abhorrence against Jewish emigrants."[7] Other international organizations abdicated responsibility during this fateful year. In August of 1938, Guillaume Favre, a member of the International Red Cross, visited the Dachau concentration camp. He did not publish an official report, but in a letter to SS leader Heinrich Himmler, he wrote that while the "very idea of a concentration camp … is an affront to free citizens' way of thinking," Dachau was well run and a "model of its kind."[8] Two years earlier, the Red Cross had made a similar observation, noting that while it was wrong to force different categories of prisoners to reside together, conditions had gotten better since the first years of the regime.

This is not to say that there were no acts of courage. Despite a mandate to enforce restrictive immigration policies, a US consular official in Vienna pleaded for more help processing visas and, when denied, paid for clerks out of his own pocket. In 1939 American Unitarian minister Waitstill Sharp and his wife traveled to occupied Czechoslovakia to study the humanitarian crisis. They then founded the Unitarian Service Committee, which aided displaced persons during the war with clothes, medicine, and food. The Vatican under Pope Pius the XI (in contrast to his successor) protested Nazi doctrines of "Aryan" superiority and noted with alarm Germany's treatment of minorities. In 1937, it issued an encyclical titled *Mit Brennender Sorge* (With Burning Anxiety), which denounced violations of the Reichskonkordat and expressed alarm at the "exalting" of one race or nation over another. Between 1938 and 1940 Jewish, Quaker, and Christian charities, along with private citizens, resettled nearly 10,000 German Jewish children in the UK through the *Kindertransport* (children's transport) rescue missions (Figure 10.3).

As Jews scrambled to leave Germany, they were, in the words of historian Armin Shmid, "lost in a labyrinth of red tape." They waited in long lines to meet with lawyers and representatives of Jewish relief organizations. They gathered affidavits and wrote letters to relatives abroad, who needed to "sponsor" them and attest to their access to gainful employment. Jews in occupied Czechoslovakia and formerly Austrian territory faced the same challenges—tangles of paperwork, crossed signals, bad luck, and fraud among foreign consular officials. One Prague family, the Strnads, exemplifies the attempt—and tragic failure—to emigrate to the US. Paul Strnad was a forty-three-year-old bank clerk, and his wife was a thirty-nine-year-old dress designer well respected in Prague fashion circles. After the Munich Agreement, the couple sensed that it was only a matter of time before the Nazis moved into the rest of the country. Paul sent desperate letters to a cousin in the United States, which included his wife's sketches and dress designs. He wrote that "for the last seventeen years (she) has been running, as proprietress, a first-class dressmaking establishment." She, Paul wrote, "enjoys a very good reputation here in Prague, as she is very diligent, has a first-class knowledge of her line, and has very good taste."[9] Unfortunately, a visa never came, and the couple was sent to Terezín and eventually met their deaths after being transported to Auschwitz.

FIGURE 10.3 *The children's transport. The children of Polish Jews upon arrival in London, February 1939 (Bundesarchiv, Bild 183-S69279/CC-BY-SA 3.0, CC BY-SA 3.0 DE, via Wikimedia Commons).*

Jews did get out. Of the 523,000 Jews living in Germany when Hitler took over, over half of them—304,000—had emigrated by 1939. From 1933 to 1939, the size of the German Jewish population under the age of forty fell by 80 percent. In the first quarter of 1939, 8,600 were able to escape Germany. But for the remaining 200,000 Jews trying to flee, sad stories abounded. In May of 1939, 937 Jewish passengers with Cuban visas boarded the German steamship SS *St. Louis* and set sail to Havana. While en route, it became clear that these visas were actually "landing permits," part of a money-making scheme that did not actually allow for Jews to disembark. The ship stayed for days in Havana harbor, with US, Cuban, and Jewish organizations frantically trying to find a home for its passengers. Goebbels tried to stir up anti-Jewish sentiments in Cuba, claiming that those on board were criminals and undesirables. The refugees were refused entry, and the ship sailed north, hugging the Florida coast and hoping to dock in Miami. But the United States also denied entry, citing official US immigration policy, and Canada also refused, arguing that if one ship were let in, others would follow. Eventually, the SS *St. Louis* was forced back to Europe. The American Joint Distribution Committee negotiated homes for most of the passengers in France, the UK, Belgium, and the Netherlands. But some of these Jews would later be trapped when the Nazis invaded western Europe.

If the Nazis wanted to get rid of Jews, why did Goebbels try to provoke a global repulsion toward them in countries that might be inclined to take some of them in? Simply put, Nazi policy was contradictory. The regime still pushed for emigration (until October 1941), and yet it also sought to rile up antisemitic sentiment abroad. The Nazis wanted to prove that the rest of the world disliked Jews and that they were addressing a global problem. The regime looked on with satisfaction as the very countries that condemned Germany for their abuses themselves did little for these accursed people. They watched the increase in antisemitism around the west, not least in the United States. In early 1939, Former US Under Secretary of State William R. Castle shared his views of Jewish requests for asylum with an audience at the American Legion: "This is a curious thing. Its basis is claimed to be purely humanitarian and yet just as many Christians have been killed in Russia as there are Jews in Germany and you never hear a cry that we ought to go to war with the Soviets to save the lives of their citizens who are still being 'liquidated' rapidly."[10] The undersecretary put the word "liquidated" in quotes, in effect offering an early form of Holocaust denial that persists to this day. But if Castle called into question the possibility of the mass murder of Jews, the Nazis themselves made little attempt to hide their violent ambitions. Nazi propaganda in the summer of 1939 was not as direct as Hitler's "prophecy" earlier in the year. But a month before the outbreak of the Second World War, Goebbels' newspaper *Der Angriff* warned that future pogroms would be in Jews' future if this group "continued behaving arrogantly" by forgetting the mercy and "empathy" Germans had shown them after the November Pogrom. In short, Jews should be grateful that their treatment had been so "humane."[11]

The Second World War and the Fate of Europe's Jews

Hitler made it clear that another war would be disastrous for Europe's Jews. And that war came on September 1. Despite their confident predictions, the Nazis were utterly unprepared for the "Jewish problem" they had inherited as they moved into Poland. Three million Jews lived in the country, but the Nazis had given little thought to how to deal with them, especially given how improvised the invasion was. Most Polish Jews were less assimilated than their coreligionists in Germany, and the Nazis saw them as conforming to the common stereotypes of the shtetl Jew: secluded, backward, and filthy. In *Mein Kampf*, Hitler had described his repulsion at the caftan-wearing, bearded, malodorous eastern European Jews he claimed to have discovered in Vienna, and it is with these propagandistic images in mind that the Wehrmacht marched eastward. Contrary to post-1945 mythology, regular soldiers—not just the SS—were intimately involved in crimes in the east. Along with the German police and the SS that followed the army, the military stole Jews' property, forced males into hard labor, and starved, beat, and humiliated men by cutting off their beards while fellow-Germans and non-Jewish civilians laughed and took photos. Amidst this chaos many Jews and Poles in western Poland, fully aware of the dangers that faced them, chose to flee into the Polish territory that the Soviets had invaded from the east. Two years later, they fell into Nazi hands again or were sent by the Soviets to Siberia.

In the early months of the war, the Nazis targeted non-Jewish Poles more directly than Jews. Hitler singled out for imprisonment or execution intellectuals, whom he saw as carrying the seeds of Polish nationalism. The Nazis combed the countryside, executing writers, musicians, professors, and partisans who were still fighting against the Nazis after the Polish army's defeat. They also put Poles into concentration camps, like the newly constructed Stutthof camp near Danzig, and deported hundreds of thousands of them further east to make way for German settlers. Over the course of the war, the Nazis murdered almost 2 million Polish civilians.

In the fall of 1939, in accordance with the Nazi-Soviet pact, Germany took over its half of Poland, absorbed the western regions of the Wartheland and Silesia into the Reich, and ruled the remainder as a colony known as the General Government. This latter area became a dumping ground for Europe's Jews while the Nazis determined their fate. The governor general of this territory was Hans Frank, a deeply antisemitic attorney and now administrator of territory that would include a vast network of concentration camps, forced labor camps, and killing installations. An army of "racial experts" followed Frank into Poland. So did a cadre of less ideologically obsessive researchers and planners who set to work designing a new future for Poland. Demographers, economists, sociologists, and historians engaged in a massive attempt to study the makeup of this territory, plan population transfers, and turn Poland into an economically vibrant German territory. They culled the Polish population for individuals who had features that would allow them to, effectively, become racial Germans. This demographic remapping provided good career opportunities for these experts who had worked in university or research centers and who now could apply their academic training to a larger nationalist cause.

Ghettos and the Western Invasions

From the start of the Second World War, the Nazis did not have a long-term plan for Polish Jews. As we saw briefly in the last chapter, those who were not murdered were kept in a state of confinement while the Nazis explored their options. In October of 1939, the Nazis opened their first Jewish ghetto in the city of Piotrkow Trybunalski, which had been the scene of fierce fighting between Germans and Poles. Over time 25,000 Jews were forced into this enclosed area. Other, much larger ghettos followed—in Krakow, Lvov, Bialystok, Lublin, and Vilna. The Warsaw ghetto, in Poland's capital and largest city, came to hold 400,000 Jews. In 1940, the Germans opened the longest-lasting ghetto in Poland's third-largest city Lodz, or Litzmannstadt in German, where 150,000 inhabitants were crammed into 1.5 square miles produced textiles and other finished goods for the German war effort. While the Nazis initially pushed only local inhabitants into these walled-off areas, soon they forced all Jews in Poland to relocate to the ghettos. Hans Frank and the SS also directed Roma populations into separate sections within the Jewish ghettos as they sought a solution, in Heinrich Himmler's words, to "the Gypsy plague" that he claimed manifested itself in constant criminality. In autumn of 1941, 5,000 Roma from Austria were sent to the Lodz ghetto. Soon Jews from around Europe would arrive as well.

The Nazis deliberately applied the term "ghetto" to these areas. In early modern Europe, Jews were confined to the ghettos of western and southern European cities, which were cramped, dingy, and enclosed. In 1940 the Nazis were now literally reversing over a century of Jewish emancipation and returning to a time when Jews were physically separated from gentile populations. As in centuries prior, the Germans wanted ghettos to be self-supporting, with little if any movement beyond their walls. The Nazis established Jewish Councils, often drawn from prewar community elders, who were tasked with governing their imprisoned populations. The Jewish Councils managed food distribution, housing, and the cultural life of the ghetto. They also maintained order and meted out punishment with the aid of a Jewish police force. Joining this force had a variety of motivations— from a desire to protect and assist one's coreligionists to an opportunist wish for more food and the protection of one's families. The Jewish Councils and police were caught in a moral gray area, at once carrying out German orders while also maintaining order, productivity, and life among ghetto populations. Their members could be brutal and tyrannical or kindly and compassionate, but whatever their characters, the Nazis would eventually force them to cooperate with the order to deliver Jews to their deaths.

Located in the worst part of town, the ghettos were overcrowded, cramped, and dirty. Small apartments had two or three people to a bed, and few had running water. With little food, Jews had to rely on the black market and smugglers, including children, who ventured outside the ghetto walls to bring back provisions. Disease was rampant. Typhus, pneumonia, tuberculosis, influenza, and dysentery ravaged the ghetto communities. The Nazis took great satisfaction in this suffering. Sometimes German vacationers even engaged in atrocity tourism amid these scenes of desperation. With Baedeker's "General Government" guidebook in hand, they could take a bus tour through the ghetto to gawk at the people who, due to the misery imposed on them, came to resemble the very stereotype of "subhuman" Jews. Some German men and women even took "romantic outings" to the ghetto. The ghetto was itself a miserable reality and a clever piece of propaganda that employed Nazi cameramen and photographers. The Nazi regime spent years warning Germans about Jewish depravity. Now they could subject Jews to conditions that could bear out this claim in film, photos, or on tours by creating a survival-of-the-fittest scenario. Ghetto dwellers with access to the black market or to more money for goods stood a better chance of surviving, while others perished of malnourishment and disease. To the Nazis, survival offered additional "evidence" that wealthy Jews hoarded money and flouted their still-fancy clothes even behind the ghetto walls. The regime, which had long derided Jews for being clannish, now portrayed them as fundamentally selfish and unconcerned with their racial brethren dying in the street.

Not everyone relished the sight of these "subhumans." A Polish visitor to the Warsaw ghetto in 1941 wrote in his diary that the majority of people "are nightmare figures, ghosts of former beings, miserable destitute, pathetic remnants of former humanity ... On the streets children are crying in vain, children who are dying of hunger. They howl, beg, sing, moan, shiver with cold, without underwear, without clothing, without shoes, in rags, sacks, flannel which are bound in strips round the emaciated skeletons, children swollen with hunger, disfigured, half conscious, already completely grown up at the age of five, gloomy and weary of life."[12] And yet life went on in the ghettos. Even as writers noted the numbers of deceased—starved, frozen to death, shot—they also documented the persistence of music, religious celebration, and occasional laughter amid the daily fear. Ghetto writings, over 10,000 pages of diaries in Lodz and countless more in other places, reflected the tragedy that befell a population but also the Jewish will to survive.

While Jews were trapped in what would grow to 457 ghettos in the annexed Polish regions and the General Government, the Nazis moved through a number of other plans to expel Jews to a confined area. The initial idea in the fall of 1939 was to concentrate Jews in a reservation in the Lublin district of the General Government or push them into the Polish territory under German occupation. Governor General Frank, however, did not look kindly upon the former. He did not want this territory to be used as a reservoir for Jews, and he pressured the regime to find a solution outside his realm. In the spring of 1940 the Nazis moved on to the idea of sending Jews in Poland to the French Island colony of Madagascar off the east coast of Africa. The "Madagascar Plan" had been bandied about for many years, including among the prewar Polish government. Even some Jews saw Madagascar, along with Palestine and even Uganda, as potential havens; for them any place was better than Europe. In September 1938, *Der Stürmer* published a cover article on the idea. In spring and summer of 1940, the Nazis, under Adolf Eichmann's leadership, took the plan seriously, predicting (and hoping) that upon arrival in Madagascar, Jews would succumb to an inhospitable climate and die in large numbers. Himmler wrote that the very "concept of the Jew will be completely eliminated by the possibility of a large emigration of all Jews to Africa." The regime eventually abandoned the plan when it realized that wartime conditions made large ship movements impossible.

The Madagascar Plan indicates that the Nazis were still exchanging ideas about what to do with Jews in 1940. In the meantime, they kept "inheriting" more and more of them. In the spring, the Wehrmacht invaded Denmark, with a Jewish population of 8,000. This was followed by Norway with a small Jewish population, the Netherlands with 140,000 Jews, Belgium with 65,000 Jews, Luxembourg with 3,500, and France in June with a population of 350,000. In each instance, the Nazis worked with local authorities to implement anti-Jewish laws. Belgium kicked Jews out of the civil service, and collaborators unleashed pogroms. From tiny Luxembourg to France, the Nazis and their local collaborators produced home-grown versions of the Nuremberg Laws, which stripped Jews of citizenship and forbade intermarriage.

In occupied northern France, the Nazis demonized Jews. In September of 1941, "Jews and France," a multimedia propaganda exhibit, ran for four months in Paris and gave visitors a survey of the political and sexually corruptive influence of a people "feasting on the blood of our France" (Figure 10.4). In a December 1941 speech at the German Institute in Paris, Louis Ferdinand Céline, a noted French antisemite, complained about how tame the German occupation was. According to bestselling novelist and soldier Ernst Jünger, who served as an intelligence officer in Paris and who attended the speech, Céline expressed frustration that soldiers "were not shooting, hanging, and exterminating the Jews" and "astonishment that anyone who had a bayonet was not making unrestrained use of it."[13] Soon Céline would get his wish, but it would happen in a more "orderly" fashion, when French Jews were transported east to ghettos and extermination camps. In Vichy France, the unoccupied southern part of the country headed by a fascist Philippe Pétain, the laws were particularly harsh and even more expansive than the 1935 legislation in Germany. Without the direct urging of the Nazis, Pétain removed Jews from all aspects of public life—business, politics, government work—and even stripped some recently naturalized Jews of their citizenship.

Back in Germany, the outbreak of war led to a collective desperation among Jews. When a boy came to his house to announce that war had broken out, Victor Klemperer and his wife considered suicide. "A morphine injection or something similar was the best thing for us; our life was over."[14] But the "racially Jewish" professor (Klemperer had converted to Protestantism before the First World War) and his "Aryan" wife did not act on this impulse, and they survived the war in a "non-privileged mixed marriage." These were marriages in which the wife was "Aryan" and the husband Jewish, as distinct from "privileged" mixed marriages, where the wife was Jewish. This word "privileged" was a misnomer, for whatever their formal status, intermarried couples suffered from persecution, social

FIGURE 10.4 *"The Jews and France" propaganda exhibition against France's Jews, September 1941 (Bundesarchiv, Bild 146-1975-041-07/CC-BY-SA 3.0, CC BY-SA 3.0 DE, via Wikimedia Commons).*

isolation, and the experience of being ostracized from both Jewish and gentile circles.

With the outbreak of the Second World War, the Klemperers were joined in their despair by non-Jews who sympathized with Hitler's victims. In her diary entry of October 10, 1939, Ruth Andreas-Friedrich wrote that "we are ashamed to face our Jewish friends; and being ashamed we go to see them more and more often."[15] Eventually, friends stopped visiting, and the laws kept coming. On the first day of the war, Jews were forbidden to be outdoors after 8:00 p.m. in winter and 9:00 p.m. in summer. Three weeks later they were barred from owning radios. When Jews appealed abroad for shipments of shoes and clothes, the Nazis warned foreigners to stop sending packages to Jews in the Reich. In November 1940, more than 50,000 Jews were conscripted into a labor force and compelled to wear special badges while they toiled on the railway and in bridge building, iron transport, and in chemical factories. In October 1940, Richard O. Boyer, a freelance American journalist, wrote that as a result of these restrictions, "all a Jew can do in Germany is to sit in his room and hope and wait for death."[16] In the meantime, Roma were confined to so-called "Gypsy camps" within the Greater German Reich.

Mass Killing and the "Final Solution"

In the summer and fall of 1940, the German military was unstoppable. It had rapidly overrun Poland and western and northern Europe, it invaded Romania in October, and it had built a network of allies and neutral states that conducted business with the Reich. The German population, once distraught by the thought of another drawn-out war of attrition, was giddy over the spate of victories, particularly over the French. Throughout Nazi-occupied Europe, the Nazis placed committed "old fighters" in positions of power, and these men began designing a racial and economic utopia. Perhaps it was now time to stop and make peace, Hitler's generals and the public wondered. But Hitler now controlled the fate of 3.2 million Jews, offering his regime an enticing opportunity to realize his "prophecy" from the prior year. For now, these prisoners—men, women, and children of all ages—were in a holding pattern. Early in the spring and summer the Nazis moved on to a third plan for expelling Europe's Jews, this time to the Soviet Union. They would be "evacuated" either to low-lying wetlands—the Pripet Marshes in Belarus and Ukraine which the Nazis planned to seize—or thousands of miles away to Siberia. Hans Frank favored any approach to get the Jews out of the General Government, and in a discussion with Croatian Military General Slavko Kvaternik in July of 1941, Hitler himself also referenced both Madagascar, which had already been abandoned, and Siberia. Neither solution was about giving Jews a permanent homeland, but about getting them out of Europe and moving them to a place where they would surely perish from the harsh elements. These initiatives for "resettlement" in the USSR, however, came to nothing, as they conflicted with Hitler's plan for war. In the western Soviet Union Jews might team up with partisans or engage in border skirmishes against German troops, and the idea of transport to Siberia was hardly practical.

As Hitler set sights on *Lebensraum* in Russia, the Nazis continued their march through Europe. In early 1941 the Wehrmacht captured parts of Yugoslavia and Greece, thus adding to their orbit over 150,000 Jews, many now pushed into newly established concentration camps in the region. They also expanded their list of allies that could help Germany solve the "Jewish problem." Already in 1938, Italy had, with some hesitation, instituted anti-Jewish laws. Despite the Italian foreign office proclaiming that there was "no Jewish problem in Italy," Mussolini forced Jewish students and teachers out of public schools and pushed professionals out of their trades. In contrast, Romania needed little goading. In 1940, it adopted the equivalent of the Nuremberg Laws and within two years passed eighty anti-Jewish statutes. Romania was the site of lootings, beatings, and pogroms. Mihail Sebastian, a Jewish Romanian playwright, novelist, and journalist, noted the visceral hatred of his coreligionists. In 1938 a neighbor, to his very face, started "ranting and raging against potbellied Jews and their bloated and bejeweled women." She was careful to make an exception, however, for "decent" Jews like Sebastian, who, the writer noted sarcastically in his diary, had "neither a potbelly nor a bloated wife."[17] Two years later, police in the capital Bucharest went house to house arresting Jews. Wrote Sebastian, "Are we facing a mass roundup of Jews? Internment Camps? Extermination?" As the Romanian Jews discovered, it would be all three.

In June 1941, while he was still trying to make a peace deal with Britain, Hitler launched Operation Barbarossa against the USSR, home to 5 million Jews. He had grown impatient as he tried to win Britain to his side, and he wanted to make his move against "Judeo-Bolshevism" and expand Germany's living space. According to historian Christopher Browning, "there was no comprehensive decision, order, or plan for the immediate mass murder of all Soviet Jews before the invasion of the USSR on June 22, 1941."[18] But now with Barbarossa, for the first time the Nazis did pair territorial acquisition with a specific project of killing as many Jews as possible. As we saw in the last chapter, Reinhard Heydrich, head of the RSHA, assembled so-called *Einsatzgruppen* (mobile killing units), which followed the Wehrmacht into Poland in 1939 and now conducted open-air shootings of Jews and "partisans" on Soviet territory. Four Units, totaling 3,000 men, divided up the territory—from the Baltics to Ukraine—where they rounded up Jews, stripped them of their possessions, made them dig pits, and shot them into these trenches, one body upon another (Figure 10.5). These mobile squads murdered over a half a million Jews in the final half of 1941 and up to 1 million total by early 1942. The men commanding these killing squads were well-educated, highly motivated professionals. Some were professors and lawyers, and others were teachers and clergymen, and there was even an opera singer. Overall, 2.7 million Jews would die on Soviet territory in the course of the war. Others, among them over 200,000 Polish Jews, survived in Soviet Central Asia, battling cold and hunger. In 1940, Stalin had ordered these Jews in Soviet-occupied eastern Poland to forced labor settlements in the country's interior, a dismal fate that, however, ultimately saved some of them.

As the Nazis pushed further into the Soviet Union, they assembled an ever-larger team of killers. They recruited Baltic, Russian, and Ukrainian civilians into militias, designated parts of the regular army and the SS for "mopping up" operations, and called upon Order Police and Reserve Police battalions

FIGURE 10.5 *Men with an unidentified mobile killing unit execute a group of Soviet Jews kneeling by the side of a mass grave, summer 1941 (United States Holocaust Memorial Museum, courtesy of National Archives and Records Administration, College Park).*

made up of volunteers back in Germany to join the slaughter in the east. Each of the four *Einsatzgruppen* was well-supplied and well-staffed—with cars, motorcycles, criminal police, auxiliary police, interpreters, and radio and teletype operators. The units included female typists, who meticulously recorded the numbers of victims. Indeed half a million German women made their way to the east in the footsteps of the army, including 35,000 female "colonizing agents" who worked on establishing new German settlements. They served as teachers, post office clerks, nurses, and railway officers.

These actions resembled the persecution of Austrian Jews after the *Anschluss*, now taken to even greater extremes and to a larger population. The invaders raped women, singled out Orthodox men for torment, and locked Jews in synagogues and cafes, forcing family and friends to pay ransom for their release. They killed Jews of all ages and set aflame some of the buildings in which they had barricaded townspeople. This happened in July 1941, in the town of Jedwabne, which lay in the eastern Polish territory ceded to the Soviet Union in 1939 and now invaded by Germany. Polish villagers—spurred on by Germans but inspired by their own antisemitism— murdered up to 350 Jews, 300 of them burnt to death in a locked barn. In twenty-two other towns, Poles participated in pogroms, killing thousands of Jews. They drew upon years of Catholic Judeophobia and more recent anti-Jewish policy. In Poland from 1935 to 1939 there existed, according to Michael Marrus, a kind of unofficial "war against the Jews," including boycotts, the segregation of Jews in universities, and sporadic pogroms. The Jedwabne massacre and other examples point to the role of non-Jews as collaborators during the Holocaust. The Nazis paid Polish gentiles to identify their Jewish neighbors. They recruited Ukrainians and Belarusians to join the SS as auxiliary police. And they encouraged local ethnic Germans to attack Jews and steal their property.

Among the Nazi elite, the mass killing of Jews in the summer of 1941, along with successes on the battlefield, unleashed a push to solve the "Jewish problem" once and for all. The euphoria of military success fueled ever more radical propositions to fulfill Hitler's genocidal aims. Two months into Operation Barbarossa, on July 3, 1941, Heydrich prevailed upon Hermann Göring, Hitler's deputy in Jewish matters, to entrust him with preparing "a total solution of the Jewish Question in the German sphere of influence." A year-and-a-half earlier, shortly before Hitler's 1939 speech, Heydrich had offered his services to come up with a final plan for Jews within Greater Germany, and now his mandate extended to the entirety of Nazi-occupied Europe. In reality, however, if anyone was presiding over the radicalization of anti-Jewish policy, it was Heydrich's boss, Heinrich Himmler, through his control of the SS and police and with the cooperation of the German military, government ministers, and party officials. Still, Heydrich sought to use Göring's mandate to develop a European-wide master plan, and in the summer and fall of 1941 he gathered data on killing methods, the location of German troops and manpower, and the opportunities to employ Jews in forced labor.

As the Nazis debated their options, the Jews still left in Germany suffered a final humiliation. In September of 1941, the Nazis proclaimed that all Jews would have to wear a yellow star, which had been introduced earlier in parts of occupied Europe. Like in the early modern ghettos, Jews were marked with a badge of shame. The fall of 1941 saw Jews purchasing cloth out of their own funds, cutting out Star of David shapes, affixing the word *Jude* on the material, and sewing these badges onto their outerwear. In October 1941, the Nazis ended all Jewish emigration (by now already near impossible) from Germany and the rest of occupied Europe. Jews' isolation was complete.

In fall 1941, the Nazis were also trying out different methods of murder in the east, though they still relied on open-air killings. Outside the town of Babyn Yar in Soviet Ukraine, the SS and the *Einsatzgruppen* killed almost 34,000 Jews from Kyiv in the course of two days on September 29 and 30, 1941. This was until that point the largest single massacre in the Holocaust, to be surpassed by Romania's killing of over 40,000 Jews in Bogdanovka in December. But in Poland, the Nazis moved toward the gassing of their victims, which had been successful in the T4 program as a method of mass killing. In early December, at the Chelmno death camp the Nazis killed Jews and Roma, mostly from the surrounding region and later from the Lodz ghetto. Fifty people at a time were pushed into vans with blacked-out windows. The SS retrofitted the vehicles to pipe in carbon monoxide exhaust fumes produced during a drive to a secluded forest. The SS guards and Jewish prisoners emptied the vehicles of asphyxiated Jews and dumped them in pits. When the smell became too great for neighboring townspeople, the SS burned the bodies. Some of the same people who had worked on the T4 program were now in Poland on this next murderous assignment in Chelmno and in the other death campus soon under construction.

Sometime in the fall or early winter 1941 during this spate of killings, the Nazi regime moved from a plan for the expulsion of Jews from Europe to one of total eradication. "Let me tell you quite frankly," Hans Frank told senior members of his administration in December, "in one way or another we will have to finish with the Jews."[19] In late November 1941, Heydrich invited top party, state, SS, and Gestapo officials to consult about his plans. The meeting was delayed because of the US entry into the Second World War after the Japanese attack on Pearl Harbor on December 7, but it came together the following month. On January 20, 1942, the RSHA leader presided over the meeting at a villa overlooking the beautiful Wannsee lake on the outskirts of Berlin. Neither Hitler nor Himmler attended the so-called Wannsee Conference. But Eichmann and other SS leaders were there, as were representatives of the interior, justice, and foreign ministries. The meeting was an opportunity for Heydrich to remind officials in the civilian ministries of the SS's claim to leadership in the "Jewish Question" and specifically of the mandate he had extracted from Göring. He reminded the meeting attendees that the ultimate goal was now murder. The conference participants reviewed a numerical breakdown of Jews still remaining in each European country, even in neutral states like Ireland and Switzerland, and considered how to deal with them. Jews would be rounded up and "evacuated to the east," a euphemism, which, as was made clear, in fact meant dispatched to be murdered—either through exhausting hard labor, or for those who refused to succumb, by direct killing. Heydrich also tried to push through hardline decisions on how to deal with mixed-race Jews and those in mixed marriage, but over time Hitler blocked any such moves against these categories, which he feared might provoke the dissent of tens of thousands of non-Jewish relatives who were otherwise loyal to the regime. Half and quarter Jews would for the most part be spared from murder for the rest of the war, as would intermarried Jews. In the latter case, the Nazis—who for two more years debated the fate of Jewish men in "non-privileged mixed marriages"—came to realize that most women were not about to divorce their Jewish husbands and send them to their deaths.

Coming out of the Wannsee Conference, we have Adolf Eichmann's summary of this meeting where well-educated representatives of a modern industrial state soberly planned a genocide at a conference table. Some historians have seen this meeting as the moment when the Nazi leadership decided on mass murder. But with Hitler and Himmler not present, that cannot have been the case. We really don't know if and when Hitler individually made a clear decision about genocide. No written order exists, though there is little question that the Führer had the final authority and that he would have known about and supported the widening of mass murder from the Soviet Union to elsewhere in Europe, which was being planned in late 1941. The death camp Chelmno, where most of Lodz's Jews were murdered, had already opened before Wannsee. Regardless of when the exact decision for mass murder was made, the genocide that would take place in extermination camps was partly a response to logistical challenges facing killing units. The Nazis recognized that open-air shootings were less efficient than they had hoped. This method depended on a highly mobile advance that would not work easily for the massive number of Jews incarcerated in Polish ghettos or in dense western European cities. The SS came to understand that face-to-face murder also hurt troop morale, drove participants to alcohol and drug abuse, led to inaccurate shooting, and even led the killers on occasion to encounter victims they knew personally from their hometowns back in Germany. (And for all that, shootings still continued in the occupied Soviet Union.) Moreover, in November of 1941 the Nazis had 250 million Europeans under their control, providing them the opportunity to exploit non-Jewish civilian labor without relying on a mass army of Jewish workers. While healthy Jews did indeed continue to slave away in labor camps and ghettos, the majority were now deemed expendable.

In the aftermath of the Wannsee Conference, in the spring of 1942, Himmler presided over the expansion of killing operations in Poland in three new camps, eventually to be known by the codename Operation Reinhard, devoted specifically to killing the 2 million Jews in the General Government. The SS conducted "actions" in the ghettos, forcing the Jewish police to aid them in raiding and rounding up Jews, who were loaded onto trains and taken to camps. In April of 1942, 50 miles to the east of Lublin, the SS opened the Sobibor camp. From this date until mid-October 1943, Sobibor was the site of 167,000 murders. Upon arrival Jews were taken from the trains, stripped of their belongings, shorn of their hair, and told they were going to take a shower. Once the Jews were inside a sealed chamber, SS guards started an engine that pumped carbon monoxide fumes into the room, killing everyone in it. The empty cargo trains returned to Lublin to begin the process again.

Another Operation Reinhard camp, Belzec, killed Jews by this method, with 435,000 perishing by the end of 1942. The largest population of Jews, from Warsaw, were brought to Treblinka, where up to 900,000 Jews and 2,000 Roma were murdered from July 1942 to October 1943. The Nazis and their eastern European collaborators engaged in a ruse to move Jews to their deaths in an orderly fashion. After disembarking at a fake passenger rail station—with numbered platforms and clocks—Jews were greeted with live chamber music, a fish farm, and manicured grounds. These beautiful surroundings would seemingly make the killers' work easier and presumably calm arriving Jews, who would assume that their miserable travel had ended in resettlement and not murder. But as in the other Operation Reinhard camps, the arrivals were in fact brutal and chaotic, with whip-wielding SS men driving crowds of Jews to their deaths in chambers filled with diesel fumes, designed and presided over by former T4 personnel.

Operation Reinhard set out to clear the Polish ghettos of their Jews. Each "action" was a scene of desperation and horror, as SS men and Jewish police violently pulled people out of hiding and led young and old to deportation trains. Each ghetto leader wrestled with his conscience in determining how closely to work with the SS in delivering Jews to their deaths. The Nazis warned that if Jews did not take charge of the operations (albeit with the SS shadowing them), the SS would conduct them in a more brutal and indiscriminate fashion. In the Vilna ghetto, Council leader Jacob Gens delivered elderly people to fulfill Nazi quotas, knowing they had already lived full lives. He hoped that the young people he spared would survive and carry on Jewish life in Europe. In Warsaw, Chairman Adam Czerniaków committed suicide rather than preside over deportation. In contrast, Lodz Chairman Chaim Rumkowski embarked on the path of cooperation. He demanded that ghetto dwellers, who by now suspected that deportation meant death, hand over their sons and daughters for murder in Chelmno. For him, the gruesome sacrifice was the key to the majority's survival. "Give me your children!" he begged to sobbing parents on September 4, 1942, in the naïve belief that appeasing the Nazis would save his community. Nazi cruelty was central to this enterprise, forcing Jews to be complicit in their own deaths and to pacify victims with the ruse that they were simply being "resettled." Some scholars have expressed disgust at the actions of people like Rumkowski, though more recently others have come to understand the untenable dilemmas these imperfect people faced.

In June of 1942, Heydrich, in whose honor Operation Reinhard was retroactively named, was murdered by Czech partisans. As reprisal, Hitler arrested 13,000 people, killed a number of them—adults and children—in mobile gas vans, and razed the entire village of Lidice, which had supposedly harbored partisans connected to the murder. This assassination did not slow down the Holocaust. The killing personnel were already in place, under the organizational command of SS and Police Leader Otto Globocnik who, along with his SS officer and camp commandant Christian Wirth, presided over the gassing of Jews in the General Government. Next to the Reinhard camps, there were three other death camps in what is today Poland. Chelmno— which lay in territory Germany annexed in 1939—remained operational, in fits and starts, until 1945. At least 150,000 Jews were murdered there. Majdanek, which began as a labor camp, improvised the use of hydrocyanide to kill the Jews of the Lublin district. The disinfectant and pesticide, also known as prussic acid, was deemed more efficient than diesel fumes in gas chambers. The crystal pellets that, when funneled through chutes, produced the gas, went under the trade name of Zyklon B. This commercial agent, once used to fumigate clothing, now killed 78,000 people at Majdanek, three-quarters of them Jews. The final, and eventually most notorious, camp was Auschwitz, which was located in the Reich's newly annexed territory in Upper Silesia. In June of 1940, the Nazis had transferred 728 Polish political prisoners to this concentration camp in the town of Oswiecim, 40 miles west of Krakow. Centrally located in western Poland (though as a result of territorial reshuffling, it was on what the Nazis were now dubbing German territory) and far from the front, with convenient rail connections, Auschwitz would become the chief site of murder for the Jews outside of the General Government and eventually a metaphor for the Holocaust. In total, over 1.1 million people lost their lives there. It also was the place where Jews of every nationality worked and died together. Starting in 1942, many of these victims now came from outside Poland.

Throughout western and central Europe, Nazi officials, together with local police, rounded up Jews, placed them in transit camps, and prepared for their deportation. On March 27, over 1,000 French Jews left the Drancy internment camp by train for Auschwitz. Three dozen additional convoys of French Jews would follow over the next two years. In July Adolf Eichmann, who was in charge of the transport of Jews to Auschwitz, saw to it that trains would leave western Europe every day. National railway companies provided passenger carriages, cattle cars, and freight trains, which the SS filled with Jews bound for the east. The process of segregation and deportation moved swiftly. For example, in April 1942, Dutch Jews were forced to wear the yellow star. On June 30, they were subjected to curfews. And on July 15, the first trains left from the Westerbork transit camp to the massive "Auschwitz II" camp in Birkenau, which was set up as an internment camp and extermination site 2 miles away from the original concentration camp. There, Himmler personally met a convoy of Dutch Jews in Auschwitz, where he inspected the killing process from beginning to end—from the unloading of the trains to the gassing with Zyklon B. One person in the Netherlands who was not on these initial transports was Anne Frank, a young Jewish German who had fled to Holland from Germany with her family and who now, like many other Jews, went into hiding. There she kept a diary of her daily life. In the following three years 100 more trains would leave Holland, bound for Auschwitz. Anne would be on on one of the last trains.

For German Jews who had held on for nine years, time had also run out. Eleven days after the Wannsee Conference, Eichmann sent a notice to all police stations in Greater Germany referring to "evacuation" and "final solution." Deportations had already begun in October of 1941, but now the Nazis moved even more decisively and with a clear sense of purpose. Partners in mixed marriages were spared, as were foreign nationals, people working productively for the Reich, and those who were particularly weak and who could not be transferred. The Gestapo consulted Jewish tax information,

Jewish charity documents, and community housing records to locate their victims. The Gestapo appeared at apartment doors early in the morning or late in the evening and warned that harsher measures would ensue if Jews did not show up at a gathering point the next day. Neighbors watched as their fellow countrymen and women filed past their a homes to the trains destined for "the east." From October 1941 to October 1942, 183,000 German, Austrian, and Czech Jews were brought to ghettos, concentration camps, and killing fields in Poland, the Baltics, and Belarus.

They were also sent to Auschwitz-Birkenau (Figure 10.6). There, upon arrival, they joined men and women from throughout Europe, who were stripped of their belongings and separated into two lines. An SS man offered a quick physical assessment, sending a person either right, for work in slave labor, or left to their death in a gas chamber. Those who went to the left were "processed" by so-called special commandos (*Sonderkommandos*), made up of prisoners, who removed dental fillings, cut hair, presided over the shower ruse, administered the Zyklon B, emptied out the bodies, and hosed down the death chamber. The *Sonderkommando* was then forced to burn the bodies in pits and, later, in industrial-grade ovens that the family firm Topf and Sons had constructed for mass cremations.

In Birkenau, those chosen for slave labor were separated into women's camps, men's barracks, "Gypsy" camps, and other quarters for Jews and non-Jews. With the exception of ethnic German inmates and "labor-education prisoners" (civilian laborers who had to be "taught" how to work under harsh conditions), each was given a tattoo with a serial number and sometimes other markings to indicate, for example, if a male-looking prisoner was in fact a woman. With few rations and the prospect of rapid physical deterioration and death, these workers toiled for the camp operations or marched to Auschwitz Camp III in Monowitz to construct a synthetic rubber factory run by the chemical conglomerate IG Farben, many dying in the process. Others chosen for labor in camp operations worked in the kitchens, as electricians, or in numerous other tasks (including as part of the killing operations) that spared them—at least temporarily—the physical torments that would lead to their collapse or their gassing. Or they toiled as slave laborers in one of forty subcamps the Nazis established around Auschwitz. They were put to work in agriculture or in building weapons for the war effort. Others mined coal, repaired machines, built air raid shelters, maintained refineries, or cleared rubble. These Auschwitz subcamps were themselves part of a larger network of forced and slave labor camps spread throughout Nazi-occupied Europe, which put into action a policy that came to be known as "extermination through labor." In the notorious Plaszów camp in Poland, the sadistic commandant Amon Goeth reveled in his ability to kill Jews for sport.

Life and death intermingled in Auschwitz. The barracks at Birkenau became an alternative universe, where a small group of prisoners with privileged jobs went to make-shift markets, brothels, and soccer games,

FIGURE 10.6 *Newly arrived Jews from Subcarpathian Rus, part of Hungary during the Second World War, get off the train in Auschwitz-Birkenau, May 1944 (United States Holocaust Memorial Museum, courtesy of Yad Vashem (Public Domain)).*

shadowed by the prospect of death and the smoke from the gas chambers that awaited the bulk of prisoners who could not fend off disease or physical decline. And some were haunted by the fear of being turned into medical guinea pigs. Twins, dwarfs, pregnant women, and others with physical deformities ended up in Dr. Josef Mengele's laboratories, where the notorious "Angel of Death" removed women's ovaries or injected prisoners with typhus or subjected them to other deadly experiments. Mengele did all this to further his anthropological studies that he had begun before the war. Mengele represents the most sadistic of preparators, but he was not alone in his cruelty. Beyond those who inflicted direct pain, there were other members of the killing machinery who played less direct roles: guarding the inmates, maintaining the camp grounds, staffing the officers' cafeteria, or compiling data on the transports and deaths. While Jews and others suffered, the Nazi guards, SS men, and a female secretarial staff that accompanied them would take a break from the killing routine to relax at a camp 30 miles south along the Sola River, where they met their families, listened to music, and happily posed for photos. The images from these sojourns reveal how professional killers were able to compartmentalize or even enjoy their work.

Some Jews under Nazi control, mainly the weak and elderly, never made it onto transports heading to the death camps. It was not worth the space on a train or the manpower to ship them as far as Poland. Aged German Jews, for example, along with famous Jews or war veterans whose murder might provoke condemnation and affect morale on the homefront were sent instead to a ghetto and concentration camp outside of Prague. Under a cruel ruse, these Jews would have to give to the SS what little money they had left to "purchase" an apartment at this "retirement community." Once at Terezín, they encountered instead the miserable conditions that soon led to their deaths or to further transport to a death camp. The fact that famous people were there helped the Nazis trick the world into thinking this was a "model camp," filled with creative activities for German elderly and young Czech Jews. The camp was "home" to musicians, playwrights, Olympic athletes, scholars, and novelists, each of whose death might spark global suspicion. One of the most famous survivors was Rabbi Leo Baeck, the chief representative of all German Jews in the prewar period.

In June 1944, the Danish and the International Red Cross visited the camp. Beforehand, on orders of the RSHA, many prisoners were deported to their deaths, and the camp underwent a beautification process. Gardens were planted, houses were painted, barracks were renovated, and the planned senior home that had not yet been built suddenly materialized. The Nazis even produced a propaganda film called "Theresienstadt" (the German name for Terezín), with the unofficial name *Der Führer schenkt den Juden eine Stadt* ("The Führer gives a city to the Jews)." The Red Cross wrote a glowing report about Terezín. Much like with the Olympics in 1936, the ruse had worked, though some Red Cross officials knew all along that this was a trick.

Propaganda and Public Knowledge

The Holocaust rested at first on deception. Jews were tricked into leaving their hometowns with fake emigration visas or with promises that they would not face another pogrom in the aftermath of "Kristallnacht" if they "kept their mouths shut." Many were deceived about their final destinations in the east, cheated out of their money and possessions, promised that "work sets you free" (the sign above concentration and death camps), and sent to "retirement homes" that were concentration camps. The Nazis even tried to deceive themselves with clinical, euphemistic language: their genocide involved "actions" (rounding up Jews), "resettlement" (imprisonment and death), and "solutions" (mass murder).

But the regime was not always so indirect, and the perpetrators regularly tallied the victims and spoke of mass killing. On October 4, 1943, Himmler addressed SS officers in Posen, telling them of their mission: "the extermination of the Jewish people." The men he addressed had all seen when "100 bodies lie together, when 500 are there, or when there are 1,000." "We have carried out this most difficult task for the love of our people," Himmler concluded, "and we have suffered no defect within us, in our soul, in our character."[20]

At the beginning of the speech, Himmler admonished his men that the mass murder "should be discussed amongst us, yet nevertheless, we will never speak about it in public." This indicates a certain squeamishness about being upfront, lest the German public be repelled by atrocities of this magnitude. But in fact, the regime did not spare the public information about the Holocaust. As they carried out the Final Solution, Nazi propagandists continually told Germans that Jews were dying en masse, and they pushed the lie that the elimination of Jews was a matter of the survival of Germany. Goebbels, in a November 1941 speech, cited Hitler's 1939 "prophecy" and reminded his countrymen and women that "the historical responsibility of world Jewry for the outbreak and spread of this war has been proven so clearly that it merits no further discussion."[21] Why say all this out loud? One answer is that the Nazis *wanted* their citizens to know that they were conducting genocide against the Jews, even if they did not speak openly of gassing. They wanted average Germans to be, in effect, co-conspirators in this "world-historical mission." Already in the fall of 1941, to rally support for the German war effort, Hitler, Goebbels, and Reich Press Chief Otto Dietrich coordinated efforts to prepare a deluge of antisemitic wall newspapers and posters in public spaces—from subway stations, to kiosks, to office lobbies. In their speeches too, Goebbels and Hitler spoke directly of extermination, thus, according to some scholars, giving everyday Germans a clear window into the genocidal intentions and policies conducted in their names. Even before they had settled on a plan for mass murder, however, the Nazis had used radical rhetoric, and the public might not have fully known that it meant outright murder. But whatever the case, during the war, in dozens of articles *Der Stürmer* referred in some fashion to the "root and branch extermination" of Jews or celebrated the "disappearance" of this "plague of pests from Poland." The Second World War was cast, like all prior German aggressions, as a defensive war, aimed at crushing the Jewish "plutocracy," which was surreptitiously guiding American, British, and Soviet foreign policy. The Nazis drew together strands of existing tropes about Jewish political influence and wove them into a public narrative about how Jews were intent on wiping out not just the German state, but the German people.

The Nazis came up with numerous excuses for the Holocaust: Jews were biologically inferior, Jews were criminals, Jews poisoned food and blood lines, and Jews wished Germans dead. The Holocaust was born of a desire to rid the world of a religion, a race, and a history. But there were also material aspects to this genocide. The Nazis wanted to provide Germans with the creature comforts that came from the dispossession of their victims. In her 1971 jailhouse interviews with Franz Stangl, journalist Gitta Sereny asked the former Treblinka commandant why the Nazis had exterminated Europe's Jews. Without hesitation Stangl answered, "They wanted their money."[22] Few scholars have taken Stangl's explanation seriously. But throughout Europe, the mass killing of Jews followed their being stripped of money and goods. Special taxes, surcharges, levies, fees, blocked bank accounts, cash withdrawal limits, and myriad confiscations were accompanied by spontaneous bouts of vandalism, harassment, and pilfering. After the deportation of their neighbors, non-Jews took over empty Jewish apartments and procured everything from furniture to tablecloths to lemon squeezers at auctions. This mass thievery benefited not only those Germans pleased by their new possessions, and the state happy to pay for the war in part through the assets of its victims, but also the moving companies, tax officers, court bailiffs, assessors, bank employees, and insurance adjusters whose livelihoods thrived on the expulsion and dispossession of Jews.

A massive bureaucracy composed of SS men, local auxiliaries, business leaders, and propagandists drove the Holocaust forward. During the Second World War, the Nazis and allied governments established more than 44,000 camps, incarceration sites, and ghettos. By the end of 1942, the majority of Polish Jews had been killed. The murder of 42,000 remaining slave laborers and camp prisoners in the so-called Harvest Festival of 1943 aimed to complete the murder of Jews in the General Government. And the Jews from Greece, Hungary, Italy, and across Europe were also drawn into the horrors of mass killing in 1943 and 1944. There would also be tremendous acts of courage by Jews and non-Jews, which will be discussed in the next chapter.

The year 1942 had been perhaps the bloodiest in human history. From August to October, 1.32 million Jews were shot or gassed, averaging about 15,000 people a day. In the beginning of 1942, a secret SD report titled "Battle against the Jews" noted that, in the spirit of the Old Testament's "eye for an eye, tooth for a tooth," Hitler's "war against the Jews shall be prosecuted unremittingly to its end."[23] Twelve months later, the job was not yet complete. But the Nazis were well on their way.

Notes

1   Evan Bukey, *Jews and Intermarriage in Nazi Austria* (Cambridge, UK: Cambridge University Press, 2011), 145.

2   "Firmen-Verzeichnis Gross-Berlin," *Der jüdische Handwerker* 30, no. 6 (June 1938): 13–14.

3   Advertisement, *Der jüdische Mittelstand*, no. 52 (October 1938): 14.

4   Hitler speech on January 30, 1939, in *Hitler: Speeches and Proclamations, 1932–1945*, Vol. III, Max Domarus, ed. (Wauconda, IL: Bochazy-Carducci, 1997), 1436–59.

5   Jewish Telegraphic Agency, "Germany Wants Only 'Aryan' Oranges," *The Wisconsin Jewish Journal*, May 12, 1939, 1.

6   Nikolaus Wachsmann, *KL: A History of the Nazi Concentration Camps* (New York: Farrar, Straus, and Giroux, 2015), 152.

7   "Nazi Summary of the Evian Conference," https://www.facinghistory.org/resource-library/text/nazi-summary-evian-conference

8   Jean-Claude Favez, *The Red Cross and the Holocaust* (Cambridge, UK: Cambridge University Press, 1999), 17–19.

9   From the exhibit *Stitching History from the Holocaust*, https://jewishmuseummilwaukee.org/exhibit/stitching-history-from-the-holocaust/

10   "Ex-US Official Sees Effort to Start War 'to Protect Jews in Germany'," *Jewish Telegraphic Agency*, February 23, 1939, 5.

11   "Goebbels Paper Hints at New Pogrom against Jews," *Jewish Telegraphic Agency*, July 31, 1939, 2.

12   Diary of a Polish visitor to the Warsaw ghetto, Stanislaw Rozycki (1941) quoted in Stephen J. Lee, *Hitler and Nazi Germany* (New York: Routledge, 1998), 85.

13   Ernst Jünger, *A German Officer in Occupied Paris: The War Journals, 1941–1945* (New York Columbia University Press, 2019), 35.

14   Victor Klemperer, *I Will Bear Witness: A Diary of the Nazi Years*, Vol. 1, 1933–1941 (New York: Modern Library, 1999), diary entry from September 3, 1939, 306.

15   Ruth Andreas-Friedrich, *Berlin Underground: 1938–1945* (New York: Paragon, 1989), diary entry from October 10, 1939, 5.

16   "German Jews Await Death," *Detroit Jewish News*, October 11, 1940, 1.

17   Mihail Sebastian, *Journal: 1935–1944* (Chicago: Ivan R. Dee, 2000), 172.

18   Christopher Browning, "When Did They Decide," *New York Review of Books*, March 24, 2022.

19   Hans Frank to senior members of his administration, December 16, 1941, quoted in Arno J. Mayer, *Why Did the Heavens Not Darken? The Final Solution in History* (New York: Pantheon, 1988), 302.

20   Heinrich Himmler, Speech to Senior SS Officers in Poznan, October 4, 1943, chrome-extension://efaidnbmnnnibpcajpcglclefindmkaj/https://www.yadvashem.org/odot_pdf/Microsoft%20Word%20-%204029.pdf

21   Joseph Goebbels, "The Jews Are Guilty," in *The Third Reich Sourcebook*, Anson Rabinbach and Sander Gilman, eds. (Berkeley: University of California Press, 2013), 737.

22   Gitta Sereny, *Into That Darkness: From Mercy Killing to Mass Murder* (New York: McGraw Hill, 1974), 232.

23   "Secret Report of the Security Services of the Reichsführer SS: 'Battle against the Jews'" (1942) in *Third Reich Sourcebook*, Rabinbach and Gilman, eds., 758.

Additional Reading

Aly, Götz. *Europe against the Jews, 1880–1945.* Translated by Jefferson Chase. New York: Picador, 2020.

Bankier, David, and Israel Gutman, eds. *Nazi Europe and the Final Solution*. New York and Oxford: Berghahn Books, 2009.

Browning, Christopher. *Nazi Policy, Jewish Workers, and German Killers*. Cambridge: Cambridge University Press, 2000.

Dwork, Deborah, and Robert J. Van Pelt. *Auschwitz: 1270 to Present*. New York: W.W. Norton & Company, 1997.

Friedländer, Saul. *Nazi Germany and the Jews: Years of Extermination, 1939–1945*. New York: HarperCollins, 2007.

Gabarini, Alexandra. *Numbered Days: Diaries and the Holocaust*. New Haven and London: Yale University Press, 2006.

Gerlach, Christian. *The Extermination of the European Jews*. Cambridge: Cambridge University Press, 2016.

Hayes, Peter. *Why? Explaining the Holocaust*. New York and London: W.W. Norton & Company, 2017.

Johnson, Eric A., and Karl-Heinz Reuband. *What We Knew: Terror, Mass Murder, and Everyday Life in Nazi Germany*. New York: Basic Books, 2005.

Roseman, Mark. *The Wannsee Conference and the Final Solution: A Reconsideration*. London: Picador, 2003.

Steinweis, Alan E. *Kristallnacht 1938*. Cambridge, MA: Belknap, 2009.

11

Resistance and Rescue

There was a time when if you asked a German what their relatives had done during the Nazi years, the expected answer would be "they were in the resistance." This is a running source of bemusement for those who study this period; if everyone was a resister, how did Hitler stay in power for twelve years? The overused claim that one's family opposed Nazism reflects Germans' post-1945 wish to distance themselves from Nazi crimes. But it also points to important issues about coercion, consent, and free will during the Third Reich. Germany was not a nation of resisters during the Nazi dictatorship. Millions of Germans from all walks of life enthusiastically supported Hitler, and it took millions to enable his crimes. Yet there *were* people who not only opposed the Nazis but also made their feelings known, at great personal risk.

Defining "resistance" is notoriously difficult. Did it only entail armed action against the Nazi leaders? Was disapproval of National Socialism without an attack on the structures of power a form of resistance? There is also a moral question. Do we have a right to judge those who did not fight against the regime? The answers to these questions depend in part on how we understand the Nazi system. This was a police state that controlled the media and murdered political, religious, sexual, and physical minorities, and opposition was dangerous. In making this case against moral judgment, some scholars argue that Nazi Germany was more than a police state; it was a totalitarian system that left people with little room to maneuver politically and ethically. According to the totalitarianism model, Nazi Germany relied on a monopoly of force and total control of the media to scare its population into submission. It created a population of atomized individuals—cut off from each other and incapable of standing up to the regime in a meaningful way.

The problem with this view is that throughout Europe people did stand up to the Nazi regime. They aired their grievances, undermined the regime in small and large ways, attempted to bring down the Nazis, and risked their lives to save Jews and undermine Hitler's genocidal program. They did so knowing that their actions could land them in jail, lead to their deaths, or hurt their families. If this minority, numbering in the tens of thousands, opposed the regime, why did the great majority not do so? Ultimately, the dictatorship brought many Germans together under the shared banner of nationalism, and it offered material and social incentives for following Nazi ideology. For most people, there was little reason to challenge the regime. But for some, the rewards that accompanied a renewed Germany were not enough.

Prewar Political Resistance

With the Nazi takeover, the regime's first victims were also its first resisters. In early February of 1933, Ernst Thälmann, the leader of the KPD, called upon its members to take vigorous action against the new government. The Nazis eventually destroyed the 360,000-person-strong Communist Party, and Thälmann's call to resist never materialized. But the communists did lay the groundwork for some opposition. They set up secret cells around the country and recruited workers to join them. For a time in 1933, one could still see red banners and hear communist slogans in working-class neighborhoods and factories. There was also some hope that the KPD and Social Democrats would put aside their bitter competition for the working-class and unite in opposition. Yet the internecine struggles on the left persisted. Communists continued to denounce SPD members as "social fascists," moderate sellouts to the capitalists the KPD felt had put the Nazis in power. Daniel Guérin, a leftist French journalist in Germany when Hitler took power, was stunned by communists who thanked fascism "from the bottom of [their] heart" for having destroyed the SPD, or who declared that they liked Hitler "a hundred times better than Severing (the former Prussian Social Democratic Minister)."[1] For their part, the Social Democrats also called for underground resistance. Their efforts fizzled quickly, especially with the destruction of labor unions and with the realization that some workers found Hitler's social policies appealing. Communist and socialist pamphleteering that did continue throughout 1933 did little to challenge Nazi power. Guérin wrote that it "broke his heart" to see the swastika flag flying in working-class neighborhoods of Berlin.

This is not to say that the left merely threw in the towel. In his Reichstag speech against the Enabling Act in March of 1933, SPD leader Otto Wels proclaimed his loyalty to the Weimar Constitution, imperfect though it was, and denounced the Nazis' supposed revolution. During his speech the SA stood guard outside the Kroll Opera house where the parliament had met since the Reichstag fire. Despite such intimidation, Wels defiantly hailed the "persecuted and oppressed," whose "unbroken optimism guaranteed a bright future."[2] This future was unfortunately far off. With the banning of their parties, many SPD and KPD leaders went into exile if they weren't already imprisoned. Two years later, the inability to bring down Hitler prompted Soviet leader Joseph Stalin and socialist leaders around Europe to embrace a "popular front" strategy that saw the parties on the left finally working together against a common fascist enemy. But there was little opportunity for action in Germany, though a web of informants did report to the exiled leadership about developments in the country.

Outside the two main parties, some Germans on the left called for a different form of politics that transcended the Weimar divide. In August 1933, the New Beginning group published a "manifesto from Underground Germany" (to cite the English translation of the pamphlet). The group bemoaned the left's lack of resistance and mocked assumptions that workers would spontaneously rise up against their oppressors. The New Beginning wanted to lead a revived left, but in 1935 and 1936, the Nazis conducted raids on the organization, arrested most of its leaders, and put an end to the group in 1938.

This is not to suggest that the workers were all happy with the Nazis or put aside their political loyalties as the regime began providing for them. By the autumn of 1933, some 60,000 communists still paid membership dues to illegal party cells and engaged in underground sports and leisure activities informally linked to the former KPD. Visible forms of left resistance would not last long, but Hitler could not simply wish away the class identities that had defined Germany for decades. During the screenings of propaganda films, for example, audience reactions might differ according to the neighborhood where the cinema was located. In middle-class areas, audiences watched dutifully, albeit with a sense of boredom. In working-class neighborhoods, however, jeering might resonate through the movie theater. Throughout the Nazi years, anti-Nazi cells persisted in working-class neighborhoods, though in increasingly few numbers. The Nazis continued to arrest fewer and fewer communists and socialists during the 1930s, indicating that there were not many people left to incarcerate: leftists were either in concentration camps, had fled the country, had come to embrace the regime, or were dead.

German Elites and Resistance

Students of Nazi Germany often pose the question of why, early on, Germans did not rise up and stop Hitler before he amassed total power. This underestimates the power of conformity and fear, and it overestimates the ability of the populace to take up arms against the regime. It also overlooks the extent to which many Germans were pleased with the regime's assault on the left. The destruction of the SPD and KPD did not lead to much hand-wringing from conservatives and moderates, who had long feared that a socialist revolution was around the corner. Nationalists reveled in a resurgent and proud Germany, but some disapproved of the Nazis' thuggery. Postwar journalist Sebastian Haffner, in 1933 a university student from a patriotic family, recounted in a wartime memoir how repellent he found Hitler. This was not about anticommunism or antisemitism per se. It was the "pimp's forelock, the hoodlum's elegance, the Viennese suburban accent, the interminable speechifying, epileptic behavior with its wild gesticulations and forming at the mouth, and the alternatively shifty and staring eyes."[3] Haffner and others could find Hitler physically and morally repugnant, but this did not mean they were ready to stand up to him. Despite the English title of Haffner's memoir, *Defying Hitler*, the author retreated into his "normal unpolitical life" and later joined the mandatory Hitler Youth before he emigrated with his pregnant girlfriend to England.

Joachim Fest, another historian and journalist, recounts how his father sat him down and explained that in a dictatorship led by a "band of criminals" one must keep one's political opinions to oneself. "Anyone with whom we exchanged a few words," he told his son, "could be a Nazi, a traitor, or simply thoughtless."[4] Yet, unlike Haffner's, Fest's father refused to have his son join the Hitler Youth when he was ten. As a result, Fest was kicked out of public school, finished his studies in a Catholic boarding academy, and stayed in Germany. He eventually joined the Wehrmacht, despite his father's protests, in order to avoid being drafted into the more brutal Waffen SS. It can be debated whether Haffner's and the Fest family's disapproval of Nazism constitute resistance. Haffner's emigration was motivated by fear, disgust, and a hope for moral self-preservation and the physical survival of his Jewish girlfriend. When a non-Jew like Haffner or novelist Thomas Mann left in disgust, colleagues who stayed behind, like Mann's brother Heinrich, portrayed this as cowardly. It was braver and more effective, they argued, to work within Germany to repel the Nazis. It was also a gesture of love for Germany to stand by one's fatherland through thick and thin. One can argue, however, that it was this very patriotism and the growing popularity of Hitler that helps account for the relative lack of resistance by the German population.

Those anti-Nazis who stayed in Germany had many reasons for doing so—nationalism, careerism, a desire not to uproot one's family, the absence of any personal danger, and support for the regime's policies if not its personalities. It can't be forgotten that many Germans hoped that Nazism was a passing phase; why leave when Hitler might be gone in a few years? In the political realm, many Weimar-era conservatives now in the Nazi government eagerly worked for the country's new leaders. They felt—at least at first—that they could mitigate Nazi excesses. In his postwar autobiography, former Finance Minister Hjalmar Schacht insisted that he had always tried to steer the Nazis down a moderate path "from within." He claimed to have promoted a free-market economics that downplayed military expenditures. He eventually turned against the regime. Yet, since he had been a member of a criminal government (and was a rabid antisemite), postwar courts found him complicit in the Nazis' policies and sentenced him to eight years of hard labor. He successfully appealed this verdict and never served the sentence.

Many of those who claimed to have pushed against Nazi excesses never in fact took up the fight. They went into what has been called "internal emigration"—retreating into private life, keeping their thoughts to themselves, and dreaming of a post-Nazi order. According to a 1936 report of the SOPADE (the SPD in exile), in Germany "all public life seems to have died out." Germans no longer read the newspaper, and "the Nazis have succeeded in achieving one thing: the depoliticization of the German people."[5] After the Second World War, some elites, questionably, portrayed their "internal emigration" as a form of resistance. And some writers insisted that they had subtly undermined the Nazis in their writing. But this "between the lines" criticism did little if anything to destabilize the regime.

The SOPADE assessment about political numbness was not true for everyone. People *did* continue to talk about politics behind closed doors, and some with access to power even planned to resist the regime. Unlike the parties on the left, the "Conservative Resistance" had the advantage of enjoying prestige and potentially working to undermine Hitler from within. It also shared some of the attitudes of the new regime, including antisemitism and a fear of the left, which for a time could insulate its members from suspicion. In the prewar years, the most active group in this vein was centered around Carl Friedrich Goerdeler. Goerdeler had come from a family of Prussian civil servants and had served as mayor of Königsberg before the Nazis came to power. He then was mayor of Leipzig, Germany's fifth largest city, until 1937. A monarchist at heart and disdainful of mass politics, Goerdeler gave the new chancellor an opportunity to prove himself an "enlightened dictator." Despite concerns about Jewish economic prominence typical of his class, Goerdeler was distressed by the antisemitic violence of the regime, not least because it made Germany look bad to outsiders. Yet, as mayor, he enforced the laws that removed Jews from the civil service and banned interracial sexual relations. In 1934 he was appointed Reich price commissioner, and along with Schacht he appealed directly to Hitler to limit massive military spending, drop its autarkic aims, and open the country to free trade. So far, this can hardly be categorized as resistance. And yet Goerdeler gradually drifted into outright opposition. He resigned as mayor when during one of his many visits with foreign leaders, the Nazis took down a statue of the "racially Jewish" composer Felix Mendelssohn-Bartholdy that stood at the entrance of the Leipzig concert hall. By 1938, he began plotting more actively against the regime, whose expansionist foreign policy he saw as reckless.

As he continued to press the leadership to avoid a war economy, Goerdeler traveled abroad to warn foreign leaders of Hitler's war plans and to ask them to denounce the Nazis' anti-Jewish and anti-Christian attitudes. He became a confidante of General Ludwig Beck, chief of the German Staff, who supported the idea of a putsch should Hitler invade Czechoslovakia.

This move, Beck felt, would lead to a war that few Germans wanted and that Germany was unprepared to fight. Beck did not deny that Germany faced "a problem of territory." But he wrote the following year: "The conclusion that the question of German living space must be resolved by 1943 to 1945 at the latest is stunning simply by virtue of its lack of substance."[6] By giving in to Hitler's Czechoslovakia demands in September 1938, however, British Premise Minister Neville Chamberlain scotched Beck's and Goerdeler's plans. Hitler had obtained a victory, and Goerdeler would have to wait for another opportunity for a coup. For his part, Beck campaigned vigorously against the planned invasion of Czechoslovakia and called for reducing the power of the SS. In August 1938, he quietly resigned his position without, per Hitler's request, drawing public attention to his discontent. Over the following years he grew determined to bring down Hitler, thinking long and hard about how to sway public opinion to his side. He feared that he would be murdered by a mob if he imprisoned Hitler, but despite such concerns, he and Goerdeler would be involved in wartime attempts to take Hitler's life.

Everyday Forms of Resistance

Next to politics and the military, religious and lay leaders could also stand against Nazi actions when they saw it as threatening their spiritual independence. Indeed, the first two years of Nazi rule witnessed a "church struggle," which brought parishioners into the street to defend their interests. Hitler had long dreamed of uniting Germans under one church and diverting their attention from sectarian divisions toward fealty to the Fatherland. In 1933 so-called "German Christians" took over the largest federation of Protestant churches, and under the leadership of Hitler-confidante and "Reich Bishop" Ludwig Müller, they aligned Christian doctrine with the Nazi precepts of "Aryan" superiority. Other Protestant leaders resisted this encroachment on their freedom, including the outspoken Württemberg bishop Theophil Heinrich Wurm and Bishop for the Bavarian Diocese Hans Meiser. Both defended the independence of their parishes, leading to their arrests and short detentions in 1934. Despite regional Gauleiters' attempts to turn the local populations—made up of many enthusiastic Nazis—against their spiritual leaders, parishioners protested in public in defense of their clergy, shouting supportive chants on "Adolf Hitler Squares" and at other gathering points. Pro-Meiser crowds even yelled "Hail Meiser," leading local leaders to fret that this struggle was turning ordinary people against the regime, after their having so enthusiastically supported the merging of the chancellor and president positions a few months earlier.

The popular demonstrations were successful, and Hitler—who was always sensitive to public opinion—intervened to release the pastors. He made it clear that, not local leaders, the pugnacious Müller, or the police but *he* would be the ultimate arbiter of any religious disputes. Hitler's dream of a united Protestant church failed. Next to Meiser and Wurm, who continued to preside over their independent regions, other oppositional clergy joined the Confessing Church, which stood against the nazification of Christianity. Led by once-enthusiastic Nazi Martin Niemöller and fellow theologians Karl Barth and Dietrich Bonhoeffer, this unsanctioned body became the home of a Christian revival and an increasing thorn in Hitler's side. Hitler did not, however, give up testing the public's resolve to keep religion a private matter. But he would moderate his stance when necessary. In 1936, a director of the ministry of churches and schools in the highly Catholic city of Oldenburg defied the spirit of the 1933 Reichskonkordat and decreed more state control of religious instruction, and even the banning of crucifixes in Catholic schools. The townspeople and regional leaders erupted in popular protest before the Gauleiter was forced to repeal the decree in November of that year. Hitler left it up to regional Nazi leaders to implement (and then rescind) these anti-Catholic rules, thus protecting himself from a public backlash and feeding a popular idea that "if only Hitler knew what was going on," he would stop such outrages. Indeed, Hitler understood better than local leaders that people could reconcile their religious identities with support for National Socialism, and it made little sense to provoke the public in this regard, especially when he needed to build support for his foreign policy aims. But he did arrest the overtly stubborn Niemöller in 1937 to keep him muzzled. Otherwise, no German bishop—Catholic or Protestant—was ever imprisoned in the 1930s.

The extent to which confessional clergymen and Catholics were "anti-Nazi" has been the source of debate since 1945. Some stood firm in defense of their faith and independence but failed to protest against the Nazis' "euthanasia" program and the persecution of Jews. Others, like the Catholic Bishop August Clemens von Galen, did protest the "euthanasia" program but were silent on antisemitism. This is not to take away from the powerful legacy of Galen, who spoke forcefully from the pulpit against the "mercy killing" of the physically and intellectually disabled. In 1941 his sermons, which attacked Nazi terror and demanded that the regime adhere to the commandment "thou shall not kill," were distributed illegally through the Reich. They inspired the German resistance and provoked popular protests, though it is possible that disdain for T4 was already so widespread that Galen felt safe protesting. Whatever the case, instead of arresting the popular von Galen, Hitler scaled back the T4 program in Germany and moved the bulk of its activities to the occupied territories of Europe. Galen was able to effect this change because he was a hero to so many Germans in ways that people like Goerdeler or Beck were not. Galen was aware of the power of overt opposition and had a weekly pulpit from which to preach.

Clearly not everyone in Nazi Germany demonstrated blind obedience to the regime. For Germans who did not have the influence that von Galen enjoyed, resistance was more subtle but possibly riskier. Here historians have debated the many meanings of resistance: Are disobedience, disapproval, dissent, and non-conformity the same as "opposition"? And is opposition the same as resistance? Certainly, many Germans did not hide their discontent about developments since Hitler had come to power. Bars and saloons, long sites of drink-infused political arguments, lost clientele as people retreated into their private lives. Pub owners registered frustration that their bars were now "silent as a grave," even on Sundays. For their part, workers complained that they could not speak up at DAF meetings because all decisions had already been made. In a depressing sign, reported the SPD in exile, most no longer expressed enthusiasm for democracy. All they cared about was steady work. Many Germans found Nazi propaganda to be incessant, annoying, and condescending. Women bristled at the state's constant guidance about how to maintain a clean home or do laundry efficiently and cheaply. Rural Germans bemoaned the flight of people from the countryside to the cities to work in the armaments factories.

And city dwellers grumbled about price increases and the disappearance of their favorite products. But this discontent did little to challenge the regime. The "if the Führer only knew" myth protected Hitler in the minds of Germans from all walks of life. The people blamed such daily outrages on the Führer's "insubordinate" underlings.

One way of channeling frustrations was through humor. One would not dare shout them from the rooftops, but friends and family exchanged witticisms. These "whisper jokes," as they were later dubbed, poked fun at the nature of German society under the Nazis, the public personas of leading political figures, the increasing demands placed on workers as war preparations ramped up, and even the creation of concentration camps. One joke made light of both the "euthanasia" program and a Nazi leader's disability: One German says to another, "Hitler is killing the disabled." The other responds, "don't tell Hitler that Goebbels has a club foot!"[7] Another poked fun at Rudolf Hess, Hitler's deputy who lost the support of the regime for his hairbrained schemes, including parachuting into Britain in 1941 to try singlehandedly to win the country over to the German side. Two old acquaintances, the joke went, run into each other in a concentration camp. Says the first: "I'm here because on May 5 I called Rudolf Hess crazy. Why are you here?" Answers the second, "I'm here because on May 15, I said Rudolf Hess *wasn't* crazy!"[8] Grumbling and joking in a dictatorship indicated that some people felt comfortable critiquing the regime as long as these words did not translate into action. Jokes about concentration camps enabled Germans to cope with the violence and erosion of the rule of law that occurred on a daily basis. Indeed, by July 1943 so many people were making fun of the regime and its leaders, according to an SD report, that it was hopeless to consider bringing all of them to trial.

Grumbling did not necessarily translate into sustained opposition to the regime. One could support Hitler's antisemitism or his foreign policy victories while carping about daily inconveniences. In the prewar years, expressing displeasure served as an outlet, and the regime, while not excited about dissatisfaction, understood that people needed to let off steam if they didn't represent a challenge to the new order. The Nazis also understood that letters to the regime were usually unthreatening. They encouraged Germans to contact authorities after witnessing suspicious activities, and some communications inevitably contained complaints and appeals. People wrote personal entreaties to Hitler asking for a relative to be released from a concentration camp or Gestapo detention. In 1933, the wife of a Nazi activist asked the Führer to personally look into the fate of her arrested husband, who had been accused of embezzling SA funds. I am turning to you, she wrote, "because my husband's existence and that of my family is being destroyed."[9] The husband was soon released.

This SA man's wife was not a resister. With her successful appeal, she burnished Hitler's credentials as compassionate and a man of the people. If opposition were to come from any group, the regime feared, it would be from young people, who were contrarians by nature and who, the Nazis felt, tended toward delinquency. With the destruction of Germany's left parties and affiliated youth organizations, the regime had banned all unsanctioned gatherings of young people. This did not stop some from starting their own groups. In the 1930s teenagers who called themselves the "Edelweiss Pirates" ditched the Hitler Youth to roam the countryside. They wore their own badges, attacked Nazi youth formations, and during the war expressed their support of the Allies. Affiliated groups bore names like the Navajos, the Kittelbach Pirates, and the Roving Dudes, all indicating an independent and adventurous spirit. Avoiding service in the Hitler Youth was risky, and so was enjoying forbidden music. The Nazis officially banned jazz and swing music, which they considered degenerate and linked to Black musical forms and Jewish vice in the United States. But enthusiasts—many of them having learned to love American popular music in the 1920s—listened to forbidden records in the privacy of their own homes or even risked detection by the authorities by going to dance halls. The Nazis branded these middle- and upper-class teenagers "swing kids." In 1940 the regime arrested over 500 young adults who were dancing the jitterbug and engaging in "deviant" behavior at a swing festival.

Non-conformist behavior varied in terms of personal risk. But overtly denouncing or condemning the Nazi regime carried with it the threat of severe penalty, including time in a prison or a concentration camp, or (during the war) execution. Nonetheless, there were people willing to produce graffiti that anonymously challenged the regime. In 1935 an employee of the Hamburg-America tourist and cargo company spotted a sticker in an office elevator that read "better to be ruled by the grace of god than by an idiot from Berchtesgaden (Hitler's mountain resort)." It also took the common phrase "The Jews are our misfortune" and replaced "Jews" with "Nazis." The shipping employee dutifully sent copies of the stickers to the Gestapo. It is unclear whether they ever found the offender. In another instance, a sign at a Berlin public swimming pool that read "Jews and Dogs Prohibited" was defaced with a caustic retort: "What if dogs can't read this?"[10]

These small acts of civil disobedience did not threaten the regime, but they reminded like-minded individuals that not everyone believed in the Nazi utopia. Taking up arms offered greater opportunities to challenge the regime, but here too, without a massive uprising, fighting back could only have a limited effect. In June of 1933, Anton Schmaus, a twenty-three-year-old carpenter apprentice and former member of the SPD's Reichsbanner organization, learned that the SA had been looking for his father, who had announced that he was "fed up with all this lawlessness."[11] When SA gangs broke into his house later that evening, Anton fired his pistol at three stormtroopers who later died from their wounds. Schmaus jumped out of a window, turned himself in to the police, and was himself shot and paralyzed in custody. Anton died the following year, a few months after the SA hanged his father in his own home.

Schmaus was defending his family. But another carpenter had a more ambitious plan. Johann Georg Elser did not fit into any of the expected categories of Hitler victims. Unlike Schmaus, he was not a socialist. He was an apolitical German who grew disillusioned with the regime. Elser's initial complaints centered on the cost of living and the curtailment of individual freedoms. But in 1938 as the country moved toward war, Elser grew determined to avert an impending catastrophe. For a year he gathered blasting cartridges, sketched plans, and cased the Bürgerbräukeller in Munich, where the Nazi elite were to meet to commemorate on site the anniversary of the Beer Hall Putsch of 1923. Elser placed a homemade bomb in a pillar near the podium where Hitler, he assumed, would ramble on for hours on the night of November 8, 1939. But the Führer left the event earlier than expected. When the bomb exploded, Elser was on a train to Switzerland. The detonation injured a waitress and killed a coworker and seven Nazi attendees. Elser was captured and sent as a "special prisoner" to Sachsenhausen where he was interrogated. He ended up in Dachau, where the SS shot him in the waning weeks of the Second World War. Hitler had survived this assassination attempt, but there would be others. By the time of Georg Elser's assassination attempt, the Nazis were already a few months into the Second World War. The following years would see continued attempts to undermine the government, rally Germans to oppose Hitler, and to bring down the regime altogether. The small acts of defiance also continued.

Opposition during the War

In September 1939, most Germans were distressed by the news of a new war. Up to that point, Hitler's foreign policy had succeeded spectacularly, and he had kept the country out of conflict. But he now seemed to be gambling his victories away. Germans' spirits would be lifted the following year when the country rode roughshod over western Europe. But again the mood shifted when Hitler invaded the Soviet Union in 1941, and members of the military and aristocracy renewed their plot against Hitler. They saw the invasions of Poland in 1939 and the Soviet Union in 1941 as foolhardy and destructive. The most significant opposition group was the Kreisau Circle, led by Count Helmuth James von Moltke. Moltke was the great-grandnephew of Field Marshal Helmuth von Moltke, who had led the German forces during the Franco-Prussian war in 1870. Before the war Helmuth von Moltke had already met with other critics of the regime in his Upper Silesian estate at Kreisau, and these gatherings accelerated in 1942 and 1943, when he and Peter Graf Yorck von Wartenburg led a diverse group of aristocrats, democrats, and leftists to map out a post-Hitler Germany. They found fault with earlier resistance efforts that focused on assassinating Hitler without planning for what happened next.

The Kreisau Circle envisioned a post-Nazi Germany not unlike the one that had preceded the Third Reich. Moltke was one of the rare aristocrats who had supported the Weimar Republic, and he proposed a decentralized political system, a renewed role for labor unions, and a reconstitution of the old political parties. The Kreisau Circle's draft plans included a revocation of the Nazis' discriminatory laws, a renunciation of racism, a banning of Nazi textbooks, a trial of the regime's leaders, and the integration of Germany into a "United States of Europe." These views can be contrasted to those of Goerdeler's group, which hoped for a more nationalistic renewal of Germany. Goerdeler was torn between his conservative instincts and his hatred of a government based on coercion. He envisioned a liberal hereditary monarchy that protected freedom of speech and civil liberties. In this, he broke from some of his co-conspirators, who longed for a more traditional authoritarian government that would maintain social order. But even Moltke hoped to hold on to some of Germany's territorial acquisitions. Members of both the Kreisau and Goerdeler circles rejected Hitler's racialized obsession with living space in the east and the murderous policy toward Jews, which they found abhorrent. While the Goerdeler circle did embrace the "polite" antisemitism of the pre-Nazi years and promoted the emigration of Jews to Palestine, its members were not virulent antisemites in the Hitler vein.

Along with Ludwig Beck, Goerdeler renewed plans to kill Hitler, but Moltke and his pacifist accomplices initially rejected violence. They moved gingerly toward the idea of removing Hitler by force only when the war effort continued to falter and news of the Final Solution reached them. The most elaborate plan to kill Hitler came to center on the figure of Claus Schenk Graf von Stauffenberg, who had loose ties to the Kreisau Circle and left-wing resisters. He had initially rejected tyrannicide but was frustrated by the lack of action among the military and aristocratic resistance. Sometime during his recovery from war injuries, which included the loss of an eye, his right arm, and two fingers on his left hand, Stauffenberg concluded that

Hitler had to be murdered, after which Germany would make immediate peace with the Allies.

By early 1944, much of the resistance had been shut down. General Beck was sidelined with cancer. Hans Oster, who worked within the German military intelligence office (Abwehr) to warn Scandinavian and western European countries in 1940 about Nazi invasion plans, had been suspended when his attempts to rescue Jews were discovered. His anti-Nazi boss, Admiral Wilhelm Franz Canaris, had lost his ability to nurture resisters when Hitler transferred the Abwehr's powers to the SD. Lastly, Dietrich Bonhoeffer, the go-between for German resistance groups and the western allies, had been imprisoned. It was now Stauffenberg who picked up the pieces and moved toward a decisive effort to kill Hitler. He, Beck, and other conspirators designed Operation Valkyrie, a plan for Berlin's reserve army and police to seize key parts of the government and communications systems in the event that forced foreign laborers should stage an anti-Nazi uprising. This was just a cover plan that would be executed in the aftermath of Hitler's murder, not after a forced labor rebellion. On July 20, 1944, Stauffenberg traveled to a meeting with Hitler and his staff at the Wolf's Lair, the Führer's headquarters in East Prussia closer to the front. He placed a briefcase with a timebomb under the oak table where Hitler was studying maps of the front. Stauffenberg left the meeting early, and the bomb went off at 12:42. The explosive destroyed the conference room, killed a stenographer, and injured over twenty people, three of whom eventually died. But Hitler had survived, with slight burns and a perforated eardrum.

Stauffenberg headed back to Berlin assuming that Hitler was dead. He put Operation Valkyrie into motion, but by that time, Himmler had taken charge and reversed Stauffenberg's mobilization order. The Count was captured and summarily executed. A furious but maniacally empowered Hitler unleashed a blood purge, with over 7,000 people arrested and almost 5,000 conspirators or associates put to death. Among those killed were Goerdeler, Beck, Canaris, Moltke, and Yorck, who were either shot on the spot or underwent a military court martial or a show trial in the notorious People's Court. Performing for the cameras, rabid Nazi and court President Roland Freisler ranted about the evils of the plotters, stripped the defendants of their military honors, and sentenced them to death by guillotine or slow strangulation by piano wire. Goodbye letters from many of the conspirators reveal a deep faith in God and a belief that their attempts to avert a catastrophe responded to a higher moral calling. Also caught up in the purge was Field Marshal Erwin Rommel, commander of the Afrika Korps in North Africa, who had maintained tenuous connections to the resistance but who argued against killing Hitler. Rommel was forced to commit suicide, and his death was reported as the result of injuries sustained during a strafing of his car in France. The regime wanted to avoid implicating a popular general and hurting troop morale.

In a secret 1943 letter to generals in the conspiracy, Carl Goerdeler wrote that "it is a great mistake to assume that the moral force of the German people is exhausted ... We must not be shaken in our belief that the German people want in the future, as in the past, justice, decency honesty and truthfulness."[12] The moral force may not have been exhausted, but few Germans had the courage to exhibit what was left of it. One exception was a group of young conspirators known as the White Rose. The resistance group, centered around the siblings Hans and Sophie Scholl, distributed anti-Nazi leaflets around the University of Munich, where they were students, and eventually around towns in central Germany (Figure 11.1). They were aided by a popular conservative Catholic psychology and music professor Kurt Huber. The Scholls hailed from an anti-Nazi family, and when they read von Galen's 1941 sermon against "euthanasia," their disdain for the regime only hardened. The brutal war in the east, along with specific news of Nazi crimes, inspired the Munich students to publish clandestine denunciations of the regime. A 1942 leaflet, written by Hans Scholl and fellow students Willi Graf and Christoph Probst, is one of the earliest denunciations of the Holocaust. Hundreds of thousands of Polish Jews, it proclaimed, had "been murdered in the most bestial way." A subsequent pamphlet implored Germans to resist the regime in any manner possible—to engage in passive resistance in factories, in writing, at rallies, and on the

FIGURE 11.1 *The White Rose resistance group: Hans Scholl, Sophie Scholl, and Christoph Probst, July 23, 1942 (© George (Jürgen) Wittenstein/akg-images).*

front: "Convince all your acquaintances, including those in the lower social classes, of the senselessness of continuing, of the hopelessness of this war, of our spiritual and economic enslavement at the hands of the National Socialists, of the destruction of all moral and religious values; urge them to passive resistance!"[13]

Eventually, the White Rose students abandoned their undercover methods and openly distributed leaflets in campus buildings and classrooms. On February 18, 1943, university janitor and SA member Jakob Schmid reported these suspicious actions to the Gestapo, which arrested the Scholls, Probst, and others, none of whom attempted to flee. Standing before the People's Court, Hans, Sophie, and Christoph were subjected to one of Freisler's vituperative tirades. The court sentenced them to death, and the three were guillotined in a prison courtyard. Professor Huber was also executed, and up to 100 other conspirators—along with their families—were arrested. In keeping with the Nazis' combination of terror and positive incentives, Janitor Schmid received a monetary reward, a promotion, and celebratory cheers at a university ceremony. The White Rose left behind a resounding condemnation of their fellow citizens: "apathy is complicity." But this did not move most of the German population. Hitler survived the bomb plot stronger than ever, with much of the war-weary public outraged that soldiers should try to murder their commander-in-chief.

Jewish Resistance

"Why do German people behave so apathetically in the face of all these abominable crimes?" This question from the White Rose's Second Leaflet echoed a common sentiment among anti-Nazi resisters. But it has also been applied to the Nazis' Jewish victims. For a long time after the Second World War, people despaired at what they saw as Jewish passivity in the face of their tormentors. They painted a picture of Jews going "like lambs to the slaughter." From a West German prison cell in 1971, former Treblinka Commandant Franz Stangl contemptuously shifted his own murderous deeds onto his victims "They were so weak ... they allowed everything to happen."[14] Indeed during and after the Nazi years, some Jews themselves bemoaned the lack of resistance by their co-religionists. Yet this image of passivity is outdated. We now have a full understanding of Jewish resistance, which was multifaceted and widespread. Some examples involve direct attacks. In 1942 a group around Herbert Baum, a young communist still in Berlin during the height of the deportations, organized an arson attack on an antisemitic and anticommunist exhibit in the center of Berlin. Baum was caught and tortured to death, and his wife and twenty co-conspirators, all in their early twenties, were executed.

Jewish resistance also involved everyday attempts to survive physically and spiritually. Until Wannsee, when mass murder became official policy,

Jewish efforts entailed undermining Nazi decrees, helping people to emigrate, and enabling family members and friends to go into hiding. Into the first years of the war, German Jews and those under occupation published underground newspapers, fostered illegal activity, and dispatched couriers to contact isolated Jewish centers. Particularly active were young people, whose goal was to foster ideological and political awareness. While many youth were involved in secular Zionist activities, with a hope of emigrating to Palestine, more devout Jews also continued their banned religious practices as a form of resistance. Every act of survival revealed a defiant population. In schools, a student might declare that they were Jewish rather than hide that fact. Likewise, bar mitzvahs and weddings, with some brides and grooms wearing yellow stars, represented a desire to continue Jewish traditions and build families for the future.

During the Second World War, Jews were also engaged in armed resistance, which was often part of individual national struggles against the Nazi occupation. There was a strong Polish Underground Army fighting for independence. But the majority of Jews, suffering from starvation and isolation and faced with extermination, could not join the nationalist resistance movements. Moreover, their ability and willingness to resist depended in part on their knowledge of their fate. The first reliable information about the *Einsatzgruppen* in the Soviet Union reached the Warsaw ghetto in the fall of 1941 in secret messages from escaped Jews. Also in January 1942, escapees from the first extermination camp, Chelmno, reached the Warsaw ghetto with eyewitness testimony of the gassings. Jewish underground newspapers published eyewitness descriptions of slaughter. With the expectation of death, some older Jews preached pacifism, faith in God, or prayer and learning in their last days. But younger generations often took a different, more sober view. On January 1, 1942, Liza Magun of the Vilna ghetto released a pamphlet calling on Jewish youth to resist attempts to assuage them:

> Hitler aims to destroy all the Jews of Europe. The Jews of Lithuania are fated to be the first in line. Let us not go as sheep to slaughter! … Resistance is the only reply to the enemy! Brothers! It is better to fall as free fighters than to live by the grace of the murderers. Resist! To the last breath![15]

While more Orthodox Jews spoke of "not by force but by strength of the spirit," even they would not counsel capitulation in the face of persecution.

With increased deportations and eyewitness accounts from death camps, some Jews remained in denial, believing that such genocidal barbarism was impossible on their advanced European continent. Some also believed that they and their fellow Jews were necessary for the war effort. Why would the Nazis kill workers, Jewish or not, whom they needed to produce arms and textiles? There were other impediments to armed resistance, including the hostility of local populations surrounding Jewish ghettos. Ukrainians, Lithuanians, and Latvians collaborated in the task of annihilation, and Western countries did not immediately assist Jews either. Throughout occupied Europe, emissaries from the west trained underground nationalist forces in armed resistance, but Jews received little help. They thus took it upon themselves to steal weapons from German arsenals and smuggle them into ghettos or to purchase poor-quality revolvers from the Polish Underground.

Knowledge of the Nazis' plans was widespread enough that by the end of January 1942, the United Partisans' Organizations (FPO) was established in the Vilna ghetto. It served as a clearinghouse for information about the Nazis' killing plans and reached out to other ghettos to organize armed resistance. It committed deliberate acts of sabotage against Nazis and joined with escapees who formed resistance groups in the forests of eastern Europe. In June 1942, the FPO derailed a German freight train en route to the front. At the end of 1942, when most Polish Jewish had already been murdered, FPO partisans began erecting barricades in streets and assembled weapons in anticipation of a ghetto liquidations. They were able to kill some Germans, with survivors slipping into the forest, where they launched new rounds of partisan combat (Figure 11.2). These groups managed to both

FIGURE 11.2 *Partisans who guarded an airfield in the Naliboki forest in Belarus, among them members of the Bielski brothers' group, July 20, 1944. Some of the individuals in the photo are escapees from the Mir ghetto (3271/72, Gosudarstvennyi arkhiv Rossiiskoi Federatsii [GAR], Yad Vashem).*

save Jews and commit acts of sabotage. Abe Asner, a former soldier in the Polish army, escaped into the woods to avoid being rounded up with fellow Jews. He led a unit of several thousand Jewish resisters, who sabotaged enemy supplies, stole food from German train convoys, and rescued Jews from ghettos. In 1942 Tuvia Bielski and his younger brother Zus established a family camp in the forests of Lithuania, where over 1,000 Jews engaged in attacks on Germans, scavenged for food, built makeshift shelters, and shared resources until the end of the war. Overall, partisans were estimated to have killed over 3,000 Germans.

The most famous example of Jewish resistance took place in the spring of 1943 in the Warsaw ghetto. By that time most Jews from the Polish capital had already been deported to Treblinka. At the end of 1942 and into early 1943, the remaining Jews, still grieving for their lost loved ones, assembled weapons and planned a final stand. Buoyed by the news of Germany's loss in Stalingrad, they stockpiled revolvers, rifles, and submachine guns and gathered food and created hiding places. On Passover, April 19, 1943, German units entered the Warsaw ghetto and quickly found themselves under attack by its inhabitants. The Germans were forced to temporarily retreat. Pitched battles resumed and continued for weeks, as a weakened population of around 40,000 Jews faced off against a well-trained and well-equipped army. Despite the Jews' powerful show of force, SS Commander Stroop's soldiers were able to beat back the Jewish fighters and arrest those who remained. As many as 7,000 Jews were sent directly to Treblinka, while others were pushed into forced labor camps, where they were eventually murdered. On May 15, Stroop blew up the central synagogue and declared the end to the Jews of Warsaw. Wrote Mordechai Anielewicz, a leader of the revolt, in his last letter two weeks before his death, "The dream of my life has risen to become fact. Self-defense in the ghetto will have been a reality. Jewish armed resistance and revenge are facts."[16] The Nazis won the day, but history, suggested Anielewicz, would remember the ghetto uprising (Figure 11.3).

The Warsaw ghetto uprising is the most famous example of organized resistance during the Holocaust. Every year in April, on the Hebrew calendar day corresponding to the beginning of the revolt, Israelis stand in a moment of silence to recall this heroism. There are numerous other examples of Jewish resistance. Within death camps, Jews blew up crematoria and attacked guards. Sobibor, Treblinka, and Auschwitz all saw resistance. The Sobibor camp was liquidated altogether shortly after 300 prisoners staged an uprising, with eleven SS men and the Deputy Commandant killed. And we have numerous examples of individual non-compliance and resistance in the direst of circumstances. Adam Czerniaków, leader of the Warsaw ghetto Jewish Council, committed suicide in July 1942, a day after the initiation of a mass deportation, mostly of children. His final letters revealed his sense of both resignation and moral uprightness: "They demand me to kill children of my nation with my own hands. I have nothing to do but to die ... My act will prove to everyone what is the right thing to do."[17]

FIGURE 11.3 *The Waffen SS arrests Jewish women and children during the Warsaw ghetto uprising, April/May 1943 (Bundesarchiv, Bild 183-41636-0002/CC-BY-SA 3.0, Public domain, via Wikimedia Commons).*

During the Holocaust it was not just Jews who stood up to the Nazis. Throughout occupied Europe, university students, religious leaders, politicians, and military officials revealed their hatred of German policies in clandestine publications. They engaged in sabotage and killed Germans in cafes and on military bases. Motivations and conditions varied from country to country, with some resisters trying to hasten the Allies' victory while others, not unlike Jews in Warsaw, hoping to leave to posterity a record of courage. In Belgium, citizens set up escape lines, provided intelligence to the British, and exposed collaborationists. In Italy, communist "Garibaldi" brigades and Catholic units fought against both the Germans and the Italian fascists. By April of 1944, up to 13,000 men were in partisan detachments, along with an equal number of female "auxiliaries." In the "Nordic" countries of Denmark and Norway, where the Nazi occupation was initially less harsh than elsewhere due to the population's supposed racial affinity to Germans, the civilian and military resistance provided intelligence officers to the British and prepared reports on the retaking of their countries. Most famously, General Charles de Gaulle led the Free

French from exile in London, where he planned a clandestine government that would take over once the Germans lost. His was not a mass movement that threatened German military control, but when De Gaulle returned from Britain with the Germans in retreat in June of 1944, he led the liberation of Paris and the dissolution of the Vichy regime in the south (Figure 11.4).

In southeastern Europe, resistance took on the form of mass movements. An Albanian National Liberation Army fought against Italian occupation. In Greece, the communist-dominated Greek People's Liberation Army and the National Liberation Front led resistance on the islands and within urban populations, first against the Italians and then against the Germans after the Italian collapse in 1943. In Yugoslavia, a communist-led partisan group was the largest resistance movement in Europe. By late 1944, 650,000 uniformed men were organized into field armies and divisions. With military

FIGURE 11.4 *An American officer and a French partisan take cover behind an auto during a street fight in a French city, 1944 (National Archives at College Park, Public domain, via Wikimedia Commons).*

assistance from the Allies, Josip Broz Tito, the postwar communist leader of Yugoslavia, led his forces against half a million Axis troops, bogging them down in mountain warfare and allowing the Americans to proceed up the Italian peninsula.

Rescue

Resistance was not the same as rescue. While many Europeans and North Americans turned a blind eye to horrors against the Jews—even those fighting against the Nazis—various institutions and individuals around the world did attempt to save as many people as they could. The Holocaust memorial in Jerusalem, Yad Vashem, has documented and honored thousands of so-called "Righteous among the Nations." These non-Jews from all walks of life risked their lives to save fellow human beings. Ranging from apolitical bystanders to even devout Nazis, these people came to recognize something so inhuman and repugnant in the persecution of Jews that they chose to save a life. Industrialist Oskar Schindler rescued Jews from the brutal Plaszów labor camp by insisting they were necessary workers in his enamelware and ammunition factory. There they would be safe from commandant Amon Goeth's brutality and could even practice their Judaism openly. The 1,200 people on "Schindler's List"—some of them elderly and unskilled—survived the war because of the chicanery and courage of one person. His ability to bribe Nazis and maintain connections with the Abwehr led him to become a "hero." In France, the Pastor André Trocmé and his wife Magda saved over 2,000 Jews in their Protestant parish of Le Chambon-sur-Lignon. Their teaching and example inspired almost everyone in the mountain village to take in Jews, the majority of whom survived. Jews from throughout France sought to make it to Le Chambon.

There are other cases of individual heroism. Berlin priest Bernhard Lichtenburg regularly protested the killing of Jews and the disabled. The Gestapo arrested him in 1941 and again in 1943, when he died en route to Dachau. Chiune Sugihara, Japanese vice-consul in Lithuania, issued thousands of visas to Jews, allowing them safe passage through Japan and on to the United States, Palestine, and the island of Curaçao. In Britain, Nicholas Winton, the son of German Jewish emigres, worked tirelessly to save German and Czech children during the *Kindertransport*. Altogether, Winton presided over the resettlement of more than 650 children. And most famous was Raoul Wallenberg, a Swedish diplomat who saved the lives of tens of thousands of Jews in Budapest in the second half of 1944. US and Jewish organizations, along with the Swedish Foreign Ministry, sent Wallenberg to the Hungarian capital in July 1944, where 200,000 Jews remained in limbo as their fellow Hungarians from the countryside were being deported to Auschwitz. Wallenberg issued thousands of Swedish protective passes and established an international ghetto of protected houses. He was even able to secure the release of Jews who had been forced onto deportation trains.

Some countries saved almost their entire Jewish populations. Shortly before Danish Jews were slated to be rounded up in 1943, the non-Jewish population got word of the impending action. It responded by hiding Jews from the SS and eventually ferrying all but a handful of the 7,000 Jews to neutral Sweden. Bulgaria, a German ally, provides a more complicated case. There, Jews were subjected to exclusionary laws, but when the Nazis sent deportation trains into the country, everyday Bulgarians and the country's King Boris III refused to send 48,000 Jews to their deaths. The Nazis were not satisfied with Boris's use of Jews as forced laborers, which some see as the king's way of saving their lives. After a meeting with a furious Hitler in August of 1943, Boris died suddenly, possibly poisoned by the Germans. These examples of countries and their leaders saving Jews prompt the question of whether the United States and its Allies should have done more to stop the Holocaust. In 1944 Jewish leaders asked the United States to bomb the gas chambers in Auschwitz and the railway lines leading to the camp with the hope of ending the killing operations. The Roosevelt administration and the air force insisted that the best way to end the slaughter would be to win the war and not "divert military power from essential war operations." Historians have since debated whether this justification was logistically true and morally defensible. While some have accused the allied powers of "abandoning" the Jews through this inaction, others have noted that such a bombing would have been imprecise and could have killed numerous Jews at Auschwitz without ending the genocide.

During the war years, everyday Germans and underground resistance groups also saved Jews. One was the "Uncle Emil" group centered around the figure of Berlin journalist Ruth Andreas-Friedrich and her partner Leo Borchard, who had briefly been the conductor of the Berlin Philharmonic. In a diary entry from February 1943, Andreas-Friedrich indicated her desperate attempts to save her friends: "In six weeks, Germany is to be Jew-free. We race around. We telephone. Peter Tarnowsky, gone. Lichtenstein, the publisher, gone. Our Jewish dressmaker, gone. Our 'non-Aryan' family doctor, gone. Gone, gone, gone! All of them! Without exception ... Are we to go and confront the SS—attack their trucks and drag our friends out? The SS is armed; we aren't."[18] Instead of engaging in futile assaults, her group found hiding places for Jews and provided them with food, ration cards, and false identification papers. They also distributed copies of the White Rose's final leaflet, which appealed to all Germans to rise up. Another group within Germany was the Bund, whose members had devoted themselves since their inception during the Weimar years to ethical living, German idealism, and physical movement. Made up of non-Jews and Jews who could pass as "Aryan," the Bund rejected sabotage, vandalism, and pamphleteering. Instead it helped Jews to go underground or obtain papers that allowed them to "hide in plain sight" by moving from house to house. They also sent food parcels to Auschwitz, when correspondence was still allowed, all the while despairing that they could not do even more to save Jews. In May of 1943, Joseph Goebbels reported that the Reich was officially *judenrein*, but thanks to the work of Uncle Emil, the Bund, and numerous other groups and individuals, 20,000 Jews remained in Germany through the war, whether in privileged mixed marriages or wearing the yellow star in non-privileged mixed marriages, whether as designated "Mischlinge," or as "submarines"—the name given to those who had gone into hiding underground.

Despite this legacy, assessing the rescuers' motivations and attitudes remains a challenge. All of them were human, with a variety of loyalties and priorities. Some who saved Jews were German nationalists and even antisemites. Resisters often had siblings and children in the Wehrmacht, and they combined a desire for Germany's military defeat with a prayer for their loved-one's safety and a squeamishness about undermining them. Some cases of courage are open to historical, not just moral, debate. In February and March of 1943, when Ruth Andreas-Friedrich was scrambling to save her friends, Berlin saw the arrest not just of "full Jews" but also of up to 2,000 "non-privileged" male Jews married to non-Jews. In the only mass public protest against Nazi policies, their wives gathered in front of the Jewish community center on Rosenstrasse, where their husbands, bearing Jewish stars on their clothes, were temporarily housed as the regime decided whether to deport them to camps in Poland. Day after day, the women shouted, "Give us our husbands." Eventually, the Nazis—who hoped to limit dissent at a time when the war was going poorly—released all but a handful of the men, most of whom survived the war. Historians have debated whether the Nazis had ever intended to send them east, given a temporary ban on deporting intermarried Jews at the time. There is strong evidence, however, that the RSHA and Gestapo leadership—which needed to fill a labor shortage in Auschwitz—were planning such a step, and indeed twenty-five of the Rosenstrasse prisoners who had no children (and thus would have fewer family members complaining about their absence) were deported to Auschwitz, only to be brought back to Berlin after twelve days of toiling in the Monowitz slave labor camp. There is also a debate about whether the wives' protests ultimately led to the release of the 2,000 men on Rosenstrasse, though Goebbels wrote as much in his diaries. Whatever the case, the Nazis concluded that these protests were "apolitical" and not a full attack on the regime, but that doesn't detract from the startling image of a mass action against a Nazi regime riven by the contradictory impulses of ridding Berlin of all Jews and avoiding public outrage. Were these women heroes? Rescuers? Good wives? Or all of them? Whatever the case, according to historian Nathan Stolzfus, calling the intermarried non-Jews "rescuers" does not turn on whether the Rosenstrasse protest alone was the cause for the men's release; intermarried non-Jews aggregately were indeed responsible for saving the vast majority of German Jews who survived the Nazi years in the Reich.

The moral and historical complexities of rescue are also revealed in the case of Wilm Hosenfeld, a member of the Nazi Party and for a time a supporter of Hitler. In the 1930s Hosenfeld rejected what he saw as the barbaric and insidious methods that were undertaken during the French and Bolshevik Revolutions; the National Socialist project, he felt, was meaningfully different. But the brutality of the war in the east and the roundups and deportations of Jews in Warsaw moved him deeply. In a July 25, 1942, diary entry, Hosenfeld noted the Nazi plan to send 30,000 Warsaw ghetto Jews to their deaths in killing chambers. "If this is true, it is (no longer) honorable to be a German officer," he declared. "I cannot go along with this."[19] Captain Hosenfeld found hiding places for Poles and Jews, including Władysław Szpilman, one of Poland's most famous pianists. After the war, the Soviets sentenced Hosenfeld to twenty-five years of hard labor because his unit had been affiliated with war crimes. Szpilman tried to get him released, but his rescuer died in 1952 in a Soviet prison camp.

Resistance and rescue continued to the very end of the Second World War. Following Nazi orders that Germans fight to the finish, the Uncle Emil group painted the word "NO" on buildings in Berlin and called for resistance to Hitler's final defense of the city. Their appeal followed other groups' acts of vandalism. In 1942, with three years still left in the war, an image was found on advertising columns and shopping display cases in Berlin that read "Permanent Exhibition: THE NAZI PARADISE: War, hunger, lies, Gestapo. How much longer?" In 1941, the Red Orchestra group of 400 anti-Nazis, some of whom worked in the Abwehr, not only defaced public buildings with calls for resistance, they also saved Jews and documented Nazi atrocities. We are still left with questions about what constituted resistance. When a former German housewife bragged during an interview in the 1980s that she had shown courage by throwing extra scraps of food to forced foreign laborers, was she justified in seeing herself as a resister? When non-Jewish Germans comforted their suffering neighbors after the November Pogrom or helped them carry their bags to deportation trains, were they engaging in acts of resistance? In both cases, these Germans engaged in behaviors that would be deemed suspicious but that had little effect on—or even enabled—the Nazis' plans. Perhaps that is beside the point. Of the many Germans after 1945 who claimed that a relative had resisted the Nazis, at least some of them were correct. Their fathers or grandmothers may have aided distraught Jews or hidden someone in their basements at tremendous risk. And yet the stark reality remains; there are simply too few of these people.

Shortly before his execution in April 1945 at the Flossenbürg concentration camp, Dietrich Bonhoeffer wrote of how he had seen much bravery and courage under Hitler but also the "power of obedience." He was saddened that Germans failed to show the moral indignance that came with a recognition that they had free will.

Notes

1   Daniel Guérin, *The Brown Plague: Travels in Late Weimar and Early Nazi Germany* (Durham: Duke University Press, 1994), 154.

2   Otto Wels, "Speech against the Enabling Act," March 23, 1933, in *The Third Reich Sourcebook*, Anson Rabinbach and Sander Gilman, eds. (Berkeley: University of California Press, 2013), 50.

3   Sebastian Haffner, *Defying Hitler: A Memoir* (New York: Farrar, Straus, & Giroux, 2002), 120.

4   Joachim Fest, *Not I: Memoirs of a German Childhood* (New York: Other Press, 2006), 72.

5   SOPADE Report, June 1936, in *Nazism: A History in Documents and Eyewitness Accounts, 1919–1945*, Vol. 1, Jeremy Noakes and Graham Pridham, eds. (New York: Schocken, 1983), 576.

6   Ulrich von Hassel diary entry, 1941, in *Third Reich Sourcebook*, Rabinbach and Gilman, eds., 863.

7   Thanks to Nathan Stolzfus for passing on this joke.

8   "'Eher jlobe ick am totalen Sieg': Flüsterwitz im Dritten Reich," *Der Spiegel*, February 12, 1964.

9   Letter from Else Menzel to Hitler, December 7, 1933, in *Briefe an Hitler*, Henrik Eberle, ed. (Bergisch Gladbach: Lübbe, 2007), 73.

10 Marion A. Kaplan, *Between Dignity and Despair: Jewish Life in Nazi Germany* (Oxford: Oxford University Press, 1998), 59.

11 Annedore Leber, ed., *Conscience in Revolt: Sixty-Four Stories of Resistance in Nazi Germany* (London: Vallentine, 1957), 4–6.

12 Francis Loewenheim, "Some People the President Ought to Honor," *The Washington Post*, April 28, 1985, https://www.washingtonpost.com/archive/opinions/1985/04/28/some-people-the-president-ought-to-honor/fe2c1600-bb2c-42ea-909b-48dd6dfc7b79/

13 For this and the following quotes from White Rose pamphlets, see https://whiteroseinternational.com/documents/?gad=1&gclid=CjwKCAjwo9unBhBTE iwAipC115Ti6DbKEUCX6TVOdcOVOn5kPOY6bi6NXG59eHIkbLr8gUtPPq BE-BoCG0IQAvD_BwE

14 Gitta Sereny, *Into That Darkness: An Examination of Conscience* (New York: Vintage, 1974), 232–33.

15 Read out loud in Vilna ghetto, January 1, 1942, https://www.yadvashem.org/vilna/during/german-occupation/responses-to-the-mass-murder.html

16 "Anielewicz's last letter," April 23, 1943, in *A Holocaust Reader: From Ideology to Annihilation*, Rita Botwinick, ed. (Upper Saddle River, NJ: Prentice Hall, 1997), 191–2.

17 Raul Hilberg, Stanislaw Staron, and Josef Kermisz, eds., *The Warsaw Diary of Adam Czerniakov: Prelude to Doom* (Chicago: Ivan R. Dee, 1979), 23.

18 Andreas-Friedrich, *Berlin Underground*, diary entry for February 28, 1943, 91.

19 Wilm Hosenfeld, "*Ich versuche jeden zu retten.*" *Das Leben eines deutschen Offiziers in Briefen und Tagebüchern* (Munich: Deutsche Verlags-Anstalt, 2004), diary entry for July 25, 1942, 630.

Additional Reading

Fogelman, Eva. *Conscience and Courage: Rescuers of Jews during the Holocaust.* New York: Anchor Books, 1994.

Gruner, Wolf. *Resisters. How Ordinary Jews Fought Persecution in Hitler's Germany.* New Haven: Yale University Press, 2023.

Hamerow, Theodore S. *On the Road to the Wolf's Lair: German Resistance to Hitler.* Cambridge, MA: Belknap, 1997.

Hoffmann, Peter. *The History of the German Resistance, 1933–1945.* Translated by Richard Barry. Third Edition. Montreal: McGill-Queen's University Press, 1996.

Mommsen, Hans. *Alternatives to Hitler: German Resistance under the Third Reich.* London: I.B. Tauris, 2003.

Orbach, Danny. *The Plots against Hitler.* Boston and New York: Houghton Mifflin Harcourt, 2016.

Roseman, Mark. *Lives Reclaimed: A Story of Rescue and Resistance in Nazi Germany.* New York: Metropolitan Books, 2019.

Stoltzfus, Nathan. *Hitler's Compromises: Coercion and Consensus in Nazi Germany.* New Haven and London: Yale University Press, 2016.

Stoltzfus, Nathan, Mordecai Paldiel, and Judy Baumel-Schwartz, eds. *Women Defying Hitler: Rescue and Resistance under the Nazis.* London: Bloomsbury Academic, 2021.

Von Klemperer, Klemens. *German Resistance against Hitler: The Search for Allies Abroad, 1938–1945.* Oxford: Clarendon Press, 1992.

12

Defeat, 1943–5

At the end of 1942, the Nazis controlled a vast expanse of territory. From the French Island of Ushant in the Atlantic Ocean, populated by 2,500 Breton speakers, to the multiethnic city of Mozdok in the Soviet Caucuses, German and Axis troops were spread across almost 2,400 miles. From north to south, exactly 3,000 miles separated the Nazi-controlled arctic settlement of Barentsburg, Norway, with its small Russian population, and the southernmost Greek Island of Gavdos. Germans occupied the British Channel Islands and manned weather stations in Greenland, and the Afrika Korps had strongholds in Morocco, Libya, Tunisia, Algeria, and Egypt. The Nazis extracted tribute from occupied governments to pay for the war, German companies exploited natural resources and labor across the continent, and Nazi U-boats and naval ships patrolled waters throughout the world, from the Gulf of Mexico and the US Atlantic seaboard to the Indian and Pacific Oceans.

As impressive as this multiethnic empire seems, this massive takeover of land and people would prove unsustainable. As he pushed to complete his war of conquest, Hitler would run up against powerful foes on the battlefield, the limits of his own military prowess, and the inability to manage diverse populations with their desires for freedom. In the final years of the Second World War, the Germans were outmanned and outgunned. The Nazis' slide toward defeat was marked by increasing brutality. The violence that Hitler had brought to Europe in the initial years of the war came home to the Reich. Bombs continued to fall on German cities, and the Nazis rooted out those who would question the "final victory." The remaining Jews in Europe would fall victim to Hitler's abiding obsession with ridding Europe of "Judeo-Bolshevism." In the final years of fighting, the defining features of National Socialist rule thus far—racial violence, ideological zealousness, and hubris—only intensified as the driving logics of the German war.

Stalingrad and Total War

Historians have posed the question, "When was Germany's loss a foregone conclusion?" Some have seen the foolhardy invasion of the Soviet Union in June of 1941 as the death knell for the regime. Others have pointed to Hitler's declaration of war on the United States in December of 1941. Whatever the long-term causes, the massive German defeat at Stalingrad in 1943 signaled to the world and to the Germans themselves that the Nazi juggernaut was vulnerable. In September of 1942, Field Marshal Friedrich Paulus and the German Sixth Army had seemed poised to conquer the strategic Soviet city of Stalingrad and push through to the Volga River and the large oil supplies in the Caucasus mountains. But the Soviets put up stiff resistance in the ensuing months, and the Nazis were incapable of supplying the troops with sufficient food and munitions during the Russian winter. Field Marshal Erich von Manstein's relief army failed to push back the Red Army, and despite Stalin's offer of surrender terms, the Germans under Hitler's "no retreat" orders fought on until February 2, when the Sixth Army finally capitulated.

The grim statistics attending the Battle of Stalingrad are staggering. The Soviets and the Axis powers deployed over 2 million soldiers. Axis casualties, including missing and wounded, totaled 800,000, while the Red Army suffered over a million casualties. A total of 70,000 Wehrmacht soldiers were killed, and 24 generals and up to 100,000 Germans surrendered (Figure 12.1) Only about 6,000 of these men ever returned home; the remaining soldiers—injured, weakened, and sick—died in harsh captivity. The battlefield was littered with 1,500 destroyed tanks, almost a thousand aircraft, and countless trucks, armored vehicles, and munitions. As many as 40,000 civilians living in or near Stalingrad had died over the course of the six-month battle, and the city was reduced to rubble.

The German surrender unleashed shockwaves in Germany. A furious Hitler wrote of General Paulus, "The man should have shot himself just as the old commanders threw themselves on their swords."[1] On February 18, Propaganda Minister Goebbels packed a sycophantic crowd of armaments workers, decorated soldiers, and party stalwarts into Berlin's Sportpalast to address the "blow of fate at Stalingrad." A feverish Goebbels urged Germans to embrace the moment. The loss in the east should inspire people to "follow [the Führer] wherever he goes," to relish total war, to commit themselves to endless work ("if necessary, fourteen hours a day"), and to "give Bolshevism the death blow." Goebbels' appeal to Germany "at this most critical hour of our national history" was greeted with wild cheers.

One wonders whether the blinded and maimed veterans placed strategically in the front rows, or the radio listeners across the Reich who had lost sons and husbands and fathers, were genuinely heartened when Goebbels issued a call to "rise up and let the storm break loose!"[2] The Security Service (SD) evidently asked itself the same thing and conducted a study of reactions to the Stalingrad speech. The SD reported that the

FIGURE 12.1 *A Soviet soldier marches behind a captured German soldier at Stalingrad, January 1943 (Bundesarchiv, Bild 183-E0406-0022-011/CC-BY-SA 3.0, CC BY-SA 3.0 DE via Wikimedia Commons).*

populace was "shocked but not despairing." This conclusion belied its actual findings. While people were happy that the government had finally "come clean" about the military situation in the east, they were pessimistic, weary, and unsure of whether the propaganda minister was even exaggerating the military loss "in order to stress the need for totalitarian measures."[3] The population, the report concluded, "is almost afraid to see any optimism." In April 1943, the Social Democrats operating from exile in London added to this assessment, citing "middle class bitterness, growing unrest in the army … and a 'hoping for the end.'"[4] Faced with the reality of war fatigue, the regime used censorship to prevent Germans from falling into further despair. A final batch of soldiers' letters from Stalingrad revealed that only 2 percent approved of the conduct of the war and that the remaining attitudes ranged from opposition to indifference to despondency. Goebbels compared the flow of sad letters to a "funeral march," filled with details of disemboweled corpses, starvation, homesickness, shell shock, and weeping soldiers. Hitler had the mail destroyed before it could reach the homes of its authors.

This funeral march would continue for over two more years, and henceforth, the Allies controlled the direction of the war. Determined never to be led astray again by professional generals and cowardly soldiers, Hitler gave more and more fighting duties to the Waffen SS, which meted out punishment to partisans and civilians. The year 1943 continued to see a series of German military losses, whose destruction was mirrored by increasing repression at home, brutal revenge actions in the east, and the continued pursuit of the Final Solution after the peak year of mass murder in 1942. On the same day as Goebbels' Sportpalast speech, members of the White Rose resistance group were arrested. In March, the Waffen SS units known as the Dirlewanger Brigade, composed of convicted criminals, burned alive the entire population of Khatyn in Belarus as retaliation for a partisan attack on a German convoy.

Such arbitrary measures became increasingly common, but they had no strategic benefit. On May 13, General Erwin Rommel's Army Group Africa surrendered to Allied troops. The "Desert Fox," whom both the Allies and Axis powers had revered as a "soldier's soldier," had failed. Three days later, the SS put down the Warsaw ghetto uprising, blew up the central synagogue, and declared the city Jew-free. In July, the Germans launched the largest tank battle in history in Kursk, only to lose in a few weeks. One million troops and 2,700 tanks could not wrest the city from the Soviets, who had possibly been warned of the assault by the "Lucy" spy ring in Switzerland. This final German military offensive on the eastern front was a decisive loss. That same month, Jews in Belarus and the Baltics took up arms against the Nazis, who had ordered the final liquidation of the ghettos and the movement of Jews to concentration camps. And three days after the Kursk assault, the Allies landed in Sicily and began the battle up the Italian peninsula.

Throughout 1943, the Red Army grew, and the German army shrank. By the end of the year, the Soviets had retaken the key cities of Orel, Kharkov, Bryansk, and Smolensk, and Kyiv fell to the Russians on November 6. The Germans suffered massive shortages of tanks and men, fielded divisions at half strength, and lost a quarter of a million soldiers that year. With the tides turning against Germany, the regime grew convinced that ideological fanaticism could induce more tenacious fighting. In the last eighteen months of the war, the most radical elements of the party and state took on new tasks, hoping to capture the energy and spirit of the *Kampfzeit* ("time of struggle") of the late Weimar years and remake Germany through a new "fighting spirit." They felt that soldiers up until that point had not been sufficiently antisemitic. Racial hygienists, in the meantime, insisted that biological purity was a key to victory; pure "Aryans" apparently made better fighters on the battlefront, despite some counter-claims that "it doesn't matter who is carrying the weapons."[5] In December of 1943, Adolf Hitler ordered the establishment of National Socialist Leadership Officers (NSFO). He hoped that these "political soldiers"—members of the Wehrmacht who received a special designation based on their commitment to racial principles—would fight harder. An implicit rebuke to the seasoned generals who had presided over German losses, these new leaders were supposedly imbued with the Nazi spirit. They would be "armed National Socialists," declared Wilhelm Ruder, who headed the commission to approve NSFO designations. "Waging war in a pure military fashion is not enough."[6] Henceforth, drafted soldiers, along with NSFO officers, sat through indoctrination courses that conveyed the importance of rooting out "the parasitic" Jewish enemy, presumably giving soldiers a newer reason—beyond patriotism or following orders—to fight to the end.

The regime also reshuffled the government to reflect this ideological urgency and the simultaneous pursuit of war and genocide. In August of 1943, Heinrich Himmler added the position of Minister of the Interior to his already massive portfolio. The Reichsführer SS was now in charge of internal security in Germany, in addition to the Waffen SS and the sprawling bureaucracy carrying out the Final Solution. He also gathered under him the remaining offices devoted to the expansion of Germandom that were not already part of his SS empire. These included the Ethnic German Working Groups and the German Foreign Institute, both of which studied race and "ethnic Germanness" abroad, and the Wannsee Institute, which studied politics and economics in the Soviet Union. Himmler took charge of the Nazis' push for *Lebensraum*, a sign that the regime was becoming ever more radical.

The Homefront and the Air War

During this same period, in the spring and summer of 1943, the bombing of German cities increased exponentially. For many years after the Second World War, the air war was a taboo topic in historical scholarship, for fear that stories of German misery "under the bombs" could eclipse Nazi crimes or establish a moral equivalence between Jews and non-Jews. Yet civilians did suffer, and one cannot understand the end phase of the war without examining the effects of the massive tonnage that fell on Germany.

In 1942 the British abandoned the strategy of precision bombing in favor of nighttime area bombing, whose broader destructiveness was aimed at shattering German morale. In March 1943 the Battle of the Ruhr saw the RAF targeting the industrial heartland of Germany with dozens of separate raids on Essen, Düsseldorf, Dortmund, Krefeld, and other cities. The results of this strategic bombing were devastating. A firestorm raged through Wuppertal, home to some of Germany's key textiles, pharmaceuticals, vehicle, and electronics companies. More than 3,500 people were killed, and 80 percent of the housing was destroyed. One observer described the city as "an ash heap around which the ruins of the houses provide the background scenery."[7] In June, the RAF launched an attack on Cologne, the latest of some two dozen sorties over the city since 1940. As many as 4,000 people were killed. During a visit to the Ruhr city of Dortmund, which was bombed at regular intervals between March and May, Goebbels conceded that the destruction was "virtually total." After thirty-nine nights of bombing the Allies had destroyed synthetic oil plants, mines, and heavy industry factories, and had induced thousands of casualties. On July 24, 1943, the British moved beyond the Rhine and Ruhr and dropped 2,300 tons of incendiary bombs on Hamburg in a matter of hours. This was followed by the Americans' daytime bombing of the city during "Blitz week," in which the United States also attacked strategic sites in Norway that provided Germany with iron ore. Operation Gomorrah, named after the biblical city God destroyed to punish its wicked inhabitants, unleashed flames that engulfed Germany's second largest city. The firestorm in Hamburg was unparalleled in the history of aerial warfare. It killed 40,000 inhabitants, and a quarter of a million homes were incinerated. The Elbe River was filled with corpses, and streets were littered with bodies, some of them mummified and others melted into the asphalt (Figure 12.2). Hans Erich Nossack, who watched the incendiary attack from across the Elbe River, returned to the city a few days later. He drove "across slopes of rubble, the vestiges of collapsed buildings, past craters and beneath bridges that had snapped in two, railroad cars dangling from them like garlands into the waters of the docks." He encountered bundles of corpses, "all of them so quiet."[8]

From 1940 to 1945, the Allies unleashed twenty-three times more tonnage on Germany than the Nazis had on Britain. Almost 40 percent of the urban-built environment was leveled, over 2 million homes were destroyed, and somewhere between 353,000 and 420,000 people were killed. The air war escalated right when Germany seemed to be already heading toward

FIGURE 12.2 *The aftermath of British aerial bombing and firestorms in Hamburg, end of July 1943 (Bundesarchiv, Bild 183-R93452).*

defeat, prompting questions among some scholars about whether it was morally justified. Almost 90 percent of the bombing raid casualties came in the last seventeen months of war, when the Allies dropped 75 percent of all their bombs. Germans came to expect nightly air raid sirens and vigilant civil defense measures. The Reich Air Defense League trained wardens and prepared firefighters for incendiary bombs and chemical attacks. It taught municipal employees and teenagers how to communicate an impending air bombardment to the public and how to lead people to gas-proof rooms, basements, and bunkers. One woman recalled "crashes and bangs" and cracking and roaring sounds as the shelter she huddled in was smashed up.[9] These air raid shelters were not always stable and could give way amid the bombs. However, during the 363 air raids on Berlin during the Second World War, Hitler, when he was in the capital, was safe in his bunker below 25 feet of reinforced concrete. When he did emerge, he showed no interest in visiting the bombed-out city to rally a spirit of resistance. Goebbels was the only major leader to visit any of the bombed cities.

For the most part, rural areas were spared the carnage, given their dearth of factories and strategic targets. Except for vulnerable villages along rail lines, farmers continued to harvest produce and livestock throughout the war, thus allowing the countryside a level of nourishment not found in the cities. In metropolitan areas, however, Germans complained about "the catastrophic state of provisions."[10] There, bombs had not just destroyed homes but also shops, utilities, communications networks, schools, and churches. The diminished civilian infrastructure led city dwellers to fan out across the countryside looking for food and shelter. Rural inhabitants often resented the arrival of these urbanites who threatened to strain resources. Trains to the countryside were clogged with city dwellers armed with toys and household items they hoped to trade for eggs, milk, and meat. By 1944, many farmhouses and village homes had been forcibly converted into army hospitals—for both wounded soldiers and bombing victims, and for sick horses necessary for work and battle. By late 1944, the NSV system was stretched thin. Soup kitchens and clothes handouts continued to the last months of the war, but as the situation deteriorated, some children and teenagers went missing or were drafted into the Wehrmacht. By the end of the war, 8.9 million Germans had been evacuated to the countryside.

Even with this destruction, Hitler remained determined to avoid a repeat of the First World War, when Germans suffered malnutrition and other privations on the homefront and eventually rebelled against the government and military. The regime offered financial compensation for the loss of property and other war damages. Germans were encouraged to take photos of their belongings and send in claims after a bombing. They also received new clothes, furniture, and other household items, some of them pilfered from occupied countries and kept in warehouses. The stolen goods of murdered Jews in particular crisscrossed the continent, making their way into Germans' apartments and houses, and the clothes and valuables stripped from Jews in concentration and death camps were placed onto non-Jewish bodies and into non-Jewish homes with little concern about the goods' racial origins. The freight carriers, financial managers, and auctioneers who trafficked in stolen Jewish property certainly relied on the public's rejection of the regime's more hysterical warnings about Jewish contagion. In 1944 alone, 18,665 train cars of Jewish property headed to cities hit hard by bombing.

The bombings grew increasingly indiscriminate as the war raged on. On March 11, 1944, the RAF pummeled the already-destroyed city of Essen, home to Krupp's main armaments factories that had suffered direct hits the year before. Krupp and other companies had relocated some manufacturing to the countryside and to concentration and labor camps, with millions of forced workers staffing the new industrial sites. But some factories remained in Essen and now faced destruction. The Allied air war culminated in the city of Dresden, where rail lines converged and where refugees had fled from the Soviet army. On the night of February 13, 1945, British planes dropped their payloads on the central city, unleashing the worst urban firestorm since Hamburg. The Americans followed a day later by bombing an already-devastated city. In his diary, Victor Klemperer described in detail the sirens, the powerful winds from the fires, the screams, his own diving into a crater, blown-out walls, shattered glass, and burning corpses. In the middle of the night, he wrote, "The street was as bright as day."[11] The Dresden air raid led to 30,000 fatalities—mostly women, children, the elderly, and many undocumented refugees. The baroque city emerged unrecognizable. Ironically, it was this gruesome chaos that allowed the Klemperers to escape the city.

Propaganda and Morale during War

The Allies hoped that the air assaults would crush the morale of the German people and hasten the end of the war. But the bombings had the opposite effect. The raids—not ideology zealotry—helped bind citizens into what some writers have referred to as a "community of fate." Civilians were unified through their daily hardships and a feeling that they were suffering a disproportionately harsh punishment. The Nazi propaganda machine presided over this narrative, and it used the privations on the homefront as an excuse to impel forward the murder of Europe's Jews. Hitler, Goebbels, and Reich Press Chief Otto Dietrich coordinated efforts to "remind" Germans that Jews had instigated the war and as a consequence were on their way to possible annihilation. Newspapers and posters that blamed Jews—both "capitalist" ones and "Bolshevik" ones—for the war found their way into subway stations, kiosks, and offices. Goebbels and Hitler spoke in increasingly direct terms about the "extermination," "extirpation," and "destruction" of Europe's Jews, thus giving everyday Germans a window into the genocidal intentions and policies of their leadership (see Plate 11). The "Jewish terror bombing," they insisted, was being answered comprehensively.

Not everyone saw Jews as the instigators. Some Germans felt that their suffering was the result of the Nazis' assault on Jews. They feared that Jews' expected "revenge" would be fierce and commensurate with the sufferings Germans had imposed on them. In the summer of 1943, a merchant in bombed-out Hamburg wrote to his family and friends that the aerial bombardment of the city had been "retaliation for our treatment of the Jews."[12] The bombing of Frankfurt, villagers farther south opined, was revenge "for the [anti-]Jewish actions of 1938."[13] This informal chatter about the murder of Jews indicates widespread public knowledge of the Holocaust during the Second World War and some level of despair over past wrongs. But even here, Nazi propagandists insisted that any acts of vengeance had resulted from "defensive" measures Germans had taken against a war "international Jewry" had started. Goebbels hoped that knowledge of Jews' supposed responsibility for German suffering would make the populace fight harder.

From the start of 1944 until the war's end in May 1945, the Wehrmacht saw 1.54 million deaths, touching every family and every community. The British, Americans, and Soviets committed themselves to totally destroying Germany's power potential. Against a backdrop of Germans' despair, defiance, and self-recrimination and Allied confidence, the regime used any opportunity to amplify Germans' self-pity and outrage to impel the country to a spirited comeback. One such moment came in late 1942 when Polish civilians pointed out an uncovered mass grave in the Katyn forest containing the remains of 22,000 members of the Polish officer corps and the intelligentsia. Stalin had ordered them murdered in the spring of 1940 to prevent the future blossoming of a Polish national movement. In the Nazi regime's estimation, Katyn was a "gift from heaven."[14] It used this discovery to try sowing divisions among the Soviets, Poles, and the western Allies. The Nazis conducted a high-profile investigation of the burial site and used this campaign to drive home the evils of their communist enemy. Goebbels wrote in his diary that a break between the Polish Government in Exile and their supposed Soviet liberators "represents a 100 percent victory for German propaganda and especially for me personally."[15]

Two years later, in October 1944 the Germans publicized harrowing accounts of events in the ethnic-German town of Nemmersdorf in Poland, which had suffered brutal civilian casualties at the hands of the Soviets. Photos of dead German bodies, an international investigation, and newsreel footage seemed to attest to the sick brutality of the Russians. Goebbels exaggerated the massacre to stir up partisan acts against the Red Army. The Nazis laid out the bodies of the victims, hitching up the skirts and pulling down the stockings of women to imply they had been raped, and readied them for the cameras (Figure 12.3). A few months later, the Nazis exaggerated the death toll in Dresden tenfold to stir a wave of outrage. Goebbels was adhering to a principle, expressed also during the discovery of Katyn, that "one might say with a 'twinkle in the eye' that the propaganda campaign need not be 'entirely accurate.'"[16] If the goal was to provoke popular rage at the Allies, this atrocity propaganda sometimes had the opposite effect. According to the SD, which surveyed public opinion, the images of German victims reminded "every thinking person of the atrocities we have committed ... Have we not murdered thousands [*sic!*] of Jews?"[17]

More important than propaganda, which many Germans recognized as exaggerated, were attempts to maintain a sense of normalcy, even amid the carnage. Escapism was essential. Light entertainment came to supplant official news and speeches on the radio waves, and the number of cinema admissions peaked in 1943 and stayed constant through 1944, representing an increase in the popularity of film over the prewar years. Movie theaters even witnessed a rise in ticket scalping and scenes of tumult in their foyers. There Germans could watch epic films and enjoy food, an ersatz coffee made of ground chicory (in the absence of coffee beans), or a Fanta soda, which Coca-Cola Germany invented when it could no longer get cola syrup from the United States. On the "higher" end of the cultural spectrum, orchestral music and literature found a ready audience of Germans eager to escape from the daily pressures on the homefront. The pleasures of

FIGURE 12.3 *The bodies of German civilians killed by the Red Army in Nemmersdorf, October 1944. German propagandists used this and other photos to stir up outrage at the communist enemy (Bundesarchiv, Bild 101I-464-0383I-26/ Kleiner/CC-BY-SA 3.0, CC BY-SA 3.0 DE, via Wikimedia Commons).*

symphonic music were shared with occupied populations, which could watch the Berlin Philharmonic during its tours of wartime Europe.

While the regime acknowledged the widespread shortages of consumer items, it ultimately depicted them as temporary inconveniences. Soon enough, this New Order would witness a "cultural and economic blossoming," offering people throughout Nazi-dominated Europe the experience of personal security and the joys of buying cars, consumer durables, and a bounty of food items. The combination of military victory, the privations of war, feelings of racial superiority, and the vision of a postwar utopia constituted a powerful tool for social control. The economy in the present was marked by shortages, but its future would be defined by an abundance earned through sacrifice. This dialectic between deprivation and wealth, between reality and promises—alongside concern for loved ones at the front and fear of international retribution following defeat—helped maintain the loyalty of the population during the war years.

Social welfare, propaganda, and cinema were not enough to keep the *Volksgemeinschaft* intact during the final stage of total war. The Nazis increasingly relied upon more repressive measures. They could do so in part because the Nazi Party began to take on the functions that nominally belonged to the state. NSDAP officials on the regional and local levels ruled the homefront with an ideological fury. Public expressions of doubt about the ultimate German victory could result in imprisonment or death. The punishment for listening to Radio Moscow or the BBC ranged from a reprimand to prison, though at some point during the war some 60 percent of the population tuned in at low volume to these and other enemy radio stations. And withholding contributions to Nazi war collection efforts would lead to social ostracization or worse. Germans were used to recycling campaigns, conservation appeals, and scrap metal drives, but the dictates from the regime came more and more regularly. This led to grumbling, arguably a risky thing in wartime. In studying what he called the "emotional geography of war," Richard Overy has written of the "psychiatric casualties" of the Second World War, which went far beyond a mundane discontent. Soldiers and their families worried endlessly, sometimes sinking into depression as the fighting and the bombing continued.[18] Others grew apathetic.

Importantly, dissatisfaction, pessimism, and private grief over the loss of loved ones did not necessarily translate into defeatism. Scholars continue to ask why the German people stayed with Hitler to the end. It has been suggested that public knowledge of the Holocaust bound Germans ever more to a genocidal war; the fate of the German people and their regime was sealed in a criminal pact. While millions of German functionaries continued to pursue the murder of Jews until the end of the war, it is questionable, however, whether this genocidal desire was a prime motivator for the majority of Germans. A more likely one was the failed assassination attempt of July 1944. While many Germans questioned Hitler's competence as a commander by this point, murdering their leader while their loved ones were dying on the front was considered a deeply unpatriotic and treasonous act. Likewise, the capture and execution of the plotters made protest in the later years even less likely. As before, citizens continued to write to Hitler, praising him as "Europe's Kaiser, oh great and wise," wishing him health and victory, and—in the case of a cousin of Hitler's by marriage—requesting favors like bringing a son home from the war so he could go back to work and help pay the bills.[19] But the number of autograph seekers and well wishers did drop precipitously. Hitler's charisma was fading, except among his most radical adherents.

Fighting to the End

Germans were able to fight for another year-and-a-half because even in their retreat they still had access to raw materials and to manpower. At the end of 1943, the Nazis still controlled iron and metal ore deposits in Ukraine, thus providing the possibility of stepped-up munitions production. The Nazi empire still included southeastern Europe, which provided cash crops and mines to the Germans. In August of 1943, Armaments Minister Speer began to transform Germany into a fully mobilized war economy. He converted civilian factories to armaments production sites. Henceforth, non-military producers of goods and services scrambled to prove their work was *kriegswichtig* (essential to the war). Companies that made household goods insisted that they had to keep Germans happy at home to keep morale high. University institutes and think tanks claimed much of their research was necessarily related to war. A consumer-research organization insisted that interviews it conducted about the public's favorite brand names were essential because the regime needed a snapshot of attitudes on the homefront.

With men at the battlefront women made up an increasingly larger portion of the workforce. In May of 1944, 2.2 million worked in factories, with the same number in commerce and banking and 5.6 million in agriculture, almost 2 million in administrative work, and 1.3 million in domestic service. And despite Nazi ideals about separate gender roles, a half million women served as auxiliaries in the armed forces, and 3,700 were guards in the Nazi camp system. But that was still not enough "manpower," and Speer and labor tsar Fritz Sauckel made up for the shortage by relying increasingly on forced laborers. In the summer of 1944, there were approximately 7.6 million foreigners from twenty different countries in Germany. As in the earlier years of the war, forced laborers from western and eastern Europe could be found on farms, in households, in government offices, in churches, in local shops, and in cemeteries. Foreign women were forced to work as waitresses, nannies, house cleaners, and railway attendants, all subject to the caprice of employers and orchestrated attempts at racial humiliation. Overall, by the end of the war, the Nazis, through Fritz Sauckel's Reich Labor Deployment office, had conscripted 8 million foreign workers.

POW and civilian labor toiled not merely for the benefit of the war economy, but also for the personal comfort and convenience of private individuals and institutions that needed a larger and inexpensive workforce. In 1944 one-third of the populations of Bremen and Hamburg were forced laborers, most of them working in a semiskilled or menial capacity for the municipal governments. In Bremen alone, approximately 200 camps were built to house and segregate these foreign workers from the German population. Two-thirds of all female Poles brought to Germany worked on farms, subject to social isolation, malnourishment, sexual abuse, forced abortions, or the removal of their newborns to dozens of state-run nursing installations, where the majority of the babies died. The actions of these foreigners were regulated and watched carefully, and they demanded the attention of countless German civilians, who would likely claim after the war to have been aloof from any aspect of Nazi criminality. Translators produced dictionaries and employee manuals to help accustom foreigners to their new roles as workers for the Reich; local authorities directed agricultural laborers to write postcards attesting to the joyful working conditions in Germany; and Nazi officials regulated the styling of foreign women's hair to mark them as non-German. And their presence in the midst of German society created fears of a rebellion.

Ironically, a regime committed to absolute racial purity had established on German soil the most multiethnic population in the country's history. Even Jews were brought back to the Reich to work, thus reversing earlier declarations that the Reich was *judenrein*. In the fall of 1944, Hungarian Jews were brought to the Thuringian town of Dora, where they were housed in a concentration camp and forced to work in underground tunnels on the V-1 rocket. This was the first of Hitler's "revenge weapons" that he promised would pummel the enemy into submission.

At the beginning of 1944, much of Europe was still under German control. But the summer saw major setbacks for the Wehrmacht. In Operation Overlord in June, 160,000 Allied forces landed in Normandy during "D-Day" to begin their fight against Germany, whose 50,000 troops on the French beach were outnumbered. This was the largest amphibious military invasion in history. By September 15, the Allies, whose presence in Europe now reached 2 million men, had made their way to the German border, entering the country in Aachen where Charlemagne, "the father of Europe," was buried. There the Americans found a "ghost town," with 20,000 of the city's original 165,000 people living in dank and dark hiding places. "We come as conquerors and not as oppressors," declared General Dwight Eisenhower, supreme commander of the Allied Expeditionary Force in Europe.

The war was hardly over. More Germans died between July 1944 and May 1945 than during the entire period of the war up to that point. In the summer of 1944, the Germans suffered more casualties on the eastern front than the entire war combined up to that point in the east. In Operation

Bagration, a powerful Red Army offensive on the eastern front from mid-June to mid-August 1944, the Soviets destroyed twenty-eight of thirty-four Wehrmacht divisions, and the German Army Group Center collapsed on a 700-mile front. It suffered 450,000 casualties. This was the biggest military defeat in German history.

As the Wehrmacht collapsed, the Nazis grew more determined to proceed with the Jewish genocide as quickly as they could. By the end of 1943, Polish Jews had almost entirely been liquidated; in November of that year, the Nazis launched Operation Harvest Festival, aimed at killing the last Jews in the Lublin district of Occupied Poland. In labor camps, concentration camps, and the death camp of Majdanek, 42,000 Jews were shot in a matter of days. It was the German army's single largest massacre of Jews during the Third Reich. In 1944 the Nazis ensnared Italian and Greek Jews, and the regime engaged in a multipronged strategy of using Jews for forced labor, keeping them in concentration camps as potential bargaining chips for leverage with the Allies, and killing as many as possible. These aims could be at cross purposes, as different members of the regime debated their priorities. This was the case with respect to so-called "Mischlinge." Some of these people with partial Jewish ancestry fought in the Wehrmacht, were forced to round up Jews for deportation, or worked for the civil and military engineering Organization Todt. For a time, the regime considered sterilizing those with mixed ancestry, but the state never embarked upon this, nor on the mass killing of this group. How much Jewish blood, the regime asked, was too much when it came to fighting the war? For some, Jews made good workers, despite years of Nazi propaganda proclaiming Jews' predatory laziness. For others, killing as many Jews as possible would be the most lasting legacy of Nazi Germany, and from the Greek island of Corfu to the south of France, they went out of their way to hunt down Jews. Ultimately, the exploitation of Jewish labor did undermine the regime's genocidal goals. If the Nazis had an overall strategy, it came to be embodied in "extermination through labor." According to the Wannsee Conference minutes, enslaved Jewish workers, most of them toiling in labor camps or in Auschwitz, would "drop out through natural reduction," and if they didn't die from exhaustion and illness, they would "require suitable treatment."[20]

This policy saw its most brutal expression in the spring and summer of 1944, when the Nazis occupied allied Hungary and sent 440,000 Hungarian Jews to Auschwitz, where able-bodied men and women were dispatched to the slave labor camp while the remaining people were murdered. At this point, the Auschwitz-Birkenau gas chambers were working at full capacity. The Nazis also began "thinning out" Austrian, German, and Czech Jews from the "model ghetto" of Terezín, near Prague, by sending them to Auschwitz. At Auschwitz itself the Nazis liquidated the "Gypsy" camp and sent surviving inmates west to Germany. As the Soviets marched toward Germany from the east, the Nazis began marching prisoners to camps farther west, where they could still be exploited for slave labor.

In December of 1944, the Nazis launched the Ardennes Offensive (also known as the Battle of the Bulge), a major campaign designed to split Allied forces in Belgium and compel a peace treaty favorable to the Axis. In what Winston Churchill called "the greatest American battle of the war," the Allies beat back the Wehrmacht. During the fighting, the Nazis summarily executed eighty-four American POWs and civilians in the Belgian town of Malmedy. In 1946 the Americans convicted seventy-three participants in this massacre, with forty-three of them sentenced to death by hanging. Due to a Cold War-era desire among the Western powers to maintain good relations among an anti-Soviet front, all of the sentences were commuted. In addition to Malmedy, up to a thousand American flyers whose planes were shot down in occupied Europe were subject to what the Nazis called "lynch justice." After years of decrying the lynching of Black Americans in the United States as barbaric, the Nazi regime now encouraged its citizens in the last years of war to kill and then hang downed airmen from trees. Most famously, on August 26, 1944, civilians and party officials in the Rhine town of Rüsselsheim beat eight downed US pilots with hammers, sticks, rocks, and shovels, killing six of them.

As the German army collapsed on all fronts, Nazi leaders and the German public put increasing faith in their rocket program, which they hoped would miraculously turn the tide of war. Over 3,000 V-2 rockets were launched. They caused casualties in London and other western European cities, but they ultimately did not succeed in reaching most of their targets, and they did nothing to alter the course of the war. These were the first long-range guided ballistic missiles and the first artificial objects to enter space in history. In addition to these "wonder weapons," Nazi researchers grasped at ever-more desperate ideas for final victory. They fed their soldiers methamphetamines sold under the brand name Pervitin to keep them awake as fighting machines. And they developed—but never implemented—a plan to build tiny, single-manned U-Boats, which would be piloted by drugged sailors up the Thames River to London on kamikaze missions. The German public began offering its own advice to Hitler about how to win the war, sending him sketches of futuristic weapons that could bring down a slew of planes using netting or unleashing artificial sandstorms in Europe that would render enemy equipment inoperable.

At the beginning of 1945, 7.5 million German men were under arms, and the regime now readied for the defense of the homeland. The Nazis had drafted ever younger men into the Wehrmacht. In August of 1943, boys aged sixteen to eighteen could be impressed into the army. In 1944 fifteen-year-olds were compelled to fight. In 1945, it was twelve-year-olds. But the armed forces were vastly underprepared. Lacking millions of rifles, ammunition, motor vehicles, communications equipment, and fuel, the Wehrmacht turned at points to horse-drawn vehicles, only to suffer from a lack of horses. In the last months of war, the Wehrmacht suffered 1.54 million deaths, or 11,846 a day on average. The Nazi regime expanded the Volkssturm, or "home guard," units to defend the Fatherland. Men from ages sixteen to sixty, who were not already involved in military functions, were trained rapidly in basic weapons handling.

This final mobilization did not mean Germans were eagerly following the Führer toward a heroic death. Many now simply wanted the war over, and when the home guard fought against the Allies, it was often under duress. Any sign of "defeatism" was risky. Courts sentenced to death "traitors of the people" along with accused "saboteurs," and in the last months of the war, the regime killed thousands of Germans, hanging them from trees, lampposts, and traveling gallows. As the Allies pushed into Germany, Wehrmacht officers shot anyone flying a white flag of surrender. As a result of fierce fighting, allied bombs, and vengeance against shirkers and defeatists, 70,000 civilians died in the last three weeks of war. This was in addition to the mass murder of thousands of regular prison inmates deemed "dangerous" and 10,000 forced laborers residing on German soil.

Adolf Hitler himself was engaged in what has been called a "choreography of doom." He imagined Germany going down in flames, with teenagers and old men meeting their deaths shoulder to shoulder as they picked off enemy troops. He called for "werewolves" to infiltrate enemy lines and engage in sabotage. This theatrical fight-to-the-death didn't pan out as Hitler wanted. Instead, a sense of foreboding enveloped the country, especially as the Holocaust became more visible. The Nazis marched death camp evacuees— Jews, Poles, Roma, and political prisoners—westward to camps on German soil, killing thousands along the way. The "death march" columns of emaciated men and women in striped prison clothing passed by Germans' apartments, workplaces, and parks—a visual testament to the crimes committed in the name of the *Volksgemeinschaft* (Figure 12.4). These prisoners had walked hundreds of miles from the camps in Poland and eastern Germany, with many of their fellow marchers having succumbed to exhaustion, a German bullet, or Allied warplanes that mistakenly strafed them.

In the spring of 1945 few Germans demonstrated the "unshakeable will to fight on," which Hitler had celebrated in his last public proclamation in February. To bolster this call to arms, cinematic feature films like *Kolberg*, which told the story of a heroic defense of a fortress town during the Napoleonic Wars and which ran in German theaters throughout the spring, were supposed to inspire the population to defend its homeland. But even leading Nazis were turning against the regime. Albert Speer worked to circumvent Hitler's March 19 "Nero decree," which demanded the scorched-earth destruction of much of Germany's remaining infrastructure—from bridges to transport and communications capabilities—in advance of Allied troops. Nazi leaders, the ideological shock troops of the movement, began saving their own skins. Nine million party members had mobilized and disciplined the population in the last years of fighting. But despite orders to protect ethnic German populations in the east from the oncoming "Soviet hordes," concentration guards and party functionaries fled with their families,

FIGURE 12.4 *Prisoners on a death march from Dachau move toward the south along the Nördliche Münchner Street in Grünwald, Germany, April 29, 1945 (Public domain, Alamy Stock Photo).*

leaving civilians to die on torpedoed refugee ships or at the hands of the Russians. They were not wrong to fear the Red Army. In the months before and after the surrender, German women were subjected to a brutal campaign of sexual violence by Soviets soldiers, who had themselves witnessed German sexual assaults on the eastern front. In the Soviet occupation zone, up to 2 million German women were raped, with at least 100,000 alone in Berlin. Teenaged girls and young women were in many cases assaulted multiple times, often carrying the trauma of their experiences well into the postwar years, when few wanted to talk about sexual violence.

Depression set in among the Nazi leadership. Hitler's deputies found his April 20 birthday a "grim and sad affair," with the Führer suffering from Parkinson's disease, ranting in the bunker, and receiving an ever-larger cocktail of drugs to relieve his gastrointestinal and anxiety symptoms. Hitler's momentary hope eight days earlier that Roosevelt's sudden death could prove a turning point came to nothing. Goebbels tried to lift Germans' spirits in a birthday radio speech, declaring boldly that "after this war Germany will blossom within a few years as never before. Her ravaged countryside and provinces will be built with new and more beautiful cities and villages in which happy people live."[21] On April 29 Hitler dictated his last will and testament from notes he and possibly Goebbels had drawn up: "Centuries will pass away, but out of the ruins of our towns and monuments will grow the hatred against those finally responsible, whom we have to thank for everything—international Jewry and its helpers."[22] The next day he and his long-time partner Eva Braun, whom he had married the day before, took their own lives. The thirty-three-year-old Braun poisoned herself, and her husband shot himself. Hitler's adjutants burned the Führer's body, which was later recovered in its charred state and submitted to forensic analysis by the Soviets. On that day on April 30, even before learning of Hitler's death, William Shirer exulted: "Berlin is finished, and Germany, and Nazism!"[23]

Among the party faithful, a wave of "suicides of despair" followed news of Hitler's death (Figure 12.5). Some could not imagine a Germany without Hitler, while others feared arrest, execution, and the wrath of the occupying forces. In Berlin alone there were 3,881 suicides. Over sixty-five of these were employees at the Siemens electrotechnical company, where managers and regular employees killed themselves and in some cases their families. On May 1 in the town of Demmin in Pomerania, up to 1,000 people committed suicide—slitting their wrists or throwing themselves into the river after weighing themselves down by rocks—to avoid the oncoming "Asiatic hordes." Himmler, the architect of the Holocaust, also took his own life after a failed attempt to make a separate peace with the Allies.

Who would lead the government after Hitler's suicide? There could be only one true "Führer," so before his death Hitler retired that title and returned the Reich leadership structure to that of before Hindenburg's death. Hitler designated Goebbels as his successor as chancellor, but the latter served only one day in his post. After failing to negotiate a separate peace with the Soviets and despairing of life without Hitler, Goebbels and his wife poisoned their six children and family dog and then took their own lives. Without a chancellor, Germans now relied on the newly installed president of the country, Supreme Commander of the German Armed Forces and naval admiral Karl Dönitz, to negotiate Germany's surrender. On May 8, 1945, the leaders of the German armed forces met with Soviet Marshal Georgy Zhukov to sign acts of unconditional military surrender. Shortly before midnight, at the USSR Military headquarters in Berlin, the Second World War ended. A month later the Allies formally dissolved the German government.

Germans reacted to the war's end with a range of emotions. Otto Faust, who was held in the USSR as a prisoner of war until 1950, recalled his feelings of dejection: "I joined the war as an idealist, as a soldier and a National Socialist, and such fierce fighting had led to such a bitter ending."[24] Recalled a German tank soldier who had fought on until May 8: "Where was the proud German Wehrmacht? Were all the sacrifices to be in vain?"[25] When Marie Jalowicz Simon, an eleven-year-old Jew who had survived the war in hiding, learned that the Allies had won, she would have liked to have celebrated. "But I felt no emotion at all."[26]

FIGURE 12.5 *The deputy mayor of Leipzig and his wife and daughter, who committed suicide in City Hall as American troops entered the city on April 20, 1945 (US Army Signal Corps, Public domain, via Wikimedia Commons).*

The Aftermath of Nazism

The Second World War had caused vast human misery and material destruction. Almost 5.3 million German soldiers, representing 6 percent of the entire population, had died or were missing. Countless others were in POW camps. There were 2 million disabled German men, and 9 million Reich citizens had been bombed out of their homes. So many soldiers had died that in 1950, there were 1,362 women for every 1,000 men in West Germany. With the absence of so many men, it was up to women to clear the rubble, take over "men's" jobs, and care for families and for their physically and psychologically damaged POW "returnees," the last of whom came back from Soviet captivity in 1955. The infrastructure of major cities was in ruins, and there were no political organizations left to administer food and medicine. As many as 740 bridges in Germany were destroyed, along with 50 percent of the railways. Before setting up a distribution system in the summer, the Allies would toss food to famished Germans as they passed through the country. In the immediate aftermath of the Second World War the German *Volksgemeinschaft* had given way to a *Trümmergemeinschaft* (rubble community).[27]

During the last weeks of the war, the true scope of the Holocaust was revealed to the world. At the same hour as Hitler's suicide, the American army liberated the 32,335 prisoners left in Dachau, the very first concentration camp. Troops of the victorious armies were stunned by the mounds of corpses littering this and other camps. One of these concentration camps was Bergen Belsen, where a young Anne Frank had died in February, having survived in hiding in Amsterdam until an unknown informer alerted the Gestapo to her family's hideout and had her sent to Auschwitz then Belsen. Over the twelve years of the Third Reich, the Nazis had slaughtered almost 6 million Jews—in camps, in killing fields, in homes, and on death marches (see Plate 15). In addition, they had murdered a quarter of million people with disabilities, 1.8 million non-Jewish Polish civilians, 5.7 million Soviet citizens (not counting the Jews in the USSR), 3.3 million Soviet POWs, and countless other national, sexual, religious, and ethnic minorities. As many as 1.7 million people, mostly non-Jews, had also died in the Nazi concentration camps (as opposed to death camps and killing fields). In this atmosphere of death, Jewish survivors and others in hiding when the guns fell silent emerged from the rubble of bombed cities, straggling toward houses and apartments that no longer existed or that had been seized by locals, or wandered into displaced person camps set up by Allied forces in the summer of 1945. For some, these camps would serve as their new homes for several years until they were resettled in Israel, the United States, or elsewhere. In these displaced person camps they met fellow sufferers, exacted occasional revenge on Germans, fell in love, married, and revived their lives and, in many cases, their religious practices.

At the same time, 10 million German refugees from the east clogged the roads, having fled before the arrival of the Red Army. Even after the surrender, the Soviets, Poles, Czechs, and Hungarians expelled ethnic German minorities. Fourteen million ethnic Germans fled or were expelled between 1945 and 1950. Over half a million of these expellees died en route to the west. The majority of these settled in the British and American zones, and throughout the coming years they became a strong political force as they memorialized and lobbied for the return of their lost "homelands." These German refugees added to a general picture of misery in Europe. Across the continent, nearly 50 million people had died and millions more were close to starvation (see Plate 16). In May of 1945, there were over 40 million uprooted people in Europe.

In the summer of 1945 the Allies officially divided Germany into four occupation zones administered by the French, British, Americans, and Soviets. And each devised ways of moving Germany materially and psychologically away from Nazism. "Denazification" was not an easy task. In 1944, the Swiss consul in Germany had marveled at the "puzzling mentality of Germans," who seemed to reside not only in "another country but another world."[28] How would the victors pull Germans out of this world? One way was to detain Nazis and their collaborators. A wave of arrests followed Germany's capitulation. The Allies captured military officers, company managers, civic leaders, and cultural figures and vetted them for their future political reliability and professional utility. The Allies interned over 400,000 Germans, some of whom spent up to three years in detention in the western zones and upwards of five years in the Soviet zone. Almost 35 percent of the detainees in Soviet captivity died. Many in the western zones were subsequently banned from professions after going through a denazification process that categorized them according to their guilt. This process was not limited to elites. Millions of Germans from all walks of life filled out questionnaires about their actions and affiliations under Nazism. They were then classified as major offenders, offenders, lesser offenders, fellow travelers, or untainted. Only the last category carried no consequences. The exceptions to this punishment system were Nazi scientists and other technical specialists who fell into an offender category but who were whisked away to the Soviet Union or the United States. There the governments exploited their expertise in weaponry, optics, physics, and chemistry to help fight the new Cold War by designing weaponry and launching the space race.

After this international tribunal, individual Allied nations, former occupied countries, and Germans themselves prosecuted leading businessmen, members of the armed forces, SS men, and the doctors who had contributed to war crimes and genocide. In the two years after the Second World War, the Americans held 462 trials of over 1,700 "lesser war criminals" on the site of the Dachau concentration camp. Poles tried over 5,300 Germans between 1945 and 1958. Courts around Europe prosecuted collaborators, who were often subjected to vigilante justice and public humiliation before their trials. With the 1949 division of Germany into a communist German

Another way to extract Germans from National Socialism was to conduct trials. In 1945 and 1946 the Allies prosecuted the leading Nazis who had not killed themselves or fled. Those who sat in the prisoner's dock in Nuremberg included Dönitz, Ribbentrop, Rosenberg, Frank, Sauckel, Jodl, and Göring (Figure 12.6). There was no legal precedent for such a tribunal, or for the prosecution of "crimes against humanity," and the trial bred a resentment in Germany that the Allies were engaging in "victor's justice." The judges, some of the great jurists of the Allied countries, sentenced twelve of twenty-four defendants to death by hanging. There were also three acquittals, and the remainder were sent to prison. This latter group included Albert Speer, who had charmed the judges into believing his claims that he was a bit player who had limited the damage Hitler caused to his nation. Göring, Hitler's one-time designated successor who had served as prime minister of Prussia, commander of the Luftwaffe, head of the Gestapo, and chief forester and weatherman for the Reich, cheated his executioners by taking cyanide the night before his scheduled hanging.

FIGURE 12.6 *International trial of Nazi leaders in Nuremberg, November 14, 1945 to October 1, 1946. Front row from left to right: Hermann Göring, Rudolf Hess, Joachim von Ribbentrop. Second row left to right: Karl Dönitz, Erich Raeder (hidden), Baldur von Schirach (BPK-Bildagentur 30018071).*

Democratic Republic (GDR) in the east and a capitalist Federal Republic of Germany (FRG) in the west, the prosecution of Nazis became caught up in the politics of the Cold War, with each side claiming that the other harbored Nazis and totalitarian tendencies. The FRG—the larger of the two countries—arguably had more high-ranking ex-Nazis than the GDR, but it also prosecuted more of them. In the 1960s West Germany put on trial some of the men who had served at Auschwitz, Sobibor, and other death camps, as well as the commanders of most large-scale concentration camps. In the forty years after the Nazi capitulation, West Germany sent almost 6,500 people to prison. This data challenges a common claim that denazification was a failure. And yet many perpetrators from the camp system were acquitted if they couldn't be linked directly to a specific death, despite their supervisory roles at camps. This stringent rule was relaxed in recent years, as one's presence within the camp architecture of destruction can now lead to a conviction, even if one did not directly kill an individual. The most famous postwar trial took place in Jerusalem and not in Germany. In 1960 Israeli agents captured Adolf Eichmann, who had organized the deportation of European Jews to their deaths. He was hiding in plain sight in Argentina. The Israelis took him to Jerusalem, tried him, and sentenced him to death. The Eichmann trial garnered much attention and led to more open discussion globally about the Nazi past.

After the war, many Germans wanted to forget about the recent past and build new lives free from reminders of the Hitler dictatorship. But the crimes and traumas of the National Socialist years were ever-present. The past appeared not just in the trials and denazification hearings, but also in the West German government's negotiation of compensation agreements with Israel and with Holocaust survivors, in devising economic and social policies that would limit the kinds of disruptions that had led to fascism, and in treading lightly on the world stage. A new West Germany used the lessons of the past to guide a way forward such that it could never threaten the world again. But these positive steps did not stop the West German government from rehabilitating former Nazis and inviting them into the halls of power. In East Germany the leadership embraced communism as a form of ideological denazification and accused the west of re-empowering Nazis, thereby setting itself against what they saw as the west's militarism and fascism.

Germany's victims were not silent either. Jews and other survivors wrote diaries, plays, and memoirs in Yiddish, English, German, French, and other languages about their suffering and losses and the need to revitalize their religion and culture. And they struggled to understand how their home countries and countrymen had succumbed to Nazi brutality. During the prosecution of Eichmann in Jerusalem, political philosopher and German-Jewish refugee Hannah Arendt covered the trial for the *New Yorker* magazine. She portrayed the SS lieutenant-colonel as an uninteresting functionary and a faceless bureaucrat who held few true beliefs, including about Jews. He was no less complicit for that, she argued, but his evil and that of the Holocaust lay in their very "banality" and unremarkable boringness.

Legacies of National Socialism

Hannah Arendt's depiction of the Nazi perpetrator encountered wide criticism. She had, for one thing, fallen for the legal defense's strategy, which portrayed the SS man as clueless about Nazi crimes (which he was not). Many generations of students since 1945 have bought into this view that all but the leading Nazi zealots were mere cogs in a wheel of a massive terror system designed by others. They have seen Germans from Eichmann down to average citizens as blinded by Hitler's charisma, seduced into complicity, or simply trying to get by in a police state. For the past eighty years, Germans have sometimes embraced this simple portrayal, but there is also no doubt that they have come a long way in acknowledging and grappling with Nazism in a process dubbed *Vergangenheitsbewältigung* ("coming to terms with the past"). They have built monuments to their victims, introduced the Holocaust into school curricula, sponsored awards and writing contests for those researching the Nazi years, and have kept a low-profile military posture as a counter to the legacy of Nazi aggression. This has been both a balm to neighboring countries and, in recent years, a source of frustration that Germans are "not doing their part" in the NATO defensive alliance.

Today, the legacy of the Third Reich is everywhere in the political culture of Germany and abroad—in a flood of books and studies about the period, in tours of former death and concentration camps, and in essays and textbooks. Many see the twelve years under Hitler as the barometer of evil, against which other historical atrocities are measured, and they mine the Nazi years for clues about how democracies fail and how an educated populace can throw its support behind a genocidal program. But the legacies of Nazi Germany can be overused. When leaders face the choice of standing up to a human rights violator, they are haunted by Neville Chamberlain's fateful decision to appease Hitler in Munich. This can lead them to a more assertive role in fighting present-day "tyrants," but it can also escalate violence and lead to military actions that can cause tremendous civilian damage. The National Socialist period is rife for comparison and abuse precisely because its crimes are so vast. Bioethicists study the actions of doctors who contributed to the Holocaust, teaching medical students about violations of the Hippocratic oath. But anti-vaccine activists cite the Nazis' forced experiments when they protest against mandates. When people marched against restrictions and lockdowns during the early 2020s in the name of bodily integrity, they likened themselves to the Scholl siblings, who stood up to those who would deny them their freedom and dignity. In short, the Nazi years beckon people to fight state oppression, advocate for human rights, and protect basic freedoms. But these people don't always study the complexities of the very history they cite.

As future students and scholars encounter examples of human rights violations and state terror, they are to be reminded that the period of National Socialism does not provide easy lessons about state power or human behavior. In Third Reich, there were Nazis who helped Jews. There were people with Jewish ancestry in the German army. There were non-party members who committed genocidal killings. There were fearful Germans, courageous Germans, and a large number of convinced National Socialists. From 1933 to 1945, Germans' lives involved more than just hatred and terror. Nationalism, belief in the Führer, racism, and concern for loved ones on the battlefield could wax and wane at different points. A constellation of emotions and commitments shaped the population in the Nazi era. But whatever the complexities, the fact remains that Adolf Hitler marshaled the energies of 80 million Germans to construct a racially exclusive, "thousand-year Reich," Fortunately, it lasted only twelve years.

Notes

1 James Taylor and Warren Shaw, *The Third Reich Almanac* (New York: World Almanac, 1976), 376.

2 Joseph Goebbels, "Now, People, Stand up and Let the Storm Winds Blow" (1943) in *The Third Reich Sourcebook*, Anson Rabinbach and Sander Gillman, eds. (Berkeley: University of California Press, 2013), 828–31.

3 Secret Report of the Security Service of the Reichsführer SS, "Reactions to Goebbels' Speech," in ibid., 832–3.

4 "Hitler's Total War and the Reaction of the German People," *Sozialistische Mitteilungen* 48 (April 1943), https://library.fes.de/fulltext/sozmit/1943-048-1.htm

5 Hermann Ernst Grobig, "Why Racial Hygiene in Wartime," in *Third Reich Sourcebook*, Rabinbach and Gilman, eds., 827–8.

6 Andreas Kunz, *Wehrmacht und Niederlage: Die bewaffnete Macht in der Endphase der nationalsozialistischen Herrschaft 1944–1945* (Munich: Oldenbourg, 2005), 241.

7 Earl Beck, *Under the Bombs: The German Homefront, 1942–1945* (Lexington: University of Kentucky Press, 1986), 59.

8 Hans Erick Nossack, *The End: Hamburg 1943* (Chicago: University of Chicago Press, 2006), 39.

9 Interview with Ursula Kretzschmar in Alison Owings, *Frauen: Women Recall the Third Reich* (New Brunswick: Rutgers University Press, 2011), 192.

10 Jill Stephenson, *Hitler's Home Front: Württemberg under the Nazis* (London: Hambledon Continuum, 2006), 165.

11 Victor Klemperer, *I Will Bear Witness: A Diary of the Nazi Years*, Vol. 2, 1942–1945 (New York: Modern Library, 1999), diary entry from February 13 and 14, 1945, 407.

12 Nicholas Stargardt, *The German War: A Nation Under Arms, 1939–1945* (New York: Basic Books, 2015), 375.

13 Ibid.

14 Secret Report of the Security Service of the Reichsführer SS, "Reactions to the Katyn Forest Massacre," in *Third Reich Sourcebook*, Rabinbach and Gilman, eds., 833.

15 Allen Paul, *Katyn: Stalin's Massacre and the Triumph of Truth* (Dekalb: Northern Illinois University Press, 1991), 230.

16 "Reactions to the Katyn Forest Massacre," in *Third Reich Sourcebook*, Rabinbach and Gilman, eds., 833.

17 Stargardt, *German War*, 472.

18 Richard Overy, *Blood and Ruins: The Last Imperial War, 1931–1945* (New York: Viking, 2022), 729.

19 Maria Schicklgruber to Hitler, August 24, 1942, in *Briefe an Hitler*, Henrik Eberle, ed. (Bergisch Gladbach: Lübbe, 2007), 414–16.

20 Wannsee Conference Protocol, January 20, 1942, https://avalon.law.yale.edu/
    imt/wannsee.asp

21 Joseph Goebbels, "Speech, April 19, 1945," https://research.calvin.edu/german-
    propaganda-archive/unser45.htm

22 Adolf Hitler, "Political Testament," April 29, 1945, https://www.
    jewishvirtuallibrary.org/hitler-s-political-testament-april-1945

23 William Shirer quoted in Walter Kempowski, *Swansong 1945: A Collective
    Diary of the Last Days of the Third Riech* (New York: Norton, 2014), 298.

24 Otto Faust quoted in ibid., 335.

25 H. St., a tank soldier, quoted in ibid., 328.

26 Marie Jalowicz Simon, *Gone to Ground: One Woman's Extraordinary Account
    of Survival in the Heart of Nazi Germany* (London: Clerkenwell, 2016), 292.

27 See Michael Wildt, *Zerborstene Zeit: Deutsche Geschichte, 1918–1948*
    (Munich: Beck, 2022), 469–502; Richard Bessel, "The End of the
    Volksgemeinschaft" in *Visions of Community in Nazi Germany: Social
    Engineering and Private Lives*, Martina Steber and Bernhard Gotto, eds.
    (Oxford: Oxford University Press, 2014), 281–94.

28 Hans Zurlinden to Pierre Bona in Bern, March 24, 1944, in *Fremde Blicke auf
    das "Dritte Reich": Berichte ausländischer Diplomaten über Herrschaft und
    Gesellschaft in Deutschland, 1933–1945*, Frank Bajohr and Christoph Strupp,
    eds. (Göttingen: Wallstein, 2012), 578.

Additional Reading

Bessel, Richard. *Germany 1945: From War to Peace*. London: Pocket Books, 2008.

Dack, Mikkel. *Everyday Denazification in Postwar Germany: The Fragebogen
    and Politics Screening during the Allied Occupation*. Cambridge: Cambridge
    University Press, 2023.

Douglas, Lawrence. *The Memory of Judgment. Making Law and History in the
    Trials of the Holocaust*. Yale: Yale University Press, 2001.

Evans, Richard. *The Third Reich in History and Memory*. Oxford: Oxford
    University Press, 2015.

Jeffrey, Herf. *The Jewish Enemy: Nazi Propaganda during World War II and the
    Holocaust*. Cambridge, MA: Belknap, 2006.

Joskowicz, Ari. *Rain of Ash: Roma, Jews, and the Holocaust*. Princeton, NJ:
    Princeton University Press, 2023.

Kallis, Aristotle A. *Nazi Propaganda and the Second World War*. London: Palgrave
    Macmillan, 2005.

Kempowicz, Walter. *Swansong: A Collective Diary of the Last Days of the
    Third Reich*. Translated by Shaun Whiteside. New York: W.W. Norton &
    Company, 2015.

Kershaw, Ian. *The End: The Defiance and Destruction of Hitler's Germany,
    1944–45*. New York: The Penguin Press, 2011.

Overy, Richard. *Blood and Ruins: The Last Imperial War, 1931–1945*. London:
    Viking, 2021.

Stephenson, Jill. *Hitler's Home Front: Württemberg under the Nazis*. London: Hambledon Continuum, 2006.

Süss, Dietmar. *Death from the Skies: How the British and Germans Survived Bombing in World War II*. Oxford: Oxford University Press, 2014.

INDEX